RESEARCHING THE SOCIAL ECONOMY

Researching the
Social Economy

Edited by Laurie Mook, Jack Quarter,
and Sherida Ryan

UNIVERSITY OF TORONTO PRESS
Toronto Buffalo London

ISBN 978-0-8020-9953-2

Printed on acid-free, 100% post-consumer recycled paper with
vegetable-based inks.

Library and Archives Canada Cataloguing in Publication

Researching the social economy / edited by Laurie Mook, Jack Quarter,
and Sherida Ryan.

Includes bibliographical references.
ISBN 978-0-8020-9953-2

1. Nonprofit organizations – Canada.   2. Cooperative societies – Canada.
3. Community development – Canada.   4. Voluntarism – Canada.
5. Economics – Canada – Sociological aspects.   6. Public-private sector
cooperation – Canada.   I. Mook, Laurie   II. Quarter, Jack, 1941–
III. Ryan, Sherida, 1949–

HD2769.2.C3R48 2010   306.30971   C2010-904484-3

University of Toronto Press acknowledges the financial assistance to its
publishing program of the Canada Council for the Arts and the Ontario
Arts Council.

 Canada Council   Conseil des Arts
for the Arts   du Canada

 **ONTARIO ARTS COUNCIL**
CONSEIL DES ARTS DE L'ONTARIO

University of Toronto Press acknowledges the financial support for its
publishing activities of the Government of Canada through the Canada Book
Fund.

Contents

Preface

In 2005, the Social Sciences and Humanities Research Council of Canada (SSHRC) funded a series of regional nodes and a national hub (the Social Economy Suite) to undertake research about the social economy in Canada. This edited collection flows from the research of the Southern Ontario Node, embracing a network of scholars and community organizations from our region as well as others from afar. *Researching the Social Economy* may represent one of the first comprehensive research collections on the social economy in Canada, but not the last. Others are being planned and should be published in subsequent years, and two other books have been published very recently: the textbook *Understanding the Social Economy: A Canadian Perspective* (University of Toronto Press) and *Living Economics*, an edited collection from Emond Montgomery Publishing. In other words, the SSHRC funding has stimulated a bourgeoning body of research and related publications. The social economy or économie sociale is a term used widely in Western Europe and Quebec, but in other parts of Canada it has had minimal currency. The fact that this book originates from English Canada is a sign of changing times. English Canada does have vibrant bodies of research around organizations and practices in the social economy – nonprofits, co-operatives, social enterprises, community economic development. However, the funding of the pan-Canadian research Social Economy Suite has facilitated thinking about commonalities between these types of organizations and practices rather than viewing them as silos. This is a difficult transition, as it is common practice to view the organizations of the social economy as distinct from each other rather than sharing common characteristics such as a social mission (see chapter 1 for a discussion of this point).

It is also common practice to view the social economy as distinct from the private and public sectors. A theme throughout this book is how the social economy, in its many manifestations, interacts in many ways with organizations in the other sectors of the economy.

Another indicator of changing times is the formation of the Association of Nonprofit and Social Economy Research (ANSER), which meets annually as part of the Congress of Humanities and Social Sciences. In addition, ANSER has started an online publication, the *Canadian Journal of Nonprofit and Social Economy Research*, publishing in both English and French. The growth of ANSER, its journal, and books such as this one are indicators that a new field has emerged to which researchers of all disciplines are gravitating.

Laurie Mook
Jack Quarter
Sherida Ryan

Contributors

Kunle Akingbola is a Researcher and Adjunct Professor at the University of Toronto and Ryerson University. His current research focus is on the environment of human resource management and strategy, particularly in nonprofit organizations. He received his PhD from the University of Toronto. He has master's degrees in Industrial Relations & HRM, Workplace Learning & Change and an MBA from Wilfrid Laurier University.

Kunle Akingbola is also a Human Resources Manager and Consultant with extensive experience in both the corporate and nonprofit sectors. He has managed and facilitated the development and implementation of HR strategies, organizational change, policies and co-ordinated negotiation of collective agreements. He has significant experience in employee relations, recruitment, labour relations and training. He has also led compensation and benefits and HR metrics/ benchmarking portfolio.

Mark C. Baetz (BA, MBA, PhD) is Professor of Business and Associate Director, Laurier Centre for Community Service-Learning at Wilfrid Laurier University. He has taught in the areas of strategic management, ethics, and corporate social responsibility. His research includes the effectiveness of university-based codes of ethics, the impact of corporate volunteer programs, and strategic management issues involved in ethical investing. He has published in the *Journal of Business Ethics*, *Journal of Management Studies*, and *Long Range Planning*.

Kathy Brock is Associate Professor, School of Policy Studies and Department of Political Studies, Queen's University, and Past Director,

Public Policy and Third Sector, School of Policy Studies. She has published books, academic articles, and reports on voluntary organizations, Canadian politics, and Aboriginal issues. Active in public affairs, she served on the National Survey of Nonprofit and Voluntary Organizations, as an advisor to the Canadian Government/Voluntary Sector Initiative, Co-Chair of the Agnes Etherington Art Centre Membership Drive, National Voluntary Sector Forum Selection Committee member, policy advisor to the Minister of Aboriginal Affairs Manitoba, political advisor to the Grand Chief, Assembly of Manitoba Chiefs, and research director of the Manitoba Meech Lake Constitutional Task Force. She is an associate editor of *Canadian Public Policy*. She received the 2008 Pierre De Celles IPAC Award for Teaching Excellence in Public Administration and the 2009 Frank Knox Award for Teaching Excellence (Queen's).

Steven D. Brown is Associate Professor of Political Science at Wilfrid Laurier University, and Director of the Laurier Institute for the Study of Public Opinion and Policy (LISPOP). His research areas include public opinion formation, political behaviour, and the factors affecting citizen engagement in Canada. He is part of a larger multi-university research team investigating the impact of high school community service programs on subsequent civic engagement.

Travis Gliedt is a PhD candidate at the University of Waterloo, Canada, in the Department of Geography and Environmental Management. His interests include community energy management, green energy solutions, and social entrepreneurship. His current research focuses on energy management in social service and environmental service organizations within the North American social economy.

Itay Greenspan is a doctoral candidate at the School of Social Policy and Practice, University of Pennsylvania. His research interests include nonprofit organizations, philanthropy and philanthropic foundations, volunteering, the Israeli environmental movement, and Middle Eastern environmental initiatives. Itay holds a master's degree in Environmental Studies (MES) from York University, Canada, and BA *cum laude* in Geography from the Hebrew University of Jerusalem, Israel. His doctoral dissertation, currently underway, is entitled 'Philanthropic Foundations and Israeli Environmental NGOs: Donor Dependency and Selection Processes.' It focuses on the *relationships* between Jewish

American philanthropic foundations and their Israeli environmental NGO beneficiaries. Itay has published in journals such as *Nonprofit and Voluntary Sector Quarterly*, *Voluntas*, and in a special issue on 'Patients, Consumers and Civil Society' of the Journal *Advances in Medical Sociology*, among others.

Denyse Guy holds degrees in Environmental Sciences and in Business Management. For close to 30 years, she has worked as a manager and educator/trainer in the co-operative sector in Canada and overseas. She has received numerous awards including national recognition in 1999 for the 'Best Managed Housing Co-operative in Canada.' In 2007, Credit Union Central of Ontario (now Central 1) and Alterna Credit Union celebrated her achievements by giving her the Garry Gillam Award for Social Responsibility. Most recently, in 2009, she was the first Canadian to be awarded the Friend of GROWMARK system, which recognizes outstanding leadership and commitment to agriculture.

In 2001, Denyse became the Region Manager of CCA Ontario, which in 2002 became the Ontario Co-operative Association and has a mission to lead, cultivate, and connect the co-operative sector in Ontario. She is currently a board member of the Community Power Fund, which supports the development of renewable energy co-operatives in Ontario, and is a trustee with the Federal Co-operative Housing Stabilization Fund.

Michael Hall established the Research Program at the Canadian Centre for Philanthropy (now Imagine Canada) and played a key role in developing and leading a number of national research initiatives such as the Canada Survey of Giving, Volunteering and Participating, the National Survey of Nonprofit and Voluntary Organizations, and the Canada Volunteerism Initiative's Knowledge Development Centre. Michael's work focuses on building and mobilizing knowledge about Canadian philanthropy, volunteering, and nonprofit organizations and he is the author of over 50 publications on these topics. He currently serves on the board of the Association for Nonprofit and Social Economy Research and is a member of the international advisory board of the *Voluntary Sector Review* and the editorial board of the *Canadian Journal of Nonprofit and Social Economy Research*.

Femida Handy is Professor at the School of Social Policy and Practice at the University of Pennsylvania. Her research interests are in the economics of the nonprofit sector and volunteering. She has published award-winning research in these fields. She is currently the editor-in-chief of the journal *Nonprofit and Voluntary Sector Quarterly*.

Ailsa Henderson is Senior Lecturer in the School of Social and Political Studies at the University of Edinburgh, and specializes in the areas of political culture and civic engagement.

Sandra Hoy has a Master of Social Work degree and is a PhD student at Wilfrid Laurier University's Faculty of Social Work. As a student, Sandra has worked as a research assistant at the Social Innovation Research Group at the Faculty of Social Work. Professionally, Sandra is the Director of Research and Evaluation at Mosaic Counselling and Family Services, a nonprofit organization in Kitchener, Ontario. Sandra's academic interests include connecting research to practice, critical mental health, and university-community collaboration.

Ginette Lafrenière is Associate Professor at the Faculty of Social Work, Wilfrid Laurier University. She is the Director of the Social Innovation Research Group, an interdisciplinary training incubator for master's and PhD students interested in community-based research. Ginette is interested in the role that universities can play in working with communities on issues relative to social justice and the social economy.

David Lasby is a Senior Research Associate with Imagine Canada. He has been involved with a number of surveys relevant to the social economy, including the Canada Survey of Giving, Volunteering, and Participating and the National Survey of Nonprofit and Voluntary Organizations. He has also worked extensively with T3010 data that registered charities are required to file with the Canada Revenue Agency. Most recently he has been involved with Imagine's new Sector Monitor, a survey program intended to regularly take the pulse of sector organizations.

David was trained as a prehistorian, specializing in the lithic technology of the Neolithic and Chalcolithic periods of the Levant. He holds a BA from the University of Toronto and an MPhil from Cambridge University.

Sophie Llewelyn is a PhD candidate in the Department of Anthropology at McGill University. She continues to explore bovine themes through her thesis research into efforts to conserve indigenous cattle breeds in North India.

Jennifer Lynes has an educational background in marketing, commerce, and environmental studies. She is currently Assistant Professor with the University of Waterloo's School of Environment, Enterprise and Development (SEED) and Associate Editor, *Journal of Fostering Sustainable Behaviour*. She has over a decade of international experience in community and organizational-based change for the promotion of environmentally sustainable behaviours, with a specific focus on youth, energy conservation, and local food issues. She has affiliations with the Waterloo Institute for Sustainable Energy and is on the Board of Directors for Waterloo Region Green Solutions (REEP). She teaches both graduate and undergraduate courses in social and green marketing.

Erica McCollum holds an MA in Adult Education and Community Development from the Ontario Institute of Studies in Education and is currently a PhD student in Sociology at the University of British Columbia. Her focus is community development and participatory governance and she is involved with ThinkCity, a citizens' engagement organization in Vancouver, BC.

Agnes Meinhard is Associate Professor of Organizational Behaviour and Theory in the Ted Rogers School of Management at Ryerson University. She is the Founding Director of the Centre for Voluntary Sector Studies at Ryerson. Her research focuses on the voluntary and nonprofit sector. Some of the areas she has researched are the formation, growth, and demise of voluntary organizations; risk management in nonprofit organizations; corporate participation in the social economy; partnerships between for-profit and nonprofit organizations; strategic responses of voluntary organizations to changing policy; women's voluntary organizations; volunteer behaviour and development; student volunteering; leadership and organizational change. Her work has been published in books and academic journals. Agnes Meinhard was instrumental in establishing Canada's first undergraduate interdisciplinary curriculum in nonprofit and voluntary sector management at Ryerson University and teaches courses in developing effective nonprofit organizations and leading nonprofit organizations through change. Voluntary organizations are not only of academic interest to Dr Meinhard; she serves on the boards of several nonprofit organizations.

Marguerite Mendell is an economist, Vice Principal and Associate Professor, School of Community and Public Affairs, Concordia University. She is also Director, Karl Polanyi Institute of Political Economy, Concordia University. She has published widely on the social economy in Quebec, local development, social finance, economic democracy, and the work of Karl Polanyi, especially as it relates to contemporary democratic economic development strategies. She has collaborated with social economy actors in developing public policy proposals at the provincial and municipal level in Quebec. Professor Mendell is a member of the Board of Directors, Chantier de l'économie sociale, the Advisory Committee of the Social Economy Partnership for Community-based Sustainable Development for the City of Montreal, and the Scientific Advisory Committee of the OECD-LEED Center on Local Development in Trento, Italy. She has also established an ART-Universitas-United Nations Development Program (UNDP) laboratory for the social economy and local development at Concordia University.

Laurie Mook is Assistant Professor in the School of Community Resources and Development at the University of Arizona and has degrees in accounting, international development, educational policy studies, and adult education. Previously she was Co-Director of the Social Economy Centre at the University of Toronto and a Social Science and Humanities Research Council of Canada doctoral fellow at the Ontario Institute for Studies in Education of the University of Toronto. She received the Gabriel G. Rudney Outstanding Dissertation Award in Nonprofit and Voluntary Action Research in 2008. Laurie is co-author (with Jack Quarter and Betty Jane Richmond) of *What Counts: Social Accounting for Nonprofits and Cooperatives, Second Edition* (London: Sigel Press, 2007) and *Understanding the Social Economy* (with Jack Quarter and Ann Armstrong, University of Toronto Press, 2009). Her research focuses on social and environmental accounting, social economy organizations, and volunteerism.

Nancy Neamtan is President/Executive Director of the Chantier de l'économie sociale, a nonprofit organization administered by 32 representatives of various networks of social economy enterprises (cooperatives and nonprofits), local development organizations, and social movements. The mission of the Chantier de l'économie sociale, a Quebec-wide organization, is the promotion and development of the social economy. She is also Co-Director of the Community-University Alliance on the Social Economy and President of the Board of the Chantier de l'économie Social Trust, an investment fund dedicated to co-operatives and nonprofits. She is one of the North American representatives on the Board of RIPESS and has been involved in international networking on the social and solidarity economy since 1997. In this respect, she is often called upon as an expert on social and solidarity economy issues by international organizations and forums.

Paulette Padanyi is Associate Professor in the Department of Marketing and Consumer Studies (College of Management and Economics) at the University of Guelph. She joined the University of Guelph in 2002 after earning her PhD from York University in 2001. She was the Chair of the Department of Marketing and Consumer Studies from 2003 to 2009. She currently teaches nonprofit marketing, and conducts research in two areas: student volunteerism at the high school level and sustainable household purchasing and consumption. She is also an advisor of master's theses; her students have conducted research in the areas of student volunteerism, donor engagement with nonprofit organizations, and pro-environmental behaviour. Paulette moved into academia in1988 after working 17 years in marketing management with two major multinational packaged goods firms. Her interest in nonprofit marketing and nonprofit issues began when she was undertaking her doctoral studies.

Paul Parker is Professor in the Faculty of Environment at the University of Waterloo and Associate Dean for Graduate Studies. He has degrees from Mount Allison University (BA, BSc), Australian National University (MA), and London School of Economics (PhD). He was the Assistant Director for Research and Statistics in the Australian federal government's Office for Local Government. He returned to Canada in 1991 and has taught in the master's program in Local Economic Development for 19 years and was the Director of the program for nine years. His research focuses on building sustainable communities by creating win-win opportunities for the environment and economy. For example, energy efficiency reduces operating costs as well as greenhouse gas emissions, so he joined two other researchers and several community partners in 1999 to launch the Residential Energy Efficiency Project, which has grown into a not-for-profit green community organization.

Jack Quarter is Professor and the Co-Director of the Social Economy

Centre at the Ontario Institute for Studies in Education, University of Toronto. He was the Principal Investigator for the SSHRC-funded Social Economy Research Alliance that led to most of the research that appears in *Researching the Social Economy*. His recent books include (with Laurie Mook and Ann Armstrong) *Understanding the Social Economy: A Canadian Perspective* (University of Toronto Press, 2009) and (with Laurie Mook and Betty Jane Richmond) *What Counts: Social Accounting for Non-Profits and Cooperatives*, 2nd edition (Sigel Press, 2007).

Matt Riehl is a Master's of Social Work graduate from Wilfrid Laurier University in Waterloo, Ontario. Currently, he works for Extend-a-Family Waterloo Region, an organization that serves people with developmental disabilities and their families, as the Community Development Coordinator. Outside of this role, he is a part-time therapist working primarily with adolescent boys, and sits on the Board of Directors for the Kitchener Downtown Community Health Centre. While attending Wilfrid Laurier University, he worked as a research assistant for the Social Innovation Research Group. During his undergraduate studies, he worked as a research assistant in the Psychology Department at the University of Waterloo.

Sherida Ryan, PhD, is the co-ordinator of a five-year Social Science and Humanities Research Council of Canada CURA, Social Business for Socially Marginalized Groups. She is also the Knowledge Mobilization and Social Media Director for the Social Economy at the University of Toronto. Sherida teaches in the Faculty of Adult Education and Community Development at the Ontario Institute for Studies in Education, University of Toronto. Her research interest focuses on the interface of emerging information and communication technology, community development, and social economy organizations.

Daniel Schugurensky is Associate Professor in the Program of Adult Education and Community Development, Ontario Institute for Studies in Education, University of Toronto. He has published extensively on adult and popular education, educational policies, higher education, citizenship education and participatory democracy, and political participation of immigrants. Among his recent publications are *Learning Citizenship by Practicing Democracy: International Initiatives and Perspectives; This is our school of citizenship: Informal Learning in Local Democracy; Ruptures, Continuities and Re-learning: The Political Participation of Latin*

Americans in Canada; and *Citizenship Learning for and through Participatory Democracy.*

Roger Spear is Chair of the Co-operatives Research Unit, Member of the CIRIEC Scientific Committee, founder member and Vice-President of EMES research network on social enterprise. He teaches organizational systems and research methods at the Open University. His most recent research projects are Governance and Social Enterprise; an EC Peer Review of the social economy in Belgium; and an OECD project on the social economy in Korea. He is Visiting Professor at Roskilde University, Copenhagen, Denmark, on a Master's in Social Entrepreneurship.

Jennifer Sumner teaches in the Adult Education and Community Development Program at the Ontario Institute for Studies in Education of the University of Toronto, where she is Director of the Certificate Program in Adult Education for Sustainability. Her research interests include organic agriculture, sustainable food systems, rural communities, and globalization. She is the author of *Sustainability and the Civil Commons: Rural Communities in the Age of Globalization* (University of Toronto Press).

Mark Ventry is the Membership and Communications Manager for the Ontario Co-operative Association, a provincial association that leads, cultivates, and connects the province's co-operatives. He has been an active part of the co-op sector since becoming a member of Guelph and Wellington Credit Union in 1976. In 2001, Mark became the credit union's inaugural Marketing Administrator, overseeing media and communications and launching the highly successful 'unBank yourself' campaign. Mark joined On Co-op in 2005 and leads the Association's member relations and recruitment strategies, and communications and marketing efforts.

His recent major projects include launching On Co-op's social media platforms, editing the award-winning *Co-op Advantage* (a full-colour magazine highlighting the Ontario co-operative sector), publication of a bi-weekly electronic newsletter about Ontario's co-operatives, the completion of Ontario's first-ever census on credit unions and co-operatives, and the launch of the province's first online searchable database of co-operatives, credit unions, and caisses populaires.

Maike Zinabou is the Resource Centre Director for a not-for-profit organization in Kitchener-Waterloo, Ontario. Maike's professional experience has been specialized in community health in a variety of capacities including clinical counselling with individuals, families, and groups, research, teaching, and service development. Her social work background has encompassed diverse experiences that include school social work, adult education, palliative care, staff and volunteer training, and fundraising. While working on her master's degree she enjoyed the opportunity to engage in community-based research within the Social Innovation Research Group.

RESEARCHING THE SOCIAL ECONOMY

1 What's in a Name?

LAURIE MOOK, JACK QUARTER, AND SHERIDA RYAN

This introductory chapter has three primary purposes: (a) to discuss differing conceptions of the social economy; (b) to consider the social economy's component organizations (nonprofit and co-operative) and component practices (community economic development); (c) to present a social economy framework that serves to integrate the collection of research papers in this book.

Social Economy

There are varying definitions of the social economy. To a certain extent, social economy has been used as a renaming of the more traditional 'third sector,' but social economy is more descriptive in that it puts up front that organizations set up for a social purpose can generate economic value – they may produce and market services, employ people, and own valuable assets (Mook, Quarter, & Richmond, 2007; Quarter, Mook, & Armstrong, 2009). In other words, even though organizations are established to meet social objectives, they may generate economic value, and most often do.

For some, social economy represents a vision of a new social order – for example, Shragge and Fontan (2000, p. 9) argue, 'a social economy implies a basic reorientation of the whole economy and related institutions.' Others, for example, Bruyn (1977) and Bruyn and Nicolaou-Smokoviti (1989), use social economy as a way of reconfiguring the field of economics. For simplicity's sake, we organize the perspectives on the social economy as follows: (a) building a social movement; (b) alternative forms of business; and (c) a conceptual framework. We shall discuss each of these in turn.

Building a Social Movement

Quebec is the one part of Canada in which the term social economy is based upon a movement perspective – that is, a fundamental challenge to social norms and a vision of an alternative social order, a point discussed in chapter 3 by Mendell and Neamtan. At the Economic and Employment Summit in Quebec in 1996, social economy organizations were defined as those that produce goods and services with a clear social mission and that have the following characteristics and objectives:

• The mission is services to members and community and not profit-oriented.
• Management is independent of government.
• Workers and/or users engage in a democratic process for decision-making.
• People have priority over capital.
• Participation, empowerment, individual and collective responsibility are key values. (Chantier de l'économie sociale, 2005)

Le Chantier's declaration was similar to one adopted in 1990 by the Conseil Wallon de l'économie sociale and inspired by the Belgian economist Jacques Defourny, who has been a highly influential figure in the European discourse on the social economy, and by CIRIEC, an international organization embracing the social and public economy (see Defourny & Monzon, 1992). Many Quebec scholars and community leaders participate in CIRIEC International, and since 1967 have had their own section, CIRIEC Canada (which could be more appropriately labelled as CIRIEC Québec). Professor Benôit Lévesque (recently retired from the l'Université du *Québec* à *Montréal*) chairs the International Scientific Council of CIRIEC (see also Roger Spear's discussion of Europe's social economy in this collection).

The criteria embraced by le Chantier in 1996 have been utilized in its efforts to build a social movement. While the dichotomous nature of some of these criteria (for example, people over capital) could be criticized as an oversimplification, they indicate a value reorientation. Moreover, the raison d'être of organizations is not only economic but also meets clear social criteria such 'democratic processes' and 'collective responsibility.' Le Chantier's website emphasizes the values of 'democracy' and 'solidarity,' and, in fact, refers repeatedly to the 'social and solidarity economy' (le Chantier, 2009).

The values of the 1996 declaration were reaffirmed in a 2006 Summit in Montreal:

> On the occasion of the *Social and Solidarity Economy Summit*, we, actors of the social economy from the community, cooperative and mutual benefit movements and associations, from cultural, environmental, and social movements, unions, international cooperation and local and regional development organizations, affirm with pride and determination our commitment to building a social and solidarity economy locally, regionally, nationally, and internationally. (Le Chantier, 2009)

The activities of le Chantier are, first, building an effective political lobby for the social economy and public services more generally at all levels of government; and second, developing social enterprises. With respect to the first, the organizations associated with le Chantier represent a broad coalition, as reflected in the declaration of the 2006 Montreal Summit. The gains of this coalition with differing levels of government are emphasized in chapter 3 by Mendell and Neamtan. Favreau (2006) argues that the organizations associated with the social economy in Quebec have gathered so much strength that they have created 'a new relationship between the economic and social sphere' (p. 13).

The second area of activity is social enterprise development through utilizing financing in the Fiducie du chantier de l'économie sociale or the Chantier Trust, a fund of $52.8 million assembled from a combination of grants from the federal and provincial governments and investments from the two labour-sponsored investment funds in Quebec, the Solidarity Fund (Quebec Federation of Labour) and Fondaction (Confedédération des syndicates nationaux) (Mendell & Rouzier, 2006). The social enterprises serve a variety of groups such as those with disabilities and those experiencing challenges because of racial and other historic forms of discrimination.

It is premature to evaluate the effectiveness of le Chantier's strategy in building a social movement. The Trust Fund is less than five years old, and the institutions that le Chantier aspires to transform have existed for many decades prior to the 1996 Summit. Nevertheless, it is evident that le Chantier has assembled a strong coalition and an impressive trust fund that operates at arm's length from the organization under a separate board. As will be argued subsequently in this chapter, the organizations and practices associated with the social economy can be found throughout Canada, and in some provinces in greater numbers than in Quebec. However, only in Quebec do these organizations fly under the flag of l'économie sociale, and only in Quebec is there a vision of a movement based upon l'économie sociale – a movement that exists not only in theory but also in practice.

Alternative Forms of Business

When the Government of Canada announced various forms of support for the social economy in its Speech from the Throne in 2004, its intention was to encourage a market-based strategy in support of social enterprises:

> And the Government will help communities help themselves. One of the best ways to do this is to get behind the remarkable people who are applying entrepreneurial skills, not for profit, but rather to enhance the social and environmental conditions in our communities across Canada. These new approaches to community development – sometimes referred to as the 'social economy' are producing more and more success stories about a turnaround in individual lives and distressed neighbourhoods – communities working to combat homelessness, address poverty and clean up the environment. The Government of Canada wants to support those engaged in this entrepreneurial social movement. It will increase their access to resources and tools. The Government will, for example, work to widen the scope of programs currently available to small and medium-sized enterprises to include social enterprises.

In the budget that followed, the federal government allocated $132 million for a series of related initiatives, $100 million over five years being for financing and $15 million for research (administered by the Social Sciences and Humanities Research Council of Canada or SSHRC). Le Chantier succeeded in obtaining $10 million under the financing allocation (the only organization to do so) before this program was cancelled by the Harper government in 2006.

It is evident from this Throne Speech and the financing program that the government's primary interest was stimulating market-based strategies that were 'not for profit' and were designed to enhance 'the social and environmental conditions in our communities across Canada.' This political initiative came from Paul Martin, the incoming and short-lived prime minister and, not coincidentally, a Quebecer who would have been conscious of the salience of l'économie sociale in Quebec. Martin embraced the dominant discourse in Quebec, but his primary interest was in social enterprise, and he has since become a passionate advocate of that form of organization and the related practice of social entrepreneurship, making speeches across Canada on this topic. This interest, it appears, preceded Mr Martin's tenure as prime minister, as in the mid-1990s as the minister of finance he engineered major cuts to government social programs in Canada. In his 1995 Budget speech, Mr Martin stated: 'Over the next three fiscal years, this budget will deliver cumulative savings of $29 billion, of which $25.3 billion are expenditure cuts ... Relative to the size of our economy, program spending will be lower in 1996-97 than any time since 1951.' In other words, Mr Martin was not an advocate of the broader social economy, but of social enterprise or market-based solutions.

The federal department responsible for administering the program, Human Resources and Social Development Canada (HRSDC), also adopted the market-based interpretation of the social economy:

> The social economy is a grass-roots entrepreneurial, not-for-profit sector, based on democratic values that seek to enhance the social, economic, and environmental conditions of communities, often with a focus on their disadvantaged members. (Human Resources and Skills Development Canada, 2005, p. 4)

Generally, academics have differentiated social enterprises from the broader social economy, though some equate the two (Chaves & Monzon, 2000; McGregor, Clark, Ferguson, & Scullion, 1997; Moulaert & Ailenei, 2005). Even among those that differentiate the two, there is a privileging of market-based organizations, as if revenues earned in the market ('earned revenues') have a higher standing than those from government and foundations. An irony in this privileging is that revenues from government and foundations generally assist organizations serving people who cannot afford the cost of market-based services – in other words, organizations with a strong social mission. Nevertheless, since the early 1990s in Canada, the neo-liberal agenda of smaller government and a greater emphasis on the market has been highly influential, and inevitably this culture has affected actors within the social economy – not simply practitioners and advocates but also intellectuals.

Although le Chantier, as discussed above, has at least a two-pronged agenda, developing social enterprises has been a centrepiece. Similarly in Europe, where the social economy has greater salience than in Canada, the emphasis has been on social enterprise development, as reflected in the influential text by Borgaza and Defourny (2001), *The Emergence of Social Enterprise.* In Belgium, the Walloon Council of the Social Market Economy utilizes the principles of the Conseil Wallon de l'économie sociale (referred to above), but adds to it that 'most of the resources of the social economy enterprises market come from the sale of goods and services' (Walloon Council of the Social Market Economy, 2008).

A Conceptual Framework

This third approach refers to the many attempts at classifying the social economy and related organizations. The simplest of these is to view the social economy as a concept by default in that it differs from the private and the public sectors – for example:

- 'A crude definition would describe it by a process of elimination, in that it is not part of the Private (For-Profit) Sector and is not part of the Public (Government) Sector.' (Blanc, Harrison, Kamat, & Fowler, 2001)
- 'Generally speaking, the term social economy designates the universe of practices and forms of mobilizing economic resources towards the satisfaction of human needs that belong neither to for-profit enterprises, nor to the institutions of the state in the narrow sense.' (Moulaert & Ailenei, 2005, p. 2042)

The problem with this type of definition is that organizations within the social economy can overlap with the private sector, in so far as they compete in the market and have similarities to a private sector firm; and they can overlap with the public sector, in that they may rely upon government funding to a substantial degree and may be influenced in part by government policies. In fact, as will be discussed later, community economic development may be viewed as both relying upon government financing and generating a portion of its revenues from the market. Therefore, viewing the social economy as completely separate

from the private and public sectors may be misleading in that all organizations are part of the same economy and relate to it in some way,
not simply to the organizations with similar characteristics but also to
parts of the economy that differ.

For that reason, in our work we use a Venn diagram (see figure 1.1),
as it emphasizes the dynamic interaction between the social economy
and the other sectors. The organizations in the social economy are an
infrastructure for society as a whole. Their members may work in the
private and public sectors, and their financing may come in part from
government and from private sector donors. In other words, even
though organizations in the social economy have some distinct characteristics, they are not a world unto themselves but one part of a society
that includes government and the private sector. The interaction between social economy organizations and the public and private sectors
is highlighted in many chapters in this collection, as discussed below in
the section on the outline of the book.

Another problem with the default approach is that the boundaries
that demarcate the social economy from the private and public sectors
are not always clear. Some social economy firms earn their revenues
from the market, much like businesses, and some businesses, albeit a
relatively small proportion, have strong social missions. These include
environmental firms that are producing alternative forms of energy,
firms like Newman's Own that donate all of their after-tax revenues
to charitable causes, and others with shares in a permanent trust that
in effect is social property much like a nonprofit (Quarter, 2000). Similarly, many nonprofits such as universities and hospitals overlap with
the public sector, rely upon government for a substantial share of their
funding, and are influenced to some degree by government policies. We
refer to such organizations as public sector nonprofits, signifying their
overlapping characteristics. We refer to those that overlap with the private sector as social economy businesses (Mook et al., 2007; Quarter et
al., 2009). While this overlap could be viewed as a weakness, it could
also be seen as a strength in that it illustrates how interconnected the
social economy is with other institutions. Distinctiveness is important,
but not to the point of being disconnected.

Interestingly, while most definitions of the social economy emphasize distinctiveness from the public sector, it is unusual to find definitions that emphasize distinctiveness from the market economy. In part,
this has to do with the influence of co-operative theoreticians and advocates in the conceptualization of the social economy, and in part, it

reflects the influence of the neo-liberal agenda that views positively the market and related concepts such as entrepreneurship and that views as a burden government and social programs financed by government. We referred to this point earlier in the discussion of the higher status accorded earned revenues as distinct from government grants.

Most conceptualizations of the social economy utilize 'democracy' as a criterion. Le Chantier, referred to above, utilizes it, and is influenced by the tradition of the Walloon Council and CIRIEC. With the exception of independence from the public sector, democracy is probably the most widely cited criterion. For this reason, some definitions exclude nonprofit organizations that serve the public, as distinct from a membership (that is, mutual associations), as they cannot claim to be a representative form of democracy. Many nonprofits serving the public have a closed board that does not represent a broader membership, unless it is hypothetical representation. Nevertheless, such boards generally follow democratic practices and may emphasize consensual decision-making. Nonprofits serving the public would also include feminist collectives that engage in participatory democracy and that may try to arrive at consensus on all decisions (Mansbridge, 1982).

As chapter 4 by Roger Spear on Europe notes, the exclusion of nonprofits from the social economy is not universally accepted in Europe, and the European Commission and European countries of Latin origin do include nonprofits. In Quebec, le Chantier, influenced by the francophone tradition in Europe, includes 'community nonprofits' only, a small subset of nonprofits in that province.

An additional problem, often overlooked, with the emphasis on democratic principles is that organizations operating according to the principle of one member/one vote may have very low member participation rates, as is common in large consumer co-operatives, credit unions, and mutual insurers. It seems inconsistent to argue that, on the one hand, democracy is essential and therefore exclude organizations with closed boards that operate democratically, but include organizations espousing the democratic principles of one member/one vote with very low participation rates. Therefore, we prefer the concept of civic engagement as a criterion for inclusion in the social economy in that it speaks to the contribution that nonprofits serving the public as well as mutual associations and co-operatives make in connecting people to each other and their communities, one form of connection being through democratic decision-making processes (Quarter et al., 2009).

The definition that we prefer is that 'the social economy is a bridging concept for organizations that have social objectives central to their mission and their practice, and either have explicit economic objectives or generate some economic value through the services they provide and purchases that they undertake' (Quarter et al., 2009, p. 3). This definition has commonalities with others that share a broad, inclusive view of the social economy (for example, Galliano, 2003; NSW Government's community builders, 2005; Vaillancourt, Aubry, Tremblay, & Kearney, 2002). Within the Quarter, Mook, and Armstrong conception, there are four broad groupings: social economy businesses, community economic development, public sector nonprofits, and civil society organizations, as shown in figure 1.1.

Briefly, social economy businesses are in the overlap between the private sector and the social economy and include organizations that balance their economic and social mission and that earn either all or a sizeable portion of their revenues from the marketplace. They would include co-operatives with shares (consumer co-ops, credit unions, worker co-ops), mutual insurers, and commercial nonprofits, both stand-alone (for example, Canadian Automobile Association, Blue Cross, Ys) and with embedded businesses (thrift shops, Travel Cuts, university presses).

Community economic development (CED, as it is usually labelled), including social enterprises serving those with disabilities, is commonly associated with economic and social needs that are addressed only partially through the market and that rely upon ongoing government support. CED would include community development corporations often depending upon regional-based programs oriented to low income communities; social enterprises for persons with disabilities; businesses owned by Aboriginal communities; and online social enterprises.

Public sector nonprofits are in the overlap between the public sector and the social economy and rely upon government agencies for a substantial portion of financing and are influenced in varying degree by government policies, but they have a separate incorporation and their own board of directors. These would include: (a) organizations that are a spin-off of government and depend totally upon a government program for their survival (e.g., Community Futures Development Corporations, Canadian Institute for Health Information); (b) organizations that were created originally by government legislation, but maintain relatively greater autonomy both in policy and finance than the spin-off organizations (e.g., universities across Canada); and (c) organizations that may have been set up apart from government but because of the

Figure 1.1. The social economy: An interactive approach

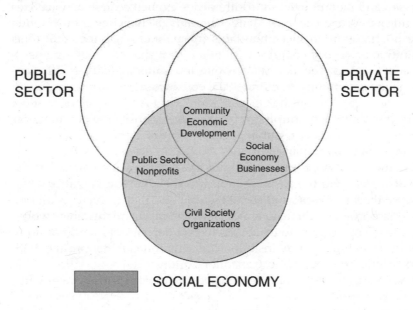

nature of their service, often to people with limited financial means, rely upon government financing (e.g., social housing development organizations, community health centres).

Including public sector nonprofits within the social economy is contentious among researchers within this field, and this viewpoint is not shared by all of the contributors to this collection (for example, Mendell and Neamtan). It also creates challenges in knowing where to draw the line between the public sector or state institutions and organizations that have one foot in the public sector and another in the social economy – public sector nonprofits. Within education, elementary and secondary schools are administered through government departments; universities have sufficient independence to be classified as public sector nonprofits. Moreover, the inclusion of public sector nonprofits does weigh heavily upon the data about the scale of the social economy (see chapter 2 by Lasby, Hall, Ventry, and Guy for a discussion of this point).

Civil society organizations are primarily the tens of thousands of associations representing the mutual needs of a membership for such functions as religion, recreation, labour rights, and professional interests, and they may also serve the public – for example, environmental associations and even political parties. Some of these associations are normative and others such as issue groups challenge norms. Often they are based upon social networks and political coalitions that form around social issues.

Following from the discussion above, four criteria are utilized to capture the social dimension of the social economy:

- Social objectives in the mission statement, meaning the organization was created to meet a social need as expressed in its objectives and including a charitable status and mutual aid for a membership;
- Social ownership, meaning that the assets belong to no one in the traditional sense but are analogous to a social dividend that is passed from generation to generation;
- Volunteer/social participation, meaning that the organization functions at least in part (for example, its board of directors) on the volunteer contributions of its members and others who engage themselves through the organization;
- Civic engagement, including democratic decision-making, meaning that the organization serves as a mechanism for people to connect with each other in a positive way.

This framework is very broad and is open to the criticism of being so diverse that it is meaningless. Put simply, what do the Canadian Chamber of Commerce, the United Church of Canada, the Canadian Red Cross Society, the University of Alberta, New Dawn Enterprises Ltd., le Mouvement Desjardins, and Arctic Co-operatives share in common? They are different, as are the many other thousands of organizations within the social economy, but we argue that they share the characteristics stated above. All of them have been set up for social purposes, are owned socially rather than in the traditional sense, rely to some extent upon voluntary contributions from members and other participants, and engage citizens in a positive way.

Organizations within the Social Economy

There are two primary organization types within the social economy – nonprofits and co-operatives. It is not uncommon to refer to the social economy in relation to these organizations as well as the practice of community economic development.

Nonprofits

Nonprofits are so varied in their services that there does not appear to be one definition that is generally accepted. The most widely cited operational criteria come from Salamon and Anheier (1992) and the Johns Hopkins Comparative Nonprofit Sector Project: (a) organized (i.e., formalized to some extent); (b) private (i.e., institutionally separate from government); (c) self-governing (i.e., equipped to control their own activities); (d) nonprofit-distributing (i.e., not returning profits to their owners or directors); and (e) voluntary (i.e., involving some degree of voluntary participation, either in their management or operations).

The Canada Revenue Agency (2009a) does attempt a definition: 'A nonprofit organization (NPO) is a club, society, or association that's organized and operated solely for: social welfare, civic improvement, pleasure or recreation, any other purpose except profit.' The definition focuses upon the functions of nonprofits. A definition that we propose, adapted from the Humboldt California Foundation (2009, p. 73), is 'A self-governing organization – including corporations without share capital, societies or trusts, but also unincorporated associations – formed not for private gain but for public or mutual benefit purposes.' This definition highlights the many forms that nonprofits can take, including not being incorporated, and that public benefit and mutual benefit are not mutually exclusive – that is, a mutual association can be viewed as a subset of the public. The definition also highlights that nonprofits can be defined by what they do – 'formed for public or mutual benefit purposes' – not just what they don't do – 'formed not for private gain.'

A Statistics Canada survey for the calendar year 2003 estimated that there were 161,000 nonprofit corporations and trusts in Canada with $112 billion of revenues, 139 million memberships, and about 2 million employees, and that participants in these organizations contributed 2 billion volunteer hours (the equivalent of about 1 million full-time jobs) (Hall et al., 2005). (Chapter 2 in this collection by Lasby, Hall, Ventry, and Guy builds upon this survey.) Moreover, another Statistics Canada survey indicates that nonprofit corporations add 7.1% to Canada's GDP (Statistics Canada, 2006).

These data do not include the many unincorporated associations or so-called 'dark matter' (Smith, 1997), as these are difficult to ascertain. There are large groups such as union locals, professional societies, tenant associations, and home and schools that tend not to incorporate, but have the basic structure of a nonprofit organization. Nor do they include the growing number of groups functioning on the Internet. Chapter 10 by Sherida Ryan, Ontario Institute for Studies in Education, University of Toronto, discusses a social economy form that has been largely invisible but is increasingly prominent – the online social economy. The Internet is increasingly the mode through which people communicate with each other, but interestingly the research on the social economy has ignored online communities. Ryan's research is path-breaking, in that regard.

About half of nonprofits in Canada have a charitable registration, 83,420 in 2008 (Canada Revenue Agency, 2009b). The criteria for a charitable registration are 'the relief of poverty; the advancement of education; the advancement of religion; or certain other purposes that benefit the community in a way the courts have said are charitable' (Bourgeois, 2002). With the exception of religious congregations, organizations serving a membership (nonprofit mutual associations) are more likely to have difficulty qualifying for charitable registration than those set up to benefit a public external to the organization. Having a charitable registration qualifies donors to an organization for a tax benefit, and therefore assists with fundraising. Organizations with a charitable status are often viewed as starving for funds, but in fact, large nonprofits such as universities and hospitals usually have a foundation with a charitable registration for fundraising drives. These organizations are among the largest employers in Canada and earn substantial revenues from the market as well.

It is common parlance to refer to a nonprofit or voluntary sector in Canada; however, there is no apex organization with the support to speak on behalf of all nonprofits or even nonprofits with a charitable status. Imagine Canada attempts to speak on behalf of organizations with a charitable registration, but there is nothing similar to the UK, for example, where the National Council of Voluntary Organisations is recognized as the voice of the sector. Nonprofits tend to organize around networks with common bonds or functions – for example, Canadian Environmental Network; National Action Committee on the Status of Women; Canadian Labour Congress; and the Canadian Ethnocultural Council. The list could fill a book, but the links across networks tend to be weak. Peter Elson's contribution to this collection (chapter 5) discusses the non-formal structure for nonprofits in Canada.

Co-operatives

Co-operatives are a much smaller group than nonprofits, and generally there is greater coherence. There is a widely used definition from the International Co-operative Alliance, the apex international organization located in Geneva, Switzerland: 'A co-operative is an autonomous association of persons united voluntarily to meet their common economic, social, and cultural needs and aspirations through a jointly-owned and democratically-controlled enterprise' (International Co-operative Alliance, 2009, ¶ 3).

There are two broad groupings of co-operatives in Canada – non-financial and financial. For the calendar year 2004 (the last year for which comprehensive data are available), there were 5,753 non-financial co-operatives, with 5.6 million members, 85,073 employees, $27.5 billion of revenues, and $17.5 billion in assets (Co-operatives Secretariat, 2007). Nearly 40% are housing co-operatives, and together with childcare and healthcare, these service co-operatives form a majority of the non-financial co-operatives. Service co-operatives are often either without or with nominal share capital, and take on the characteristics of a nonprofit. By comparison, many other forms of co-operatives with share capital take on the characteristics of a business, albeit a social economy business, and are in such fields as farm marketing, where co-operatives have a strong presence in such services as poultry, dairy, and hogs, and in consumer retailing (e.g., Mountain Equipment Co-operative). The co-operative presence, however, in farm marketing is in decline partly because of the demutualization (conversion into conventional businesses) of large grain marketing and poultry co-operatives.

Financial co-operatives in Canada (credit unions or caisses populaires) organize the bulk of the 12 or so million Canadians associated with a co-operative. There are two federations, Desjardins, named after the founder of Canada's first credit union in Lévis, Quebec in 1900, and the Credit Union Central of Canada. These federations reflect Canada's two major solitudes – French and English – though recently the lines have blurred as Desjardins has expanded its operations into Southern Ontario with its purchase of savings and loan societies from the provincial government. There are 1,140 credit unions and caisses populaires in Canada (divided about equally between the two federations), with 3,400 service locations, 10.5 million members, 64,600 employees, and $248.8 billion in assets (Co-operatives Secretariat, 2007). Financial co-operatives transact 12.67% of the Canadian financial GDP for the financial sector. Based upon asset size, the Desjardins Group, which is the largest employer in Quebec, is the sixth largest financial institution in Canada.

Like nonprofits, co-operatives are also organized by networks based upon their service – for example, the Co-operative Housing Federation of Canada, and the Credit Union Central of Canada. Unlike nonprofits in Canada, though, co-operatives have links across the networks and recognized apex organizations that speak on behalf of co-operatives – Canadian Co-operative Association and Conseil canadien de la co-operation et de la mutualité – based upon a membership of co-operative organizations.

Historically, co-operatives have thought of themselves as a movement, referred to as the co-operative commonwealth (MacPherson, 1979). One vision, as articulated by British social reformer Beatrice Potter and her husband Sidney Webb, was for the provision of services through networks of consumer co-operatives (Webb & Webb, 1921). Although co-operatives participate actively in broader social movements such as fair trade and micro credit, the movement culture among co-operatives is weak, and in Canada at least the term co-operative commonwealth is rarely used.

Nonprofits and co-operatives function in all parts of Canada, though the strength of their presence varies. Quebec, as mentioned, is the only province with a social economy movement, but it is not the only province in which organizations that make up the social economy are developed. Indeed, if one looks at size of the nonprofit and co-operative sectors as indicators of the strength of the social economy, there is impressive development throughout Canada, with Quebec by no means the strongest. For example, for nonprofits, the Statistics Canada survey taken for the year 2003 shows that, while Quebec had more nonprofit organizations per capita than the Canadian average, the Territories, Saskatchewan, Manitoba, Prince Edward Island, and Nova Scotia had more nonprofits per capita than Quebec (Hall et al., 2005). For nonprofit revenues, Ontario had almost double those of Quebec, with 43% of Canada's total. Ontario's nonprofits also have 47% of paid staff and 40% of volunteers, more than Quebec on both counts.

For non-financial co-operatives, Quebec has a very strong presence relative to the rest of Canada with 39% of the total in the year 2004 (Co-operatives Secretariat, 2007). However, on a per capita basis, Saskatchewan is larger. Utilizing membership for non-financial co-operatives, both British Columbia and Alberta are larger than Quebec, and for membership per capita, Saskatchewan again exceeds the other provinces. For employees, Saskatchewan has more per capita than Quebec, and for revenues, Saskatchewan, Manitoba, and Alberta are larger than Quebec on a per capita basis. For financial co-operatives, however, Quebec is the largest in Canada, whether in absolute terms or per capita.

The point is not to be critical of Quebec and the obvious strength of the organizations in its social economy, but to argue that even though Quebec is the only province with a social economy movement, it isn't necessarily the province with the largest number of social economy organizations. It is premature to evaluate the impact of le Chantier and the related social movement in Quebec because le Chantier was formed in 1996 and the funding for its investment fund is relatively recent, and even more so when one bears in mind the time that it takes for such a fund to become operational. The more appropriate criterion is growth among social economy organizations since the movement has been in place. Those data are not readily available, and the problem is compounded by the fact that it is not clear what year is the appropriate base line.

Nevertheless, it can be seen that in other provinces, there are vibrant nonprofits, social enterprises, co-operatives, credit unions – the same manifestations of the social economy as in Quebec, but without a movement culture. Therefore, we come full circle and ask again – does having a social economy movement add value to the development of organizations that normally are viewed as fitting within it? At this point, the answer is not clear. However, it is an important issue to follow.

Even though le Chantier and its investment fund may be a stimulus to developing the social economy of Quebec, there are other stimuli, some with a historic role. These include public sector nonprofits like Société d'aide au développement des collectivités (SADC) or Centre d'aide aux enterprises; community development corporations and regional development co-operatives, of which there is an extensive network.

In varying degrees, these forms of stimuli to development exist in other parts of Canada, though the names may differ. The public sector nonprofits working at arm's length from the government are referred to as Community Futures Development Corporations. There are also community development corporations, investment funds, and government support programs. The approach goes under different labels – community economic development in Manitoba and Nova Scotia; co-operative development in Saskatchewan; social enterprise development in Ontario. Even within each province, there are variations on the predominant theme and many points of development reflecting the dynamism that underlies the social economy.

This argument can be seen as calling into question the utility of the social economy concept. However, the utility of the social economy concept is its bridging and interactive qualities. The social economy, as we conceptualize it, forces researchers to look at the commonalities that may exist in differing organizational forms and to seek out common denominators.

Let us illustrate this point by taking the example of a Toronto-based organization called Common Ground. It is a co-operative, nonprofit with charitable registration, and houses four businesses (a catering firm and three coffee sheds) for the developmentally disabled (people with Down's syndrome). The developmentally disabled work within these businesses or social enterprises, and are partners within them, participating to a degree in decision-making. The charitable status is important because the businesses do not break even and the charitable registration allows Common Ground to raise funds more easily. All of these differing organizational forms are directed to a common social goal of gainful employment for members of a disabled group. The social economy concept is helpful in understanding this type of interaction in that it breaks down the rigidities associated with labels such as business, co-operative, nonprofit, and charity. While each of these organization forms has a meaning, all operate in the same society, and the norms of the society affect how they operate. Similarly, the norms for business are changing as concern is growing about the deterioration of the physical environment. Environmental groups (nonprofits) are pressuring for that change, government is responding to a degree, and market-based organizations are being forced to adapt their business practices. The social economy, as a dynamic concept, is a way of viewing this interaction; it is a way of recognizing that all organizations are part of the economy and that all share social responsibilities. Development in the social economy is affected by government policies and by support from the private sector. Moreover, the social economy, by creating a social infrastructure, strengthens the qualities of the private and public sectors.

Having a portion of society referred to as the social economy differentiates it to a degree from the private and public sectors, but also emphasizes that these forms of organization overlap (social economy businesses, public sector nonprofits, community economic development). Thus, it becomes evident that the social economy and the rest of the economy are not dichotomous but partially overlapping and interactive. While the norms within the social economy may differ from the private and public sectors, it is a difference in degree. Additionally, development in the social economy is affected by government policies and by support from the private sector. Moreover, the social economy and its social infrastructure strengthen the qualities of the private and public sectors.

The interaction between the social economy and other sectors, which we emphasize, has been expressed in other ways – for example, in Polanyi's concept of the economy as an 'instituted process' (Polanyi, 1957), in Granovetter's subsequent elaboration upon 'embeddedness' (Granovetter, 1985), and in the more recent development of the social capital concept (Putnam, 1995, 1996, 2000). Each of these formulations addresses a unique set of issues, but they share the common denominator of viewing the economy within a social context. Although this viewpoint may seem self-evident to some, it does fly in the face of the tradition that views the economy as an end in itself and the part of society not specifically within the mainstream economy as an 'externality' – that is, in some other space. The interactive approach put forward in this chapter helps us to understand that organizations created for social purposes yield economic results and that businesses have social responsibilities, much like the organizations of the social economy.

Outline of the Book

The chapters that follow in this collection reflect this interactive approach. In other words, they represent the breadth of the social economy and the many ways that social economy organizations interact with the other sectors of the economy.

Many of the chapters discuss the interaction between the social economy and the private sector. For example, chapter 11 by Agnes Meinhard, Ryerson University and Femida Handy and Itay Greenspan, University of Pennsylvania, examines employer-supported volunteering programs of major financial institutions in Canada; chapter 9 by Travis Gliedt, Paul Parker, and Jennifer Lynes, University of Waterloo, discusses how environmental organizations have created strategic partnerships with the private sector in response to cuts in government funding; and chapter 13 by Jennifer Sumner and Sophie Llewelyn, University of Guelph, discusses challenges faced by organic farmers, and how they address these challenges through a farm-marketing co-operative.

Other chapters discuss the interaction with the public sector. For example, chapter 8 by Paulette Padanyi, University of Guelph, Mark Baetz and Steven Brown, Wilfrid Laurier University, and Ailsa Henderson, University of Edinburgh, discusses mandatory high school community service, a program initiated by the Ministry of Education in Ontario during the mid-90s; chapter 7 by Daniel Schugurensky and Erica McCollum, OISE/University of Toronto, examines the gap between the presence of the social economy in the business world and their portrayal in business and economics textbooks; chapter 5 by Peter Elson, Mount Royal University, Calgary, undertakes a comparative analysis of the nonprofit sector in the U.K. and its relationship to government and why the sector has not evolved similarly in Canada; chapter 6 by Kathy Brock, Queen's University, analyses effective collaboration with government in a post-welfare society and economy.

Issues that are more specific to social economy organizations are explored in several chapters, and reflect the institutional structure of the society in which they are embedded. Chapter 12 by Olakunle Akingbola, OISE/University of Toronto, explores the causes, impacts, and dimensions of work stoppages in social economy organizations in Ontario between 1994 and 2005; chapter 10 by Sherida Ryan examines online social economy enterprises; and chapter 14 by Ginette Lafrenière, Maike Zinabou, Matt Riehl, and Sandy Hoy, Wilfrid Laurier University, looks at the role of co-operatives in the integration of minority francophones in Ontario.

Several chapters focus on the many debates about the characteristics of social economy organizations. Chapter 3 by Marguerite Mendell, Concordia University, and Nancy Neamtan, le Chantier de l'économie sociale, reflects the movement culture found in Quebec; chapter 4 by Roger Spear, Open University, UK, discusses the debates about the social economy within a European context, and chapter 2 by David Lasby and Michael Hall, Imagine Canada, and Mark Ventry and Denyse Guy, the Ontario Co-operative Association, presents a statistical profile of the social economy in Ontario.

This collection of research papers is diverse, but in that regard it reflects the social economy, as a diverse form of organizations that interact with society as a whole and in so doing provide an essential social infrastructure.

REFERENCES

Blanc, T., Harrison, D., Kamat, A., & Fowler, T. (2001). *Mapping the social economy in Bristol: Evaluating the barriers and drivers for growth*. Bristol: Bristol Social Economy Development Project.

Borgaza, C., & Defourny, J. (2001). *The emergence of social enterprise*. New York: Routledge.

Bourgeois, D.J. (2002). *The law of charitable and not-for-profit organizations*. (3rd ed.). London: Butterworths.

Bruyn, S. (1977). *The social economy*. New York: John Wiley.

Bruyn, S., & Nicolaou-Smokoviti, L. (1989). *International issues in social economy: Studies in the United States and Greece*. New York: Praeger.

Canada Revenue Agency. (2009a). *Non-profit organizations*. Retrieved December 6, 2009, from http://www.cra-arc.gc.ca/tx/nnprft/menu-eng.htm

Canada Revenue Agency. (2009b). *Charities Directorate*. Retrieved December 6, 2009, from http://www.cra-arc.gc.ca/charities/

Chantier (Le) de l'économie sociale. (2005, September). *Social economy and community economic development in Canada: Next steps for public policy*. Montreal: Author.

Chantier (Le) de l'économie sociale. (2009). *Mission*. Retrieved December 6, 2009, from http://www.chantier.qc.ca/

Chaves, R., & Monzón, J.L. (2000). *Public Policies*. In CIRIEC (International Centre of Research and Information on the Public and Co-operative Economy), The Enterprises and Organizations of the Third System: A Strategic Challenge for Employment. Retrieved December 7, 2009, from International Centre of Research and Information on the Public and Co-operative Economy http://www.ciriec.ulg.ac.be/fr/telechargements/dgv_ciriec_fulltext_english.pdf#page=87

Co-operatives Secretariat. (2007). *Co-operatives in Canada (2004)*. Ottawa: Government of Canada.

Defourny, J., & Monzon, J. (Eds.). (1992). *Économie sociale*. Brussels: CIRIEC.

Favreau, L. (2006). Social economy and public policy: The Quebec experience. *Horizons, 8* (2), 7-15.

Galliano, Renato. (2003). *Social economy entrepreneurship and local development*. Milan: North Milan Development Agency: European Association of Development Agencies.

Granovetter, M. (1985). Economic action and social structure: The problem of embeddedness. *American Journal of Sociology 91* (3), 481–510.

Hall, M., de Wit, M.L., Lasby, D., McIver, D., Evers, T., Johnson, C., et al. (2005, June). *Cornerstones of community: Highlights of the National Survey of Nonprofit and Voluntary Organizations.* (Catalogue No. 61-533-XPE, Rev. ed.). Ottawa: Statistics Canada.

Human Resources and Skills Development Canada. (2005). *What is the social economy?* Retrieved December 7, 2009, from http://www.hrsdc.gc.ca/en/cs/comm/sd/social_economy.shtml

Humboldt California Foundation. (2009). *Glossary of terms.* Retrieved November 4, 2009, from http://www.hafoundation.org/haf/about-us/glossary.html

International Co-operative Alliance. (2009). *Statement on the Co-operative Identity.* Retrieved November 19, 2009, from http://www.ica.coop/coop/principles.html

MacPherson, Ian. (1979). *A history of the co-operative movement in English-Canada: 1900–1945.* Toronto: Macmillan.

Mansbridge, Jayne. (1982). Fears of conflict in face-to-face democracies. In Frank Lindenfeld & Joyce Rothschild-Whitt (Eds.), *Workplace democracy and social change* (pp. 125-37). Boston: Horizon.

McGregor, C., Clark, S. Ferguson, Z., & Scullion, J. (1997). *Valuing the social economy and economic inclusion in lowland Scotland.* Glasgow: Communities Enterprise in Strathclyde.

Mendell, M., & Rouzier, R. (2006). *Some initiatives that enabled the institutionalization of Quebec's social economy: Civil society's crucial role and the state's essential role.* Montreal: Concordia University, Unpublished document.

Mook, L., Quarter, J., & Richmond, B.J. (2007). *What counts: Social accounting for nonprofits and cooperatives* (2nd ed.). London: Sigel Press.

Moulaert, F., & Ailenei, O. (2005). Social economy, third sector and solidarity relations: A conceptual synthesis from history to present. *Urban Studies 42* (11), 2037–53.

NSW Government's Community Builders. (2005). *Social enterprise – Definitions, examples, links and readings.* Retrieved December 7, 2009, from http://www.communitybuilders.nsw.gov.au/building_stronger/enterprise/soc_ent.html

Polanyi, Karl. (1957). The economy as instituted process. In Karl Polanyi, Conrad Arensberg, & Harry Pearson (Eds.), *Trade and market in the early empires* (pp. 243-70). New York: Free Press.

Putnam, R. (1995). Bowling alone: America's declining social capital. *Journal of Democracy 6* (1), 65–78.

Putnam, R. (1996). *The decline of civil society: How come? So what?* Ottawa: John L. Manion Lecture.

Putnam, R. (2000). *Bowling alone: The collapse and revival of American community.* New York: Simon & Schuster.

Quarter, J. (2000) *Beyond the bottom line: Socially innovative business owners.* Westport CT: Greenwood/Quorum.

Quarter, J., Mook, L., & Armstrong, A. (2009). *Understanding the social economy: A Canadian perspective.* Toronto: University of Toronto Press.

Salamon, L.M., & Anheier, H.K. (1992). *In search of the nonprofit sector II: The problem of classification.* Baltimore: Johns Hopkins University, Institute for Policy Studies, Center for Civil Society Studies.

Shragge, E., & Fontan, J.M. (2000). Introduction. In E. Shragge & J.-M. Fontan (Eds.), *Social economy: International debates and perspectives* (pp. 1-21). Montreal: Black Rose.

Smith, David Horton. (1997). The rest of the nonprofit sector: Grassroots associations as the dark matter ignored in the prevailing 'flat earth' maps of the sector. *Nonprofit and Voluntary Sector Quarterly 26* (2), 114–31.

Statistics Canada. (2006). *Canada's nonprofit sector in macro-economic terms.* Satellite account of Nonprofit institutions and volunteering. 13-015-XWE.

Vaillancourt, Y., Aubry, F., Tremblay, L., & Kearney, M. (2002, November). *Social Policy as a determinant of health and well-being: The contribution of the social economy.* Paper presented at the Social Determinants of Health across the Life-Span Conference, Toronto, ON.

Walloon Council of the Social Market Economy. (2008). *Mission.* Retrieved July 29, 2008, from http://www.wallonie.be/fr/index.html

Webb, S., & Webb, B. (1921). *The consumers' co-operative movement.* London: Longmans, Green.

Yunus, M. (2007). *Creating a world without poverty: Social businesses and the future of capitalism.* New York: Public Affairs.

2 A Portrait of the Ontario Social Economy

DAVID M. LASBY, MICHAEL H. HALL,
R. MARK VENTRY, AND DENYSE GUY

Ontarians benefit from the contributions of a wide array of organizations that have, at their core, a social mission. Until recently, research and knowledge of the contributions of these organizations has been divided into separate streams, with one devoted to studying nonprofit organizations and another focusing on the contributions of co-operatives. Recent interest in the concept of the social economy has provided an opportunity to combine our understandings of these two types of organizations with social or nonprofit-maximizing missions. In this chapter, we present the first unified portrait of Ontario's social economy, outlining its size and scope as well as some of the challenges it is facing.

Canada has one of the largest nonprofit sectors in the world when one considers the size of its paid staff and volunteer workforce. Out of the 37 countries that participated in Johns Hopkins University's Comparative Nonprofit Sector Project (CNP), Canada's nonprofit sector was second only to the Netherlands, with a paid staff and volunteer workforce that accounted for 11.1% of the economically active population (Hall, Barr, Easwaramoorthy, Sokolowski, & Salamon, 2005).[1,2] It was far larger than the nonprofit sectors in countries such as the United States, the United Kingdom, France, Germany, and Australia.

According to the 2003 National Survey of Nonprofit and Voluntary Organizations (NSNVO), there are 45,360 nonprofit organizations in Ontario, making up 28% of organizations in Canada and accounting for 43% of total revenues (Hall, de Wit, et al., 2005; Scott, Tsoukalas, Roberts, & Lasby, 2006). Based on a 2004 survey of non-financial co-operatives (n = 928), the Co-operative Secretariat estimates that the revenues of non-financial co-operatives in Ontario total at least $2.1 billion. Together they are believed to make up 16% of all non-financial co-operatives in Canada and account for 11% of total revenues (McMartin, 2007). There are more than 200 credit unions and caisses populaires in Ontario with combined assets of almost $26 billion (Deposit Insurance Corporation of Ontario, 2008).

This chapter explores the relative contributions that nonprofits and co-operatives make to the social economy and presents a portrait of their areas of economic activity. It highlights the significant economic contribution that social economy organizations make in Ontario and shows some of the differences among organizations in terms of the types of resources they rely upon to make their contributions. Two key features of social economy organizations will be evident – the role that citizens play as volunteers and the role that government plays as the primary funder of a small number of institutions. It also examines the challenges that nonprofits and co-operatives face in fulfilling their missions. Finally, we close by discussing implications for the development of public policy concerning the social economy, an area in which Ontario's efforts lag considerably behind those of a number of other provinces in Canada.

Defining the Social Economy

Definitions of the social economy range from the narrow to the broad (e.g., Mook, Quarter, & Richmond, 2007; Neamtan & Downing, 2005; Quarter, 1992, 2000). The definition employed in this chapter includes organizations with a social mission that take a nonprofit organizational form or, like co-operatives, have social goals other than the maximization of profit. It excludes businesses that have been established primarily for a social purpose, organizations that have not incorporated, and mutuals.[3] This definition is similar to that presented by Mook, Quarter, and Ryan in the first chapter of this collection, but much broader than that applied in Quebec, as discussed in the chapter by Mendell and Neamtan, or in francophone parts of Europe, as discussed by Spear. In applying this definition, hospitals, universities, and colleges are included within the social economy, as are business and professional associations, unions, and places of worship.

Data Sources for Studying Ontario's Social Economy

This chapter draws on two primary sources of data to provide a portrait of the social economy in Ontario: the 2003 National Survey of Non-profit and Voluntary Organizations (NSNVO) (Hall, de Wit, et al., 2005) and the Ontario Co-operatives Survey (OCS), conducted in 2007 by the Ontario Co-operative Association and Imagine Canada. The NSNVO collected information from approximately 12,995 incorporated non-profit and voluntary organizations across Canada (2,251 from Ontario). Using a definition of nonprofit organizations derived from Salamon and Anheir (1997), it studied a set of organizations that were:

- institutionally separate from government;
- self-governing;
- nonprofit-distributing (i.e., devoting any profits realized to the mission of the organization rather than distributing them to owners or shareholders);
- beneficiaries of voluntary contributions of money and/or involve volunteers' governance and/or organizational activities; and
- incorporated or registered in some way with the provincial or federal governments.

The NSNVO excluded most co-operatives, capturing only a small number of nonprofit housing co-operatives. In order to collect more comprehensive information on co-operatives, the Ontario Co-operatives Survey was developed, using a questionnaire modelled on the one used by the NSNVO. The survey attempted contact with all known co-operatives in Ontario and obtained responses from 692 of the estimated 1,300 such co-operatives, producing 576 complete interviews.

For the analyses reported here, data from the NSNVO has been combined with data from the Ontario Co-operatives Survey. The NSNVO financial data has been adjusted to account for inflation in order to make it more comparable with the 2007 OCS data. In addition, NSNVO data dealing with Ontario co-operatives was removed to eliminate any possible duplication of data from the two data sets.

Data from the two surveys has been weighted to provide unified estimates for Ontario. OCS data was weighted according to region of the province, co-operative size, and sub-sector to adjust for total non-response. Responses for a limited number of parameters (e.g., paid staff, total revenues) were imputed to adjust for item non-response. For information on the weighting and imputation strategy used in the NSNVO, readers are referred to appendix B of the NSNVO Highlights Report (Hall, de Wit, et al., 2005).

Figure 2.1. Annual revenues of Ontario social economy organizations compared to selected Ontario industries

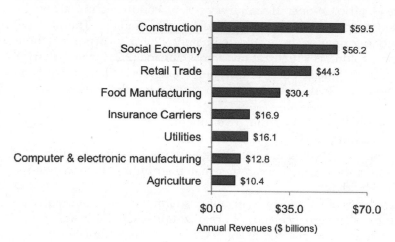

Annual Revenues ($ billions)

An Economic Force in the Province of Ontario

Based on findings from the NSNVO and the Ontario Co-operatives Survey, there are at least 46,000 social economy organizations in Ontario. Collectively their total annual revenues are estimated to be approximately $56.2 billion for 2007. The 1% of organizations that are Hospitals, Universities, & Colleges account for $19.8 billion of these revenues, while the remaining organizations account for $36.3 billion.

Ontario's social economy is larger than many key Ontario for-profit industries. In terms of revenues, Ontario's social economy is almost as a large as the Construction industry and larger than Retail Trade. It is almost twice the size of the Food Manufacturing industry and more than three times the size of Insurance Carriers or Utilities (see figure 2.1).[4] Even with the influence of Hospitals, Universities, & Colleges removed, it is still larger than the entire Food Manufacturing industry and more than twice the size of Insurance Carriers or Utilities.

Ontario social economy organizations draw on paid labour from just over 970,000 full-time and part-time staff and unpaid labour from 7.8 million volunteers.[5] Collectively, we estimate that the labour contributed by volunteers and paid staff is the equivalent of approximately 1.2 million full-time positions.[6] Hospitals, Universities & Colleges account for the equivalent of approximately 280 thousand full-time posi-

Figure 2.2. Labour force of Ontario social economy organizations, compared to selected Ontario industries

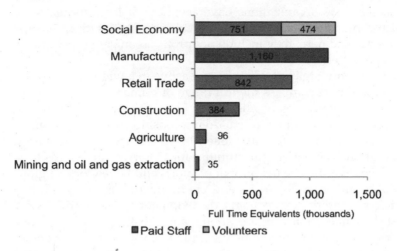

Full Time Equivalents (thousands)

■ Paid Staff   ▢ Volunteers

tions, while the remaining organizations account for the equivalent of 940 thousand full-time positions. Collectively, the labour contributed to social economy organizations amounts to approximately 17% of the economically active population of Ontario. Paid employment alone accounts for 11%.

To put our findings in broader context, when expressed in terms of Full-Time Equivalents (FTEs) the total labour consumption (both paid and volunteer) of Ontario's social economy organizations exceeds that of the entire Manufacturing industry of the province (see figure 2.2).[7] Even with the influence of Hospitals, Universities, & Colleges removed, total labour consumption (940 thousand FTEs) exceeds that of Retail Trade. Focusing on paid staff only, social economy labour consumption is somewhat smaller than that of Retail Trade. When the influence of Hospitals, Universities, & Colleges is removed, paid staff labour consumption is somewhat larger than Construction (484 thousand FTEs vs. 384 thousand FTEs).

Key Features – The Contours of Ontario's Social Economy

The social economy construct brings a broad variety of organizations into a single framework based upon their common pursuit of a social mission and their pursuit of goals other than the maximization of profit.

Underlying their common roles as vehicles for collective action is considerable diversity.

Social economy organizations have a variety of legal forms, some of which confer particular privileges such as exemption from income taxes. As defined here, they include nonprofit organizations, charities, and co-operatives.

Social economy organizations are also active in a wide range of economic areas that encompass the full range of human needs and interests. Social economy organizations provide a variety of services that range from daycare centres for children to hospices for the terminally ill. They provide housing and shelter, healthcare, renewable energy, and education. They offer opportunities for Ontarians to express their interests, whether this be the pursuit of sports and recreation, religious worship, or advocacy for social and environmental issues. And they provide opportunities for economic development and solidarity.

Finally, social economy organizations can be distinguished from one another on the basis of where they get the majority of their revenues. Some are 'commercial' and derive most of their revenues from the sales of goods and services. Others rely more on gifts and donations of money and volunteer time. A small but economically important group relies mainly on funding from government.

Legal Status

Social economy organizations can be categorized into three broad groups based on their legal status: incorporated not-for-profit corporations and associations (nonprofit organizations), organizations that have registered charity status (registered charities), and co-operatives.[8]

Organizations can incorporate as not-for-profit corporations, either with the Province of Ontario or federally. Registered charities are usually, but not always, nonprofit organizations that have also applied to the federal government to be registered as charities. To qualify for registration, they must work in one of four areas: the relief of poverty, the advancement of religion, the advancement of education, or other charitable purposes that benefit the general community. Both nonprofit organizations and registered charities are exempt from income taxes and may qualify for rebates on sales taxes in specific instances, but registered charities have a number of advantages over both nonprofit organizations and co-operatives.

Registered charities are able to provide receipts for donations that donors can use to claim tax credits. As Hall, de Wit, et al. (2005) point out, this gives an advantage over other nonprofit and voluntary organizations in their ability to attract donations from individual Canadians and from corporations. Moreover, registered charities benefit from the provision that charitable foundations can disburse funds only to qualified donees, of which registered charities are the largest single group.

Co-operatives are organizations that are owned by the members who use their services or purchase their products. Co-ops can provide virtually any product or service, and can be either nonprofit or for-profit enterprises. They operate in a broad range of areas such as housing, childcare centres, financial services (e.g., credit unions and insurance), renewable energy, social services, arts and culture, retail sales, and the provision of agricultural goods and services.

Co-ops offer a unique type of business model that shares some commonalities with both business corporations and not-for-profit organizations, but there are some key differences between the three types of organizations in how they are organized and carry on activities. For example, one of the defining features of co-operatives is that they operate on a democratic system that specifies 'one member, one vote.'

Co-ops have multiple bottom lines that include social as well as economic (or financial) objectives. While the financial viability and stability of a co-operative is important to its members, the primary objective is to maintain access to the product or service supplied by the co-op, not solely to increase the rate of return on their investment. As a result of commitment to this principle, in many communities, co-operatives have stayed to serve their members long after other businesses have fled to more profitable locales. For example, there are numerous communities in Ontario where credit unions are the only source of financial services.

The majority of social economy organizations are charities. Almost two-thirds (59%) of the 46,000 social economy organizations in Ontario are registered charities and over a third (38%) are incorporated nonprofits. The remaining 3% are co-operatives.

Area of Economic Activity and Organizational Function

Social economy organizations work in a variety of areas that touch on the lives of Ontarians. We employ a modified version of the International Classification of Nonprofit Organizations (ICNPO) to categorize social economy organizations on the basis of their main area of economic activity (see table 2.1).[9]

Following Salamon (1999), organizations can also be broadly grouped into two types of functions:

- *Service functions* involve the direct delivery of services such as education, social welfare, health, community and economic development, housing, and animal welfare and habitat conservation; and,
- *Expressive functions* are those that enable individuals to express their interests and/or beliefs – examples of this type of function include organizations supporting arts and culture, religious organizations, sports and recreation, labour, trade and professional associations, and advocacy groups.

Most social economy organizations serve expressive functions. As table 2.2 shows, 55% of all social economy organizations serve expressive functions, predominantly in the areas of Religion (23%) and Sports & Recreation (16%). Arts & Culture organizations are the next largest type of organization serving an expressive function (8% of all organizations), followed by Business & Professional Associations & Unions (5%) There are relatively few organizations working in areas of the Environment (2%) or Law, Advocacy, & Politics (2%).

Just under a third (31%) of Ontario social economy organizations provide service delivery functions. Most of these organizations work in the areas of Social Services (12% of all organizations), Development & Housing (10%), and Education & Research (5%). In contrast, Hospitals, Universities, & Colleges make up only 1% of all organizations, although, as will be seen, they play a much larger economic role than their numbers would suggest.

Not all organizations can be readily categorized as having a service or expressive function. For example, organizations working in the area of Granting, Fundraising, & Volunteerism Promotion may support either type of function.

Charities are the dominant legal form for service delivery organizations. With the exception of Development & Housing organizations, 73% or more of the organizations in each service delivery activity type are charities. Expressive function organizations, in contrast, are dominated by nonprofit organizations. The only exception to this is Religious organizations, which are almost exclusively comprised of charities (97%). Co-operatives make up a significant component (18%) of Development & Housing organizations.

Table 2.1
Primary activity areas of social economy organizations

Primary Activity Area	Number of Organizations	Description
Arts & Culture	3,478	General or specialized fields of arts and culture
Sports & Recreation	7,457	General or specialized fields of sports and recreation, co-operatives
Education & Research	2,322	Education and research, excluding school boards, universities, colleges, and post-secondary institutions
Health	1,138	General and specialized healthcare services, health support services, excluding hospitals
Hospitals, Universities, & Colleges	430	Hospital facilities that provide inpatient or out-patient medical care, universities, colleges and other postsecondary institutions
Social Services	5,387	Social services to a community or target population; childcare and aboriginal services co-operatives
Environment	937	Environmental conservation, pollution control and prevention, environmental education and health, and animal protection
Development & Housing	4,694	Improving communities and promoting the economic and social well-being of society; housing co-operatives, credit unions, and caisses populaires
Law, Advocacy, & Politics	1,023	Protecting and promoting civil and other rights advocating the social and political interests of general or special constituencies, offering legal services and promoting public safety
Grant making, Fundraising, & Volunteerism Promotion	5,416	Philanthropic organizations and organiza tions promoting charity and charitable activities, including grant-making foundations, volunteerism promotion and support, and fund-raising organizations
Religion	10,437	Religious organizations such as churches, mosques, synagogues, temples, shrines, seminaries, monasteries, and similar religious institutions and their related organizations and auxiliaries
Business & Professional Associations & Unions	2,215	Organizations promoting, regulating and safe-guarding business, professional and labour interests, federations and associations
Organizations Not Elsewhere Classified	1,364	International development and relief organiza-tions, organizations encouraging cultural understanding, agricultural and food co-operatives, wholesale, retail and transportation-co-operatives, energy and primary resources co-operatives, organizations unable to locate their primary activity within any of the specified activity categories

Table 2.2
Distribution of Ontario social economy organizations by primary activity area and legal basis of organization

Primary Activity Area	% of Organizations	Legal Basis of Organization		
		Registered Charities	Nonprofits	Co-operatives
Expressive Functions		57%	43%	0.2%
Religion	23%	97%	3%	0%
Sports & Recreation	16%	19%	81%	0%
Arts & Culture	8%	59%	40%	1%
Business Associations & Unions	5%	7%	92%	1%
Law, Advocacy, & Politics	2%	38%	62%	0%
Environment	2%	48%	52%	0%
	55%*			
Service-Related Functions		55%	36%	9%
Social Services	12%	73%	23%	4%
Development & Housing	10%	17%	65%	18%
Education & Research	5%	73%	27%	0%
Health	2%	83%	17%	0%
Hospitals, Universities, & Colleges	1%	87%	13%	0%
Other Co-ops	0.4%	0%	0%	100%
	31%*			
Other Functions		75%	25%	0%
Granting, Fundraising, & Volunteerism	12%	82%	18%	0%
Other NPOs	3%	44%	56%	0%
	14%*			
Total/All Organizations	100%	59%	38%	3%

*Reported total differs from independently calculated total due to rounding of sub-components.

Revenue Orientation

Social economy organizations can also be categorized according to their main source of revenue. *Government-oriented* groups receive 50% or more of revenues from government.[10] Similarly, *earned income-oriented* organizations receive 50% or more of their revenues from the sale of

Table 2.3
Distribution of Ontario social economy organizations by revenue orientation and legal basis of organization

Revenue Orientation	% of Organizations	Legal Basis of Organization		
		Registered Charities	Nonprofits	Co-operatives*
Government	12%	13%	10%	34%
Earned Income	46%	29%	72%	60%
Gifts & Donations	32%	48%	7%	3%
Diverse	10%	10%	11%	3%
Total	100%	100%	100%	100%

*Results incomplete – revenue orientation could be determined for only 30% of Co-operatives.

goods, products, and services, while *donation-oriented* organizations receive at least 50% of revenues from gifts and donations. *Diversified funding* organizations do not rely on any single source of revenue for more than 50% of their income.

Most social economy organizations are oriented predominantly either to earning income or to obtaining donations. More social economy organizations derive the majority of their revenues from earned income than from any other source (46% are Earned-income organizations). About a third (32%) rely mostly on gifts and donations to finance their operations. Close to one in ten (12%) receive the bulk of their funding from government either as grants or as payment for services rendered. The remaining 10% of organizations have diversified funding sources.

Nonprofit organizations and co-operatives are more likely to be earned income–oriented. As table 2.3 shows, charities are much more likely than other organizations to rely on grants and donations for 50% or more of their revenue. This is no doubt a reflection of the fact that they are better able to attract donations from individuals because of their ability to issue charitable tax receipts to donors. Charities are also privileged with respect to nonprofit organizations and co-operatives in their unique ability to receive grants from charitable foundations. Owing perhaps in part to the disadvantages they face relative to charities with respect to grants and donations, nonprofit organizations and co-operatives are much more likely to be oriented to earned income as a source of revenue. Co-operatives may also be somewhat more likely than other types of organizations to rely on government funding, though this finding should be viewed with caution, given the incompleteness of recall among co-operatives and other factors.[11]

The Financial and Human Resources of Social Economy Organizations in Ontario

Ontario's social economy organizations marshal substantial financial and human resources in pursuit of their social missions. They range along a continuum that includes at one end a large number of volunteer- or citizen-driven organizations that provide venues for self-expression including advocacy, social justice, sports, recreation, or religious worship. At the other are a relatively small number of large service institutions working in education, health, and social services. The volunteer-driven organizations rely mainly on donations of time and money to support their efforts, while the service institutions rely on government and earned income and a paid, professional workforce.[12]

Most organizations have less than $100,000 in annual revenues. While social economy organizations as a group report annual revenues totalling $56 billion ($36.3 billion when Hospitals, Universities, & Colleges are excluded), most individual organizations have very modest annual revenues. As table 2.4 shows, 54% of organizations report annual revenues of less than $100,000, while only about a tenth of organizations receive $1 million or more per year.

Economic activity is concentrated in a small group of large organizations. Although the majority of organizations are small, with annual revenues less than $100,000, the 2% of organizations that report annual revenues of $10 million or more account for 65% of total social economy revenues.[13] As table 2.4 shows, 35% of all revenues go to the 1% of organizations that are Hospitals, Universities, & Colleges.

Co-operatives have larger annual revenues than charities or nonprofit organizations. Co-operatives typically report much higher revenues than do charities or nonprofit organizations. More than half of co-operatives earn revenues of $505,000 or more. In contrast, the median revenues of registered charities are $81,000 while those for nonprofits are $71,000.

Health organizations report the largest organizational revenues. Health organizations and Hospitals, Universities, & Colleges lead the social economy in terms of the size of their annual revenues (median annual revenues of $909,000 and $1.2 million, respectively). With the exception of Business & Professional Associations & Unions, the median revenues

Table 2.4
Distribution of Ontario social economy organizations and annual revenues and median
annual revenues by annual revenue size class and primary activity area

Annual Revenue Size Class	% of Organizations	% Total Revenues	Median Annual Revenues ($,000's)
<$30,000	33%	0.3%	$9
$30,000–$99,999	21%	1%	$56
$100,000–$249,999	16%	2%	$163
$250,000–$499,999	10%	3%	$331
$500,000–$999,999	8%	5%	$644
$1,000,000–$9,999,999	10%	24%	$2,019
>=$10,000,000	2%	65%	$17,379
Total/All Organizations	*100%*	*100%**	*$78*
Primary Activity Area			
Expressive Functions			*$68*
Religion	23%	6%	$87
Sports & Recreation	16%	5%	$39
Arts & Culture	8%	3%	$36
Business Associations & Unions	5%	10%	$282
Law, Advocacy, & Politics	2%	2%	$105
Environment	2%	1%	$20
	*55%**	*26%**	
Service-Related Functions			$209
Social Services	12%	11%	$140
Development & Housing	10%	7%	$234
Education & Research	5%	3%	$166
Health	2%	5%	$1,235
Hospitals, Universities, & Colleges	1%	35%	$909
Other Co-ops	0.4%	4%	$150
	*31%**	65%	
Other Functions			*$33*
Granting, Fundraising, & Volunteerism	12%	5%	$18
Other NPOs	3%	4%	$118
	*14%**	9%	
Total / All Organizations	*100%*	*100%*	*$78*

*Reported total differs from independently calculated total due to rounding of sub-
components.

of expressive organizations are smaller than those of service organizations.

Government-oriented organizations have larger annual revenues than organizations relying on other types of income. Organizations that are mostly oriented towards government funding typically have much larger median annual revenues (50% have annual revenues of $508,000 or more) than organizations that are oriented towards earned income ($67,000) or grants and donations ($71,000). Organizations with diverse funding sources have the smallest median revenues ($43,000).

Human Resources of the Social Economy

The role of volunteers is a key factor distinguishing the social economy from the private and public sectors. Substantially all social economy organizations involve volunteers, either as board members or in the day-to-day functioning of the organization. Although paid staff provide most workforce hours for the social economy as a whole, more than half of social economy organizations have no paid staff and rely entirely on volunteers for their labour needs. Volunteers provide 39% of total workforce hours in Ontario's social economy while paid staff provide 61%.[14] Five percent of volunteers serve as board members, collectively contributing 3% of total workforce hours.[15] The remaining 95% of non-board volunteers account for 36% of hours.

Social economy employment is more likely to be part-time and temporary. Paid staff in social economy organizations are less likely to have full-time and permanent positions than is the case in the general Canadian labour force. Fifty-six percent of paid staff in the social economy are full-time employees and 69% are employed on a permanent basis (i.e., their employment does not have a set termination date). In contrast, 82% of employees in the general Ontario labour force are engaged on a full-time basis and 87% are permanent employees (Statistics Canada, n.d.-a, n.d.-c).

Paid staff resources are concentrated in the same group of organizations that receive most of the revenues. As might be expected, paid staff tend to concentrate among organizations that have greatest access to financial resources. Organizations with annual revenues of $1 million or more account for almost three-quarters of total hours worked by paid staff (see table 2.5). Similarly, Hospitals, Universities, & Colleges account for 36% of hours worked by paid staff. Social Services and Development & Housing organizations together account for another 33% of hours.

Table 2.5
Distribution of Ontario social economy organizations, annual revenues, and paid staff hours by annual revenue size class and primary activity area

Annual Revenue Size Class	% of Organizations	% Total Revenues	% Total Paid Staff Hours
<$30,000	33%	0.3%	1%
$30,000–$99,999	21%	1%	18%E
$100,000–$249,999	16%	2%	2%
$250,000–$499,999	10%	3%	2%
$500,000–$999,999	8%	5%	4%
$1,000,000–$9,999,999	10%	24%	24%
>=$10,000,000	2%	65%	49%
Total	100%	100%*	100%

Primary Activity Area			
Expressive Functions			
Religion	23%	6%	5%
Sports & Recreation	16%	5%	4%
Arts & Culture	8%	3%	3%
Business Associations & Unions	5%	10%	7%
Law, Advocacy, & Politics	2%	2%	1%
Environment	2%	1%	0.4%
	55%*	26%*	20%
Service-Related Functions			
Social Services	12%	11%	13%
Development & Housing	10%	7%	20%
Education & Research	5%	3%	2%
Health	2%	5%	5%
Hospitals, Universities, & Colleges	1%	35%	36%
Other Co-ops	0.4%	4%	1%
	31%*	65%	77%
Other Functions			
Granting, Fundraising, & Volunteerism	12%	5%	1%
Other NPOs	3%	4%	2%
	14%*	9%	3%
Total	100%	100%	100%

*Reported total differs from independently calculated total due to rounding of sub-components.
EUse with caution.

Figure 2.3. Distribution of total Ontario social economy workforce full-time equivalent positions, showing additional contribution of volunteers, by annual revenue size class

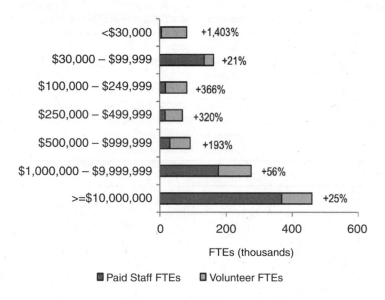

Most organizations rely mainly on volunteer labour. Although the paid labour supply tends to be concentrated among organizations with the most financial resources, the volunteer labour supply is not. For example, volunteers contribute 14 times more labour than paid staff among organizations with annual revenues less than $30,000 and over 3.5 times more among organizations with annual revenues between $100,000 and $249,999 (see figure 2.3). Similarly, as shown in figure 2.4, volunteers contribute more than four times the workforce hours of paid staff to Sports & Recreation organizations, more than three times the hours to Fundraising, Grant making, & Voluntarism Promotion organizations, and more than double the hours to Education & Research and Religion organizations.

Government-oriented organizations, particularly those working in health areas, rely more on paid labour. On average, paid staff accounts for 62% of total workforce hours for government-oriented organizations (see table 2.6). In contrast, organizations that depend on donations and earned income typically receive about three-quarters of their workforce hours

Figure 2.4. Distribution of total Ontario social economy workforce full-time equivalent positions, showing additional contribution of volunteers, by primary activity area

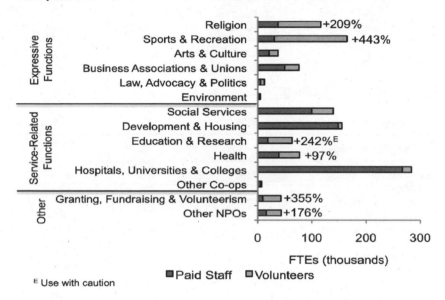

E Use with caution

from volunteers. Similarly, on average, over 60% of workforce hours for Hospitals, Universities, & Colleges and Health organizations come from full-time and part-time paid staff, as do over half of the hours for the typical Social Services organization. In general, with the exception of Business & Professional Associations & Unions and Law, Advocacy, & Politics organizations, expressive organizations tend to be more dependent on volunteers than are service organizations.

The Capacity Challenges Faced by Social Economy Organizations

While they are a significant force in Ontario's economy, there are signs that social economy organizations may be under strain. In both the NSNVO and the OSC respondents were asked to indicate the extent to which their organizations were experiencing problems in five general areas:

• human resources – the capacity to recruit and retain volunteers and paid staff;

Table 2.6
Average workforce hours from full-time and part-time paid staff and volunteers by revenue orientation and primary activity area

Revenue Orientation	Full-Time Paid Staff	Part-Time Paid Staff	Volunteers
Government	42%	19%	38%
Earned Income	20%	7%	73%
Gifts & Donations	21%	5%	74%
Diverse	14%	4%	83%
All Organizations	*23%*	*8%*	*70%*
Primary Activity Area			
Expressive Functions	*19%*	*6%*	*75%*
Religion	24%	5%	70%
Sports & Recreation	7%	6%	87%
Arts & Culture	17%	5%	78%
Business Associations & Unions	37%	12%	52%
Law, Advocacy, & Politics	30%	11%	59%
Environment	13%	7%	80%
Service-Related Functions	*33%*	*12%*	*54%*
Social Services	37%	14%	49%
Development & Housing	29%	9%	63%
Education & Research	29%	10%	61%
Health	45%	17%	38%
Hospitals, Universities, & Colleges	34%	26%	39%
Other Co-ops	40%	9%	50%
Other Functions	*11%*	*4%*	*85%*
Granting, Fundraising, & Volunteerism	10%	3%	88%
Other NPOs	20%	8%	72%
All Organizations	*23%*	*8%*	*70%*

- demand – the level of demand for services and products;
- policy development – the capacity to participate in the development of public policy;
- relationships and networks – the capacity to utilize relationships

with clients, members, funders, partners, government, and other stakeholders; and

- external financial issues – for organizations that had received funding from an external organization during the previous three years, factors related to external funding.

The NSNVO also asked charities and nonprofit organizations to report problems they were experiencing with respect to the following:

- volunteer issues – the capacity to train and manage volunteers;
- internal financial issues – internal capacity to obtain and deploy revenues;
- planning – the capacity to plan for the future and adapt to change; and
- infrastructure and processes – the capacity to deploy or rely on internal administrative systems, information technology, software, or databases.

As table 2.7 shows, the challenges that were most cited as problems by organizations were those pertaining to volunteering; for example, *recruiting the type of volunteers the organization requires* (57%), *retaining volunteers* (49%), and *obtaining board members* (49%). Other important challenges were *planning for the future* (reported to be a problem by 59% of organizations and a *serious* problem by 14%) and *increasing demands for services and products* (a problem for 42% of organizations and a *serious* problem for 14%). Areas associated with paid staff such as recruitment, retention, or training were among the least likely to be reported to pose a problem for organizations.

Internal financial challenges were also significant for charities and nonprofit organizations.[16] Close to half (48%) reported difficulties *obtaining funding from individual donors* and 44% reported difficulties *competing with other organizations for funding or revenues*. Difficulties with earned revenues were reported by 38% of organizations. A significant group (42%) of nonprofits and charities reported problems *obtaining funding from other organizations such as government, foundations, and corporations*, and 20% reported that it was a *serious* problem.

For organizations that reported having received funding from another organization at some point during the previous three years, challenges with their external funding were perceived to be much more serious than any other capacity area (see table 2.8).[17] For example, 69%

Table 2.7
Capacity challenges faced by Ontario social economy organizations

	A Small Problem	A Moderate Problem	A Serious Problem	Total Reporting a Problem
Human Resources – Volunteers				
Difficulty recruiting the type of volunteer the organization needs	21%	25%	12%	57%
Difficulty obtaining board members	18%	22%	9%	49%
Difficulty retaining volunteers	20%	19%	9%	49%
Difficulty providing training for volunteers*	20%	14%	7%	40%
Difficulty providing training to board members	14%	15%	6%	35%
Lack of paid staff to recruit or manage volunteers*	11%	12%	11%	34%
Human Resources – Paid Staff				
Difficulty obtaining the type of paid staff the organization needs	8%	12%	7%	28%
Difficulty providing staff training & development	11%	11%	6%	28%
Difficulty retaining paid staff	6%	7%	5%	19%
Internal Financial Issues				
Difficulty obtaining funding from individual donors*	12%	23%	13%	48%
Competition with other organizations for funding or revenues*	11%	20%	12%	44%
Difficulty obtaining funding from other organizations including government, foundations, or corporations*	7%	16%	20%	42%
Difficulty earning revenues*	9%	18%	11%	38%

Table 2.7 (Concluded)

	A Small Problem	A Moderate Problem	A Serious Problem	Total Reporting a Problem
Demand				
Increasing demands for services or products	11%	17%	14%	42%
Planning & Policy Development				
Difficulty planning for the future*	20%	24%	14%	59%
Difficulty adapting to change*	20%	16%	4%	40%
Difficulty participating in the development of public policy	11%	16%	9%	36%
Relationships & Networks				
Difficulty collaborating with other organizations	14%	8%	2%	25%
Infrastructure & Processes				
Lack of internal capacity (e.g., admin. systems or technology) *	17%	17%	7%	41%

*Co-operatives were not asked this question.

reported difficulties because of reductions in government funding and 40% indicated that these reductions were a *serious* problem. Sixty-four percent reported problems with the unwillingness of funders to fund core operations of the organization and 33% indicated that these caused *serious problems.*

Government-oriented organizations are much more likely to report problems than are organizations that are oriented to other funding sources. As table 2.9 shows, government-oriented organizations are much more likely to report capacity problems than are organizations that rely on other funding sources. The two exceptions to this trend are with difficulty earning revenues and difficulty collaborating with other organizations, for which organizations with diverse funding are more likely to report problems.

Government-oriented organizations also generally report more difficulties with external funding than do donation- or earned income–oriented organizations (see table 2.10). However, their pattern of problems is quite similar to that of the diverse funding–oriented organizations.

Co-operatives report more problems than other organizations. Co-operatives were generally more likely to report capacity problems than were charities or nonprofit organizations (see table 2.11). In turn, charities were generally more likely to report problems than nonprofit organizations. However, they were appreciably less likely to report difficulties in three main areas: obtaining board members, obtaining funding from other organizations such as government, foundations, and corporations, and earning revenues.

In terms of external capacity challenges, with the exception of reductions in government funding, registered charities that had received funding from another organization in the previous three years were more likely to report problems than were nonprofits or co-operatives (see table 2.12).

Conclusion

Ontario's social economy organizations touch almost all aspects of daily life through their role in delivering human and social services and the opportunities they provide to pursue personal and collective interests. Highly diverse, they have a substantial economic impact and a social impact that, if it were to be assessed, would no doubt be more impressive. Yet many organizations appear to be struggling to fulfil their so-

Table 2.8
External capacity challenges faced by Ontario social economy organizations that have received external funding during previous three years

		A Small Problem	A Moderate Problem	A Serious Problem	Total Reporting a Problem
External Financial Issues	Reductions in government funding	9%	19%	40%	69%
	Unwillingness to fund core operations	10%	21%	33%	64%
	Over-reliance on project funding*	10%	20%	23%	53%
	Need to modify programs	12%	24%	11%	47%
	Reporting requirements of funders	15%	20%	11%	46%

*Co-operatives were not asked this question.

Table 2.9
Capacity challenges faced by Ontario social economy organizations by revenue orientation

	Government	Earned Income	Gifts & Donations	Diverse
Human Resources – Volunteers				
Difficulty recruiting the type of volunteer the organization needs	69%	56%	53%	56%
Difficulty obtaining board members	64%	53%	37%	52%
Difficulty retaining volunteers	59%	48%	45%	45%
Difficulty providing training for volunteers*	54%	40%	38%	35%
Difficulty providing training to board members	56%	31%	31%	34%
Lack of paid staff to recruit or manage volunteers*	60%	30%	28%	40%
Human Resources – Paid Staff				
Difficulty obtaining the type of paid staff the organization needs	53%	22%	24%	30%
Difficulty providing staff training & development	56%	24%	23%	26%
Difficulty retaining paid staff	27%	15%	16%	21%
Internal Financial Issues				
Difficulty obtaining funding from individual donors*	63%	40%	50%	58%
Competition with other organizations for funding or revenues*	69%	42%	34%	57%
Difficulty obtaining funding from other organizations including government, foundations, or corporations*	76%	41%	27%	56%
Difficulty earning revenues*	45%	43%	24%	50%
Demand				
Increasing demands for services or products	67%	38%	37%	40%

Table 2.9 (*Concluded*)

	Government	Earned Income	Gifts & Donations	Diverse
Planning & Policy Development				
Difficulty planning for the future*	75%	58%	55%	63%
Difficulty adapting to change*	50%	39%	40%	32%
Difficulty participating in the development of public policy	60%	35%	29%	37%
Relationships & Networks				
Difficulty collaborating with other organizations	31%	24%	19%	36%
Infrastructure & Processes				
Lack of internal capacity (e.g., admin. systems or technology) *	67%	34%	40%	43%

*Co-operatives were not asked this question.

Table 2.10
External capacity challenges faced by Ontario social economy organizations that have received external funding during previous three years by revenue orientation

		Government	Earned Income	Gifts & Donations	Diverse
External Financial Issues	Reductions in government funding	83%	62%	45%	79%
	Unwillingness to fund core operations	79%	54%	51%	82%
	Over-reliance on project funding*	60%	47%	47%	62%
	Need to modify programs	61%	35%	42%	61%
	Reporting requirements of funders	59%	36%	34%	59%

*Co-operatives were not asked this question.

Table 2.11
Capacity challenges faced by Ontario social economy organizations by legal basis of organization

	Registered Charities	Nonprofits	Co-operatives	All Organizations
Human Resources – Volunteers				
Difficulty recruiting the type of volunteer the organization needs	57%	56%	73%	57%
Difficulty obtaining board members	45%	55%	63%	49%
Difficulty retaining volunteers	47%	49%	76%	49%
Difficulty providing training for volunteers*	42%	37%	–	40%
Difficulty providing training to board members	36%	32%	51%	35%
Lack of paid staff to recruit or manage volunteers*	36%	31%	–	34%
Human Resources – Paid Staff				
Difficulty obtaining the type of paid staff the organization needs	30%	23%	43%	28%
Difficulty providing staff training & development	30%	24%	40%	28%
Difficulty retaining paid staff	19%	16%	29%	19%
Internal Financial Issues				
Difficulty obtaining funding from individual donors*	55%	36%	–	48%
Competition with other organizations for funding or revenues*	45%	42%	–	44%
Difficulty obtaining funding from other organizations including government, foundations, or corporations*	41%	44%	–	42%
Difficulty earning revenues*	35%	43%	–	38%

Table 2.11 (*Concluded*)

		Registered Charities	Nonprofits	Co-operatives	All Organizations
Demand	Increasing demands for services or products	45%	36%	53%	42%
Planning & Policy Development	Difficulty planning for the future*	60%	59%	42%	59%
	Difficulty adapting to change*	42%	37%	–	40%
	Difficulty participating in the development of public policy	36%	37%	–	36%
Relationships & Networks	Difficulty collaborating with other organizations	24%	25%	31%	25%
Infrastructure & Processes	Lack of internal capacity (e.g., admin. systems or technology)*	44%	36%	–	41%

*Co-operatives were not asked this question.

Table 2.12

External capacity challenges faced by Ontario social economy organizations that have received external funding during previous three years by legal basis of organization

		Registered Charities	Nonprofits	Co-operatives	All Organizations
External Financial Issues	Reductions in government funding	69%	67%	79%	69%
	Unwillingness to fund core operations	71%	56%	51%	64%
	Over-reliance on project funding*	59%	43%	–	53%
	Need to modify programs	55%	36%	36%	47%
	Reporting requirements of funders	48%	42%	44%	46%

*Co-operatives were not asked this question

cial missions, which suggests that Ontarians are unlikely to be reaping all the benefits that these organizations are capable of providing.

As we have shown, the 46,000 social economy organizations in the province have a larger economic presence than many key industrial sectors of the economy. They are widely diverse, varying along a number of key dimensions. The majority are registered charities that rely on donations or government funding for their operations. However, they also include nonprofit organizations and co-operatives that rely on earned income.

Although the role of co-operatives in the social economy is relatively modest, compared to the role of nonprofit organizations, they play important roles in a number of areas within the social economy such as Development & Housing, and Social Services. Analysis that includes both co-operatives and nonprofits under the same umbrella presents a more comprehensive view of the social economy, but there are some risks with this approach. Because the numbers and contributions of co-operatives are relatively modest, constant care must be taken not to overlook their specific concerns and challenges. This is all the more important given that co-operatives are more likely than nonprofits to report many capacity challenges.

Social economy organizations are instruments that citizens are able to use to pursue missions that they believe to be worthwhile. Most obtain their revenues either from the sales of goods and services or from gifts and donations. And many also rely upon substantial contributions of volunteer time to operate their organizations. Co-operatives are an exception, with most commanding substantially more revenues and relying much more on paid staff than other organizations.

However, a significant number of social economy organizations also serve as instruments for the delivery of government-funded services. These organizations working in health, social services, and higher education are much larger than others in terms of financial resources and account for the bulk of paid employment in the social economy.

The use and reliance on volunteers is one of the key features of social economy organizations. Most organizations rely mainly or solely on volunteers rather than paid staff and many organizations with paid staff also benefit from contributions of volunteer labour.

Most employment is concentrated in the organizations that receive the bulk of the revenues, with co-operatives and government-oriented organizations generally relying much more on paid staff than volunteers. While social economy organizations are major employers in

Ontario, the nature of this employment is more part-time and temporary than is the case for the general labour force.

Are Ontarians receiving the full benefit that social economy organizations can provide? Our research suggests that they may not be. Many social economy organizations reported facing a variety of problems that keep them from fulfilling their missions. Government-oriented organizations and co-operatives were much more likely than others to report problems with respect to almost every capacity area we assessed.

Despite the sizeable economic impact of Ontario's social economy organizations, Ontario has given little attention to supporting their development. In comparison, provinces like Quebec, Alberta, and New Brunswick have developed, or are in the process of developing, a variety of initiatives to support the development and sustainability of their social economy.

Quebec has implemented a variety of programs and policies to support the social economy (e.g., Favreau, 2006; Loxley & Simpson, 2007; Vaillancourt, Aubry, Jetté, & Tremblay, 2003). Among these are initiatives to include social economy organizations in the development of social and economic policy at local and provincial levels, policies to promote the social economy in key areas such as daycare, homecare, and social housing, and the creation of dedicated pools of funding for the development of social economy organizations.

Other provinces such as New Brunswick and Alberta, for example, have more recent public policy initiatives. In 2006, New Brunswick appointed a minister responsible for Community Non-Profit Organizations as well as a deputy minister for Community Non-Profit Organizations whose primary task is to address the recommendations of the Premier's Task Force on the Community Non-Profit Sector (Premier's Community Non-Profit Task Force, 2007). The Government of Alberta along with key social economy partners has created the Alberta Nonprofit Voluntary Sector Initiative and a Framework for Collaboration that is intended to 'create solutions for commonly shared issues, build the capacity of both sectors to participate in the partnership as well as capacity to better serve Albertans and engage both sectors in an integrated policy dialogue' (Government of Alberta, n.d.).

While this chapter is not intended to present a detailed analysis of areas for policy development in Ontario, our findings do provide some direction for further exploration. Our research is one of the first to take a combined view of three distinct types of social economy organizations: charities, nonprofit organizations, and co-operatives. It reveals that each pursues social objectives in distinct ways and relies on different types of financial and human capital. Charities, for example, are more likely to rely on donations and/or government funding, while nonprofit organizations and co-operatives are more likely to rely on earned income. Charities and nonprofit organizations tend to rely much more on volunteers for their labour while co-operatives depend more on paid staff.

Efforts to improve the human and financial resources available to social economy organizations merit attention. However, these should be considered through the lens of current resource dependencies. Many social economy organizations, especially co-operatives and nonprofit organizations, rely mostly on income from the sale of goods and services to support their operations. Initiatives that improve access to capital may help these organizations to further develop their capacities to earn their own revenue.

Other organizations, mostly charities, rely mainly on donations from individuals and foundations to support their operations. While the federal government has improved tax incentives for charitable donations, provinces such as Alberta have shown that provincial governments can also play a role in efforts to stimulate donations to charities by improving provincial tax incentives (Government of Alberta, 2007).

The portrait of the social economy that emerges from this study places government in a central role when one considers the role that organizations play in the delivery of higher education, hospital services, and health and social services. Not only does government provide significant funding to the social economy as a whole, but government-oriented organizations are also among the largest organizations in the social economy and command a significant amount of the financial and human resources within it.

Ironically, while government-oriented organizations tend to receive the lion's share of the dollars in the social economy, they also are much more likely to report capacity problems. The types of problems these organizations experience have been well documented. The funding regime for many nonprofits changed significantly during the 1990s, and, as Hall (2006) and Scott (2003) have noted, many are still coping with changes such as

- reductions in funding;
- the introduction of competitive bid processes for government funding;

- a focus on funding projects rather than broad support for the organization's activities;
- a restriction of funding to direct program costs with little allowance for administrative overhead and infrastructure costs;
- shorter duration of funding;
- frequently changing funding priorities;
- mandated collaborations with other organizations; and
- increased requirements for financial accountability.

Together these changes make for a difficult operating environment for government-oriented organizations. The lack of stable and long-term funding makes long-term planning difficult and it undermines the ability of organizations to develop and maintain the human and intellectual capital they require. Efforts to improve the funding arrangements that governments have with their social economy service delivery 'partners' would be well received.

It is also worth considering the unique resources that social economy organizations rely upon – donations of money and time. Our research shows that some types of social economy organizations appear to be better positioned to access these resources than others. Charities have been privileged in their ability to provide tax credits for donations. It is not surprising then to see that they benefit more from such donations than do nonprofit organizations or co-operatives. It may be worth exploring the benefits of widening access to tax credits for donations beyond the organizations that now qualify for registered charity status.

Finally, the role that volunteers play in the social economy is striking and not well appreciated. Most social economy organizations rely entirely on volunteers for their operations, and the most frequently reported challenges that organizations face in fulfilling their mission pertain to their ability to engage volunteers. Policy initiatives that improve the ability of social economy organizations to engage volunteers in their efforts are likely to be particularly valuable.

Ontario's social economy organizations are an impressive economic and social force. Ranging in scale from the numerous volunteer-driven community organizations to large and mostly government-funded institutions, most harness voluntary contributions of time and money in pursuit of social missions that touch all aspects of Ontarians' lives. These social economy organizations are playing a key role in Ontario yet receive only modest attention in terms of public policy. Given the extent to which Ontario lags behind other provinces in development of public policy to support the social economy, there are opportunities to improve the already substantial impact these organizations make.

NOTES

1 The study included 17 advanced, industrial countries from North America, Western Europe, and Asia; 15 developing countries across Latin America, Africa, the Middle East, and Asia; and five countries in Central and Eastern Europe.
2 International comparisons performed by the CNP exclude religious organizations.
3 Chum (2008) reports that there are 82 mutuals in Ontario which essentially are insurance companies operating within a broad co-operative model. Together these account for approximately 13% of the property and casualty insurance market in Ontario.
4 Source: Statistics Canada, CANSIM Table 381-0016 – Provincial gross output at basic prices in current dollars, System of National Accounts (SNA) benchmark values, by sector and North American Industry Classification System (NAICS), annual (Statistics Canada, n.d.-d) [2004 figures adjusted for inflation].
5 The number for volunteers is the total number of volunteers reported by Ontario organizations (i.e., the number of volunteer positions). Many individuals volunteer for more than one organization. According to the 2004 Canada Survey of Giving, Volunteering, and Participating, there were approximately 5.1 million Ontario volunteers (Hall, Lasby, Gumulka, & Tryon, 2006).
6 Assuming 35 hours per week, 48 weeks per year.
7 Source: Statistics Canada, CANSIM Table 282-0022 – Labour force survey estimates (LFS), by actual hours worked, class of worker, North American Industry Classification System (NAICS) and sex, annual (Statistics Canada, n.d.-b) [2003 figures].
8 In this chapter organizations incorporated as not-for-profit corporations and associations that also have charitable status are classified as charities.
9 Following our work with the NSNVO (Hall, de Wit, et al., 2005), we employ a modified version of the International Classification of Nonprofit Organizations (ICNPO) (Salamon & Anheier, 1997) to describe the economic areas in which social economy organizations are working in Ontario. It should be noted that many organizations work in more than one area, but for analysis purposes they have been placed in the category

in which they devote the greatest portion of their time and resources. While the ICNPO was not designed to describe the activities of co-ops, we are able to classify the majority of co-operatives into three main ICNPO categories: Social Services (childcare co-operatives), Development & Housing (housing co-operatives and credit unions), and Other (producer co-operatives, agricultural marketing co-operatives, etc.). Small numbers of co-operatives were placed in other classes, such as Sports & Recreation and Arts & Culture.

10 Although predominantly comprising service delivery organizations, government-oriented organizations include a variety of activity types: 28% are Social Services organizations, 16% Development & Housing, 11% Health, 11% Arts & Culture, and 4% Hospitals, Universities, & Colleges.

11 Due to incomplete recall by survey respondents, revenue orientation could be determined for only 30% of co-operatives. Because of the way the survey was structured, it may have response bias leading to an overestimation of the percentage of co-operatives with a government revenue orientation.

12 In a survey conducted by the HR Council for the Voluntary & Nonprofit Sector (2008), paid staff worked mainly in the following job categories: senior management (12%), mid-level manager or supervisor (20%), accredited or certified professional (15.3%), other profession requiring a university degree (14.5%), technical staff and paraprofessionals (11.6%).

13 Twenty-five percent of the organizations in this category are Business & Professional Associations & Unions, 20% are Hospitals, Colleges, & Universities and 17% are Social Services organizations.

14 Workforce hours include both paid staff and volunteer hours.

15 Board volunteers may also contribute to the operational activities of organizations in addition to their board service.

16 These items were not employed in the Ontario Co-operatives Survey. These findings therefore pertain only to nonprofit organizations and charities.

17 External funding questions were asked of the 41% of organizations that 'were incorporated, had been active for at least three years, and that had received funding from governments, foundations or corporations over that period' (Hall et al. 2005).

REFERENCES

Chum, A. (2008). *Mapping the mutuals and co-operative insurance movement in the*

Ontario and Canadian context: Challenges and opportunities for the social econo-my. Paper presented at the Southern Ontario Social Economy Community-University Research Alliance Symposium, Toronto, ON. Retrieved November 26, 2009, from the Social Economy Centre http://sec.oise .utoronto.ca/english/pdfs/2008_symposium/1_chum_0508.pdf

Deposit Insurance Corporation of Ontario. (2008). *2007 Annual Report*. Retrieved November 22, 2009, from http://www.dico.com/Design/ AnnualReport2007.pdf

Favreau, L. (2006). Social economy and public policy, the Quebec experience. *Horizons, 8*(2), 7-15.

Government of Alberta. (2007). *Revised (Backgrounder): Charities and Albertans benefit from increased tax credit*. Retrieved November 26, 2009, from http://www.gov.ab.ca/home/NewsFrame.cfm?ReleaseID=/ acn/200704/21364345FB08B-EC79-7432-700BA7ECC6219175.html

Government of Alberta. (n.d.). *Alberta nonprofit/voluntary sector initiative*. Retrieved November 26, 2009, from http://culture.alberta.ca/anvsi/

Hall, M.H. (2006). The Canadian nonprofit and voluntary sector in perspec-tive. In V. Murray (Ed.), *Management of Nonprofit and Charitable Organizations in Canada* (pp. 25-51). Markham, ON: LexisNexis, Butterworths.

Hall, M.H., Barr, C.W., Easwaramoorthy, M., Sokolowski, S.W., & Salamon, L.M. (2005). *The Canadian nonprofit and voluntary sector in comparative per-spective*. Toronto: Imagine Canada.

Hall, M.H., de Wit, M.L., Lasby, D., McIver, D., Evers, T., Johnson, C., et al. (2005). *Cornerstones of community: Highlights of the national survey of nonprofit and voluntary organizations. 2003 revised*. (No. Catalogue No. 61-533-XPE). Ottawa: Statistics Canada.

Hall, M.H., Lasby, D., Gumulka, G., & Tryon, C. (2006). *Caring Canadians, involved Canadians: Highlights from the 2004 Canada survey of giving, volun-teering, and participating* (No. Catalogue No. 71-542-XPE). Ottawa: Statistics Canada.

HR Council for the Voluntary & Non-profit Sector. (2008). *Toward a labour force strategy for Canada's voluntary & non-profit sector*. Ottawa: Author.

Loxley, J., & Simpson, D. (2007). Government policies towards community economic development and the social economy in Quebec and Manitoba. *Linking, learning, leveraging social enterprises, knowledgeable economies, and sus-tainable communities*. Retrieved November 26, 2009, from the Canadian CED Network http://www.ccednet-rcdec.ca/files/ccednet/Loxley_Simpson.pdf

McMartin, A. (2007). *Co-operatives in Canada (2004 data)*. Ottawa: Co-operatives Secretariat.

Mook, L., Quarter, J., & Richmond, B.J. (2007). *What counts: Social accounting for nonprofits and cooperatives* (2nd ed.). London: Sigel Press.

Neamtan, N., & Downing, R. (2005). *Social economy and community economic development in Canada: Next steps for public policy.* Montreal: Chantier de l'Économie Sociale.

Premier's Community Non-Profit Task Force. (2007). *Blueprint for action: Building a foundation for self-sufficiency.* Fredericton: Government of New Brunswick.

Quarter, J. (1992). *Canada's social economy: Co-operatives, non-profits, and other community enterprises.* Toronto: James Lorimer.

Quarter, J. (2000). The social economy and the neo-conservative agenda. In E. Shragge & J.M. Fontan (Eds.), *Social economy: International debates and perspectives* (pp. 54-65). Montreal: Black Rose.

Salamon, L.M. (1999). *America's nonprofit sector: A primer* (2nd ed.). New York: The Foundation Center.

Salamon, L.M., & Anheier, H.K. (1997). Toward a common definition. In L.M. Salamon & H.K. Anheier (Eds.), *Defining the nonprofit sector: A cross-national analysis* (pp. 29-50). New York: Manchester University Press.

Scott, K. (2003). *Funding matters: The impact of Canada's new funding regime on nonprofit and voluntary organizations.* Ottawa: Canadian Council on Social Development.

Scott, K., Tsoukalas, S., Roberts, P., & Lasby, D. (2006). *The nonprofit and voluntary sector in Ontario.* Toronto: Imagine Canada and Canadian Council on Social Development.

Statistics Canada. (n.d.-a). Table 282-0002 – Labour force survey estimates (LFS), by sex and detailed age group, annual (persons unless otherwise noted), CANSIM (database), using E-stat (provider). Retrieved October 20, 2008

Statistics Canada. (n.d.-b). Table 282-00022 – Labour force survey estimates (LFS), by actual hours worked, class of worker, North American Industry Classification System (NAICS) and sex, annual, CANSIM (database), using E-stat (provider). Retrieved October 26, 2009

Statistics Canada. (n.d.-c). Table 282-0080 - Labour force survey estimates (LFS), employees by job permanency, North American Industry Classification System (NAICS), sex and age group, annual (persons), CANSIM (database), using E-stat (provider). Retrieved October 20, 2008

Statistics Canada. (n.d.-d). Table 381-0016 – Provincial gross output at basic prices in current dollars, System of National Accounts (SNA) benchmark values, by sector and North American Industry Classification System

(NAICS), annual, CANSIM (database), using E-stat (provider). Retrieved October 8, 2008

Vaillancourt, E., Aubry, F., Jetté, C., & Tremblay, L. (2003). Regulation based on solidarity: A fragile emergence in Quebec (S.A. Stilitz, Trans.). In Y. Vaillancourt & L. Tremblay (Eds.), *Social economy: Health and welfare in four Canadian provinces*. Montreal: Fernwood Publishing and LAREPPS, École du travail sociale, Université du Québec à Montréal.

3 The Social Economy in Quebec: Towards a New Political Economy

MARGUERITE MENDELL AND NANCY NEAMTAN

Although the vocabulary is new, the social economy has been well established in Quebec for more than a century. Its development has been an integral part of Quebec's social and economic history (D'Amours, 2007; Laville, J.-L., Lévesque, B., & Mendell, M., 2007; Lévesque, 2001; Lévesque & Mendell, 1999; Mendell, 2002; Mendell, 2008; Neamtan, 2005). The co-operative movement has a long and established presence and has contributed to the well-being and economic growth of Quebec. Numerous associations and nonprofit organizations have played a vital role in meeting socio-economic needs over the years. In Quebec, these collective enterprises, whatever their juridical status, are recognized as economic actors alongside the private and public sectors. What distinguishes the social economy in Quebec, however, is its broad reach, which extends beyond these collective enterprises to include social movements and territorial intermediaries that identify themselves as part of the social economy. Together they are represented by the Chantier de l'économie sociale, a multi-scalar and multi-sectoral institutional space that is unique in its diversity and in its unity. This does not imply consensus on all issues. Rather, the Chantier's commitment to constructing an alternative model of economic development embedded in a process of deliberative, democratic decision-making is the basis for this innovative network of networks.

The focus of our chapter is on how the social economy not only challenges the prevailing economic model through its *outcomes*, but also on the institutional changes that this requires, the *processes* of re-engaging government in new ways, and of working across boundaries to participate in new policy design. For this to happen, social economy actors had to also tear down the boundaries between groups, organizations, and movements accustomed to working separately in the interests of their members. This also distinguishes the Quebec experience. Working across boundaries has meant establishing spaces for dialogue and working towards collective objectives or in the *general interest* of the many organizations and movements involved.

The social economy in Quebec is a history of mobilization and political action. The view of the social economy upon which this chapter is based is different from that outlined in chapter 1 by Mook, Quarter, and Ryan and in chapter 2 by Lasby et al. In Quebec, the social economy is seen as a social movement that challenges norms, as distinct from a classification system that attempts to understand the many ways that organizations with a social mission interact with other parts of the economy. This view is similar to that proposed in francophone Europe and advocated by CIRIEC, and as outlined in chapter 4 by Roger Spear.

The numerous public policies outlined in this chapter are the result of this innovative institutional design. Without this structure, without the leadership provided by the Chantier and the capacity for the social economy to speak with a single voice, many of these policies would not exist or would not be as far reaching.

Quebec: A Distinct Society in North America

The unique characteristics of Quebec society have provided fertile ground for the current expansion of the social economy. Quebec is a small French-speaking nation within Canada with a population of 7.5 million people. As a distinct society, it has had to wage an extensive political struggle for its survival and recognition as a nation. This context has contributed to its social cohesion unique in North America. Until the middle of the twentieth century, outside interests dominated the economy of Quebec. The 'Quiet Revolution' in the 1960s, under the government of Jean Lesage, was a turning point that radically transformed Quebec and established the present institutional infrastructure. The 1960s was marked by the extensive intervention of government in the economy, including the nationalization of hydro-electricity (Hydro-Québec) and the creation of the *Caisse de dépôt et de placement*, the public-sector pension fund, which in 2007 had $257.7 billion in total assets (Caisse de dépôt, 2008).[1] Most significant, however, were the emergence of a new entrepreneurial class among Francophones and the growth of the labour movement. Today, more than 40% of the province's workers are unionized, the highest rate in North America (Jackson & Schetagne, 2004).

The Quiet Revolution led to the rapid decline of the Catholic Church's influence and to the emergence of a dynamic community movement (*mouvement populaire*). This movement of primarily nonprofit associations not only defended the rights of the disadvantaged but also became engaged in service provision including healthcare, housing, social services, childcare, literacy, and employment training. During the same period, co-operatives and mutual associations maintained and increased their presence in the financial, insurance, and agriculture sectors and, to a lesser degree, in forestry and some retail services.

The strong presence of government during this period reflected its drive to modernize Quebec. Institutional changes in all sectors of life, including education, accompanied this objective. For example, the Hautes études commerciales (HEC) was established to develop a francophone business class. Government also played a central role in redistributing wealth through the creation of universal social security programs and the delivery of education and health and social services. Although this state-led development strategy succeeded in radically transforming Quebec, the limits of this model became apparent by the early 1980s. Economic restructuring and the recession, experienced throughout all OECD countries at that time, had severe negative impacts in Quebec. A declining manufacturing sector and the progressive depletion of natural resources called for state action that was not forthcoming, confirming the substantial limits on the ability of the Quebec government to act. A sharp increase in unemployment combined with reduced public spending capacity was devastating for local communities confronting poverty and marginalization. These conditions led to a major cultural shift within the labour and community movements in Quebec; it also marked the rebirth of the social economy (Lévesque & Mendell, 1999). Indeed, the legacy and earlier achievements of the social economy in Quebec were critical to this new phase, which represents both continuity and transformation in response to new realities.

Labour Solidarity Investment Funds

In 1983, the establishment of a workers' investment fund, the Fonds de solidarité (FTQ), by the Fédération des travailleurs et travailleuses du Québec (FTQ), Quebec's largest union, was the first manifestation of this cultural shift.[2] Following extensive internal debates, the FTQ decided that the labour movement had to become proactive in the search for solutions to the economic crisis and massive job losses in the early 1980s. It successfully negotiated tax measures with both the federal and provincial governments to establish the Fonds that would create and maintain jobs in Quebec by investing in small- and medium-sized businesses (Lévesque, Belanger, Bouchard, & Mendell, 2001). The Fonds de solidarité is obliged by law to invest a minimum of 60% in enterprises in Quebec. We refer to this as development finance to distinguish the Fonds from more traditional venture capital, given its commitment to job creation and economic development (Lévesque, Mendell, & Rouzier, 2003). Development finance conforms to double bottom line or triple bottom line objectives, if environmental goals are also included. In 2008, assets of the Fonds de solidarité were $7.3 billion. Over the years, the Fonds has invested nearly $4.1 billion in Quebec and created over 100,000 jobs (FTQ, 2008).[3]

To fully meet its objectives, the Fonds de solidarité diversified its investment tools by creating sectoral and territorial or *place-based* funds, often in partnership with municipalities and other regional development actors. Two of these funds, *SOLIM*, a real estate fund, and a number of *SOLIDES*, local investment funds, invest in social economy enterprises. In 2006, the Fonds de solidarité became a financial partner of the Chantier d'économie sociale Trust, investing $12 million in a $52.8 million patient capital investment fund that provides long-term capital for social economy enterprises (Fiducie du Chantier de l'économie sociale, 2008).[4]

This is but one of several examples of an innovative socio-economic initiative in which a Quebec social movement organization has engaged directly in a partnership with the private and public sectors. In an earlier article (Lévesque et al., 2003), we suggested that while the Fonds de solidarité primarily meets the needs of small and medium businesses in general, its investment in the Chantier Trust confirms its growing commitment to the social economy. Moreover, the Fonds is itself a social economy enterprise, controlled by workers, with clearly stated goals of profitability, job creation, and socio-economic development.

In 1996, the second largest union organization in the province, the Confédération des syndicats nationaux (CSN), established Fond*Action*, a development fund for co-operation and employment that adds to an already existing network of innovative financial instruments developed by the CSN.[5] Fond*Action* benefits from the same tax measures created for the Fonds de solidarité by the federal and provincial governments. However, the mandate of Fond*Action* differs somewhat in that it prioritizes investments in enterprises that practise participatory management, collective ownership, and a commitment to sustainable development. Fond*Action* has also developed some specialized financial tools with various partners specifically for social economy enterprises. It has created or maintained over 8,000 jobs since it was established; in 2008 Fond*Action* had assets of $635.6 million (Fond*Action*, 2008).[6]

Citizen-Based Initiatives in Economic Development

Parallel to the establishment of the first labour fund in 1983, the community movement also embarked on a process of redefining its relationship with economic development, and established the first community economic development corporations (CDECs) in disadvantaged districts of Montreal. These new local development intermediaries, financed by the federal, provincial, and municipal governments, created strategies to revitalize neighbourhoods hard hit by economic restructuring, the recession, and job losses. Community organizers and social activists had to shift their action from oppositional politics to economic development, and work with the labour movement and business community to co-design a blueprint for economic recovery. Despite the depth of the economic crisis, collaboration did not come easily. Debate, dialogue, and a collective learning process were necessary to break with traditional roles and strategies. More than twenty years later, CDECs are part of the socio-economic landscape of Quebec. Other organizations and associations have also emerged as key actors in local and regional development.[7] Together, these represent numerous citizen-based initiatives that are instituting processes of economic democratization in Quebec and have stimulated a favourable environment for a revitalized social economy movement today.

We referred earlier to working across boundaries as a defining characteristic of the social economy in Quebec. The experience of these early CDECs has, in many ways, shaped the strategic orientation and the institutional infrastructure of the social economy and its capacity to work horizontally across numerous sectors and regions involving many social movements in the process. While the private and public sectors are not part of this innovative institutional network, the social economy engages with the public sector directly in negotiating policy innovation and with the private sector more indirectly by presenting the social economy as a credible and significant economic player and, more recently, as a possible source for investment opportunities (Mendell & Nogales, 2008).

New Recognition of the Social Economy

A key moment in the evolution of today's social economy occurred in 1996, when the government of Quebec organized the *Sommet sur l'économie et l'emploi* (Summit on the Economy and Employment), bringing together representatives of large corporations, employers' associations, labour federations, financial institutions, municipalities, and social movements. The objective of the Summit was to enable a broad consultation on the economic and fiscal crises in Quebec. Consultations of this sort were not new in Quebec; however, the so-called Quebec model of 'concertation' had, until that time, included only the 'big' players – government, business, and labour. Given the serious difficulties faced by government, the Sommet invited representatives of social movements to participate for the first time and issued a challenge to both the private sector and civil society to propose economic renewal strategies. Three task forces were established and given six months to prepare for the Summit, including a working group on the social economy that drafted an ambitious action plan. This plan, called 'Osons la solidarité' (Daring Solidarity), offered a consensual definition of the social economy, drew attention to the socio-economic contribution of the social economy, and suggested initiatives that would create thousands of jobs, while meeting the social, environmental, and cultural needs of Quebec. The working group, the Chantier de l'économie sociale, was given two years to meet the objectives of its action plan. Because it exceeded these objectives, participating networks and social movements decided to transform the Chantier, a temporary structure created by the provincial government, into an independent nonprofit organization to continue to promote and develop the social economy. As will be discussed, since the establishment of the Chantier, the government of Quebec has adopted numerous measures and public policies that were the fruit of this action plan and beyond (Mendell & Rouzier, 2006).

Twelve years later, the social economy continues to develop and is an integral part of the political economy of Quebec. Despite its numerous achievements, visibility, and recognition in Quebec, the rest of Canada, and internationally, the social economy in Quebec does not have adequate data to reflect its activities. This limitation is not specific to Quebec; it exists elsewhere in Canada and internationally. Official data provided by the *Bureau de l'économie sociale* (social economy office) and the *Direction des coopératives* (co-operatives' directorate) is for 2002. There are currently many efforts to improve upon this information, but they have not yet been incorporated into official statistics (CESIM, 2008; Chantier, 2008).[8]

The Social Economy in Quebec 2002

- 7,822 businesses (3,881 co-operatives and 3,941 NPOs)
- 935 childcare centres
- 671 credit unions
- 180 worker co-operatives
- 103 social economy enterprises providing domestic assistance
- 72 worker shareholder co-operatives (Workers in a business may create a workers' shareholder co-operative and may jointly acquire shares in the business in which they are employed.)
- Total sales without credit unions: $17.2 billion ($15.9 billion for co-operatives and $1.3 billion for NPOs)
- Total sales with credit unions: $102.5 billion ($101.2 billion for co-operatives; $1.3 billion for NPOs)
- Job creation in Quebec (2002): without credit unions: 124,302 jobs (79,222 in co-operatives and 45,080 in NPOs); with credit unions: 161,302 jobs (116,222 in co-operatives and 45,080 in NPOs)

The Social Economy: A Contribution to a Redefinition of Social and Economic Policy

The social economy is contributing to a broader reflection on social and economic policy. In Quebec, we have created a political economy framework to situate the social economy within a new model of development in which its role in the production of goods and services is recognized. The contribution of the social economy to sustainable local and regional development, to the creation of jobs for marginalized groups, and to the efficient provision of services is increasingly acknowledged. What is less well documented and conceptualized is the realignment of state, market, and civil society that this implies as well as the implications for public policy. The specific activities that define the social economy in different communities require corresponding policy flexibility and ultimately a new political culture. Not only do existing policy environments have to open up and encourage dialogue and collaboration, but they also have to adopt flexible governance (Amin & Hausner, 1997).

The Co-Construction of Public Policy

The objective of this article is to provide an overview of Quebec's social economy. We have chosen to focus on the policy environment to illustrate the innovative process of policy formation in Quebec that involves ongoing dialogue between social economy actors and different levels of government. In November 2008, the government of Quebec announced an action plan for the social economy, its most comprehensive policy initiative since the 1996 Summit (Gouvernement du Québec, 2008). The need to involve nine ministries in this plan confirms the recognition of the need for horizontal policy development. But most significant is the *process of co-construction* that led to this important initiative. It is this process that we summarize below.

A major challenge for policy makers has been developing consensus on a clear definition of the social economy. Over the recent years, several definitions have been proposed by researchers and stakeholders, based on different histories and analytical frameworks. For these reasons, the development of public policy for the social economy has been complex, not only in Quebec but also throughout Canada and internationally. Governments are increasingly recognizing the benefits of inter-sectoral and multi-stakeholder dialogue as they design appropriate measures for the evolving social economy. The menu of existing policy measures is inadequate. Not only does this call for policy innovation, but it also strongly suggests that the *processes* of policy formation have to change. Growing references to collaborative planning, policy dialogue, and communities of practice refer to the need for new *processes* that require new institutional dialogic spaces.

In Quebec, where public policy to facilitate the social economy has made considerable strides, each new strategic initiative is the result of proposals made by social economy actors. The relationship between the Quebec government and the social economy is based on the mutual understanding that government alone does not have the capacity to identify needs and new practices in the social economy. The co-construction of public policy is a sine qua non in devising effective policies to support the social economy. While it might be a stretch to suggest that these processes are the seeds for a new regulatory environment, this no longer seems as improbable.

Flexible Policy Formation

The government of Quebec maintains an ongoing partnership agreement with the Chantier de l'économie sociale, a network of networks, which, in collaboration with its various members and partners, is expected to make an active contribution to the development of public policy. Furthermore, the government of Quebec recognizes the Conseil québécois de la coopération et de la mutualité (Quebec council of co-operatives and mutual associations) as the main interlocutor on issues relating specifically to co-operatives and mutual benefit organizations. These relationships are dynamic and consultative and, in recent times, have risen to the challenge set by the innovative nature of the social economy. Indeed, the long history of dialogue and *concertation* makes this somewhat easier in Quebec. That said, even *concertation* has, over time, established fixed patterns of behaviour and expectations that have to be transformed and become more flexible. The social economy represents an ongoing process of innovation originating in communities actively engaged in processes of 'learning by doing.' New approaches to economic development, new forms of partnership, and new social initiatives are being tested on a continuing basis; this underlies the invention and expansion of exemplary practices. Innovation exerts considerable pressure on both government and social economy actors, who must be able to ensure proper accountability for public funds, while encouraging the emergence of innovative practice. Unlike traditional public policy, which discourages experimentation and change, social innovation and the social economy necessitate the ongoing creation of precedents in public policy.

Four Main Categories of Public Policies[9]

Since the Summit in 1996, numerous public policies have been adopted in Quebec to support the growth of the social economy, both directly and indirectly. We group these into four main categories: (a) territorial policies; (b) generic development; (c) sectoral policies; and (d) policies for target populations (Downing & Neamtan, 2005).

Territorial Policies

Social economy enterprises have emerged in communities that mobilize to promote development. The example of the tripartite support given to community economic development corporations (CDECs) in most urban centres in Quebec is an important illustration of the role of enabling public policy. As we noted earlier, these not-for-profit development organizations at the service of communities have inspired some of the most original and successful social economy initiatives in Quebec.

The creation of local development centres (CLDs) across Quebec in 1997, to which we referred earlier, was, in fact, a strategic gain for the social economy as they were also mandated by law to support the development and consolidation of social economy enterprises, with subsidies designated for these enterprises. This policy changed somewhat under the Liberal government elected in 2003, but the obligation to support the social economy remains, and the governance of the CLDs, now predominantly locally elected officials, must include at least one representative from both the social economy and the private sector.

The government of Quebec's comprehensive Action Plan includes support for regional social economy poles (nodes) in each administrative region as well as for new initiatives in the social economy, signifying its role in regional development. The recent transfer of responsibility for the social economy to the Ministry of Municipal Affairs and Regional Development has reinforced the commitment of the Quebec government to the social economy, a more horizontal policy location that is better able to address the diversity of the social economy. In addition, the City of Montreal launched a municipal policy to promote the social economy, based on a broad and inclusive partnership between social economy actors and the municipal actors in March 2009. Social economy actors from numerous sectors, researchers, and representatives of the municipal government jointly drafted this policy proposal that represents a continuity of this process. The central recommendation calls for embedding an ongoing multi-stakeholder dialogue in municipal policy formation. These social economy policy initiatives at the municipal and provincial levels are important illustrations of an embedded deliberative regulatory culture in Quebec.[10] Social economy actors have spearheaded this culture and its underlying processes of policy formation.

Generic Development

During the past decade, the federal and Quebec governments have developed several generic policies to accommodate social economy enterprises in all sectors and regions. These measures were initially proposed by social economy actors demanding policies for social enterprises that corresponded with those favouring small and medium enterprises. Since the economic crisis of the early 1980s, policies and programs to assist small and medium businesses have been among the strategic priorities of governments. They include increased access to finance, support for research and development, improved management skills and human resource development, and greater access to new markets. Similar policies exist for the social economy in Quebec, excepting measures to promote access to new markets. Pressure is mounting for a public procurement policy that would favour social economy enterprises, as found in Europe and the United States.[11]

For research and development, the federal government has been the main source of support. The federally funded Social Sciences and Humanities Research Council of Canada (SSHRC) was an international pioneer in developing the Community-University Research Alliances (CURA). This was reinforced in 2004 by an additional injection by government of $15 million to create a new CURA program focused on the social economy. These research partnerships have played a critical role in advancing the social economy in Quebec. Moreover, the 'communities of practice' or 'learning communities' established by these partnerships are contributing to new research methodologies and to an epistemology that better captures organizational and institutional transformation embodied in the social economy. After almost a decade of successful research collaboration, with concrete results for practitioners and for policy makers, the need for ongoing public support needs little emphasis.

Access to finance has been a central element of generic policy, both provincially and federally. The availability of capital was identified as a priority soon after the Summit in 1996. Social economy enterprises, considered high risk by private investors, require small investments, and therefore have difficulty accessing mainstream financial markets. As noted earlier, a supportive finance sector was essential, and over the last ten years, this sector has evolved considerably. A network of solidarity finance, CAP Finance, established in December 2009, now provides a range of investment products from micro-credit to patient capital. Founding members of this network include RISQ (Réseau d'investissement social du Québec), established by the Chantier in 1997; the Réseau du crédit communautaire, the network of micro-credit across Quebec; the Caisse d'économie solidaire Desjardin, founded in

1971; the two labour solidarity funds, Fonds de solidarité (FTQ) and FondAction (CSN), Filaction, a local development fund established by FondAction and the recently created Fiducie du Chantier de l'économie sociale (Chantier de l'économie sociale Trust). The creation of the Chantier de l'économie social Trust in 2007 responded to the unmet need for long-term investment capital. The Trust is an intermediary that provides secure and profitable investment for investors and makes long-term capital available for social economy enterprises. The principal financial contribution came from the federal government (a $22.8 million grant), and additional investments came from the Fonds de solidarité and FondAction and the Quebec government.[12]

These innovations are civil society initiatives that have successfully involved government both as a financial contributor and through enabling policies. They are significant illustrations of a process of co-construction. The barriers erected by financial institutions became the incentive to design alternatives that overcome the resistance of mainstream finance. Moreover, it was necessary to create lending and investment opportunities comparable to the private sector, to dispel the myth that social economy enterprises are not investment worthy. The investment threshold of the Trust is $1.5 million, dispelling another myth that solidarity finance is synonymous with micro-credit. The Trust is currently working on the development of a secondary market, a social stock exchange for which there are precedents in other parts of the world.[13]

Labour force development has been another area in which public policy has supported the strengthening of the social economy. A recommendation in the Chantier's action plan, presented at the 1996 Summit, was the creation of a sectoral council on labour force development for the social economy, based on the model in a wide range of industries. The Comité sectoriel de main-d'oeuvre en économie sociale et action communautaire (CSMO-ÉSAC) began its work in 1997 and has provided strategic support and resources for training of managers, workers, and administrators of social economy enterprises. The CSMO-ÉSAC has also developed evaluation tools, portraits of sectors, and apprenticeship or training programs in new professions. The Ministry for Employment and Social Solidarity provides ongoing funding for the sectoral council.

Strengthening managerial capacity has been another target for public policy. In 1997, a specific program to support networking and the development of management skills in the social economy was created by the Quebec government. This program was cancelled in 2002. The federal government social economy initiative in 2004 also provided funding for initiatives to develop managerial capacity. While support by the local development centres (CLDs) in Quebec contributes to managerial capacity within the social economy, this need has been identified as a priority by numerous social economy enterprises.

The policy needs we have identified were included in the *dialogue* with the government of Quebec and have resulted in concrete measures. Below, we provide examples of the major generic policy initiatives that have supported the social economy from the early 1980s to the current period.[14]

Measures prior to 1995:

- 1982: Worker shareholder co-operatives (coopératives de travailleur actionnaire);
- 1983: 35% provincial and federal tax credit for the creation of labour funds; the tax credit was reduced to 15% in 2000;
- 1985: Co-operative investment plan (Régime d'investissement coopératif); this measure combined with a tax benefit allows the members and employees of a co-operative to invest in their business by purchasing preferred shares. The maximum deduction is 150%. From 1985 to 2003, more than $200 million was invested in businesses.

Measures after 1995:

- 1996: Following the Summit, the social economy working group was integrated into the office of the premier (Conseil exécutif);
- 1997: The working group became le Chantier de l'économie sociale;
- 1997: Creation of the Sectoral Committee on Workforce Development in the Social Economy and the Community Sector (Comité sectoriel de main-d'oeuvre/Économie sociale et action communautaire);
- 1997: Modification of the law on co-operatives to include *solidarity co-operatives* (recognizing the role of multiple stakeholders);
- 1997: Modification of Quebec's loan guarantee program for small and medium businesses and co-operatives to include nonprofits;
- 1997: Creation by the Chantier of the Réseau d'investissement social du Québec (RISQ), a $10 million fund ($5 million in donations and

$5 million in grants) offering non-guaranteed loans up to $50,000 for social economy enterprises;

- 1997: Creation of a program to support networking activities by social economy enterprises;
- 1999: The Chantier de l'économie sociale becomes a legal entity (nonprofit organization) administered by networks of social economy enterprises, social movements, and local development organizations and receives funding from the Quebec government ($450,000 annually; recently increased to $650,000);
- 2000: Establishment of the Bureau d'économie sociale in the Ministry of Finance (Quebec): transferred to the Ministry for Economic and Regional Development in 2003, to the Ministry for Economic Development, Export and Innovation in 2004, and most recently to the Ministry of Municipal Affairs and Regional Development in 2007;
- 2000: Community/University Research Alliance in the social economy;
- 2001: The Quebec government creates a new investment fund for collective enterprises within its investment entity, La Financière. An envelope of $15 million is allocated for the social economy. In 2008, an additional $10 million is invested in this program;
- 2006: $10 million investment in the Chantier d'économie sociale Trust in collaboration with the Chantier, with additional investments from the two labour funds and the federal government.

At the federal level:

- 2004: Creation of the Secretariat for the Social Economy and a round table bringing together numerous stakeholders and a social economy initiative in the federal budget that included:
- $100 million for the creation of patient capital funds ($30 million for Quebec; later reduced to $23 million by the Conservative government);
- $17 million for capacity building ($3 million for Quebec);
- $15 million for research partnerships in the field of the social economy.

The social economy initiative was cancelled in 2006 by the newly elected Conservative government; Quebec was the only region where the funds were spent, with the exception of the funds made available across Canada through the SSHRC for research partnerships.

Sectoral Policies

Social economy enterprises emerge in response to needs that neither the market nor the government is able to meet. Combining market resources, volunteer contributions, and government support in many cases, social economy enterprises have played a strategic role in structuring markets and efficiently meeting social and economic needs. Policies that promote the emergence or strengthening of specific sectors of the economy (including the environment, personal services, housing, new technologies, communications, social tourism, food services, and culture) have offered important tools for the development of the social economy.

Over the past decade, several major sectoral policies have resulted in the rapid development of social economy enterprises. We provide a few examples:

- In 1997, the Programme d'éxonération financière pour les services d'aide domestique (financial support for homecare services) created the context for the development of a network of 100 collective enterprises, covering the entire province of Quebec. Those who use these services, mainly the elderly, receive financial support to allow them to pay between $4 and $10 an hour for housework and other related services, depending on their level of income. The government budget for this program increased from $26.4 million annually in 1997 to $48.3 million in 2004-5. These enterprises have become an essential part of the health and social service network in Quebec and employ almost 8,000 people.
- In 1997, the new family policy in Quebec supported the development of a large network of social economy enterprises providing childcare services. The concept for Centres de la petite enfance (early childhood centres) was proposed by the Chantier de l'économie sociale at the Quebec Summit in 1996, based on an innovative proposal by the existing network of parent-controlled daycare centres. An initial budget of $230 million annually allowed parents to have quality educational daycare at $5 per day offered by parent-controlled nonprofit centres. This policy has evolved, and despite the introduction of support for private for-profit daycare by the Liberal government in 2004, the vast majority of childcare services (200,000 places in 1,000 nonprofit early childhood centres) continue to be offered through the social economy, but at $7 per day. These centres

employ 40,000 people, making this network the third-largest employer in Quebec. Over 7,000 parents are volunteers on the boards of directors. The Quebec government invests over $1.7 billion annually in these early childhood centres.

- In 1999, the Quebec government introduced a program to support social economy enterprises involved in recycling waste. This program aimed to create and maintain permanent and high quality jobs in collective enterprises while increasing the recycling of waste materials and diminishing the use of landfills by municipalities and industry. Between 1999 and 2004, $23.4 million was invested by the government of Quebec; this program was renewed in 2005 with a reinvestment of $5.7 million.

Policies for Target Populations

Social economy enterprises play an active role in ensuring that marginalized groups have access to jobs and services. Rather than investing exclusively in income security programs, the social economy works to find the means to integrate individuals perceived as unproductive by conventional employers. This trend exists in several countries in Europe that have made substantial investments in programs designed to support the socio-economic integration of target groups (youth, the disabled, recently arrived immigrants, ex-convicts). In some countries, these social enterprises are an integral part of labour force development strategies. In Italy, for example, public procurement is used to support social co-operatives, defined by law as co-operatives that hire a minimum of 30% of their workers from identified marginalized groups (Gruet, 2008)

In Quebec, this approach is reflected in several initiatives. For the past few decades, the Quebec government has supported a network of nonprofit businesses (*entreprises adaptées*) whose mission is to create employment for the disabled. A government program compensates these social economy enterprises for the reduced productivity of these employees. In 2006-7, $48.4 million was invested in 44 enterprises offering employment to over 4,000 people, of whom over 3,000 people living with severe disabilities would otherwise be on social assistance. Two successive studies by Quebec economist Pierre Fortin have confirmed that governments saved money through this investment (Fortin & VanAudenrode, 2006, 2007). However, these studies do not measure the increase in pride and human dignity inherent in the impacts of these enterprises.

Conclusions

In this chapter, we have provided a brief overview of the social economy in Quebec, focusing especially on the contribution it makes to social innovation and public policy. We have noted how the design of these public policies breaks with traditional policy formation, in which government departments devise and implement programs in isolation and from a top-down perspective. The experience of the past decade has made it clear that traditional processes of public policy formation are not adapted to citizen-driven social innovation. The co-construction of public policy that describes a new process of policy formation requires a radical cultural shift. This is neither a 'top-down' nor a 'bottom-up' approach; rather it is a horizontal and dialogic approach involving many stakeholders in society. As we have shown, dialogue takes place at the local, regional, and national levels. Government must be open to such dialogue, both within and between ministries and with non-government actors. Jurisdictional boundaries are porous; the linkages between different levels of government have to be continuous and fluid.

In Quebec, policies enabling the social economy are the result of a process of co-construction and of broad and inclusive collective learning; it involves the co-construction of new ideas and approaches arising out of a multi-stakeholder dialogue. Indeed, many have interpreted the public policies we have described as pragmatic responses by governments unable to resolve existing socio-economic problems. Governments are quick to adopt programs that produce results, without a genuine commitment to broader and more structural change. It is also true, however, and much more important in our opinion, that the public policies we have described have had and will continue to have a much greater impact for at least two reasons. The social economy is now recognized as an important actor in the economy and, secondly, for its pivotal role in the development of new ways of thinking about public policy.

In Quebec, a culture of dialogue has existed for almost 40 years. However, prior to 1996, social movements had never been invited to participate in this dialogue. Ironically, in 2006, it was the Chantier de l'économie sociale that extended an invitation to government representatives to participate in a Summit to celebrate its 10th anniversary. The Chantier's 2006 Summit drew more than 700 delegates as well as international representatives from more than 20 countries. Both levels of government were present; the premier of Quebec spoke to the successes of the last 10 years and expressed his firm commitment to the social economy. This can no longer be interpreted as one of the pragmatic responses by government. It confirms the institutionalization of a process of dialogue and co-construction of public policy. This process has shaped many enabling policy initiatives for the social economy – sectoral, territorial, generic, and those favouring targeted populations. The process challenges a culture of public policy formation that has much to learn if it is to contribute more effectively to the well-being of society, the primary goal of all public policies.

We cannot conclude this chapter without referring to the recent global financial crisis and the response of governments around the world to avert a global economic catastrophe. This is not the first time that the deregulation of the financial markets has led to re-regulation. The exchange rate crisis in the 1990s, for example, forced governments to buy and sell currencies to shore up the international financial market. While the recent crisis is beyond the scope of this chapter, we do wish to point out that it, like those that preceded it, will not be resolved by chaotic interventions, regardless of the staggering sums of money committed by governments. The recent intervention by several governments, however inadequate, is, for the first time, a sign of recognition that a coherent policy framework and a defined and interventionist role for government are necessary. The social economy in Quebec, in many ways, is a microcosm of the relations that shape all economies. There is production, consumption, and exchange. But these activities are embedded in societal objectives that stress the ethical values of citizenship, democracy, and the sustainable livelihood of people and the planet. These values must inform the response to the global crisis and respond to the moral outrage it has generated. They are already embedded in the social economy that is participating in the design of an enabling policy environment to enshrine these values.

NOTES

1 www.lacaisse.com
2 Today the FTQ has approximately 500,000 members.

3 www.ftq.qc.ca

4 www.fiducieduchantier.qc.ca.

5 The CSN has approximately 300,000 members.

6 www.fondaction.com

7 In 1998, the Quebec government passed a law creating local community centres (CLDs), modelled on the CDECs. While government created these centres, they inherited the distributed governance of the CDECs with civil society organizations involved in decision-making. Despite a reduced institutional role for some organizations by the current government, their engagement and influence continues.

8 A new data base on the social economy in Montreal produced by the Committee for the Social Economy on the Island of Montreal (CESIM) provides a broad portrait that includes all community organizations. However, CESIM also produced an inventory of social economy enterprises engaged in market activity, which is much smaller. This inventory conforms with the provincial data for 2002 that focuses on those enterprises engaged in the market. The government of Quebec has expressed its commitment to provide updated information on the social economy.

9 These were first presented to the federal government and outline the policy needs for the social economy.

10 The work of Erik Olin Wright and Archon Fung on empowered participatory governance is a theoretical inspiration (Fung & Wright, 2003; Mendell, 2006).

11 Examples of procurement policies include the Public Service Delivery Action Plan adopted by the Cabinet Office of the Third Sector in the United Kingdom in 2006. In the United States, several programs created by the Office of Small Business to promote public procurement for SMEs can be applied to social enterprises. In Italy, Law 381/91 allows public authorities to give direct contracts to type B social co-operatives (work integration, 30% disadvantaged members). This also relieves them of social charges for disadvantaged members and reduces VAT rate to 4% (Gruet, 2008).

12 ARUC completed a survey of investment in social economy enterprises by solidarity finance actors from 1996 to 2006. The total invested was $750 million ('Investir Solidairement,' www.Chantier.qc.ca).

13 In 2003, a social stock exchange, the Bolsa de Valores Socials (BVS), was created in Brazil. Currently, the Rockefeller Foundation has contributed $500,000 to study the feasibility of developing such an exchange in the United Kingdom (Mendell & Nogales, 2008; Skoll Center for Social Entrepreneurship, 2007).

14 This is a synthesis of Mendell and Rouzier (2006).

REFERENCES

Amin, A., & Hausner, J. (1997). *Beyond market and hierarchy: Interactive govern-ance and social complexity.* Cheltenham: Edward Elgar.
ARUC en économie sociale. (2009). *Accueil.* Retrieved November 16, 2009, from http://www.aruc-es.uqam.ca
Chaire de recherche en économie sociale. (2009) *Accueil.* Retrieved November 16, 2009, from http://www.chaire.ecosoc.uqam.ca
Chantier de l'économie sociale (2008). *Portrait statistique de l'économie sociale sur l'Île de Montréal,* Chaire de recherche du Canada en économie sociale, UQAM
Chantier de l'économie Sociale. (2009). *Accueil.* Retrieved November 16, 2009, from http://www.chantier.qc.ca
Comité d'économie sociale de l'Ile de Montréal (CESIM). (2008). *Répertoire des entreprises d'économie sociale de Montréal.* Retrieved November 16, 2009, from http://www.achatsolidaire.com/
D'Amours, M. (2007). *L'économie sociale au Québec: Cadre théorique, histoire, réal-ités et défis.* Anjou: Editions Saint-Martin.
Downing, R., & Neamtan, N. (2005). Social economy and community eco-nomic development in Canada: Next steps for public policy. *Issues Paper.* Retrieved November 16, 2009, from Chantier de l'économie sociale http://www.chantier.qc.ca/uploads/documents/categories_publications/issues_paper21sept_final.pdf
Fortin, P., & VanAudenrode, M. (2006). *Les entreprises adaptés: une aubaine économique et sociale pour le Québec.* Montréal: Groupe d'Analyse.
Fortin, P., & VanAudenrode, M. (2007). *Entreprises adaptés au Québec et réalités économiques.* Quebec: Université Laval.
Fung, A., & Wright, E.O. (2003). *Deepening democracy: Institutional innovations in empowered deliberative democracy.* London: Verso.
Gouvernement du Québec (2008). Economie sociale. Pour des communautés plus solidaires. Retrieved November 16, 2009, from http://www.mamrot.gouv.qc.ca/publications/regions/regi_econ_soci_plan_acti.pdf
Gruet, E. (2008). *Marchés publics et économie sociale. Pour une orientation sociale des politiques d'achat du Québec.* Chantier de l'économie sociale.
Hartzell, J. (2007). *Creating an ethical stock exchange.* Retrieved November 16, 2009, from Skoll Centre for Social Entrepreneurship http://www.universitynetwork.org/sites/universitynetwork.org/files/files/Skoll_EthicalStockExchange.pdf
Jackson, A., & Schetagne, S. (2004). Solidarity forever? – An analysis of chang-es in union density. *Just Labour* 4: 53–82.

Laville, J.-L., Lévesque, B., & Mendell, M. (2007). The social economy: Diverse approaches and practices in Europe and Canada. In A. Noya & E. Clarence (Eds.), *The social economy: Building inclusive economies* (pp. 155–87) Paris: OECD .

Lévesque. B. (2001). Système québecois d'innovation en économie sociale. *ARUC-ÉS*. Rapport Annuel.

Lévesque, B., Belanger, P., Bouchard, M., & Mendell, M. (2001). Le Fonds de solidarité FTQ : Un cas exemplaire de nouvelle gouvernance. Montreal : Fonds de solidarité FTQ.

Lévesque, B., & Mendell, M. (1999). L'économie sociale au Québec: Eléments théoriques et empiriques pour le débat et la recherche. *Cahiers du CRISE*, no. 9908.

Lévesque, B., Mendell, M., & Rouzier, R. (2003). New forms of financing social economy enterprises and organizations in Québec. In *The non-profit sector in the 21st century: A stakeholder for economy and society* (pp. 106-30) Paris: OECD.

Mendell, M. (2006). L'empowerment au Canada et au Québec: Enjeux et opportunités. *Economie, Géographie et Société, 8*(1) 63-86.

Mendell, M. (2009). The three pillars of the social economy. In Ash Amin (Ed.), *The social economy: International perspectives on economic solidarity*. London: Zed Books

Mendell, M., & Leys, C. (Eds.). (1992). *Culture and social change: Social movements in Ontario and Quebec*. Montreal: Black Rose Books,

Mendell, M., & Nogales, R. (2009). Social enterprises in OECD member countries: What are the financial streams? In A. Noya (Ed.), *The changing boundaries of social enterprises*. Paris: OECD

Mendell, M., & Rouzier, R. (2006). Some initiatives that enabled the institutionalization of Quebec's social economy: Civil society's critical role and the state's essential role. *Working Paper*. British Columbia and Alberta Research Alliance on the Social Economy (BALTA).

Mendell, M., et al. (2006). Investir solidairement: Bilan et perspectives. *Rapport du comité investir solidairement*. Report submitted for the Sommet de l'économie sociale. Retrieved November 16, 2009, from Chantier de l'économie Sociale http://www.chantier.qc.ca/uploads/documents/categories_publications/rapport-investir-v3.pdf

Neamtan, Nancy. (2005). The social economy: Finding a way between the market and the state. *Policy Options*, July/August, 71-6.

4 The Social Economy in Europe: Trends and Challenges

ROGER SPEAR

This paper gives an overview of the social economy in Europe. Drawing on the most recent statistical data the paper examines the social economy's size in different European countries and current trends and challenges in Europe; it also reviews its status and political context at the EU level. The paper draws on the CIRIEC (2007) study of the Social Economy in the European Union and the contribution on social enterprise draws on the work of the EMES Network.

Origins

The social economy includes a wide range of types of organizations – from those formed in the 19th century to relatively new organizations; and from large organizations to small enterprises often with a stronger value base. In terms of overall employment, social economy organizations play an important role in the European economic landscape, both in terms of combating social exclusion, and in providing alternative (social) enterprise models.

There are different approaches to examining the origins of the social economy, but here we emphasize the historical development of the sector in relation to its changing context. The starting point for many theorists is the great period of social and political ferment in the first half of the 19th century, although there were many relevant developments in previous centuries. However, during the 19th century many of the current themes and structures of the social economy became more developed and institutionalized. In broad terms there were two major themes: on the one hand, self-managed initiatives for mutual benefit – either for producers or for users/consumers; and on the other, charitable initiatives to support others (disadvantaged) for general/public interest.

One origin of the social economy in the first half of the 19th century was self-help initiatives developed in the context of strengthening the wage-earning classes. Similarly, there was a flourishing of initiatives to support consumer co-operation among the working class to combat poor quality supplies and exploitation by private business. In the second half of the 19th century, rural social economy initiatives developed to support co-operation between family-run enterprises. Thus, through its different forms of mutualization, the social economy developed and exhibited a traditional divide between the interests of producers and those of consumers. For example, the well-known Rochdale pioneer consumer co-operative, created in 1844 in Manchester, sought to counter the power of manufacturing industry and agricultural production by uniting consumers and distributing its profits between consumers and its salaried workers. This division or conflict between different mutual players led to a separation between co-operation among users (savings and loans, consumer spending, insurance, tourism), and co-operation among producers (individual entrepreneurs, farmers, and associated workers). These roots led to the great pillars of co-operation and mutuality in agriculture, financial services, and retail, with workers' and housing co-operatives being strong in certain countries.

With regard to charitable or associational[1] (voluntary sector) initiatives to support others, different traditions emerged with implications for the role of the state in relation to associational activity – in the following ways. The concept of charity developed towards one's fellows as an essential component of citizenship in democratic society; and in this view (typical of the UK), charities enjoyed a high degree of autonomy and the state saw its role as providing a framework for citizens and society to manage themselves. In other countries, associational activity was strongly based on a sense of solidarity, which supported philanthropic activity. This was also an inter-generational solidarity where a sense of responsibility was developed between generations; and this led to the state taking initiatives to impose compulsory schemes/contracts of social insurance. The different forms of welfare system influenced the nature of the relationship between the state, the family, and associational/charitable activity. Thus in the universalistic systems typical of Scandinavia, associations' advocacy role was prominent; in contrast, in Anglo-Saxon liberal systems, a dual system operated where the state provided for the most disadvantaged, with associations supporting others; and in the corporatist regimes (Germany, France, Belgium, etc.) a close partnership has developed between the state and associations. In Mediterranean and some other countries the family has played a key role, with the state and associations supporting that system (CIRIEC, 2000). One of the factors underlying this considerable diversity between sectors within the social economy in Europe is the extent of religious influence over education, social protection, and welfare provision.

This historical contextual perspective on the development of the social economy helps explain current preferences for particular institutional forms. Thus in some countries, like Italy or Spain, co-operatives and mutuals are quite prominent, while in others, like Belgium, they form a very small proportion compared to charities or associations.

Today new forms of multi-societal and lateral networks of social economy organizations are emerging. In a solidaristic manner these networks are also bringing together, within a single organization, various types of stakeholders: consumers, workers, beneficiaries, volunteer workers, and/or institutional partners. Such networks and organizations operate to combat social exclusion and to regenerate communities, and to provide work integration services in order to bring about new jobs for the disadvantaged.

Definitions and Perspectives on the Social Economy

Defourny and Borzaga (2001) argue that there are two different bases for conceptualizing the social economy such as *institutional form*, co-ops, mutuals, associations or voluntary organizations, and foundations (CMAF) and *normative criteria* based on values. The CMAF view is fully recognized in Latin countries in Europe and is the one that is recognized at the European level (European Commission, 2008). Thus the CMAF perspective is probably the most influential basis for defining the sector, but the term social economy is not well understood in many countries, and people frequently intuitively adopt a normative/values perspective if they are not so well informed about European and other international experiences.

The normative/values view is based on the idea that there are different values and principles that underlie the distinctiveness of the sector. These values/principles for example might include the seven co-operative principles, and more generally they would include the following:

- Owned by and serving the community (general interest) or members (mutual interest) (rather than serving financial stakeholders and profit);
- Independently managed;
- Participative structures;
- Primacy of people and labour over capital.

Although the CMAF view is the predominant basis for defining the social economy, at least in Europe, there are other perspectives. A third perspective is the *indigenous view*. Based on historical development and legal frameworks, this view suggests that although a country may not have specific legislation for different CMAF sectors of the social economy, it may well have legislation for organizations located between the private market and the state – and those organizations that occupy this space usually have some degree of recognition; although the extent to which they constitute a coherent unified sector differs from country to country. Thus in the UK this area of socio-economic activity is represented by Industrial and Provident societies and Friendly societies. More recently (1980) Company law has been adapted to enable the 'company limited by guarantee' form to be exclusively for social economy organizations and to exclude the option of allowing share capital (beyond nominal value). This may be contrasted with Belgium, where the preferred legal form for social economy activity is the nonprofit association (asbl – *association sans but lucratif*). The UK also has new legislation for social enterprise with the Community Interest Company.

Supporters of the social economy have been concerned that many older social economy organizations seem to have moved somewhat from their original founding values and become, to varying degrees, similar to capitalist business (this is referred to as 'isomorphism'). This has provoked reactions about what has always been a central part of the social economy, a set of distinctive values – such as democracy, solidarity, independence, nonprofit or limited profit distribution, ownership not based on financial stake. And linked to these values, a distinctive relational characteristic based on embedded social capital networks has been emphasized. In the last quarter of the 20th century this has led to some attempts to redefine the social economy itself – possibly mainly in those countries where the predominant definition is not well established; in France, for example, debate around such issues centres on new terms such as '*économie solidaire*' or the new social economy – and it is now commonly linked with the traditional form – as the *social and solidarity economy.*'

Finally, another perspective on the sector that has gained increasing interest, as the market has moved into more and more spheres of activity, is the *social enterprise perspective.*

Data and Definitions

Over the last 10 to 15 years there has been considerable effort applied to defining the third sector and social economy so that statistical data can be collected on an international comparative basis. This began with the the Johns Hopkins Comparative Nonprofit Sector Project, which has collected data on 41 countries and produced a UN handbook for national statistics bodies to use in gathering data on nonprofit organizations through satellite accounts – 26 countries have committed to developing this system.

The Johns Hopkins Comparative Nonprofit Sector Project defines nonprofits as having the following characteristics:

- Formal (institutionalized/legal structure)
- Private (structural independence from the government)
- Self-governing
- Nonprofit distribution constraint
- Voluntarism (some voluntary contribution (time/money)

In other words: those organizations which are self-governing and constitutionally independent of the state; which do not involve the distribution of profits to shareholders; and which benefit to a significant degree from voluntarism (Salamon & Anheier, 1997).

Within Europe there was a strong feeling that this approach was more oriented to the U.S. experience than the European one, where co-operatives and mutuals seemed to carry out similar activities to nonprofits, i.e., where some countries would use nonprofit legal forms while others would use co-operative ones. In addition, within certain parts of Europe there is more of a political project to broaden the third sector from the U.S. view of it just being the nonprofit sector, and integrate different elements (co-ops, mutuals, associations, foundations) under the same umbrella: that of the social economy. This has resulted in attempts to define and map the 'rest of the social economy,' essentially the co-operative and mutual part, since, as Mertens (2007, p. 7) argues, 'the satellite account of nonprofit institutions covers (alongside founda- tions) the associative component of the social economy.' CIRIEC (an international research network) has made an important contribution to this by defining companies of the social economy, and producing a manual which specifies how data on them may be collected through satellite accounts (linked to national data collection systems).

Barea and Monzón (2006) propose the following working definition of the social economy company:

> The set of private, formally-organised enterprises, with autonomy of deci- sion and freedom of membership, created to meet their members' needs through the market by producing goods and providing services, insur- ance and finance, where decision-making and any distribution of profits or surpluses among the members are not directly linked to the capital or fees contributed by each member, each of whom has one vote. (p. 33)

The main areas of difference between the social economy perspective and the Hopkins nonprofit perspective relate to goals, democratic con- trol, and profit distribution. This has implications for what is included and excluded: thus as mentioned above Hopkins excludes co-ops and mutuals because the Hopkins criteria emphasize the non-distribution constraint, whereas the social economy view allows limited distribu- tion of net income to members. And in relation to goals, social economy organizations are set up to fulfil members' or community needs, but this is not explicit in the Hopkins criteria; and the social economy view emphasizes democratic control by members, which is not mentioned in the Hopkins criteria. These differences of emphasis about the character- istics of the nonprofit or associative component of the social economy could also have implications for what is included or excluded. That said, there are also areas of similarity; for example, the Hopkins criteria of voluntarism are similar to the social economy emphasis on freedom of membership (i.e., voluntarily entered into), and most social economy boards operate on a voluntary basis (Defourny & Borzaga, 2001). But as Mertens (2007) argues, there is an unresolved issue about the link between the 'NPI Satellite Account' and the 'Satellite Accounts of Com- panies in the Social Economy.' Thus, if these two systems of data col- lection are to be complementary, there is still some work to be done to ensure compatibility (and no overlap).

Figure 4.1. Diagram of the social economy adapted from Pestoff (1998)

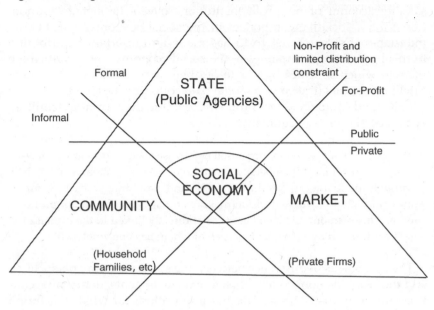

The boundaries of the social economy are not well defined, but are based on its location between the adjacent sectors of the state, market, and community, as Pestoff (1998) shows in the diagram (figure 4.1). This diagram also uses three criteria to delineate the sector (represented by three lines that pass through the large triangle) – public/private, formal/informal, and nonprofit/for-profit – but as the discussion above indicated, there could be an additional line differentiating between nonprofits and limited profit or surplus distribution (of co-ops and mutuals). And it is important to note that the social economy is viewed as overlapping with the state, market, and community, not simply distinct.

The Size and Status of the Social Economy in Europe

The data in the CIRIEC Social Economy study are based on the following sources: CIRIEC International (2000), the Co-operatives Europe study (2006), and various other sectoral and national studies. The data include nonprofit organizations, such as charities, and voluntary sector organizations, such as those providing welfare and other services to

Table 4.1
Paid employment in co-operatives, mutual societies, and associations. European
Union (2002–3)

Country	Co-operatives	Mutual Societies	Associations	Total
Belgium	17,047	12,864	249,700	279,611
France	439,720	110,100	1,435,330	1,985,150
Ireland	35,992	650	118,664	155,306
Italy	837,024	*	499,389	1,336,413
Portugal	51,000	*	159,950	210,950
Spain	488,606	3,548	380,060	872,214
Sweden	99,500	11,000	95,197	205,697
Austria	62,145	8,000	190,000	260,145
Denmark	39,107	1,000	120,657	160,764
Finland	95,000	5,405	74,992	175,397
Germany	466,900	150,000	1,414,937	2,031,837
Greece	12,345	489	57,000	69,834
Luxembourg	748	n/a	6,500	7,248
Netherlands	110,710	n/a	661,400	772,110
United Kingdom	190,458	47,818	1,473,000	1,711,276
Cyprus	4,491	n/a	n/a	4,491
Czech Republic	90,874	147	74,200	165,221
Estonia	15,250	n/a	8,000	23,250
Hungary	42,787	n/a	32,882	75,669
Latvia	300	n/a	n/a	300
Lithuania	7,700	0	n/a	7,700
Malta	238	n/a	n/a	238
Poland	469,179	n/a	60,000	529,179
Slovakia	82,012	n/a	16,200	98,212
Slovenia	4,401	270	n/a	4,671
Total	3,663,534	351,291	7,128,058	11,142,883

*The data on mutual societies are integrated with those of co-operatives for Italy and
with those of associations for Portugal.

the public through state contracts. As can be seen the associative sector
is about twice the size of the co-op/mutual sector in terms of employment – though the picture would be different for turnover.

Table 4.1 shows that the social economy in 25 countries of Europe
(data on Bulgaria and Romania were not available) comprises over 11
million paid employees, with associations being the largest sector in
terms of employment, about twice the size of the co-operative sector,
and mutuals being a much smaller part. Table 4.2 shows that this is

Table 4.2
Paid employment in social economy compared to total paid employment.

Country	Employment in Social Economy	Total Employment*	%
Belgium	279,611	4,048,499	6.9
France	1,985,150	23,859,402	8.3
Ireland	155,306	1,730,381	9.0
Italy	1,336,413	21,477,906	6.2
Portugal	210,950	4,783,988	4.4
Spain	872,214	16,155,305	5.4
Sweden	205,697	4,252,211	4.8
Austria	260,145	3,786,969	6.9
Denmark	160,764	2,684,311	6.0
Finland	175,397	2,354,265	7.5
Germany	2,031,837	35,850,878	5.7
Greece	69,834	3,832,994	1.8
Luxembourg	7,248	187,809	3.9
Netherlands	772,110	8,089,071	9.5
United Kingdom	1,711,276	27,960,649	6.1
Cyprus	4,491	307,305	1.5
Czech Republic	165,221	4,707,477	3.5
Estonia	23,250	565,567	4.1
Hungary	75,669	3,831,391	2.0
Latvia	300	960,304	0.0
Lithuania	7,700	1,378,900	0.6
Malta	238	146,500	0.2
Poland	529,179	13,470,375	3.9
Slovakia	98,212	2,118,029	4.6
Slovenia	4,671	888,949	0.5
Total	11,142,883	189,429,435	5.9
Europe-15	10,233,952	161,054,638	6.4
New members-10	908,931	28,374,797	3.2

*Working population aged between 16 and 65 years, Eurostat, 2002.

equivalent to just under 6% of paid employment in the EU, with the proportion of paid employment in the EU 15 having double the proportion of employment as that of the new EU 10.

It is possible to make some commentary on this diverse perform-ance, but it is also difficult to make generalizations, since the diversity seems to depend on specific historical contextual factors. Firstly, the top three countries (in terms of % employment) are France, Ireland, and Finland. France and Finland have strong traditions in the social economy, but have also suffered high levels of unemployment; while Ireland has a strong tradition of church involvement in education and welfare (rather than state provision) – although the state provides most of the finance and regulates the sector strongly – so there is some debate about including the Irish schools in the voluntary sector. Portugal, Greece, and Luxembourg have the lowest levels within Europe 15; clearly the family in Mediterranean countries may play a role for the first two countries, by taking more responsibility for social insurance and welfare services.

The new EU member countries have undergone severe transitional economic restructuring which has had drastic effects on their social economies. Privatization and restitution have had negative impacts particularly on what were often thriving co-operative sectors, agriculture and co-ops for disabled people in particular, while the withdrawal of the state has provided a stimulating effect on civil society, and we have seen considerable growth of associational life in some of these countries, for example, Poland (Gumkowska, Herbst, & Wyganski, 2008).

It is also noteworthy that, overall, associations clearly form the largest segment of the social economy, in terms of employment – 64%, with co-ops forming 33% – and with the state withdrawing from welfare service provision, nonprofits serving the public are likely to increase. But there are certain countries where co-ops are the larger segment: Italy, Spain, and the Scandinavian countries Sweden and Finland, which have managed to maintain a strong tradition. And strong traditions may increase the legitimacy of a particular form – thus for example in Italy social co-operatives have been formed to provide welfare services which in many countries would typically be provided by nonprofits.

Status of the Social Economy

Although most countries will have political recognition and representation for the CMAF members of the social economy family, some countries give the social economy a high level of recognition. France, Portugal, and Spain fall into this category, with Belgium, Ireland, Italy, and Sweden close behind. The development of institutions to represent the social economy and co-ordinate its activities is likely to facilitate a win/win game for its members. And since the social economy often needs to link up transversally to address multi-dimensional issues, sector co-ordination improves the policy context between the different social, economic, and other ministries involved.

At the other end of the scale are those countries where the concept of the social economy is not well known. This includes Germanic countries (Austria, Germany) and the Netherlands, which is among the highest in table 4.2 (% of the workforce), and new members of the EU (Czech Republic, Estonia, Hungary, Lithuania, Slovenia). Part of the reason for this lack of recognition may be to do with the terminology – the word 'social' has different meanings in different national contexts with different societal traditions; for some countries 'social' means social security, while for others, 'social' is not compatible with the idea of business enterprise. In such countries certain members of CMAF may be better recognized – like nonprofits or NGOs among the newer EU members.

Political Representation

At the European Union level there are parts of the European Commission that have responsibilities for the social economy. In the 1980s the European Commission gave a high level of recognition to the social economy through the Social Economy Unit in DG Enterprise (and before that in DG XXIII). And the profile of the sector was raised through a number of European Social Economy conferences held during the 1990s – in Paris 1990, Rome 1991, Lisbon 1993, Brussels 1994, Seville 1995, and Birmingham 1998; then, more recently, Prague 2002, Krakow 2004, and Luxembourg 2005. But in 2000, as a result of reorganization in the European Commission, the responsibilities of the Social Economy Unit were integrated into the Unit 'Crafts, Small Enterprises, Co-operatives and Mutuals' that focused more on entrepreneurial aspects.

With regard to representative structures for lobbying and consultation on policy matters, the Consultative Committee for Co-operatives, Mutual societies, Associations and Foundations (CCCMAF) operated from March 1998 to November 2000; but again due to reorganization this was replaced by the autonomous European Standing Conference of Co-operatives, Mutual societies, Associations and Foundations – CEP-CMAF – which took the name 'Social Economy Europe' in 2007. The social economy is also represented in other European institutions and consultative bodies, and federal bodies for its component parts also operate at the European level. Also since 1990, the Social Economy Intergroup has operated as an observatory with a watching brief over

European policies linked with the social economy (social cohesion, social protection, health, insurances, Social Services of the General Interest, competition, CSR, employment policies, etc). And finally, within the broadly based European Economic and Social Committee, there is a social economy category comprising 36 members from co-operatives, mutual societies, associations, foundations, and social NGOs. This committee commissioned and disseminated the CIRIEC 2007 study on the social economy in the European Union (which this chapter draws on).

Trends and Challenges

There are many trends and challenges in the social economy and its changing context, so this review is necessarily very selective. Clearly the changing European policy context is one very important influence on trends in the sector. Thus the European Union agendas around social cohesion and social exclusion have helped shape the new wave of social economy initiatives in the area of work integration and community regeneration, particularly work integration social enterprise like many of the social co-operatives in Italy; similarly, agendas have operated at regional and national levels with regard to integrating new regions, nations, and neighbouring (Euro-Mediterranean) partners. Changing legislative and fiscal trends are tending to give less support for the sector while it becomes more isomorphic with business. The changing shape of welfare systems and public service provision is creating new challenges particularly as contracting increases, either directly with the state or via voucher systems, and the nonprofit or voluntary sector is playing an increasing role here, but not without reservations about losing some of its values and mission.

The themes addressed here are legislative and fiscal, contracting for public/welfare services, competition issues which are becoming more pressing, establishing the value of the social economy, and social enterprise trends.

Legislative and Fiscal Trends (CIRIEC, 2007)

Following on from the approval of the Statute for a European Company (SE) in 2001, a Statute for a European Co-operative Society (SCE) was adopted by the European Council in 2003. This aimed to improve the legal structures available for co-operatives to engage in cross-border and trans-national activities. But new European statutes for mutuals and associations have fallen off the EU agenda.

In many countries the members of the CMAF family enjoy some degree of tax advantage (especially nonprofits), and in a few cases this position has been strengthened in recent years. For example, Portugal, Italy, and Spain have been able to maintain their special tax regimes. But the trend is for these advantages to be eroded. A similar isomorphic change may be seen in the liberalization or degeneration of rules linked to co-operative principles – for example, giving some members more than one vote (usually based on size/patronage), allowing financial partners, and allowing demutualization (the conversion of co-operatives and mutual associations into businesses).

Thus in general there are pressures towards isomorphism; and maintaining the distinctiveness of the social economy has become more and more of a challenge.

Contracting for Public and Welfare Services

In many countries traditional partnership arrangements between the state and the social economy for welfare and public service provision are changing towards more market-like arrangements. Similarly there have been general trends from grants to contract funding. There is a trend towards more mixed economies where public, private, and social economy players compete. As such, there is the issue of smaller providers (like social economy organizations) managing the transaction costs of large contracting, since there is a growing tendency for contracts to be packaged into larger units to achieve economies of scale. Additionally, since social economy organizations often provide multiple social outcomes, there is the problem of transversal benefits, i.e., where a contract delivers a positive outcome to another budget area.

But procurement (by the state) of services varies considerably. Firstly, 'hard' or tightly specified contracting models based on an adversarial approach have sometimes given way to 'soft' relational contracting models which allow for more flexibility because a more trusting relationship has been developed. Secondly, larger contracts are subject to the full EU procurement regime, which is quite complex, and EU Treaty free market rules (fair, open, transparent, and non-discriminatory competition) apply to most contracts. However, it is possible under the EU framework[2] to include social requirements ('social clauses') in contracts and in the whole procurement life cycle (provided the social value/

outcome is properly specified); the proviso being should the *contract-ing authority be predisposed* to do so – the main barriers are motivation and affordability. After all why shouldn't public sector organizations begin to address social issues in their supply chains! Nonetheless there is pressure on costs, and although 'best value' (which can include so-cially valued outcomes) is often the official criterion, it is easy to see that contracts might be awarded by lowest price. In addition there may be a tendency for public authorities not to pay the full cost of services provided by nonprofits, assuming that voluntary work and donations can compensate for the difference. (A large proportion of UK contract-ing voluntary organizations report this.)

Voucher systems where users purchase services directly rather than through the quasi-market of state procurement are generating consid-erable interest. A recent Belgian voucher system (Defourny & Henry, 2009) operating to develop proximity services in a mixed economy (with public/private/social economy players) proved effective in elim-inating the informal economy and creating 80,000 new jobs in four years (with subsidies to service users and providers). But only 10% of these vouchers had been spent in the social economy, and there were issues of avoiding 'creaming' by private sector providers.

In the European debate on social services of the general interest (SSGI), there is a changing pattern of social/welfare service provision that is increasingly being commissioned through market mechanisms. This has led to considerable debate both among social economy actors, which are traditionally very active in this sector, and among policy makers. The European Parliament passed resolutions in March 2007 on social services of general interest in the European Union – and two ex-cerpts illustrate the nature of the debate:

The European Parliament:
Reaffirms its commitment to modern and high-quality SSGI based on the values of equality, solidarity, rule of law and respect for human dignity, and the principles of accessibility, universal service, efficiency, economic management of resources, continuity, proximity to service users and trans-parency, which contribute to the implementation of the Community's tasks as defined in Articles 2 and 3 of the Treaty. (European Parliament, 2007, ¶ 25)

Considers that it would be a mistake to adopt an approach to SSGIs which juxtaposes the rules on competition, State aid and the internal market on the one hand, and concepts of public service, general interest and social cohesion on the other; considers, on the contrary, that it is necessary to reconcile them by promoting positive synergies between the economic and social aspects; asserts, however, that in the case of SSGIs, the rules on competition, State aid and the internal market must be compatible with public service requirements, and not vice versa. (European Parliament, 2007, ¶ 28)

The policy framework is now taking shape, with the European Union about to adopt a *quality framework for social services,* which will include a set of principles for social services that all 27 European member states will have to implement. Concerns have been expressed by social economy actors about this framework; thus in June 2008, the Platform of European NGOs advocated that the EC 'adopt a favourable regulatory framework to go beyond the strict market logic' (Platform of European NGOs, 2008, p. 5). The organization argued that quality services should be 'provided on the basis of solidarity' and that public procurement rules should be reformed to ensure that public authorities give priority to 'affordable quality services accessible for all with a strong user involvement, and to service provision that reflect[s] social considerations over cost effectiveness criteria' (Platform of European NGOs, 2008, p. 5). They also argue that the contribution of the social economy should be better acknowledged in public procurement processes and state aid procedures.

Contested Terrain – Competition Issues

There is continuing pressure on traditional frameworks for the social economy. With regard to co-operatives there have been legal complaints from private competitors against co-operative legal and fiscal frameworks in Italy, Spain, and France. These private competitors demand that certain of these legal/fiscal provisions be considered as state aid and against European competition law. The representative body, Co-operatives Europe, is opposing this, but the outcome is still undecided.

In some cases responding to such challenges involves being more specific about the social outcomes of social economy players. Thus, for example, in the case of Italian social co-ops there was in the early 1990s a preferential purchasing arrangement with municipalities. But this was contested by the European Commission as a breach of competition law. However, further legislation in 1996 clarified the situation and implemented EC procurement law by allowing municipalities to specify tenders for some contracts from organizations so that they would meet specific social requirements to employ a minimum number of disadvantaged people – and social co-operatives have continued to demonstrate their effectiveness in this respect.

Another area where the social economy has been under pressure has been in one of their key areas of effectiveness – their capacity to form federations and co-operative groups. The CIRIEC study (2007) notes that 'these forms of association have been queried by the European Court of Justice, being interpreted as illicit agreements contrary to free competition.'

Establishing the Value of the Social Economy

There is considerable interest in measuring the values, outputs, and outcomes of social economy organizations. This is partly because of the above trends towards being more specific about these measurements for contracting purposes; but also because of increasing developments in social investment and measuring social return on investment; and the need to be more explicit in policy, evaluation studies, and other discourse about the added value of the social economy (Bouchard, 2009).

This also links with the need to protect this difference and the development of measures to ensure that this difference is legitimized and secured through, for example, the use of asset locks (where the assets cannot be privatized but are transferred to another social economy organization on dissolution of the organization), and social audits (e.g., Mook, Quarter, & Richmond, 2007).

Growth and Development of Social Enterprise

Social enterprises are organizations that have enterprise characteristics (trading in the market or contracting, employing people), but also have social goals (participation, user involvement, community benefit). For the last 20 years these organizations have been growing in many countries such as Italy with large numbers of social co-operatives formed both for welfare services and for work integration; and in Sweden, where a few thousand nursery co-ops (childcare) have been formed. Many of these initiatives combine associative and co-operative dimensions within the same structure. This trend is partly a result of new organizations being formed, but also because existing organizations are

Table 4.3
Legislation for social enterprise

Country	Type of Structure	Date	Type of Enterprise	Numbers
Italy	Social co-operative	1991	A+B	7000+
Portugal	Social solidarity co-operative	1996/8	B	500+
Spain	Social initiative co-operative	1999	A+B	
Spain	Work integration enterprise	2007		
Greece	Limited liability social co-operative	1999	B mental health	
France	Collective interest co-operative society	2002	A	94
Lithuania	Social enterprise	2004		
Poland	Social co-operative	2006	B	
Belgium	Social finality enterprise	1996	All	400
Finland	Social enterprise	2004	B	69
UK	Community interest company	2005	All	2000+
Italy	Social enterprise	2005/2006	All	
South Korea		Planned legislation		
Japan		Planned legislation		
South America		Planned legislation		

Note: A = providing social services; B = work integration

being transformed by contexts, becoming more and more influenced by markets (Borzaga & Defourny, 2001; Nyssens, 2006). (See the work of the EMES Network for more detail on empirical and theoretical perspectives on this field.)

Recent work by the EMES Network (Defourny & Nyssens, 2008) has shown a number of trends in social enterprise. Firstly there has been a broadening of the fields of activity. The field of work integration social enterprise (WISE) has become increasingly recognized as an area of social enterprise effectiveness. But social enterprises are also gaining recognition in proximity services, health/social services, and even more broadly, in recent Italian legislation, social utility. Social utility includes environmental/ecological activities, culture, heritage, social tourism, research, and education.

At the same time there has been innovation in institutional forms, with increasing interest in new legal structures for social enterprise, which bring together co-operative entrepreneurial aspects with non-profit social aspects, thereby providing a better fit with welfare services and labour market services. Table 4.3 above shows the country, type of structure, date, type of enterprise (A/B), and numbers formed (where known).

This blossoming of legislation requires some commentary. It represents new legislation for social enterprise which embodies hybrid legal forms, blurring boundaries between traditional social economy structures, for example, with regard to nonprofit market operation and multi-stakeholder boards. The legislation indicates an increased recognition of social enterprise as a brand. But given the very different numbers of social enterprises formed under each legal form (where data are available), it is clear that there is varying effectiveness of different legislations. Several are overly restrictive or do not provide sufficient advantage compared to existing social economy legislation – this appears to be the case in Greece, France, Finland, and Sweden (where the 'Firm with Limited Profit Distribution' (2006) has attracted little interest). There are only two clearly popular structures: in Italy and the UK (plus Portugal). And the picture is still that most social enterprises use the most flexible legal form available for the social economy, according to national preferences; for example, in Belgium the nonprofit (*association sans but lucrative:* asbl), and in Sweden the co-operative.

Social Entrepreneurship

In the USA there is a rapidly emerging field of social entrepreneurship, which can be seen in the activities of the University Network for Social Entrepreneurship (University Network for Social Entrepreneurship, 2008). And there are growing developments in this area in Europe too – for example, the first European master's degree in Social Entrepreneurship has been set up at Roskilde University (Denmark) (Psychology and Educational Studies, 2008). Another indication of the rapid growth of this area is the number of publications; for example Bornstein (2004), Dees, Emerson, & Economy (2002), Leadbeater (1997), Austin, Howard, and Wei-Skillern (2003), Nicholls (2006), and Mair, Robinson, and Hockerts (2006). Some of these authors, such as Austin, Howard, and Wei-Skillern (2003) adopt frameworks drawn from the conventional entrepreneurship literature, which focus on entrepreneurial processes (of opportunity recognition/construction, and deal-making) rather than on the entrepreneur or on the specific form of organization formed. Indeed the type of organization formed is not considered important (in this perspective) – social enterprise, NGOs, and socially responsible business could all be outcomes of social entrepreneurship.

Conclusion

The social economy is most commonly understood in Europe as the family of co-operatives, mutuals, associations (nonprofits), and foundations (CMAF) that operate between private business and the state. They have their origins in civil society movements throughout history, but most can be more directly linked to the movements and civil society dynamics of the 19th century and community action and the new social movements of the 20th century. The social economy has different levels of recognition in Europe, with Latin countries having the strongest commitment to unifying this family of organizations under the Social Economy umbrella. Its size varies considerably from country to country depending partly on the roles of the state and the family in welfare provision, and partly on the historical development of the different parts of the sector; post-communist restructuring of Eastern Europe has seen substantial changes to both co-operatives and nonprofits in those countries. Recent work to more rigorously define the social economy company complements the earlier work on nonprofits, and facilitates the collecting of data on much of the social economy through satellite accounts. The social economy faces many new challenges, including how to resist isomorphic pressures in increasing global markets, how to play its full part in mixed economies of welfare provision, and how to continue to compete in increasingly deregulated markets. Interesting new approaches to the social economy such as the social enterprise perspective and social entrepreneurship are proving influential in contexts where market dynamics are increasingly dominant.

NOTES

1 The term 'associations' is drawn from the social economy usage to mean voluntary sector organization, including charities or nonprofits. They often are based on associational activity of different kinds, as noted below, but typically they are for other groups rather than for self-help, e.g., a small group of people with disabilities getting together to help all people with the same disability, or a group of people creating a philanthropic organization to help others – usually disadvantaged or disabled. Associational activity for members would more often be through co-ops or mutuals, although there are some self-help voluntary organizations.

2 Commission of the European Communities (2001) Interpretative Commu-

nication on the Community law applicable to public procurement and the possibilities for integrating social considerations into public procurement. Brussels. COM (2001) 566 final.

REFERENCES

Austin, J., Howard, S., & Wei-Skillern, J. (2003). Social entrepreneurship and commercial entrepreneurship: Same, different, or both? *Social Enterprise Series, 28, Working Paper*, Division of Research, Harvard Business School.

Barea, J., & Monzón, J.L. (2006). *Manual for drawing up the satellite accounts of companies in the social economy: Co-operatives and mutual societies.* Retrieved November 3, 2009, from European Commission http://ec.europa .eu/enterprise/newsroom/cf/document.cfm?action=display&doc_ id=3837&userservice_id=1&request.id=0

Bornstein, D. (2004). *How to change the world: Social entrepreneurs and the power of new ideas.* Oxford: Oxford University Press.

Bouchard, M.J. (2009). *The worth of the social economy: An international perspective.* Peter Lang.

CIRIEC. (2000). *The enterprises and organisations of the Third System: A strategic challenge for employment.* Retrieved November 10, 2009, from http://www .uv.es/uidescoop/TSE-DGV-CIRIEC-Contents%20index-English.pdf

CIRIEC. (2007). The Social Economy in the EUROPEAN UNION. *Report N°. CESE/COMM/05/2005.* The European Economic and Social Committee (EESC).

Dees, J., Emerson, J., & Economy, P. (2002). *Strategic tools for social entrepreneurs: Enhancing the performance of your enterprising nonprofit.* Indianapolis: Wiley.

Defourny, J., & Borzaga, C. (2001). *The emergence of social enterprise in Europe.* Andover, UK: Routledge.

Defourny, J., Favreau, L., & Laville, J.L. (1998). *Insertion et nouvelle économie sociale.* Paris: Desclée de Brouwer.

Defourny, J., & Henry, A. (2009, July). *The comparative performance of for-profit, public and third-sector providers in the field of 'Voucher Services' in Belgium: A DEA frontier approach.* Second EMES International Conference on Social Enterprise. Trento, Italy.

Defourny, J. & Monzon, J.L. (1992). *Economie sociale – entre économie capitaliste et économie publique.* Bruxelles: De Boeck Université.

Defourny, J., & Nyssens, M. (2008). Social enterprise in Europe: Recent trends and developments. *EMES Working Paper number 08/01.* Retrieved from http://www.emes.net/index.php?id=49

Desroche, H. (1983). *Pour un traité d'économie sociale.* Paris: CIEM.

European Commission. (2008). *Social economy enterprises.* Retrieved November 2, 2009, from http://ec.europa.eu/enterprise/policies/sme/promoting-entrepreneurship/social-economy/index_en.htm

European Parliament. (2007). European Parliament resolution of 14 March 2007 on social services of general interest in the European Union. *Texts adopted.* Retrieved November 2, 2009, from http://www.europarl.europa .eu/sides/getDoc.do?pubRef=-//EP//TEXT+TA+P6-TA-2007–0070+0+ DOC+XML+V0//EN&language=EN

Eurostat (2002). *Le secteur coopératif, mutualiste et associatif dans l'Union européenne.* Luxembourg: Office des publications officielles des Communautés européennes.

Gumkowska, M., Herbst, J., & Wygnanski, K. (2008). Poland. In C. Borzaga, G. Galera, & R. Nogaler (Eds.), *Social Enterprise: A new model for poverty reduction and employment generation* (pp. 78–103). Retrieved from http://europeandcis .undp.org/poverty/show/2F171313-F203-1EE9-B687694A1F8C9AEC

Leadbeater, C. (1997). *The rise of the social entrepreneur (Demos Papers).* London: Demos.

Mair, J., Robinson, J., & Hockerts, K. (2006) *Social entrepreneurship.* New York: Palgrave Macmillan.

Mertens, S. (2007). *Measuring the social economy in the framework of the national accounts.* Liège, Belgium: Center for Social Economy, Business School of the University of Liège.

Mook, L., Quarter, J., & Richmond, B.J. (2007). *What counts: Social accounting for nonprofits and co-operatives.* (2nd ed.). London: Sigel Publishing.

Nicholls, A. (Ed.) (2006). *Social entrepreneurship: New models of sustainable social change.* Oxford: Oxford University Press.

Nyssens, M. (Ed.) (2006). *Social enterprise, public policy and civil society.* London: Routledge.

Pestoff, V.A. (1998). *Between market and state: Social enterprise and civil democracy in a welfare society.* Aldershot: Ashgate.

Platform of European NGOs (2008). *Quality of social and health services: Social NGOs' recommendations to EU decision makers.* Retrieved November 19, 2009, from http://cms.horus.be/files/99907/MediaArchive/Policies/Services_ of_General_Interest/08–06–26%20Final%20common%20position%20on%20 quality%20social%20and%20health%20services.pdf

Psychology and Educational Studies. (2008). *The Centre of Social Entrepreneurship.* Retrieved November 3, 2009, from http://www.ruc.dk/paes_en/cse/

Salamon L.M., & Anheier, H.K. (1997). *Defining the non-profit sector: A cross-*

national analysis. Baltimore: Institute for Policy Studies, Johns Hopkins University.

University Network for Social Entrepreneurship. (2008). *About us*. Retrieved November 3, 2009, from http://universitynetwork.org/admin/menu/item/edit/74?q=about_us

5 A Comparative Analysis of Voluntary Sector/Government Relations in Canada and England

PETER R. ELSON

This chapter compares voluntary sector/federal government relations in Canada with voluntary sector/central government relations in England between the years 1994 and 2008. While similar policy developments took place in Northern Ireland, Scotland, and Wales, there are important differences such as the existence of distinct representative organizations, which are beyond the scope of this study to address, and thus this analysis focuses on England. The voluntary sector, using the framework introduced in chapter 1 by Mook, Quarter, and Ryan, includes public sector nonprofits and civil society organizations. It was during the time period of this study, 1994 to 2008, that long-standing voluntary sector/government relations issues pertaining to policy relations, advocacy, funding, and the definition of charity came to the fore in both Canada and England.

Yet the consequences of these similar short and intense periods of policy dialogue resulted in two very different policy outcomes. In Canada at the federal order of government the policy outcome was weak and only partially enforced, whereas in England there was and continues to be a strong and consistent financial and political reinforcement for progressive voluntary sector policies. This research investigates, through the lens of historical institutionalism, the influence of institutional regime type on these two distinct voluntary sector policy outcomes and the implications of regime type for the future direction of voluntary sector/government relationships.

Canada, like Australia, is a federated state and as such, provinces play a significant role in the lives of voluntary sector organizations. In fact, provinces are a dominant funder of voluntary organizations which deliver social, health, and educational services (Hall, Barr, Easwaramoorthy, Sokolowski, & Salamon, 2005). However, the federal government, not the provinces, has assumed the dominant regulatory role over charities, which account for half of all nonprofit organizations. The federal order of government in Canada, like the central government in the UK, has ultimate taxing authority over charities and has used this position in Canada to regulate a variety of related activities such as registration requirements and public advocacy. Because only charities can issue tax receipts for donations, and private foundations can only disburse funds to registered charities, charities enjoy a preferential fundraising position.

Provinces, in spite of their important role as a funder and their primary jurisdictional responsibility for social policy, have only recently emerged as a place of collective political dialogue (Elson, 2009b). In chapter 3, Marguerite Mendell and Nancy Neamtan profile the emergence of a new political economy in Quebec. This is a development which has attracted a great deal of interest by voluntary sector leaders across Canada who are striving to find their voice in their own provincial climate. The next chapter, by Kathy Brock, on the complexity of relations between social economy organizations and the Ontario government, highlights how individualistic this relationship becomes when there is no collective voice to represent the sector. It is this collective voice, or the lack thereof, which lies at the centre of this comparative analysis.

Before undertaking this comparative analysis, I introduce historical institutionalism as the framework I utilize to analyse voluntary sector/government relations at the federal level in Canada and with the central government in England.

Historical Institutionalism

Historical institutionalism makes the assumption that institutions constrain and shape the actions of actors and, ultimately, policy outcomes. Streeck and Thelen (2005, p. 9), two leading historical institutionalism scholars, define institutions as 'building-blocks of social order: they represent socially sanctioned, that is, collectively enforced expectations with respect to the behaviour of specific categories of actors or to the performance of certain activities.' This is the operational definition of institutions adopted for this chapter. It is the extent to which expectation of behaviour or performance is reinforced which defines the relative formality of an institution and thus its regime type (Streeck & Thelen, 2005). Institutional regime type in this chapter refers to the

Table 5.1
Institutional regime type

Regime Type	Features	Example
Formal	Well established and sanctioned representational and reporting protocol which is transferable across time and issues	A government department enforces clear reporting protocols for their representatives which are consistent from issue to issue
Non-formal	Transitory representational and reporting protocol which is non-transferable across time and issues	A group of voluntary sector representatives make deputations to government on an issue; but there is no consistency in representation or reporting across issues
Informal	Ad hoc representational and reporting protocol which is non-transferable across time and issues	Independent representation by voluntary sector organizations to government committees where there is no co-ordination of representation

degree to which sectoral representation and reporting is formally monitored and reinforced within the public and voluntary sectors.

Historical institutionalism will be used to analyse the regime types associated with the voluntary sectors in Canada and England as each defined and presented their policy agenda and engaged their respective central governments in policy dialogue. This analysis will then be extended to include the influence of regime type on the subsequent policy outcomes.

To facilitate the analysis of regime types, an institutional regime type classification scheme was created, based on the degree to which regime rules are formally established and enforced (Elson, 2010 (forthcoming)). This scheme, outlined in table 5.1, differentiates institutional regime types into three categories: formal, non-formal, and informal. The formal regime type, typically associated with government-policy-representative regimes, is characterized by an established and sanctioned representational and reporting protocol that is transferable across time and issues. The non-formal institutional regime type features a transitory representational and reporting system that is non-transferable across time and issues. The informal institutional regime type reflects an ad hoc representational and reporting protocol that is also non-transferable across time and issues. This scheme classification is an extension of an accepted differentiation between formal and informal regime types (Lawson, 1993; Streeck & Thelen, 2005). Regime formality is a reflection of the degree to which representational and reporting protocols and sanctions are formalized and reinforced over time and circumstance.

Before the Shift

In Canada, the period from 1994 to 1997 was a time in which voluntary sector/federal government relations were at an all-time low. This was due to massive budget cuts, constricted service contracts, constrained policy dialogue, and neo-liberal labelling of the voluntary sector as representative of 'special interests' (Evans & Shields, 2000; Phillips, 2001b).

In England, the 1990s started with a similar low ebb in voluntary sector/central government relations. The Thatcher and Major governments each relegated the voluntary sector to a marginal policy position and the role of the sector to one of charity provider, that is, utilizing volunteers to fill the social service gaps created by massive reductions in government funding (Kendall, 2003). In this regard, the voluntary sectors in Canada and England found themselves in a similar marginalized policy position, the Canadian policy arena being dominated by fiscal constraint and the English position by political ideology.

While historically the voluntary sectors in both Canada and England had prior experience participating in centralized policy forums (e.g., the National Advisory Council on Voluntary Action [1977] in Canada and the Wolfenden Committee [1978] in England), neither voluntary sector had collectively defined a made-in-the-sector policy agenda (National Advisory Council on Voluntary Action, 1977; Wolfenden Committee, 1978). The marginalized policy position facing both sectors in the 1990s catalysed leading national voluntary organizations in both countries, for the first time, to act on their own behalf.

Canada

A Made-in-Canada Policy Agenda

In Canada, the response at the federal level to this political marginalization and policy isolation by leading voluntary sector organizations was the creation of the Voluntary Sector Roundtable in 1995 (Voluntary Sector Initiative, 2008). The absence of a dedicated national organization with the legitimacy to speak for the sector as a whole catalysed a group of 12 national organizations to create the Voluntary Sector Roundtable[1] to act (Hall et al., 2005; Phillips, 2003a). The Voluntary Sector Roundtable's primary goals were (a) to enhance the relationship between the charitable sector and the federal government and (b) to encourage a supportive legislative and regulatory framework for organizations in the community (Voluntary Sector Roundtable, 1998). The Voluntary Sector Roundtable soon realized it needed to promote sectoral accountability, good governance, and public trust (Phillips, 2003a). To this end, in October 1997, the Voluntary Sector Roundtable set up the Panel on Accountability and Governance in the Voluntary Sector (PAGVS), an arm's-length panel chaired by former leader of the federal New Democratic Party, Ed Broadbent.

The Panel's 1999 report, *Building on Strength: Improving Governance and Accountability in Canada's Voluntary Sector*, not only laid out recommendations for better self-regulation and governance but also presented steps for the federal government to take in order to create a more enabling environment and stronger relationship with the voluntary sector (Panel on Accountability and Governance in the Voluntary Sector, 1999).

While a pan-Canadian consultation with voluntary sector organizations took place following the release of a draft of the Broadbent Report, there was no ongoing attempt to consolidate or formalize the representation of the sector beyond the select membership in the Voluntary Sector Roundtable. This representational and reporting protocol was non-formal, and ongoing communication with the voluntary sector-at-large took the form of the broad release of updates and reports (Voluntary Sector Roundtable, 1999). This non-formal representation and reporting regime continued through the next series of policy discussions between the Voluntary Sector Roundtable and the federal government. These policy discussions took the form of three joint (voluntary sector/government) tables designed to address relationship, capacity, and regulation issues, and resulted in the release of the report *Working Together* (Joint Tables, 1999).

In June 2000, in response to the Broadbent Report, the Joint Table *Working Together* Report, and their own political priorities, the federal government announced the creation of the federally funded Voluntary Sector Initiative (VSI) (Voluntary Sector Initiative, 2006). The VSI was a five-year, $94.6 million initiative to fund the work of seven Joint Tables, designed on the collaborative model created by the Voluntary Sector

Task Force. These seven Joint Tables were (1) Co-ordinating Committee, (2) Accord, (3) Awareness, (4) Capacity, (5) Information Management and Technology, (6) Regulatory, and (7) National Volunteerism Initiative. In addition, two independent working groups on funding and advocacy were funded by the voluntary sector (Brock, 2005). The regime type which prevailed over the five-year Voluntary Sector Initiative will be profiled under the section entitled *Canadian Voluntary Sector Initiative*.

Policy Dialogue and New Labour

Unlike Canada during the 1990s, England did have a lead national organization with the presence and legitimacy to speak for the voluntary sector. This organization, the National Council for Voluntary Organisations, had already created a Parliamentary Working Group in the late 1980s to strategically and consistently lobby MPs to ensure that the organization was seen as the premier representative for the sector (6 & Leat, 1997).

The National Council for Voluntary Organisations saw the need to reach out to the broader voluntary sector if it was to legitimize its position as a representative body and collective voice for that sector (National Council for Voluntary Organisations, 1994). Positive changes within the opposition Labour Party and the ongoing political marginalization by the Conservative government provided the impetus for the voluntary sector to take action. This action took the form of the creation of the Commission on the Future of the Voluntary Sector under chair Nicholas Deakin in 1994 (National Council for Voluntary Organisations, 1994). The mandate of the Deakin Commission (1996) was to

- provide a clear vision for the voluntary sector;
- articulate the contribution of the voluntary sector and its place in society;
- promote constructive inter-sectoral relationships;
- improve the performance and governance of voluntary organizations; and
- make the case for new fiscal, legal, and regulatory arrangements for the sector.

The Deakin Commission consulted widely, contracted the completion of background position papers, and received numerous deputations from voluntary and intermediary organizations and agencies, such as the Charity Commission, throughout its one-year consultation period.

The Deakin Report, for the first time, positioned the voluntary sector as a distinct and viable public policy partner (6 & Leat, 1997; Wolfenden Committee, 1978). The Deakin Report declared that the voluntary sector was a major force in its own right, not only because of its size and flexibility but also because it was the backbone of civil society and an essential precondition for a healthy democracy (Commission on the Future of the Voluntary Sector, 1996). Deakin (1996) saved for last his flagship recommendation for the relationship of the voluntary sector with central government, namely, a meaningful partnership which would take the form of a concordat that would lay down basic principles for future relations. The release of the Deakin Report coincided with both a growing recognition of the voluntary sector by the opposition Labour Party and a pending national election. As a result, in 1997 the voluntary sector was well placed to engage in policy dialogue with the newly elected Labour government (New Labour, as it was called), who in turn were equally interested in negotiating a Compact and establishing a central role for the voluntary sector in the delivery of public services.

At the same time, a national conference of umbrella voluntary and community organizations established the Working Group on Government Relations under the auspices of the National Council for Voluntary Organisations to develop the Compact with government (Compact Working Group, 2001). The National Council for Voluntary Organisations consolidated its own national leadership role in the development of the Compact, as it heavily supported the Working Group on Government Relations.

The Working Group on Government Relations in England can be seen as a parallel development to the Voluntary Sector Roundtable in Canada, as both comprised leading national voluntary sector organizations, were experienced in national policy dialogue, and were politically astute. The fact that the Working Group on Government Relations in England came out of a national voluntary sector conference, rather than being self-appointed, as was the case in Canada, helped to establish the transparency and representative legitimacy that was needed in subsequent negotiations with government. Thus while a representational and reporting protocol was not yet established in either country, the elements of a more formal regime were clearly present in England.

The Canadian Voluntary Sector Initiative

The Canadian Voluntary Sector Initiative in 2000 followed the release of the independent report on the voluntary sector (undertaken by the Panel on Accountability and Governance in the Voluntary Sector) and joint Voluntary Sector Roundtable/government policy discussions in 1999 (Joint Tables, 1999; Panel on Accountability and Governance in the Voluntary Sector, 1999).

The Voluntary Sector Initiative allocated $95 million over five years in two phases. This budget funded seven joint policy discussion tables pertaining to voluntary sector/federal government relations: accord negotiations; capacity building; regulation; volunteering; awareness; information technology; and a Joint Coordinating Committee; and their respective representatives approved the initiatives (Voluntary Sector Initiative, 2008). Two independent working groups on financing and advocacy were established by the voluntary sector because the federal government, particularly the Department of Finance and Treasury Board, flatly refused to make any tax-related policy issue a subject for mutual negotiation. These two powerful federal departments had no intention of yielding ground to outside groups or setting a policy-making precedent. Politically, the government wanted to avoid any contentious areas (e.g., advocacy, financing) in order to achieve a concrete 'deliverable' (e.g., the Voluntary Sector Accord) by the end of the International Year of Volunteers in 2001 (Brock, 2004; Phillips, 2003a, 2004).

The most visible Phase One event was the signing of the Accord between the Government of Canada and the Voluntary Sector to coincide with the International Year of Volunteers in December 2001 (Robillard & Deboisbriand, 2001). This signing was followed by the development and wide circulation of two codes of good practice: a Code of Good Practice on Policy Dialogue, and a Code of Good Practice on Funding (Voluntary Sector Initiative, 2002a, 2002b). In Phase Two, modifications to regulations concerning how much advocacy could be conducted and under what conditions followed in 2003 (Canada Revenue Agency, 2003), but there was no movement by the government on two areas which were of utmost concern to the voluntary sector, the definition of charity and funding practices.

Regime Types during the Voluntary Sector Initiative

Leadership for the voluntary sector during the voluntary sector ini-

Table 5.2
Institutional regime type: Voluntary Sector Initiative

Voluntary Sector Initiative (Canada)	Regime Features	Regime Type
Government representation to Joint Tables		
Collective representation strong throughout and beyond the negotiation process	Established and sanctioned representational and reporting protocol which is transferable across time and issues	Formal
Voluntary Sector representation to Joint Tables		
Collective representation weak throughout and beyond the negotiation process	Transitory representational and reporting protocol which is nontransferable across time and issues	Non-Formal

tiative was carried forward from the *Working Together* process by the Voluntary Sector Roundtable. In order to cope with the complexity of co-ordinating seven Joint Tables and establishing voluntary sector representatives for each of these tables, two steps were taken. First, the Voluntary Sector Roundtable expanded its membership to include appointed voluntary sector chairs of the Joint Tables, chairs of the sector-only Working and Reference Groups,[2] and sector members of the Joint Coordinating Committee (Social Development Canada, 2004). Second, a general call for representatives was sent out to the voluntary sector community and a broad pan-Canadian representative group was selected to sit on the Joint Tables. While representative of the broad voluntary sector, most often these individuals had limited national policy skill or experience. Exacerbating this skill deficit was that voluntary sector representatives within the Joint Tables operated without any predetermined policy platform or priorities (Social Development Canada, 2004).

Federal government representatives saw part of their role at the Joint Tables as one of safeguarding their respective ministers from any unwanted political or fiscal repercussions or direct political intervention from the voluntary sector outside the established negotiation process (Good, 2003; Social Development Canada, 2004). These government representatives were directed and constrained by their departments (Social Development Canada, 2004). As an official observer to the Joint Accord Table, Phillips (2003a) has revealed that government members reported through an executive committee of assistant deputy ministers to a reference group of eight ministers who were responsible for providing political leadership on the file at the Cabinet table. At several times in the process of developing the Voluntary Sector Accord, government members had to seek approval or guidance from the executive committee or reference group of ministers (Phillips, 2003a).

This protocol is evidence that government representatives operated under a formal institutional regime type (see table 5.2). This formal regime protocol constrained the actions of government department representatives with the voluntary sector and reinforced government representatives' internal relationship to a formal institutional structure.

United Kingdom

The English Compact

The Compact in England was negotiated between a Working Group on Government relations established by the voluntary sector and a Ministerial Working Group of leading cabinet ministers. Rather than addressing details that would be more bureaucratic than policy-focused, the voluntary sector's Working Group on Government relations deliberately kept the language and tone at a level which was appropriate for direct ministerial participation: shared principles, reciprocal obligations, followed by proposed implementation, monitoring, and dispute resolution mechanisms (Stowe, 1998). When necessary, the chair of the Working Group on Government relations, Sir Kenneth Stowe, directly represented the collective voluntary sector policy position to the Ministerial Working Group[3] (Stowe, 1999).

The focus on general principles in the Compact made the agreement politically palatable and deferred more contentious issues such as funding policies, the definition of charity, and governance. This was a deliberate strategy, for through the process of negotiating the Compact, the Working Group on Government Relations established its political credibility with its government counterparts, and then was able to use this credibility to later advocate for a resolution of funding, governance, and statutory issues.

Following the agreement to the terms of the original Compact in England and its counterpart throughout England, five codes of good practice were subsequently developed by the Compact Working Group. These codes outlined detailed practice guidelines for funding and procurement; consultation and policy appraisal; community groups; volunteering; and black and minority ethnic groups.

Regime Types during Compact Negotiations

In England, the National Council for Voluntary Organisations worked to establish a formal regime of representational and reporting protocols as the sectoral partnership (The Compact) with central government was negotiated. Evidence of this developing formality is found in the funnelling of sector-wide consultations to the Government Relations Working Group and its complementary Reference Group of voluntary organizations.

The Reference Group to the Government Relations Working Group comprised 65 voluntary sector organizations that had national policy experience, were leaders in the sector, and had a broad grasp of the voluntary sector as a whole.[4] The Reference Group acted as a sounding board for the Working Group prior to discussions with government (Stowe, 1998). For example, a draft consultation document on the components of the Compact was circulated for feedback to the Reference Group and then circulated even wider for feedback from the sector. Stowe contends that this extensive consultation process was key to its acceptance by the sector (Stowe, 1998).

In excess of 10,000 copies of a draft consultation document on the proposed content for the Compact were distributed, and 11 consultation meetings were held (Stowe, 1998). It has been estimated that more than 25,000 organizations were consulted during this process. The Government Relations Working Group consolidated the feedback from these sectoral meetings and only then were the results presented to its central government counterpart, the Ministerial Working Group (Commission for the Compact, n.d.).

The strength of the sectoral consultation document on the proposed Compact developed by the Working Group was such that the actual Compact embodied the approach, structure, and content of the consultation document (Stowe, 1998). One of the clearest messages the Working Group received from its consultations was that there was no appetite in the voluntary sector in England for a Compact solely with the Labour Party. Any agreement needed to be a Compact with parliament (Stowe, 1999). This was accomplished by making representation to both the Conservative and the Labour parties and forging a common agreement by both parties that there was a need for the Compact (Stowe, 1999).

The draft Compact document was created by the voluntary sector and formally presented to the Ministerial Working Group. Both the

Table 5.3
Institutional regime type: England compact

Compact	Regime Features	Regime Type
Government Relations Working Group (England)		
Collective representation strong throughout and beyond the negotiation process	Established and sanctioned representational and reporting protocol which is transferable across time and issues	Formal
Ministerial Working Group (England)		
Collective representation strong throughout and beyond the negotiation proces	Established and sanctioned representational and reporting protocol which is transferable across time and issues	Formal

Ministerial Working Group and the Government Relations Working Group had access to a larger constituency reference group and the results of their own sectoral consultation on the same draft. In this regard, the formality of the regime type of the two groups was matched (see table 5.3). Through a series of meetings, the two sides negotiated a final position, which formed the final version basis of the Compact. The continuity of the representational and reporting protocols for the working groups has extended past the signing of the Compact and throughout the ten years of Compact implementation. The strategic agenda of the Compact Voice, as the Compact Working Group is now called, has been maintained and transferred across changes in both government and voluntary sector representation.

Comparison of Policy Outcomes

As Phillips (2003b) has noted, there is no organizational equivalent in Canada to the National Council for Voluntary Organisations in terms of resources and legitimacy to represent the voluntary sector as a whole. The consultation process during the development of the Broadbent Report and following its release served to reinforce this non-formal voluntary sector regime type for three reasons. First, the timing of the consultation was such that it could only reinforce the policy agenda the Voluntary Sector Roundtable had already established. Second, because the key issues, which were identified by the sector (e.g., funding, advocacy, and definition of charity), were not open to negotiation, the process proceeded largely for its own sake. Third, the breadth of the representation by the voluntary sector provided representative voices at the Joint Tables, but the lack of policy experience and expertise only reinforced the non-formal regime type. There was no continuity between the policy capacity, which was developed during the Voluntary Sector Initiative, and subsequent policy deliberations.

The Voluntary Sector Accord in Canada was only afforded the policy priority government departments chose to give it; political interest in the Accord quickly dissipated; and Accord implementation surveys only lasted two years and then stopped (Elson, 2006). After five years, the Voluntary Sector Initiative was terminated, and long before this point in time departments had moved on other policy priorities.

Notwithstanding changes which have taken place within the Charities Directorate, a partnership with government departments may have been important to the sector, but to most government departments, the Voluntary Sector Initiative was peripheral to other policy priorities (Phillips, 2001b). Since the election of the minority Conservative government in 2006, any form of overt advocacy, research, or policy analysis has been shunned by policy makers, a climate which has been reinforced with corresponding funding cuts to policy and research related initiatives and programs (Department of Finance Canada, 2006). A Blue Ribbon Panel was announced with great fanfare in June of 2006 following massive cuts to the sector to address issues related to grants and contributions. Three years later the recommendations are crawling through the bureaucracy and there is little concrete evidence that changes are imminent. Policy consultations are highly orchestrated and selective, with virtually no opportunity for broad policy dialogue involving the voluntary sector. This cold climate at the federal level could be one reason why there is a spirit of optimism in relations at the provincial level (Elson, 2009a).

The non-formal regime type, which characterized voluntary sector representation during the Voluntary Sector Initiative, continued with its successor, the Voluntary Sector Forum. This meant that there was no concerted or collective movement to resist the aforementioned funding cuts which the voluntary sector experienced in October 2006 (Levy-Ajzenkopf, 2006). Umbrella voluntary sector organizations in Canada have worked hard to maintain a relationship with the federal government, but no apex organization has systematically and collectively provided a voice for voluntary organizations throughout Canada. More often than not, voluntary sector organizations are isolated from mainstream policy processes. At no time has responsibility for a voluntary sector policy agenda rested in one federal department or minister.

In England, however, the voluntary sector, with the lead of the National Council for Voluntary Organisations, has built a formal representational and reporting institutional process framework (e.g., the Government Relations Working Group) to ensure that the voluntary sector was both well informed and represented (Phillips, 2003a; Stowe, 1998).

The Government Relations Working Group transitioned itself into the Compact Working Group upon the signing of the Compact and continuity was maintained, as was the pressure to implement the Compact and to develop and monitor the five Codes of Good Practice. The most recent transformation of the Compact Working Group to Compact Voice reflects its ongoing representational role. The Compact continues to provide a focused, clear, and continuing sense of purpose and direction for both the government and the voluntary sector.

Evidence of the institutional regime differences between the national representative voices for the voluntary sector in Canada and England can be seen in the eventual demise of the Coalition of National Voluntary Organizations in Canada and the corresponding growth of the National Council for Voluntary Organisations in England. In Canada, the dominant focus by lead organizations representing the sector during the Voluntary Sector Initiative was on relationship building to maintain a collegial relationship with the government in power to the detriment of representing and defending the core issues facing the sector at the time (e.g., definition of charity, advocacy regulations, and funding regimes).

In terms of comparing the actual content of the Canadian Accord and the Compact for England, the Accord is long on shared values and principles and short on commitment and monitoring mechanisms. For example, in the Accord the government commits itself to recognizing the need to engage the voluntary sector in dialogue. Specifically, the Accord states:

> Recognize its need to engage the voluntary sector in open, informed and sustained dialogue in order that the sector may contribute its experience, expertise, knowledge, and ideas in developing better public policies and in the design and delivery of programs. (p. 8)

Contrast this with a similar section on policy development and consultation in the Compact:

To appraise new policies and procedures, particularly at the development stage, so as to identify as far as possible implications for the sector.

Subject to considerations of urgency, sensitivity or confidentiality ... to consult the sector on issues which are likely to affect it, particularly where the government is proposing new roles and responsibilities for the sector. Such consultation should be timely and allow reasonable timescales for response, taking into account the need of organizations to consult their users, beneficiaries and stakeholders. (para 9.5, 9.6)

The Compact is more consistently specific than the Accord in terms of principles and commitments, such as the one noted above, in areas relating to funding, advocacy and consultation, inclusion, and account-ability. The Compact Working Group deliberately deferred the question of the definition of charity because of the perception that it would be contentious for some groups in the sector and the timing was not right. In contrast, the Voluntary Sector Roundtable worked to push the policy agenda on as many fronts as possible because it felt the policy win-dow was very narrow. As it turned out, the two-year policy timetable, typical of the federal government's attention span, achieved what was principled, possible, and palatable.

The implementation of the Compact was reinforced through a number of mechanisms, including a detailed annual implementation report by both the voluntary sector and government, which was tabled at the annual meeting to review the Compact. This annual Compact Action Plan is mutually agreed upon and has consistently included ex-plicit targets, an outline of actions to be taken, measures of success, and accompanying lead agencies. The successes and shortfalls in adhering to the Action Plan by each sector have been reported at each annual meeting and subsequently recorded in the annual report to Parliament (Compact Voice, 2007; Compact Working Group, 2001, 2003).

Following the signing of the Compact, the Ministerial Steering Group and the voluntary sector Reference Group each asked the Working Group on Government Relations to continue its representational work for the sector. This they did under the name Compact Working Group (now renamed Compact Voice). The specific mandate for the Compact Working Group was to take the Compact forward for mutual advan-tage with a specific focus on continuing development, implementation, monitoring, and representation at the Compact Annual Meeting (Com-mission for the Compact, n.d.; Compact Working Group, 2001).

In addition to the work of the Compact Voice and the representa-tional role of both the voluntary sector and central government, the Labour government has made substantial investments in voluntary sector infrastructure since 2002, the year of their first Cross Cutting (i.e., budget) Review, including the development of national hubs of expertise in governance, performance, finance, volunteering, workforce development, and ICT, and geographical support networks (Capacitybuilders, 2007).

This voluntary sector partnership policy direction continues to be reinforced both politically and fiscally at the highest levels in government. In 2006 the Office of the Third Sector was transferred to the Cabinet Office, in recognition of the increasingly important role of the third sector in both society and the economy (Office of the Third Sector, 2008). This development included moving the responsibilities of the Active Communities Directorate from the Home Office and the Social Enterprise Unit from the Department for Trade and Industry into the Office of the Third Sector as part of the Cabinet Office (Office of the Third Sector, 2008).

The overall commitment to creating a viable third option for the delivery of a blend of social inclusion and economic growth includes the Office of the Third Sector's national policy on social enterprise. Their social enterprise activity is focused on working across government to create an environment for social enterprises to thrive. The central government's commitments include a substantial financial investment in research, infrastructure, and resources to nurture social enterprises (Office of the Third Sector, 2009). For example, the Department of Health's Social Enterprise Investment Fund announced in the summer of 2009 that more than £70 million ($140 million CDN) would be available through Futurebuilders England for start-up and existing social enterprises over three years (Partnerships UK, 2009). Futurebuilders England, funded by the Office of the Third Sector, is a specific £215 million ($430 million CDN) fund that offers support and investment to help Third Sector organizations win contracts to deliver public services.

Between 1998 and 2008, the National Council for Voluntary Organisations successfully addressed outstanding policy issues not included in the Compact, including permissive political activities and campaigning, and most recently, wholesale changes to the Charities Act that was passed in 2006. This was accomplished by collaborating with other leading voluntary sector organizations using a formal representation and reporting regime similar to the one that was established during the Compact negotiation process (e.g., commissioning research; developing a reference group, and engaging the broader voluntary sector in a consultation process).

Discussion

The process of negotiating and signing the Compact enabled the voluntary sector and the National Council for Voluntary Organisations to formally create a representative voice for the voluntary sector. This voice, the Compact Working Group, created continuity in representation and reporting as progressive targets for Compact implementation were established, monitored, and implemented (Etherington, 2000). The representation on the Compact Working Group was a continuation of the Working Group on Government Relations, which had been created at the national conference held in 1997 to discuss the Compact.

The process and design in Canada leading to the Voluntary Sector Initiative and signing of the Voluntary Sector Accord were initiated with a similar consultation document, the Broadbent Report (Panel on Accountability and Governance in the Voluntary Sector, 1998). The Voluntary Sector Roundtable in Canada, like the English Working Group on Government Relations, was a relatively small, but influential group of national voluntary organizations (Joint Tables, 1999). Together with government representatives, the Voluntary Sector Roundtable created a Joint Table and formulated many of the policy positions which formed the basis of the Voluntary Sector Initiative and the Accord (Phillips, 2004).

The political climates in which these two voluntary sector policy initiatives were undertaken were significantly different. In the United Kingdom, a newly elected Tony Blair was committed to implementing his transformative 'Third Way' public policy, which saw at its core the voluntary sector as both an alternative delivery agent for government services and a catalyst for citizenship participation (Giddens, 1998; Kendall, 2003). Both political capital and financial resources were allocated to support this intended transition.

In Canada, a similar mood of collaboration was developing within government, but for reasons that were peripheral to the voluntary sector. According to Susan Phillips (2001a), this relationship shift was a result of: (a) key citizen engagement advocates located in the Privy Council Office; (b) limited government fiscal resources which the voluntary sector could help to mitigate; and (c) the visibility and community-based credibility which the government could gain by affiliating with the voluntary sector. The Liberal Party, wanting to overshadow its neo-liberal fiscal policies and the three years of cuts to social programs contained in its 1994 through 1996 budgets, gave considerable attention to the voluntary sector in its 1997 election campaign program and then followed through after its re-election (Phillips, 2003a). The commitment to the voluntary sector and the Voluntary Sector Initiative by the federal government in Canada was motivated by short-term political relations policy, devoid of any overarching strategic policy shift.

The key difference in the direction taken to address these policy dialogue overtures came in 2000 when the Voluntary Sector Roundtable in Canada decided to expand its representation to be seen as more legitimately 'representative' in the eyes of the government. While the Voluntary Sector Roundtable diffused and diluted its policy expertise and political capital by opening up its representative voice to a wide spectrum of voluntary organizations across Canada, the Working Group on Government Relations in England consolidated and formalized its policy expertise and political capital by creating a reference group of 65 national organizations with which they consulted and by having as its lead spokesperson Sir Kenneth Stowe, a well-respected individual with significant political credibility in Whitehall.

The decision in Canada to expand representation by the Voluntary Sector Roundtable diluted existing policy expertise and resources, distanced key voluntary sector leaders from politicians, and eliminated any opportunity to build a pan-Canadian institutional presence. The Accord negotiations then became more focused on projects than policy; more ambitious than politically practical; and more individually inclusive than collectively representative.

In England, the voluntary sector in general, and the National Council for Voluntary Organisations in particular, have created a partnership with government in which engagement is communication, not conflict; differences call for dialogue, not rhetoric; and expectations are measured and met, not left behind as empty promises. The investment in voluntary sector infrastructure, such as the interconnected hubs of expertise and training for voluntary organizations provided through Capacitybuilders and Futurebuilders, at the national, regional, and local level has reached almost £1 billion [$2 billion CDN] since the first Cross Cutting Review in 2002 (HM Treasury, 2008).

During this time, the Active Communities Unit expanded within the Home Office and is now incorporated within the Office of the Third Sector in the Cabinet Office, at the very centre of government. This ongoing political access is in addition to Compact Voice meetings and the annual Report to Parliament on the Compact.

The institutional regime differences between the representative

Table 5.4
Institutional regime type: England/Canada comparison

Case	Regime Features	Regime Type
Government Relations Working Group (England)		
Collective representation strong throughout and beyond the negotiation process	Established and sanctioned representational and reporting protocol, which is transferable across time and issues	Formal
Voluntary Sector Roundtable (Canada)		
Collective representation weak throughout and beyond the negotiation process	Transitory representational and reporting protocol, which is non-transferable across time and issues	Non-formal

voices for the voluntary sector in Canada and England are seen in the representational uncertainty, which prevailed following the end of the Voluntary Sector Initiative and the corresponding growth of the National Council for Voluntary Organisations in England (see table 5.4). In Canada, the dominant focus by lead organizations representing the sector during the Voluntary Sector Initiative was on relationship building to the detriment of representing and defending the core issues facing the sector at the time (e.g., definition of charity, advocacy regulations, and funding).

In England, the voluntary sector, with the lead of the National Council for Voluntary Organisations, built a formal representational and reporting process (e.g. the Government Relations Working Group) to ensure that the voluntary sector was both well informed and represented. Weaknesses, such as the representation of black and ethnic minorities, were explicitly acknowledged and later addressed within the representational regime which had been established (Phillips, 2003a; Stowe, 1998).

The Government Relations Working Group transitioned itself into the Compact Working Group upon the signing of the Compact and continuity was maintained, as was the pressure to implement the Compact and to develop and monitor the five Codes of Good Practice. The most recent transformation of the Compact Working Group to Compact Voice reflects its ongoing representational role. The Compact continues to represent a focused, clear, and continuing sense of purpose and direction for both the government and the voluntary sector.

Conclusion

There are still substantial challenges ahead, particularly in relation to support for Local Compacts across England. Not everyone is convinced that this partnership with government will come without a price; namely, the degree of independence which is so important to both voluntary organizations and Local Authorities (National Council for Voluntary Organisations, 2004). This research has shown that the formal institutional regime type developed by the voluntary sector, with the capacity to legitimately engage and represent its constituency, has succeeded in moving forward an ambitious policy agenda of its own creation. In circumstances where a critical juncture takes place in voluntary sector/government relations, institutional regime type can have an impact on policy outcomes.

The voluntary sector may be better served by a more formal institutional regime type when engaged in formal policy dialogue with governments. The non-formal regime type which dominates the Canadian voluntary sector at the national level has, for example, hindered the ability of the voluntary sector to translate general public support for common cause advocacy into policy changes (Ipsos-Reid, 2006). To summarize the view of an interviewee within a central government agency, 'we see very little evidence of [voluntary sector] engagement in permissible political activities. When we do hear from organizations, their concerns are often very particular and not germane to our policy making process.'

A more formal representation regime type for the voluntary sector may be beneficial to its long-term relationship with the federal government in Canada. However, as demonstrated by the National Council for Voluntary Organisations in England, this institutional regime representation must be broad, consistent, legitimate, and linked to national as well as community organizations. This formal regime type would require a consistent investment in increasing the depth of stakeholder participation and greater continuity of representation and reporting across policy arenas. This increased regime formality would need to be underpinned by policy research, deep stakeholder consultation processes, and a strong political and media presence. This will take time, dedication, foresight, and financial and human resources. What this research has demonstrated is that there is a way, over time, to systematically identify, articulate, and achieve policy goals which are driven from within the voluntary sector for the benefit of the sector and a more equitable and just society.

NOTES

1 The twelve national organizations were Canadian Centre for Ethics in Sport, Canadian Centre for Philanthropy, Canadian Conference of the Arts, Canadian Council for International Cooperation, Canadian Council on Social Development, Canadian Environmental Network, Canadian Parks/Recreation Association, Community Foundations of Canada, Health Charities Council of Canada, the Coalition of National Voluntary Organizations, United Way of Canada/Centraide Canada, and Volunteer Canada (Voluntary Sector Roundtable, 1998).
2 Two tables for advocacy and financing were established to enable sector representatives to discuss these two areas of concern.
3 Members of the Ministerial Working Group were departments with an existing relationship with the voluntary sector: the Home Office; Department for Culture, Media and Sport; Department for Education and Employment; Department of Environment, Transport and the Regions; Department of Health; Department of Social Security; Northern Ireland Office; Scottish Office; and Welsh Office.
4 The Working Group on Government Relations included the National Council for Voluntary Organisations; National Centre for Volunteering; National Association for Voluntary and Community Action; Association of Chief Executives of Voluntary Organisations; Progress Trust; Council for Ethnic Minority Voluntary Organisations; National Association of Volunteer Bureaux; and the Charities Aid Foundation (Compact Working Group, 2001).

REFERENCES

6, P., & Leat, D. (1997). Inventing the British voluntary sector by committee: From Wolfenden to Deakin. *Non-Profit Studies, 1*(2), 33–45.

Brock, K.L. (2004). The devil's in the detail: The Chrétien legacy for the Third Sector. *Review of Constitutional Studies, 9*(1&2), 263–82.

Brock, K. L. (2005). Judging the VSI: Reflections on the relationship between the federal government and the voluntary sector. *The Philanthropist, 19*(3), 168–81.

Canada Revenue Agency. (2003). *Political activities [CPS – 022]*. Ottawa: Charities Directorate, Canada Customs and Revenue Agency.

Capacitybuilders. (2007). *Destination 2014: Our strategy for the delivery of ChangeUp*. Birmingham: Capacitybuilders.

Commission for the Compact. (n.d.). History of the Compact. Retrieved April

3, 2008, from http://www.thecompact.org.uk/information/100020/100212/
history_of_the_compact/

Commission on the Future of the Voluntary Sector. (1996). *Meeting the challenge
of change: Voluntary action into the 21st century*. London: National Council of
Voluntary Organisations.

Compact Voice. (2007). *Joint Compact Action Plan 2006–2008: Report to Parliament of the seventh annual meeting to review the Compact on relations between
government and the voluntary and community sector*. London: Compact Voice.

Compact Working Group. (2001). *Annual review of the Compact, October 2001:
Progress report by the Compact Working Group*. London: National Council for
Voluntary Organisations.

Compact Working Group. (2003). *Report to Parliament of the fifth annual meeting to review the Compact on relations between government and the voluntary and
community sector*. London: Home Office.

Deakin, N. (1996). *Meeting the challenge of change: Voluntary action into the 21st
century*. London: NCVO.

Department of Finance Canada. (2006). Canada's New Government cuts
wasteful programs, refocuses spending on priorities, achieves major debt
reduction as promised Retrieved September, 26, 2006, from http://www.fin.
gc.ca/news06/06–047e.html

Elson, P. (2006). Tracking the implementation of voluntary sector – government policy agreements: Is the voluntary and community sector in the
frame? *International Journal of Not-for-Profit Law, 8*(4), 34–49.

Elson, P. (2009a). Independence in a cold climate: A profile of the nonprofit
and voluntary sector in Canada. In M. Smerdon (Ed.), *The first principle of
voluntary action: Essays on the independence of the voluntary sector from government in Canada, England, Germany, Northern Ireland, Scotland, United States of
America and Wales*. London: Baring Foundation.

Elson, P. (2009b). *Straw, sticks, bricks: A framework for examining voluntary sector/
government relations*. Paper presented at the Second Annual Conference of
the Association of Nonprofit and Social Economy Research.

Elson, P. (2010 (forthcoming)). *High ideals and noble intentions: Voluntary sector –
government relations in Canada*. Toronto: University of Toronto Press.

Etherington, S. (2000). Developing collaborative relationships between civil
society and government: The Compact between the UK government and
voluntary sector in England. *Asian Review of Public Administration, 12*(1),
99–107.

Evans, B.M., & Shields, J. (2000). *Neoliberal restructuring and the Third Sector:
Reshaping governance, civil society and local relations, working paper No. 13*. Toronto: Centre for Voluntary Sector Studies, Ryerson University.

Giddens, A. (1998). *The Third Way: The renewal of social democracy*. Cambridge: Polity Press.

Good, D.A. (2003). Promises and pitfalls: Experience in collaboration between the Canadian federal government and the voluntary sector. *Journal of Policy Analysis and Management, 22*(1), 122–7.

Hall, M.H., Barr, C.W., Easwaramoorthy, M., Sokolowski, S.W., & Salamon, L.M. (2005). *The Canadian nonprofit and voluntary sector in comparative perspective*. Toronto: Imagine Canada.

HM Treasury. (2008). Spending reviews. Retrieved April 11, 2008, from http://www.hm-treasury.gov.uk/spending_review/spend_index.cfm

Ipsos-Reid. (2006). *Talking about charities 2006: Tracking Canadians' opinions about charities and issues affecting them*. Edmonton: Muttart Foundation.

Joint Tables. (1999). *Working together: A government of Canada/voluntary sector joint initiative – report of the Joint Tables*. Ottawa: Voluntary Sector Task Force, Privy Council Office.

Kendall, J. (2003). *The voluntary sector: Comparative perspectives in the UK*. London: Routledge.

Lawson, S. (1993). Conceptual issues in the comparative study of regime change and democratization. *Comparative Politics, 25*(2), 183–205.

Levy-Ajzenkopf, A. (2006). Surprise! Budget cuts 2006. Retrieved October 2, 2006, from www.charityvillage.com

National Advisory Council on Voluntary Action. (1977). *People in action: Report of the National Advisory Council on Voluntary Action to the government of Canada*. Ottawa: Secretary of State.

National Council for Voluntary Organisations. (1994). *Managing the present, planning the future: Annual review 1993–1994*. London: National Council for Voluntary Organisations.

National Council for Voluntary Organisations. (2004). *Standing apart, working together: A study of the myths and realities of voluntary and community sector independence*. London: National Council for Voluntary Organisations.

Office of the Third Sector. (2008). About us. Retrieved April 5, 2008, from http://www.cabinetoffice.gov.uk/third_sector/about_us.aspx

Office of the Third Sector. (2009). Social enterprises. Retrieved September 18, 2009, from http://www.cabinetoffice.gov.uk/third_sector/social_enterprise.aspx

Panel on Accountability and Governance in the Voluntary Sector. (1998). *Helping Canadians Help Canadians: Improving governance and accountability in the voluntary sector – a discussion paper*. Ottawa: Voluntary Sector Roundtable.

Panel on Accountability and Governance in the Voluntary Sector. (1999). *Building on strength: Improving governance and accountability in Canada's voluntary sector*. Ottawa: Voluntary Sector Roundtable.

Partnerships UK. (2009). Futurebuilders England to manage Social Enterprise Investment Fund. Retrieved March 6, 2009, from http://www
.partnershipsuk.org.uk/View-News.aspx?id=97

Phillips, S.D. (2001a). From charity to clarity: Reinventing federal government-voluntary sector relationships. In L.A. Pal (Ed.), *How Ottawa spends 2001–2002: Power in transition*. Don Mills: Oxford University Press.

Phillips, S.D. (2001b). More than stakeholders: Reforming state-voluntary sector relations. *Journal of Canadian Studies, 35*(4), 182–202.

Phillips, S.D. (2003a). In accordance: Canada's voluntary sector accord from idea to implementation. In K.L. Brock (Ed.), *Delicate dances: Public policy and the nonprofit sector* (pp. 17–62). Kingston: McGill-Queen's University Press.

Phillips, S.D. (2003b). Voluntary sector – government relationships in transition: Learning from international experience for the Canadian context. In K.L. Brock (Ed.), *The nonprofit sector in interesting times: Case studies in a changing sector* (pp. 17–70). Montreal and Kingston: McGill-Queen's University Press.

Phillips, S.D. (2004). The limits of horizontal governance: Voluntary sector – government collaboration in Canada. *Society and Economy, 26*(2–3), 393–15.

Robillard, L., Hon., & Deboisbriand, M. (2001). *An accord between the government of Canada and the voluntary sector*. Ottawa: Voluntary Sector Task Force, Privy Council Office.

Social Development Canada. (2004). *The voluntary sector initiative process evaluation: Final evaluation report*. Ottawa: Audit and Evaluation Directorate, Social Development Canada.

Stowe, K. (1998). Professional developments: Compact on relations between government and the voluntary and community sector in England and Wales. *Public Administration and Development, 18*(5), 519–22.

Stowe, K. (1999, April 26–7). *England's new model – a compact*. Paper presented at the Canadian Centre for Philanthropy's Fifth Annual Symposium: Terms of Engagement; Forging New Links between Government and the Voluntary Sector, Toronto.

Streeck, W., & Thelen, K. (2005). Introduction: Institutional change in advanced political economies. In W. Streeck & K. Thelen (Eds.), *Beyond continuity: Institutional change in advanced political economies*. Oxford: Oxford University Press.

Voluntary Sector Initiative. (2002a). *A code of good practice on funding: Building on an accord between the government of Canada and the voluntary sector*. Ottawa: Voluntary Sector Initiative (Canada).

Voluntary Sector Initiative. (2002b). *Code of good practice on policy dialogue:*

130   Peter R. Elson

Building on an accord between the government of Canada and the voluntary sector.
   Ottawa: Voluntary Sector Initiative (Canada).
Voluntary Sector Initiative. (2006). Goals of the voluntary sector Initiative. Re-
   trieved June 29, 2006, from http://www.vsi-isbc.org/eng/about/goals.cfm
Voluntary Sector Initiative. (2008). History of the VSI. Retrieved July 29, 2008,
   from http://www.vsi-isbc.org/eng/about/history.cfm
Voluntary Sector Roundtable. (1998). VST up-date – January 1998. Retrieved
   June 29, 2006, from http://www.vsr-trsb.net/newsletters/news-jan98.html
Voluntary Sector Roundtable. (1999). Update on the Voluntary Sector Round-
   table. Retrieved August 27, 2008, from www.nben.ca/egroups/groupnews/
   groupnews_archives/pre00/chpna1.htm
Wolfenden Committee. (1978). *The future of voluntary organisations: Report of the
   Wolfenden Committee.* London: Croom Helm.

6 Capturing Complexity:
The Ontario Government Relationship
with the Social Economy Sector

KATHY L. BROCK

Too often, the relationship between the state and the social economy is characterized as antagonistic or harmonious, complementary or competitive, conflictual or co-operative, depending on the type of policy or agency involved. While these attributes might feature in a relationship, they are not helpful in understanding what type of relationship between the state and sector is most beneficial, effective, or efficient under what circumstances. As the earlier work of Gidron, Kramer, and Salamon (1992) and Coston (1998) demonstrated, an understanding of power relations, linkages, and history between the state and social economy sector is critical for determining how to restructure or improve the relationship. This chapter devises a continuum of relations between the two sectors in an attempt to capture the complexity of arrangements and to understand when certain dimensions of the relationship should be emphasized to achieve policy goals. Using this continuum, the chapter assesses the state of relations between the Ontario government and social economy organizations. Following the definitions presented by Mook, Quarter, and Ryan in chapter 1, this study primarily addresses public sector nonprofits and civil society organizations much like Elson in chapter 5. However, Elson's focus is on organizations at the national level in Canada compared to England. This Ontario case study yields insight into more general criteria for determining when a state actor should function in a facilitative or coercive manner to ensure that sector and citizen needs are well served.

Data were gathered for this study through three means. First, a literature search was conducted to provide knowledge of the relationships in existence between the state and social economy sector. The continuum was developed based on this research. Second, an extensive

review of Ontario government websites, literature, and policy documents revealed the contact points between the two sectors in that province. Third, rolling informal interviews were conducted with officials
from the two sectors in Ontario to deepen the understanding of current relations. This material provided the basis for testing and applying the continuum to characterize the type and nature of relationships
in Ontario and then to offer insights into state actions useful for other
jurisdictions.

This study uses a broad and inclusive definition of the social economy,
as mentioned above. The definition encompasses voluntary organizations, registered charities, incorporated nonprofits, co-operatives, credit
unions, mutual insurers, community economic development corporations, and unincorporated formal associations that pursue a wide range
of social objectives (Quarter, 2000; Browne, 2000). As Lasby, Hall, Ventry,
and Guy mention in chapter 2, there are approximately 45,360 nonprofit
and voluntary organizations, including registered charities and incorporated nonprofits with a reported $47.7 billion in annual revenues,
950,000 employees, and 7.8 million volunteers (cf. Scott, Tsoukalas,
Roberts, & Lasby, 2006), and over 1,900 co-operatives, credit unions, and
caisses populaires with over 2.3 million members in Ontario (Ontario
Co-operative Association, 2008). While many social economy organizations receive substantial government funding or perform government
services (Foster and Meinhard, 2002), others are autonomous market
actors or operate independently of government support and have limited or no formal contact with government but are included in the study
since they are affected directly or indirectly by government legislation,
regulations, or activity. Social economy organizations, by definition
then, are a varied group that form a vibrant part of Ontario's social and
economic life. Judging from trends in other jurisdictions, the Ontario
government is likely to expect more of the social economy in servicing
society and in maintaining the provincial social and economic fabric
(Brock, 2000; Hudson, 1999; Kendall, 2003; Salamon, 2003, 1995).

The Changing Relationship between the State and Social Economy

The new century is one of contradictions that are fundamentally challenging the operation of the public, private, and social economy sectors
as well as relations among and within each sector (Broadbent, 2000;
Sagawa & Segal, 2000; Wood, 1995). According to the Independent Sector's *Working Better Together* report (Scott, 2002), the nonprofit and by

extension the social economy sector is redoubling its efforts to meet rising demands by reflecting on its role, rethinking means of obtaining mission goals, aspiring to be a more equal and stronger partner with the other two sectors without sacrificing values or missions, adapting to the new·generation of philanthropists and volunteers, and striving to build core capacity to meet demands and rise to public and private sector expectations including the renewed emphasis on accountability and transparency. And, I would add, organizations are learning to be competitive with rival public and private agencies while building skills for collaboration (Brock & Webb, 2006). Governments are moving towards governance and away from the command-and-control form of state leadership, adopting accountability and performance measures, rethinking the roles of social institutions, establishing more effective social, economic, and policy frameworks to guide the sectors, developing roles and instruments as catalysts, brokers, and partners, and adopting best practices from the other sectors.

In this new environment, the traditional view of relationships between social economy organizations and governments as conflictual, competitive, and unequal is not helpful. In this view, organizations were cast as critics of the state or as threatened by state intervention. Gidron, Kramer, and Salamon (1992) refute this depiction, arguing that relationships are determined by the functions each side performs, the method of financing, and the historical context, as well as the political and social context. Indeed, state and non-state agencies might have multiple sets of relationships. The nature of relationships ranges from insular to collaborative, to partnering, to mergers; with benevolence or animosity characterizing each stage depending on the underlying power relations (Parker, 1999; Phillips & Graham, 2000). While relations that are less integrated may be characterized as government dominant with nonprofits financially dependent, relationships that are more integrated and functional will see the sectors sharing decision-making authority and responsibility (Gidron et al., 1992). In some cases, social economy organizations may operate independently of government but still be affected by the legal regime.

The state orientation to the sector in this broad range of relationships can be best described using a continuum (see table 6.1). At one end of the continuum, governments act as enablers. In the fullest expression of this role, governments open the policy process to relevant organizations as partners and provide any necessary support to ensure that the organizations take advantage of this opportunity while respecting their

Table 6.1
Continuum of government relationships with the social economy sector

	State as Enabler				State as Enforcer						
	Hard				Soft	Soft				Hard	Hard
Partners	Accord	Seeks out opportunity to support	Promotes common goals	Provides Information	Exhort Action Praise	Exhort Action Threat	Eligibility rules	Tied to Aid	Regulations	Legislation	Legislation
Co-operative Equal	Collaborative	Benevolent	Kind	Passive	Parental	Parental	Guardian	Directive	Imposing	Mandate	Coercive Unequal

autonomy and independent decision-making process. Social economy organizations have an equal part in the design and implementation of policy and identify where monetary or other support is needed to ensure full participation with government or in the market as the case may be. Full partnerships are relatively rare.

At the other end of the spectrum, government acts as an enforcer. In the strongest expression of this role, the government enacts legislation, most often unilaterally defined or with limited consultation, and attaches penalties and sanctions, to force compliance with expected standards or behaviours. Penalties are applied through special tribunals and administrative bodies or the police and courts. Government acts in a directive and activist role, assuming the responsibility of defining the necessary behaviours or standards, policing the agents, and ensuring compliance. Social economy organizations operating as autonomous market organizations are at this end of the spectrum, mainly affected by the legislative regime.

Between these two extremes are a range of actions from co-operative to coercive that governments might adopt to support and promote the social economy. As partners, the state and organizations engage as equals in the promotion of mutually defined policies and goals. This may be the case where an accord between the state and the sector has been signed defining the relationship and setting out the rules of conduct, and both actors respect the autonomy of the other and abide by the accord. However, where government respects and heeds the advice of an organization but retains final decision-making authority or regulatory or monetary control, the relationship will resemble collaboration more than partnership (Brock, 2005; Phillips 2003). This has occurred in Canada at both the federal and provincial levels of interaction.

In the third category of enabling actions, the state actively seeks opportunities to support the sector; for example, by offering organizations money to assist with a responsibility without requiring the agency to submit an application for the funds or to report back on the expenditure, or by providing start-up funds to create an autonomous organization to provide a public service or function. The state is empowering the sector but acknowledging its independence. In a more passive but still positive role, the state provides information or resources necessary for organizations that the organizations access themselves through the Internet, newsletters, applications, or other means. The onus is on organizations to seek opportunities. Finally, in its softest role as an enabler, the state exhorts action and offers praise or rewards when compliance is evident.

On the other side of the continuum, the state acts in an enforcement capacity with its hardest form of action consisting of legislation or common law rules with defined penalties and sanctions. Legislation without penal sanctions is a more moderate form of coercive action. Regulations still impose the will of government on the organizations but are easier to change (e.g., setting standards in service provision). Funding can be an enabling mechanism but, when directly tied to ensuring certain behaviour or standards, it is coercive, particularly if the central mission of an organization is affected. Eligibility rules for programs, service provision, or funding are also coercive but less onerous than those tied to aid if the exclusion is voluntary and similar support is available elsewhere. On the soft side, the state may exhort or prohibit certain types of action but with threats, such as loss of funding or a licence, attached if an organization does not 'voluntarily' comply. Threats (enforcement) and praise (enabling) merge into each other.

Relationships between government and organizations often fall into multiple categories simultaneously. Similarly, while an organization might be a partner with a government department in providing a service to the public, another part of its organization may be engaged in a more adversarial relationship with that same department in trying to effect policy changes on a more general issue, and its communications strategy might be dependent on government funding. Thus, the continuum helps identify the different aspects of a relationship and which is primary, determine whether a relationship is more likely to be responsive to enabling or enforcement actions, and ascertain whether enabling or enforcing actions are more appropriate at any given time. While the continuum is generally helpful in characterizing the different types of actions that the state might take to support the sector, it should be noted that enabling actions may shade into more coercive ones in certain contexts and vice versa. Coercive or enabling state actions may be positive or beneficial to the sector. Positive enabling state support for the sector may have an implicit enforcement clause. The next section applies the continuum to the case of Ontario. Examples of these types of relations are cited throughout.

The Ontario Government: Cautious Enabling and Enforcement

Two features of the relationship between social economy organizations and the Ontario government stand out. First, the relationship between social economy organizations and the Ontario government lacks an overall framework agreement or structure regulating relations, despite the recent example set by the federal government's Voluntary Sector Initiative (VSI) and the signing of an Accord to frame that relationship (2000–5) and similar examples in other provinces like Newfoundland and Labrador, Manitoba, and Alberta. In Ontario, relations between the state and social economy sector are more fragmented owing in large part to the absence of a corporate body to speak on behalf of this sector and the exceptionally diverse nature of the sector.

Second, the relationship is embedded: as Alan Cairns has explained, the relationship between the state and non-state actors may be termed embedded when a complex network of programs, obligations, and interests tie government departments to, in this case social economy, organizations (Cairns, 1995). Mutual embeddedness occurs when the state and sector organizations become reliant upon and deeply entwined with each other. In the neo-liberal shift in the 1990s, this web of mutual embeddedness deepened as streamlined governments became more dependent on organizations for program delivery, research, and insight into public needs; and organizations became more dependent on government funding, recognition, and regulations (Meinhard, Foster, & Berger, 2003). Emphasizing individual responsibility and a reduced role for the state (Evans & Shields, 2000), the government emphasized both volunteering and an expanded role for community organizations (Meinhard, Foster, & Wright, 2006). The government-established Advisory Board on the Voluntary Sector held four months of consultations and in early 1997 recommended that the government 'act as an enabler of voluntary action not as a director or a controller' (Browne, 2000, p. 68; Ontario Advisory Board on the Voluntary Sector, 1997). In response, the government began more active promotion of citizen volunteering, encouraged organizations to work collaboratively, worked to build the capacity of organizations, and involved private corporations in sharing this sense of social responsibility (Burke-Robertson, 2005). But, unable to relinquish its traditional role of enforcer, the government increasingly turned away from contributions and grants to contractual arrangements with organizations, often with stringent conditions (Browne, 2000). Despite organizations questioning the viability and sustainability of this type of relationship (Reed & Howe, 2000; Richmond & Shields, 2004), the model of cautious enabling and enforcement with the government reluctant to relinquish its directive role, particularly in core program and policy areas, has persisted.

The Ontario Government as an Enabler: Not So Hard

The Ontario government tends towards the softer forms of enabling action. Rare is the instance of equal partnerships where the public and social economy sectors co-operate and share information fully; and certainly not on a more than small and episodic basis. However, the government does actively promote the social economy and voluntary sector and engages in some fairly robust forms of collaborative behaviour.

The most tangible evidence of the government's desire to support the social economy and voluntary sector is the dedication of a unit to volunteerism within the Ministry of Citizenship and Immigration (Ontario Ministry of Citizenship and Immigration, 2007c). Tasked with the responsibility of co-ordinating government efforts to strengthen volunteerism in the province, this unit is essentially a one-stop shop for social economy and voluntary organizations and volunteers to learn about programs and services within government that support their activities (Ontario Ministry of Citizenship and Immigration, 2007b). Softer forms of enabling comprise the bulk of the unit's activities. The unit provides toolkits on technology and media relations for organizations, information on grants, incorporation, and effective operations and management, and various services, and disseminates data on volunteering and giving in Ontario through printed and electronic media. Its 'Citizenship in Action' initiative recognizes volunteering among different segments of the population through awards and provides support for programs that build the contribution 'that volunteers and not-for-profit organizations make to our economic and social well-being.' For example, one such project, Agencies Board Commissions Greater Toronto Area (ABC GTA), provides resources and tools 'to recruit, train and match candidates from diverse backgrounds to volunteer for leadership positions in agencies, boards, and commissions and not-for-profit organizations in the Greater Toronto Area,' while another program, Seniors Mentoring Newcomers, develops opportunities to engage new retirees and newcomers to Canada in their communities (Ontario Ministry of Citizenship and Immigration, 2007a). Such initiatives promote volunteering among groups that may have limited experience with citizen engagement, and include training activities to build the capacity of organizations to incorporate these volunteers (Deboisbriand, 2005).

While the unit and its proponents speak of building capacity within the sector and promoting volunteerism (interviews 6, 3, 9), its focus towards volunteer organizations and activities is problematic. First, while volunteers play a vital role in many social economy organizations, and recruiting volunteers and board members has been identified as a key challenge for Ontario organizations (Scott et al., 2006), the focus on volunteering conveys a limited understanding of the sector. For many social economy organizations, the priority is not volunteering but rather obtaining supports similar to those available for 'small and medium sized enterprises' (Goldenberg, 2006). Second, the unit's co-ordinative function across government departments is limited to promoting 'volunteerism' and lacks enforcement mechanisms. As a result, the disparity in the way in which various ministries interact with organizations adversely affects the sector's ability to influence policy at a macro level or to call for a 'focused, strategic approach to working with, convening and engaging the nonprofit and voluntary industry in formal collaboration' (Council of Ontario Voluntary Organizations, 2006). Further, the sector lacks a champion within government to promote its interests (Browne & Welch, 2002; O'Connor, 2005).

Individual ministries have developed a wide range of relations with the sector, with the most robust type being collaborative where policy development and delivery are shared with organizations. These types of relations are more likely to occur in ministries like Community and Social Services or Health or Citizenship and Immigration where a history of co-operative engagement in the delivery of services has produced a mutual trust. While tensions might enter these relationships, they are mitigated by the established reputation of the social economy actors as reliable and mutual agreement on policy goals and instruments. Even in these cases, though, government caution is exercised through agreements or contracts guiding their work.

Both the Ministry of Community and Social Services and the Ministry of Citizenship and Immigration regularly engage organizations as collaborators to deliver services under transfer payment agreements. The ministries define and develop policies and programs but treat organizations as autonomous actors with self-defined missions, providing resources to support and enhance organizational capacity. The Ministry of Community and Social Services developed *Thriving Communities* as a broadly consultative document that outlines the framework for building 'partnerships' with community organizations to assist citizens struggling to succeed (Ontario Ministry of Community and Social Services, 2006). The Ministry of Citizenship and Immigration developed the Labour Market Integration Unit's initiative to expedite the inclusion of professionals and immigrants into the labour market (Ontario ServiceOntario Info-Go, 2006a). Such initiatives indicate that government officials engaging with well-established professional associations and regulatory bodies, immigrant community agencies, and educational institutions will feel sufficiently comfortable with the organizations to treat them as collaborators in policy development. However, one interview participant observed that such programs were more consonant with furthering the ministry's objectives than supporting social economy organizations as part of a distinct sector (interview 7). This would be an example of government arrangements that enable the sector becoming tinged with government control and enforcement of outcomes and objectives. Still, the work of Sagawa and Segal (2000) shows that mutual self-interest may be the sustaining factor in collaboration or partnership.

The Ministry of Health offers two important examples of collaboration. The Aboriginal Healing and Wellness Strategy (AHWS) brings together Aboriginal people and 15 organizations with four government ministries to combat conditions of 'poor health and family violence that Aboriginal people in Ontario have endured' (AHWS, 2006). Aboriginal communities and organizations are involved in the design of programs and are allocated formal responsibility for program delivery with government support (interview 5). The government created Local Health Integration Networks (LHINs) as nonprofit agencies that engage in planning, integrating, and funding health services. While LHINs are independent and community based, the government still sets priorities for healthcare, outlines principles, goals, and requirements for LHINs, and appoints their boards of directors (Ontario Local Health Integration Networks, 2009). Government control creeps in, even in more robust examples of enabling arrangements.

Many of the Ontario government's activities fall into the middle categories of enabling action and range from seeking out opportunities to support organizations to promoting common goals with organizations. Too numerous to list, a few examples of these activities will suffice. The government-funded Ontario Trillium Foundation, an agency of the Ministry of Culture, provides over 1,500 grants to social economy organizations involved in arts and culture, environment, human and social services, and sports and recreation from the proceeds of charity casinos (Ontario Trillium Foundation, 2007). While the grants build the capacity of these organizations to engage citizens more actively, the increasingly strict terms of the adjudication process and contracts could qualify this and similar funding relationships as examples of the government acting as an enforcer of standards in the social economy rather than as an enabler of civic engagement through autonomous organizations (Browne, 2000; Struthers 2004).

Community economic development programs are a second area where the Ontario government is seeking opportunities to support the social economy sector. The government provides resources such as fact sheets and a wide range of materials on managing organizations. On a more active level, regional economic development staff host workshops in Southern Ontario rural communities to bring together individuals, organizations, municipal government, and local businesses with a mutual interest (Ontario Ministry of Agriculture, Food and Rural Assistance, 2006; interview 9). Given that both market conditions and funders are increasingly requiring organizations to engage in the time- and resource-intensive activities of building partnerships or sharing ideas, this initiative is sector friendly. One interviewee remarked that their government department had recently recognized the partnering challenges facing organizations and provided funds and structural support specifically to help agencies partner and work together to integrate services and fill gaps in service delivery (interview 6). Still, such support may become less friendly if funding or support is contingent on a forced merger.

Numerous programs build sector capacity and promote common goals with organizations. The Ministry of Citizenship and Immigration developed and expanded its Ontario Screening Initiative with the endorsement of organizations like Junior Achievement to assist organizations in risk reduction strategies by screening individuals in positions of trust. The ministry's Ontario Community Builders program provides grants to organizations for educational projects that build awareness of Ontario's diverse heritage. Other examples include the Children and Youth Services programs for youth justice, the Ministry of the Attorney General's victims' services secretariat, and the Community Safety and Correctional Services programs for volunteer parole and counselling for offenders and community policing.

As mentioned above in the area of economic development, the Ontario government is supporting organizations to build alliances with the private sector. In a softer form of enabling program where the onus is upon organizations, the government provides tools and resources to help organizations attract private sector interest and participate in joint projects, and encourages private sector corporations to donate to social economy organizations. Government programs assist organizations in bringing private sector representatives onto their boards and in developing program evaluations consistent with private sector expectations (interview 5). In a firmer example of encouraging trisector partnerships, the Ontario Ministry of Citizenship and Immigration's Skills Training Program for At-Risk Women promotes partnerships among a violence-against-women organization, a training organization, and an employer. Similarly, the 2006 high profile Youth Challenge Fund in Toronto allocated $15 million to community organizations in underserved neighbourhoods and challenged the private sector to contribute another $15 million that the government would then match (Ontario Office of the Premier, 2006). One interview participant commented on the meagreness of trisectoral efforts like these (interview 8), despite evidence suggesting corporate partnerships are 'a viable way to augment funding' (Meinhard et al., 2003).

While these programs are significant examples of moderate to more active enabling, the vast majority of government efforts to support the voluntary sector fall in the range of soft or passive enabling – information provision, advice, and exhortations to volunteer or community service. For example, the government provides information on Internet technology, drawing on resources from projects undertaken from 1999 to 2005. Several government interviewees commented on this type of consultative and resource role as their primary interaction with the sector (interviews 6, 3, 9). Other interviewees emphasized that the government role in developing policy research and sharing information and resources among organizations extended the impact of individual projects to a broader audience (interviews 5, 6, 9). For example, as Ryan documents in her chapter here, DAWN, an organization against violence perpetrated on women and children, has developed a website to consolidate information and provide easier access for smaller organizations with limited capacity to track this material. Information dissemination and knowledge development of the sector provide direction for future capacity building (Richmond & Shields, 2004). However, too often organizations with limited resources must themselves navigate through the bewildering array of government departments and services to locate relevant funding sources, programs, and information.

Finally, the Ontario government promotes volunteering and awareness of its benefits to the community through its Volunteer Service Awards that recognize more than 9,000 Ontarians a year for their community service efforts. These activities of government are examples of soft enabling but should not be underestimated, because 'volunteering

... "does not just happen." It must be nurtured and supported' (Debois-briand, 2005, 34).

Therefore, on the enabling side of the continuum, government relations with the social economy sector range from soft (common) to active or semi-hard enabling (infrequent). The state engages in capacity building among organizations on a regular but not systematic basis. While the government is supportive of the sector, relations remain decentralized and department or program specific with little interest evident in further centralization or codification of the relationship or mobilizing organizations as a self-identifying sector. Even in their more supportive relations with organizations, government departments still tend to define objectives and standards governing relations. The Ontario government is a cautious enabler of the sector and tends towards a more directive and controlling role that is even clearer in its role as an enforcer.

The Ontario Government as Enforcer: Comfort in Direction

Enforcement may be either positive or punitive. The state is most active in its role as enforcer when questions of accountability and trust are involved and then to a lesser extent in areas of capacity building. We begin with the hardest forms of enforcement – legislation and regulations.

The primary piece of legislation defining the relationship of the Ontario government to the social economy is the *Corporations Act*. An organization may incorporate as a nonprofit (not-for-profit in Ontario legalese) or corporation without share capital, 'for the purpose of carrying on, without pecuniary gain, objects of a patriotic, charitable, philanthropic, religious, professional, sporting or athletic character' which benefit the community (Ontario Ministry of the Attorney General, 2007b). All Ontario nonprofit corporations are subject to this act and its accompanying regulations, overseen by the Ministry of the Attorney General. Benefits of incorporation include recognized legal status, limited protection to members from lawsuits and damages awarded therein, public legitimacy from government recognition, and tax relief. The incorporated nonprofit must comply with applicable statutes pertaining to board governance, the organization's constitution and by-laws, rules for meetings, and reporting and disclosure requirements. Noncompliance entails sanctions ranging from self-help remedies, to director and officer liability, to penalties and fines, to cancellation of the corporate charter and dissolution of the corporation. While this legislation provides important benefits and support to nonprofits, its punitive measures are significant.

Charities in Ontario have a different legal status. By law, charities are required to incorporate under the Letters Patent issued under the Corporations Act, under the Standing Orders of the Legislative Assembly, or under Letters Patent under the *Canada Corporations Act* through Industry Canada. The Public Guardian and Trustees Office oversees charities in Ontario (Ontario Ministry of the Attorney General, 2007a). Charities are subject to the same plus additional requirements as not-for-profits. For example, a charity's activities must be devoted to relief of poverty, advancement of education, advancement of religion, and/ or other purposes beneficial to the community, as determined under common law, and its ability to engage in political activities and advocacy is restricted. Benefits include issuing tax receipts for donations and government sanction of the organization.

These acts are among the clearest examples of the government as enforcer setting clear standards and rules governing organizations with associated penalties for noncompliance with Ontario laws including human rights. While the legislation is in part punitive, it also supports the sector by providing financial benefits, lending recognized organizations public legitimacy, and setting standards of good governance and accountability. Other legislation with compliance mechanisms governs particular organizations or types of organizations, such as universities, colleges, hospitals, and care centres, or sets market standards. Regulations attending each piece of legislation are softer forms of enforcement since they are generally easier to amend and may be eased through the discretion allowed officials drafting and implementing them.

In a move largely praised by the sector, the Ontario government engaged in a surprisingly strong form of enforcement in the late 1990s. Responding to concerns about fluctuations and trends in volunteering, the government mandated the participation of high school students in community service as a graduation requirement, as explained in detail in chapter 8 by Padanyi, Baetz, Brown, and Henderson in this volume. The program is intended to 'encourage students to develop awareness and understanding of civic responsibility and of the role they can play in supporting and strengthening their communities' (Ontario Ministry of Education, 1999, 9). Students must complete 40 hours of community involvement activities throughout their four years of high school. One interviewee noted that many students are completing only the minimum hours (interview 4). Early studies of the program indicate it may not be achieving its objectives (Meinhard et al., 2006; Ontario Network, 2006) and may overtax the capacity of organizations to train and manage the influx of short-term volunteers (Scott et al, 2006; cf. Padanyi, Baetz, Brown, and Henderson). One interviewee commented that organizations in larger centres simply could not accommodate the large numbers of student volunteers (interview 4). Similar concerns apply to mandated community service programs for convicted offenders. Enforcement, even when well intended, may sometimes go awry.

Enforcement may involve imposing controls on the sector through funding models tying support to conditions and eligibility requirements that may have an impact on the mission or operations of organizations. Such types of state action are prevalent. Even enabling actions such as Trillium Foundation grants and Community Economic Development initiatives have conditions or eligibility requirements that may be activated to make an organization ineligible for support or to revoke funding or participation. The move from grants and unconditional block funding to contribution agreements and dedicated contracts also introduces constraints on organizations. For example, the Ministry of Municipal Affairs and Housing operates an affordable housing program described as a partnership with nonprofit and co-operatives but uses contribution agreements rather than grants, tracks progress of funded projects, requires regular reporting, monitors and addresses issues arising in the course of a project, manages cash flow, ensures timely and accurate payments, and undertakes joint communications with the Canada Mortgage and Housing Corporation (Ontario ServiceOntario Info-Go, 2006b). Flexibility and discretion of the organization are seriously circumscribed even in the event of an unanticipated emergency or urgency. Such constraints may impair the ability of organizations to execute their missions or force organizations to alter mission objectives (interview 8; O'Connor, 2005; Foster & Meinhard, 2002).

Forced partnerships have mixed results but are not uncommon. One funding program encourages social economy organizations to partner with the private sector by giving organizations that comply with this stipulation priority in the grant process (Ontario Ministry of Small Business and Entrepreneurship, 2007). The government and Trillium Foundation have required organizations applying for funding to collaborate or merge with other social economy organizations (interview 8). However, some organizations finesse this constraint by collaborating on paper but not in practice, thus compromising the success of this approach in achieving government objectives of efficiency and effectiveness (interview 8). To circumvent this avoidance behaviour, some departments have adopted a funding model requiring organizations to document these partnerships in detail (interview 6). These forced arrangements may be unduly costly in terms of time and resources and may fail if not appropriate to specific circumstances or if the organizations do not share common goals and clash over issues of culture, autonomy, and other interests (Council of Ontario Voluntary Organizations, 2006; Burke-Robertson, 2005). Forced partnerships may lack the foundation of trust and reciprocity so critical to functional relationships and are inimical to the democratic, participatory, and voluntary nature of the sector.

Conclusion: Cautious Encouragement

As the Ontario government has become more embedded in society through its relations with organizations and as organizations have become more embedded in the policy development and service delivery work of government, the ties between the two sectors have multiplied, creating a diverse array of arrangements. While embracing organizations to different degrees as policy participants, government officials retain concerns about the accountability, legitimacy, and good governance of organizations. The underlying importance of these concerns in the relationship can be seen in the areas where government takes some of its boldest actions as an enforcer. The legislative and regulatory framework for social economy organizations generally and nonprofit corporations and charities more directly operates to ensure that organizations are well governed and meet set standards. Noncompliance is punished. Here, government is within its comfort zone, adopting a traditional, directive, and, at times, coercive stance towards social economy organizations. Even in its enabling role, government is reluctant to relinquish control over policy priorities, design, and execution, rendering it a cautious and infrequent policy partner or collaborator.

Government endeavours to build the capacity of organizations are inconsistent. On the one hand, it embraces certain organizations as collaborators in the development of social policy and delivery of healthcare. It actively seeks opportunities to fund and support organizations and promote common goals to meet social and economic needs. It supports volunteering through exhortation but is reluctant to adopt stronger measures, as witnessed in the anemic community service program in schools. Government support is the most robust where organization objectives parallel those defined by a particular ministry or government. Passive support is offered to organizations more generally in the guise of providing information and services. Funding arrangements are tending towards more stringent conditions. The state's caution in action is inconsistent with supporting the sector's vibrancy and health as it becomes an even more central player in the social and economic life of the province.

When are enabling and enforcement activities most appropriate for state actors in general? This research is too preliminary to develop hard criteria but permits some speculations. When addressing capacity-building questions, enabling activities defined in consultation with the sector yield the most promising results. Similarly, more emphasis on enabling activities that bridge into full collaborations and extend into partnerships seems desirable where organizations have the expertise and skills required to engage in policy design, development, and implementation. Similarly, the public interest might be better served by a broad consultative exercise engaging organizations than by applying political criteria in setting policy priorities. Enabling activities should build on organizations' strengths and range from soft actions to harder ones if the social economy is to be encouraged to mobilize as a collective voice and become a conscience for the state. While this mobilization could result in a challenge to state authority in the development and implementation of policies and programs, it could strengthen the quality of democracy.

Enforcement or coercive activities are an essential part of the state's function. On a positive side, legislation, penalties, regulations, tied aid, eligibility requirements, and threats can all be effective means of ensuring that the social economy sector in all its diversity remains accountable and efficient in serving Canadians. The state can set clear standards to govern the effective operation of autonomous, market-oriented social economy organizations. On the negative side, if the government is too restrictive or directive it may inadvertently undermine the vitality, innovativeness, and diversity within the sector that make it effective. As is the current orientation in the Ontario government, the preference should be towards enabling, not enforcing or coercion, with the first remedy in case of malfunction to be assistance in correcting the problem rather than punitive measures. In all cases, preservation of the unique contribution of social economy organizations to the life of citizens should be the objective that guides the choice of policy instrument.

The policy implications of the state of relations between the Ontario government and the social economy are rather disappointing. As mentioned at the outset of this chapter and as documented more thoroughly in the Lasby, Hall, Ventry, and Guy chapter, the social economy sector in Ontario is vibrant and richly diverse, and comprises a significant portion of the overall Canadian social economy. It possesses a wide array of talent and knowledge of all facets of life in Ontario. And yet, this chapter has indicated that the social economy sector is being under-utilized in the development and delivery of policy to Ontarians. As shown in chapter 5 by Elson, presented above, social economy organizations can be valuable and productive partners in the policy process with clear benefits to citizens. By embracing the social economy with caution and a reluctance to yield or share authority, the Ontario government is losing a significant opportunity. Ontario social economy organizations could deepen government knowledge of most areas of society and the economy and offer critical feedback on programs and services. As the Ontario government becomes increasingly constrained by rising deficits and debt and as it faces continuing economic challenges, it should rethink its cautious enabling of the sector and engage in a partnership with organizations to redefine the relationship and bring the sector more fully into the policy process in a way that will benefit its citizens. The continuum presented in this chapter offers a means of beginning that policy dialogue.

REFERENCES

Aboriginal Healing and Wellness Strategy. (AHWS). (2006). *About AHWS*. Retrieved November 8, 2009, from http://www.ahwsontario .ca/about/about_top.html

Broadbent, E. (2000, March). *Democracy and corporations: What's gone wrong?* The Corry Lecture, Queen's University, Kingston, Ontario.

Brock, K.L. (2000, November). *Enablers or enforcers? Understanding the government role in promoting voluntary action and civil society.* Paper proposed for the 29th Annual Conference of the Association for Research on Nonprofit Organizations and Voluntary Action. New Orleans, Louisiana, USA.

Brock, K.L. (2005). Judging the VSI: Reflections on the relationship between the federal government and the voluntary sector. *The Philanthropist, 19*(3), 168–81.

Brock, K.L., & Webb, K. (2006, July). *Creating sustainable relations among the pub-*

lic, private and nonprofit sectors to prevent human tragedy: The global road safety initiative. Paper presented to the Seventh International Conference of The International Society for Third Sector Research, Bangkok, Thailand.

Browne, Paul Leduc. (2000). The neo-liberal uses of the social economy: Non-profit organizations and workfare in Ontario. In Eric Shragge and Jean-Marc Fontan (Eds.), *Social economy: International debates and perspectives* (pp. 65–80). Montreal: Black Rose Books.

Browne, P., & Welch, D. (2002) In the shadow of the market: Ontario's social economy in the age of neo-liberalism. In Yves Vaillancourt and Louis Tremblay (Eds.), *Social economy health and welfare in four Canadian provinces* (pp. 10134). Montreal: Fernwood Publishing.

Burke-Robertson, J. (2005). Strategic alliances in the voluntary sector in Canada. *The Philanthropist, 17*(1), 49–74.

Cairns, A. (1995). The embedded state: State-society relations in Canada. In Alan Cairns (Ed.), *Reconfigurations: Canadian citizenship and constitutional change.* Toronto: McClelland and Stewart.

Coston, J.M. (1998). A model and typology of government-NGO relationships. *Nonprofit and Voluntary Sector Quarterly, 27*(3), 358–82. doi: 0.1177/0899764098273006

Council of Ontario Voluntary Organizations (COVO). (2006). *Ontario's nonprofit voluntary industry pre-budget submission to the Ministry of Finance December 2006.* Retrieved March 13, 2007, from http://www.covo.on.ca/pdfs/2006_PreBudget_Submission_COVO.pdf

Deboisbriand, M. (2005). Strategies for boosting volunteerism in Canada. *The Philanthropist, 20*(1), 23–36.

Evans, B., & Shields, J. (2000, May). *Neoliberal restructuring and the Third Sector: Reshaping governance, civil society and local relations.* Paper presented to the Annual General Meeting of the Canadian Sociology and Anthropology Association, University of Alberta, Edmonton, Alberta.

Foster, M., & Meinhard, A. (2002). A contingency view of the responses of voluntary social service organizations in Ontario to government cutbacks. *Canadian Journal of Administrative Sciences, 19*(1), 27–41.

Gidron, B., Kramer, R., & Salamon, L. (1992). Government and the Third Sector in comparative perspective: Allies or adversaries? In Benjamin Gidron, Ralph Kramer, and Lester Salamon (Eds.), *Government and the Third Sector: Emerging relationships in welfare states* (pp. 1–30). San Francisco: Jossey Bass.

Goldenberg, M. (2006). *Building blocks for strong communities: Key findings and recommendations.* Retrieved November 8, 2009, from Imagine Canada and Canadian Policy Research Networks http://www.cprn.com/documents/44482_en.pdf

Hudson, P. (1999). The voluntary sector: The state and citizenship in the U.K. In Dave Broad and Wayne Antony (Eds.), *Citizens or consumers: Social policy in a market society* (pp. 212–24). Halifax: Fernwood.

Kendall, J. (2003). *The voluntary sector: Comparative perspectives in the UK.* London: Routledge.

Meinhard, A., Foster, M., & Berger, P. (2003). *The evolving relationship between government and the voluntary sector in Ontario.* (Working Paper Series No. 23). Retrieved November 8, 2009, from Centre for Voluntary Sector Studies, Ryerson University Faculty of Business http://www.ryerson.ca/cvss/WP23.pdf

Meinhard, A., Foster, M., & Wright, P. (2006). Rethinking school-based community service: The importance of a structured program. *The Philanthropist*, 20(1), 5–22.

O'Connor, Denise. (2005). The dark side of contracting with government: The case of VHA Hamilton and the Province of Ontario. *The Philanthropist, 19*(3), 201–10.

Ontario Advisory Board on the Voluntary Sector. (1997). *Sustaining a civic society: Voluntary action in Ontario.* Retrieved November 10, 2009, from http://www.cdhalton.ca/dispatch/cd0204.htm

Ontario Co-operative Association. (2008). *Co-op statistics.* Retrieved November 8, 2009, from http://www.ontario.coop/pages/index.php?main_id=302

Ontario Local Health Integration Networks. (2009). *About Local Health Integration Networks.* Retrieved November 16, 2009, from http://www.lhins.on.ca/aboutlhin.aspx?ekmensel=e2f22c9a_72_184_btnlink

Ontario Ministry of Agriculture, Food and Rural Affairs. (2006). *Rural Economic Development (RED) Program.* Retrieved November 8, 2009, from http://www.omafra.gov.on.ca/english/rural/red/about.html

Ontario Ministry of the Attorney General. (2007a). *Charities.* Retrieved November 8, 2009, from http://www.attorneygeneral.jus.gov.on.ca/english/family/pgt/nfpinc/charities.asp

Ontario Ministry of the Attorney General. (2007b). *Not-for-profit incorporator's handbook.* Retrieved November 8, 2009, from http://www.attorneygeneral.jus.gov.on.ca/english/family/pgt/nfpinc/default.asp

Ontario Ministry of Citizenship and Immigration. (2007a, February 22). *McGuinty government opening doors to volunteer sector for new-comers.* News Release. Retrieved March 19, 2007, from http://www.citizenship.gov.on.ca/english/news/2007/n20070222-2.shtml

Ontario Ministry of Citizenship and Immigration. (2007b). *Volunteerism: Tools and information*. Retrieved November 8, 2009, from http://www.citizenship.gov.on.ca/english/volunteerism/tools/

Ontario Ministry of Citizenship and Immigration. (2007c). *Volunteerism*. Retrieved November 9, 2009, from http://www.citizenship.gov.on.ca/english/volunteerism/

Ontario Ministry of Community and Social Services. (2006). *Thriving communities: A strategic direction for the Ministry of Community and Social Services*. Retrieved November 9, 2009, from http://www.mcss.gov.on.ca/NR/rdonlyres/0BEC9ACD-3112–4A2E-8F6A-E30DB2278731/100/En_ThrivingCommunities_Jan2006.pdf

Ontario Ministry of Education. (1999). *Ontario secondary schools, grades 9 to 12: Program and diploma requirements*. Retrieved November 9, 2009, from http://www.edu.gov.on.ca/eng/document/curricul/secondary/oss/oss.pdf

Ontario Ministry of Small Business and Entrepreneurship. (2007). *Youth entrepreneurship partnerships grants for non-profit organizations*. Retrieved November 9, 2009, from http://www.ontariocanada.com/ontcan/1medt/smallbiz/en/sb_ye_partnerships_projects_en.jsp

Ontario Network. Canada Volunteerism Initiative. (2006). *Mandatory community involvement activities ... 40 hours well spent?* Retrieved November 9, 2000, from http://www.pavro.on.ca/ocvi/docs/40_hours/40hourswellspent.pdf

Ontario Office of the Premier. (14 December 2006). *Youth Challenge Fund announces $3.5 million to support neighbourhood programs for at-risk youth*. News Release. Retrieved November 9, 2009, from http://www.premier.gov.on.ca/news/Product.asp?ProductID=843 >

Ontario ServiceOntario Info-Go. (2006a). *Ministry of Citizenship and Immigration: Immigration Branch: Labour Market Integration Unit*. Retrieved November 9, 2009, from http://www.infogo.gov.on.ca/infogo/office.do?unitId=UNT0021109&actionType=servicedirectory&infoType=service&keyword=community%20agencies&organizationName=ALL&locale=en>

Ontario ServiceOntario Info-Go. (2006b). *Ministry of Municipal Affairs and Housing: Housing Division: Delivery Branch*. Retrieved November 16, 2009, from http://www.infogo.gov.on.ca/infogo/office.do?unitId=UNT00259-17&actionType=servicedirectory&infoType=service&keyword=non-profit&organizationName=ALL&locale=en

Ontario Trillium Foundation. (2007). *How we work*. Retrieved November 9, 2009, from http://www.trilliumfoundation.org/cms/en/about-how_otf_works.aspx?menuid=5

Parker, M. (1999). *Partnerships: Profits and not-for-profits together*. Edmonton: Muttart Foundation.

Phillips, S.D. (2003). In accordance: Canada's Voluntary Sector Accord from idea to implementation. In K. Brock (Ed.), *Delicate dances: Public policy and the nonprofit sector* (pp. 17–61). Montreal and Kingston: McGill-Queen's University Press.

Phillips, S.D., & Graham, K.A. (2000). Hand-in-hand: When accountability meets collaboration in the voluntary sector. In Keith G. Banting (Ed.), *The nonprofit sector in Canada: Roles and relationships* (pp. 149–90). Montreal and Kingston: McGill-Queen's University Press

Quarter, J. (2000). The social economy and the neo-conservative agenda. In Eric Schrage and Jean-Marc Fontana (Eds.), *Social economy: International debates and perspectives* (pp. 54–80). Montreal: Black Rose Books.

Quarter, J. (2001). An analytic framework for classifying the organizations of the social economy. In Kathy L. Brock and Keith G. Banting (Eds.), *The nonprofit sector and government in a new century* (pp. 63–100). Montreal and Kingston: McGill-Queen's University Press.

Reed, P., & Howe, V. (2000). *Voluntary organizations in Ontario in the 1990s*. Retrieved November 9, 2009, from Statistics Canada http://www.statcan.ca/english/research/75F0048MIE/75F0048MIE2002002.pdf

Richmond, T., & Shields, J. (2004). *Third Sector restructuring and the new contracting regime: The case of immigrant serving agencies in Ontario*. (Working Paper Series. No. 24). Centre for Voluntary Sector Studies. Ryerson University Faculty of Business.

Sagawa, S., & Segal, E. (2000). *Common interest, common good: Creating value through business and social sector partnerships*. Boston: Harvard Business School Press.

Salamon, L. (1995). *Partners in public service: Government–nonprofit relations in the modern welfare state*. Baltimore: Johns Hopkins University Press.

Salamon, L. (2003). *The resilient sector: The state of nonprofit America*. Washington: Lester Salamon, Brookings Institute, Aspen Institute.

Scott, K., Tsoukalas, S., Roberts, P., & Lasby D. (2006). *The nonprofit and voluntary sector in Ontario: Regional highlights from the National Survey of Nonprofit and Voluntary Organizations*. Toronto. Retrieved November 3, 2009, from Imagine Canada http://www.ccsd.ca/pubs/2003/fm/regional_reports/nvso_2006.pdf

Scott, R. (2002). *Working better together: How government, business, and nonprofit organizations can achieve public purposes through cross sector collaboration, alliances, and partnerships*. Retrieved November 9, 2009, from Independent Sector http://www.independentsector.org/PDFs/working_together.pdf

Struthers, M. (2004, July). *Supporting financial vibrancy in the quest for sustaina-bility in the not-for-profit sector*. Paper prepared for the Community of Inquiry Symposium, Toronto, Ontario.

Wood, E. (1995). *Democracy against capitalism*. Cambridge: Cambridge University Press.

7 Notes in the Margins: The Social Economy in Economics and Business Textbooks

DANIEL SCHUGURENSKY AND ERICA MCCOLLUM

In this chapter, we argue that there is a gap between the presence of the social economy in Canada and throughout the world and its coverage in business and economics textbooks used in high schools and universities. Our interest in this topic was ignited by a study undertaken in 1995 that analysed the representation of the social economy in high school business and economics textbooks used in the province of Ontario (Davidson, Quarter, & Richmond, 1996). After examining over 30 textbooks, the study found a bias against the social economy. A decade later, we conducted a follow-up study to explore if any changes had occurred. Our findings revealed that during those ten years, the size of the social economy increased, but its presence in high school business and economics textbooks actually decreased.

To complement our primary data on Ontario high school textbooks and curricula, we reviewed studies from other jurisdictions on the presence of the social economy in high school and university textbooks and curricula. These studies show that the social economy is underrepresented in business and economics textbooks, and occasionally portrayed in a negative light. The titles of some of those studies are self-explanatory:

- The case of the missing organizations: Cooperatives and the textbooks (Hill, 2000);
- The disappearance of co-operatives from economics textbooks (Kalmi, 2006);
- The portrayal of labor in reporting textbooks: Critical absences, hostile voices (Bekken, 1994);

- Alternative economics: A missing component in the African American studies curriculum (Nembhard, 2008);
- De-emphasis on cooperatives in introductory economics textbooks (Lynch, Urban, & Somner 1989).

Educational researchers use the term 'missing curriculum' to refer to contents that, deliberately or not, are marginalized or entirely excluded from the classroom experience. One possible explanation for the low profile of the social economy in business and economics textbooks is the prevailing view that the only purpose of business is to increase profits for shareholders (Friedman, 1970). From this perspective, any producer of goods and services whose main mission is not to maximize profits but to maximize the well-being of its members or the community is likely to be excluded because it is not seen as a genuine economic actor. We argue – along with other contributors to this book – that the social economy sector is indeed part of the 'real' economy, and in many areas is more productive, efficient, and socially responsible than the for-profit sector. Hence, we suggest that students need to be adequately exposed to the social economy in high schools and universities, and this should include appropriate coverage in economics and business textbooks.

It is important. to clarify that our study focused on textbooks and curricula, and hence we cannot make any claims about what actually happens in classrooms (a topic for other research) or about learning acquired by students through extracurricular activities like community service (see chapter 8). However, considering that textbooks are largely aligned with the curriculum, and that teachers seldom deviate considerably from the official curriculum, we suggest that an analysis of textbook content is an appropriate strategy to explore students' exposure to the social economy.

Does the Social Economy Matter?

Someone could argue that low attention paid to the social economy in the textbooks can be justified by the marginal presence of this sector in society. However, available data suggest that both in Canada and internationally, the social economy makes a significant contribution to the social, economic, cultural, and environmental well-being of communities. Moreover, by stressing an emphasis on the most disadvantaged members of society and on democratic values and practices, the social economy provides an alternative paradigm to the dominant for-profit business model, which is currently enduring its deepest crisis since the 1929 Depression. Furthermore, in recent decades, the social economy has been growing in size, vibrancy, and importance throughout the world. Consider, for instance, the following facts:

Co-operatives

- The co-operative movement brings together over 800 million people around the world. The United Nations estimates that the livelihood of nearly three billion people (half of the world's population) is made secure by co-operative enterprises. Co-operatives can be seen in many different parts of the economy, including daycare, housing, forestry, farming, banking, and retailing (International Cooperative Alliance, 2009).
- The 2006 listing of the top 300 global mutual and co-operative organizations revealed combined assets of US$30–40 trillion and an annual turnover of approximately US$1 trillion. This is almost equivalent to the assets of Canada, the world's ninth largest economy. Among these 300 organizations, we can find Switzerland's largest employer, Europe's largest dairy business, France's largest bank, and the world's largest miller and marketer of rice (International Cooperative Alliance, 2006).
- Co-operatives and mutual enterprises appear particularly strong in banking and insurance. For example, mutual insurers as a whole cover 25% of the world market. In some countries (e.g., Cyprus), the market share of co-operative banks is around one-third, and in France co-operative banks handle 60% of the total deposits. The share of agricultural marketing by co-operatives was very strong in many countries and close to 100% for some products. Co-operatives and mutuals remain important all over the world in several other sectors including housing, agriculture, retailing, commerce, and healthcare (International Cooperative Alliance, 2009).
- In Canada, about 12 million people belong to at least one co-operative corporation, and 75% of jobs created by co-operatives are full-time positions. In 2004, there were 5,753 non-financial co-operatives that held over $17.5 billion in assets, brought in $27.5 billion of revenues, and employed around 85,000 people; the largest of them had 2006 revenues of $5.4 billion. Moreover, Canadian co-operatives

produce 35% of the world's maple sugar production (Co-operatives Secretariat 2007, 2006).

- Co-operatives have a higher survival rate than other business enterprises. In Quebec, for instance, the survival rate of co-operatives is 62% after five years and 44% after 10 years. In contrast, the survival rate of other forms of Quebec business enterprise is almost half (35% after five years and 20% after 10 years). More strikingly, after the first year alone, only 6.7% of co-ops closed their doors, compared to 24.6% of other businesses (Ontario Co-operative Association, 2008).
- Le Mouvement des caisses Desjardins, the umbrella organization for credit unions/caisses populaires in francophone Canada, is the largest employer in Quebec and, with a workforce of 40,000 and almost 5.8 million members, is the sixth largest financial institution in Canada with assets of $144 billion in 2007 (Desjardins, 2009).

Nonprofits

- In many countries, nonprofit organizations are the fastest growing segment of the economy. In the US, from 1977 to 2001, the number of employees in this sector doubled. By 2001, there were 12.5 million employees in the nonprofit sector, representing 9% of all employment (Gunn, 2004; Independent Sector, 2004; Myers & Stocks, 2008; Van Til, 2000). In Canada, between 1997 and 2003, the GDP for the core nonprofit sector increased at an annual average rate of 7.6%, which was significantly faster than the average of 5.6% for the economy as a whole (Hall et al., 2004; Hamdad & Joyal, 2005).
- Presently, there are nearly 1.3 million charitable and philanthropic organizations in the U.S. that employ approximately 11.5 million people (Panel on the Nonprofit Sector, 2005). In New York City alone, in 2000 there were over 9,000 nonprofits, which accounted for $65 billion in annual revenues, over 500,000 jobs (14% of total city employees), and a collective payroll of about $23 billion (Myers & Stocks 2008; Seley & Wolpert, 2002).
- In Canada, there were 161,000 incorporated nonprofits in 2003. That year, Canadian nonprofits had revenues of $112 billion, employed two million people (54% of them full-time), and had a volunteer labour force estimated to be another one million full-time equivalent jobs (Hall et al., 2004; Statistics Canada 2006).
- Contrary to the stereotype that nonprofits' revenues are 'unearned'

(donations and grants), 35% of their revenues are earned through the marketplace; indeed, a significant number of nonprofits compete successfully in the market with private firms.

- The nonprofit sector accounts for 7% of the overall Canadian GDP. In 2003, the GDP for the core nonprofit sector was two times larger than each of the motor vehicle manufacturing and agriculture industries and larger than the entire accommodation and food services industry. Moreover, the overall nonprofit sector's GDP was larger than the mining industry, the oil and gas extraction industry, and the entire retail trade industry. These figures do not include the imputed value of volunteering, which in 2001 increased the overall sector's share of the economy by another 1.4% (Statistics Canada, 2006).

While these figures and others (for further information on the significance of the social economy in Ontario, Quebec, and Europe see chapters 2, 3, and 4, respectively) are impressive in their own right, it is important to stress that in addition to their significant economic impact, nonprofits and co-operatives make a significant social impact, as they often solve many social problems in areas in which the business sector does not intervene because it would not be profitable. This includes efforts aimed at alleviating poverty, promoting the local economy, nurturing civic engagement, providing social support, increasing democratic processes in local organizations and workplaces, and fostering community development. Moreover, social economy organizations mobilize large numbers of volunteers to serve society. If volunteer contributions were included in conventional accounting (Mook, Quarter, & Richmond, 2007), the figures above would be even more impressive.

Interestingly, not much is known about the social economy, even by the government. For instance, the official website of Human Resources and Social Development Canada (2005) acknowledges that 'the Government of Canada is just beginning to understand the power and potential of social economy enterprises and organizations.' Given that the social economy has such a significant presence in our economies, and that we know little about it, it is pertinent to ask to what extent the sector is represented in business and economic textbooks, be it in higher education institutions or in high schools.

The Social Economy in Textbooks: Prior Studies

To inform our research, we reviewed previous studies that analysed the representation of the social economy in textbooks used in post-secondary institutions and high schools. Although our focus was on economics and business textbooks, we also included relevant studies on other subjects in our literature review.

Post-secondary Institutions

Some studies that focused on the portrayal of unions in college textbooks have found both a poor representation of the topic and an anti-union bias in the texts. For instance, Bekken (1994) conducted a content analysis on 14 textbooks and workbooks used in journalism programs in U.S. colleges, and found that labour unions were either ignored or portrayed in a negative light. Similar findings have been reported by subsequent research (e.g., Shaffer, 2002).

By and large, research on the representation of the social economy in business and economics textbooks in higher education has focused on co-operatives. Lynch, Urban, & Sommer (1989) reviewed 19 leading introductory economics texts used in U.S. and Canadian universities and found co-operatives mainly absent from these texts. More than half of these textbooks did not make any reference to co-operatives, and the few that devoted some space limited coverage to less than one page. A few years later, Parnell (1995) noted that the co-operative form of business has been largely ignored in post-secondary textbooks. At the same time, Hill (2000) examined the coverage of co-operatives in 25 introductory economics textbooks used in Canadian universities. Four were textbooks published in the USA, 10 were Canadianized versions of U.S. textbooks, and the remaining 11 were Canadian textbooks. He found that in most introductory textbooks, co-operatives were either entirely ignored or received only a passing mention and concluded that by neglecting democratic forms of economic institutions like co-operatives, the introductory textbooks 'fail to describe adequately actually existing institutions, ignore questions for economic democracy, and miss an opportunity to offer some interesting lessons in the basic principles of economic organizations and their development' (Hill, 2000, p. 293).

A few years later, Chamard (2004, p. 34) analysed economic and management textbooks and also found that the coverage was minimal. He concluded that the dominant paradigm is investor-owned, for-profit businesses competing for market share and profit, and that for this reason few graduates of business programs are well prepared to manage in co-operative environments.

From a historical perspective, probably the most interesting study on this topic was the one conducted by Panu Kalmi, a scholar at the Helsinki School of Economics, and published in a paper suggestively entitled 'The disappearance of co-operatives from economics textbooks.' He analysed 22 economic textbooks used at the University of Helsinki from 1905 to 2005 and found that both the quantity and the quality of the coverage of co-operatives decreased after the Second World War. Kalmi (2006) suggested a number of possible causes for this decline, including a change in the role of government and a move towards a neoclassical top-down economic paradigm. Although Kalmi's study was conducted in Finland, we would like to suggest that its findings are relevant internationally because most of the economics textbooks used in Finnish universities (as in many universities around the world) were Anglo-American books or domestic books largely modelled after Anglo-American books.

Moreover, Kalmi managed to identify that the first author to ignore co-operatives in an introductory economics textbook was Paul Samuelson, who won the Nobel Prize in 1970 for his work on neoclassical economics. In his textbook, Samuelson omitted co-operatives from the list of business organizations that includes proprietorships, partnerships, and corporations. This is an important detail because Samuelson's introductory economics textbook was very influential internationally; indeed, it has been reprinted many times in different languages and has been used for decades in many countries. So, when Samuelson omitted co-operatives, it is possible that many other economists followed suit. Today, many economics textbooks do not recognize co-operatives as a form of business organization.

Of course, the best way to find out to what extent Kalmi's findings are relevant beyond Finland would be to conduct similar studies in other parts of the world, exploring the coverage of co-operatives in textbooks published in the first half of the 20th century. For instance, a 1940s study of curricula in southern 'Negro' colleges in the USA found that 37 of 57 respondents from universities, colleges, or junior colleges said that they taught about the co-operative movement, and mentioned entire courses devoted to this topic (Brooks & Lynch, 1944; Nembhard, 2008). This suggests that Kalmi is on the right track, and that more research on this topic is needed.

High Schools

In a review of 78 Ontario textbooks, Babin and Knoop (1975) found many biases against labour unions and other groups. They reported that in most textbooks the description of the labour movement and its history was rarely present, and when unions were mentioned it was generally in negative terms, such as blaming unions for inflation, strikes, and slow economic growth.

Ross (2001) examined the portrayal of charitable activity in U.S. high school history textbooks from 1930 to 1995, and found that charitable organizations were mentioned, but only in terms of playing a supportive role in a historical event, with no discussion of their particular missions and their specific roles in history. Antonelli (2003) analysed textbooks used in career studies in Ontario, and noted that the only work alternatives presented by the texts were job sharing, flex-time, part-time, self-employment, and temporary work:

> Throughout all of the Career Studies textbooks, the authors choose not to empower students so that they can directly challenge the problematic trends in the modern world of work. Other workplace options like co-operatives or worker-run industries that would provide students with an alternative for workplace control are not mentioned in any of the texts. Instead, the textbooks ask students to adapt to the demands of the market. (Antonelli, 2003, p. 112)

As noted in the introduction, a prior study that caught our interest was the one conducted in 1995 by Jack Quarter and two OISE doctoral students (Alison Davidson and Betty Jane Richmond), who undertook a project to determine the representation of the social economy in high school textbooks used in the province of Ontario. After examining 34 popular textbooks, they concluded that there was a bias against the social economy (Davidson et al., 1996). A decade later, we conducted a similar study to find out if the situation had changed.

The Social Economy in Business and Economics Textbooks: A Ten-Year Follow-Up

In order to estimate changes from 1995 to 2005, we examined the most popular business and economics textbooks used in Ontario high schools in 2005. Moreover, we also analysed all updated versions of the original textbooks used in the 1995 study to assess any changes over that decade. Additionally, we reviewed the current Ontario curriculum guidelines to analyse the correspondence between curriculum guidelines and textbooks.

In order to select the business and economics textbooks that were the most popular in 2005, our first criterion was inclusion on the Trillium List, which is the official list of approved textbooks in Ontario high schools. Because schools were also using textbooks that were not included in the Trillium list, the second criterion to define our sample was textbooks in common use in Ontario high schools. We identified those textbooks by canvassing schools and consulting with teachers in this area. In total, we selected 22 texts with 11,375 pages. In a separate analysis, we examined nine updated texts from the 1995 study.

Using the same methodology of the 1995 study, our analysis of textbook coverage of the social economy covered five themes: co-operatives, nonprofits serving the public, mutual nonprofits, unions, and reformist tendencies in the private sector (e.g., worker participation in management decisions). Likewise, to identify the type and extent of coverage, we used the following categories: mentioned (one sentence to one paragraph); discussed (one or more paragraphs); included (one or more sections of a chapter); and featured (one or more chapters). We also paid attention to the presence of the social economy in pictures, textboxes, and case studies.

Findings I: Texts Used in 2005

As noted above, in our study we examined 22 economics and business textbooks used in Ontario high schools in 2005. The findings are presented according to the five main themes: co-operatives, nonprofits serving the public, nonprofit mutual associations excluding unions, unions, worker participation and reformist tendencies in the private sector.

Co-operatives

Co-operatives were mentioned in 18 of the 22 texts analysed (82%). Of the 22 texts, only 12 (54%) provided at least a discussion of a quarter page. The coverage of co-operatives did not exceed a brief discussion or a very short case study in any of the texts. There were no sections of chapters or full chapters dedicated to the topic. Business English texts provided the highest proportion of coverage at 0.53% of the pages, and this was due to one book that described the writing activities of a person working at a credit union. Overall, only 0.31% of the pages analysed were devoted to co-operatives. When co-operatives were discussed, the typical approach was a brief description followed by their advantages and disadvantages. Although coverage was generally neutral, in four texts there was no mention and in six others the reference was passing. For example, *Canadian Entrepreneurship and Small Business Management* states

> the vast majority of businesses take one of the following forms: sole proprietorship, partnership, or corporation. A co-operative, which is a business owned and run jointly by its members, is significant in certain sectors and regions but is overall a less popular option. (Balderson, 1998, p. 96)

Interestingly, the textbook describes sole proprietorship, partnership, and corporation in detail without any further reference to co-operatives.

Nonprofits Serving the Public

Nonprofits received substantially more coverage than co-operatives (0.65% of pages compared to 0.31%) and were mentioned at least in 18 of the 22 texts (82%), with 17 (77%) allowing a quarter of a page or more. One text included a full section of a chapter and another dedicated two chapters to the topic. Entrepreneurship and marketing texts dedicated the highest proportion of pages to this topic at 0.86%, but the 22 textbooks averaged only 0.65% of a page on this form of organization.

The statements in the texts ranged from recognizing the important role of nonprofits in the economy to excluding them. One textbook on marketing (Barnes, 2001) recognized the importance of the nonprofit sector by stating that 'in recent years, we have been giving some long overdue marketing attention to the multimillion dollar market made up of so called non business or not-for-profit organizations' (p. 193). Interestingly, the book does not give the topic extensive attention, with only 3.15 pages out of 736 (0.44%) dedicated to all nonprofits (both public service and mutuals combined).

Nonprofit Mutual Associations (Excluding Unions)

Mutual associations are a special type of nonprofits whose main purpose is to serve their members. Those members have a common interest, and seek to fulfil it through the association. Mutual associations can be professional groups, social clubs, burial societies, religious congregations, ethno-cultural groups, business associations, academic societies, sports clubs, and neighbourhood associations. Although unions are mutual associations, we treat them separately, in keeping with the methodology of the 1995 study.

Of all the categories analysed, mutual nonprofits were mentioned in the highest percentage of textbooks, 20 of the 22 (91%). However, only 15 of the 22 texts (68%) provided at least some discussion, and there was nothing in excess of a quarter page. General business textbooks had the highest coverage on mutual nonprofits with a mention on 0.37% of their pages. Overall, the proportion of pages in all of the texts dedicated to mutual nonprofits was 0.25%.

Unions

Only 10 of the 22 texts (45%) provided a mention of unions even though about 30% of Canada's workforce belongs to a union. Only six of the 22 texts (27%) include a discussion beyond a quarter page. Overall, 0.58% of the pages were dedicated to this topic (a relative low coverage considering that almost one-third of the Canadian workforce belongs to a union) and the figure is inflated because when unions are covered in a text, they tend to be extensively discussed – two textbooks dedicate a complete chapter and three dedicate at least one section of a chapter. Economics textbooks have the highest proportion of coverage on unions, with 2.40% of their pages dedicated to the topic. Moreover, all textbooks with extensive coverage of unions (except one) were economics texts, a general business textbook being the one exception.

The coverage of unions generally consists of some information on collective bargaining, history, strikes, and arbitration. Some texts recognized the role that unions have played in increasing the wages of workers. New challenges and constraints facing unions in the global competitive business environment were discussed, and a number of texts suggested that this has created a need for unions to change their historically adversarial relations with management. In *Understanding Canadian Business*, for instance, Nickles, McHugh, McHugh, Berman, and Cosa (2003) raise the need for less adversarial employee/management relationships:

Every firm seeks to have a highly motivated workforce, which requires good labour-management relations. That means each side has to appreciate the needs of the other. A progressive union with modern attitudes can co-operate with a progressive, modern management to arrive at workable compromises (p. 440).

The same text, in a discussion of the future of labour/management relations, asks if there is still a need for unions, and cites Wal-Mart (a firm that rejects unions) as an example of the new kind of management/employee relationship. Indeed, some textbooks argued that worker participation in the management of the company is a new approach that would make unions redundant.

Reformist Tendencies in the Private Sector: Worker Participation

Only 12 of the 22 texts (55%) mentioned worker participation and six (27%) had coverage of a quarter of a page or more. No text had coverage of even a section within a chapter. General business texts provided the highest proportion of coverage on worker participation (0.71%). Of all the topics covered in this study, worker participation had the lowest proportion of pages in the texts (0.13%).

Some texts described worker participation as a form of business management that is becoming popular. It was portrayed as a method to empower employees and give them more pride in their work. Interestingly, the businesses used as exemplars of this model did not always have an admirable record when it came to empowering their employees. As noted above, *Understanding Canadian Business* (the textbook with the most extensive coverage of worker participation) cites Wal-Mart and dubs it as a model for the future (Nickles et al., 2003). In discussing the virtues of encouraging worker participation, the textbook celebrates the success of the three partnership goals set by Wal-Mart's owner: 'treat employees as partners,' 'encourage employees to question and challenge the obvious,' and 'involve associates [the Wal-Mart label for employees] at all levels in the decision-making process' (Nickles et al., 2003, pp. 376–8).

Wal-Mart is an intriguing choice to illustrate worker empowerment because this company has been criticized extensively for its labour practices and lost several court cases for labour law violations in the USA and in Canada (Austen, 2007; CBC News, 2005; Human Rights Watch, 2007[1]). Adams (2005) argues that Wal-Mart has created a template for 21st century business that is premised on low wages, short hours, little individual job security, and aggressive denial of collective representation. The official website of the National Labor Relations Board (a federal agency created by the U.S. Congress to administer legislation on labour/management relations) lists 428 files on Wal-Mart.

Overall, our study of Ontario business and economics textbooks used in Ontario high schools in 2005 revealed that the coverage of the social economy was generally low across the board. However, coverage varied by topic. For example, economics texts provided coverage of unions, whereas marketing texts rarely even mentioned the topic. Nonprofits in the public service and mutual nonprofits received scant coverage in economics texts, but fared better in entrepreneurship texts. The latter texts, however, scarcely mentioned co-operatives (0.06%) and worker participation (0.03%).

When all categories are combined, organizations in the social economy and the reformist tendencies in the private sector averaged 1.93% of the coverage in the 22 texts reviewed in 2005. This is a decrease from the 2.55% in the textbooks analysed in 1995. When the representation of the social economy is broken down into categories, there is a slight increase in each category from 1995 to 2005 except for unions. However, overall the main finding of this study is that the coverage of the social economy in economics and business textbooks in Ontario high schools was low in 1995 and remained low in 2005. See table 7.1.

Findings II: Updated Texts

To have a better understanding of changes in the last decade, we decided to look at the nine 2005 textbooks that were updated from 1995 and examined in the Davidson et al. study. The analysis revealed trends that were similar to the previous section, with the overall coverage of the social economy remaining low and dropping slightly in the updated texts. In these nine texts, the proportion of pages devoted to co-operatives dropped slightly from 0.28% to 0.23%, and the coverage of nonprofits in the public service improved from 0.24% to 0.30%. There was also a slight improvement in the representation of mutual nonprofits (from 0.10% to 0.12%) and a small decrease in the coverage of unions (from 1.74% to 1.60%). Coverage of unions had the largest decrease in any category. Finally, there was increased representation of worker participation in the updated texts with four additional texts mentioning worker participation and coverage increasing from 0.02% to a scant 0.03%.

Overall, the proportion of pages dedicated to the social economy and worker participation was 2.39% in the nine 1995 texts and 2.29% in the 2005 updated versions. The analysis of the nine texts confirms the pattern in the larger group of business texts, with the co-operative category being the exception. In the comparison of the nine updated texts, the coverage of co-operatives slightly decreased, but in the larger comparison we found a slight increase.

Table 7.1
Social economy citations in 2005 Ontario high school business textbooks

SE Category	Texts	M	D	C	I	F	Pgs of SE in texts	% of pgs dedicated to topic in 2005	% of pgs dedicated to topic in 1995
Co-ops	22	13	11	5	0	0	35.32	0.31	0.25
Public Nonprofit	22	16	14	8	1	1	74.21	0.65	0.31
Mutual Nonprofit	22	17	09	8	0	1	28.48	0.25	0.08
Worker Participation	22	8	06	1	0	0	15.24	0.13	0.05
Unions	22	8	03	3	3	2	66.16	0.58	1.86
Total SE	22	62	43	25	4	4	219.41	1.93	2.55

Note: Total# of pgs in Section: 11375; M = Mentioned (1 sentence to 1 paragraph); D = Discussed (1 or more paragraphs); C = Case Study; I = Inclusion (1 or more sections of a chapter); F = Featured (1 or more chapters)

In addition, some textbooks have made changes to the conceptualization of business in their more recent editions. For instance, a look at three editions of a business book (1987, 1994, and 2001) reveals a progressive narrowing of the definition of business, with an increasing shift from a broad understanding that included social economy organizations to one more oriented towards the for-profit sector. Indeed, the 1987 edition of this book stated that a business 'can be defined or described by its type of ownership, the goals produced or services offered [or] the types of jobs provided or by the different functions that it performs in your community.' This understanding of business was rather inclusive and encompassed nonprofit organizations. The 1994 edition of the same book explained, 'the goal of business is to supply goods and services to meet consumer demands.' Although this was a narrower definition than the 1987 edition, it still included nonprofits. However, the 2001 edition of the same book stated that 'the goal of business is to make a profit,' a definition that clearly excludes nonprofits (Murphy et al., 1987, p. 21; 1994, p. 18, and 2001, p. 16).

Findings III: Curriculum Guidelines

To complement our data on textbooks, we explored the 2006 Ontario Curriculum guidelines for high school business classes. Like textbooks, the curriculum refers to some aspects of the social economy, but not in proportion to their presence in society. Throughout the curriculum for grades 9 through to 12, co-operatives only appear as suggested examples and never as a required topic, although they are regularly given as suggested examples for business ownership. For grade 11 accounting, however, co-operatives are not even mentioned.

Nonprofits appear in the grades 9/10 business curricula only as suggested examples but receive increased attention in certain 11/12 classes. Nonprofits or related activities such as volunteering were mentioned in the requirements of one grade 11 and one grade 12 Entrepreneurship class. Nonprofits received a marked inclusion in the curriculum for a grade 11 Marketing course. In this curriculum, nonprofits were listed in the general requirements of the course. In addition to knowing the marketing needs of nonprofits, students were asked to 'identify the characteristics and features of not-for-profit organizations.' Finally, one International Business grade 12 course required students to know the ways that non-governmental organizations and international development agencies promote economic progress in developing countries. Mutual associations, unions, and worker participation are not required teaching material in any of the high school business courses and only appear a couple of times as suggested examples. Overall, the only aspect of the social economy that is represented as required material in at least some upper-level business curricula is nonprofits. The other actors of the social economy are suggested as possible examples in the Ontario curriculum, but not as required material.

Subsequent Studies

The findings from two studies undertaken in 2007 by our research associates in the U.S. and Canada are consistent with the findings from Davidson et al. (1996) and our own study. In the U.S., Myers and Stocks from Pittsburgh University conducted a study examining 13 popular economics and business textbooks used in U.S. high schools, and concluded that the social economy is weakly represented (Myers & Stocks, 2008). At the same time, the Social Economy Hub at the University of Victoria carried out a study to assess social economy contents in the British Columbia curriculum by examining Prescribed Learning Outcomes in different subject areas (e.g., Social Studies, Business, Career and Personal Planning). The authors found very few or no references to the social economy and questioned why the concepts of the social economy were not part of the discussions that help students define their career choices (Cormode, McKitrick, & Smith, 2008).

The findings arising from these studies and from our own research suggest that the representation of the social economy in business and economics high school textbooks is disproportionately low relative to its role in the economies of Canada and the US, and that the information is sometimes biased against certain social economy actors. However, more research is needed to have a more accurate picture of the situation. We will elaborate on this in the next sections.

Summary, Discussion, and Conclusions

As noted in the introduction to this chapter, organizations of the social economy have a significant role in Canada and internationally. Co-operatives and nonprofits have millions of members and manage millions of dollars every day. The social economy shows, contrary to the prevailing neo-liberal paradigm, that it is possible to run businesses that put people before profit and still be economically viable. Moreover, it shows that democratic management and socially oriented businesses are not utopian dreams but viable alternatives to organizing economic enterprises. This is particularly important in the context of the current economic crisis, which originated in the speculative practices of the mainstream financial system.

While the social economy is important in terms of both its social mission and its presence, and while this sector has grown significantly in recent decades, students are seldom exposed to it when they take economics or business courses in high schools and universities. As Kalmi's (2006) study of university textbooks suggests, this omission is not an unintentional oversight, but the result of changes in economic paradigms that can be traced to the post-Second World War period. Today, it is clear that there is incongruence between the Canadian business reality and what students are learning in textbooks. This shortcoming is significant because, as Hill (2000) suggested, the social economy has key differences from the mainstream business models, providing useful examples of how differing structures, incentives, democratic processes, and goals play out in the economy. It is also significant because a high percentage of instructional time in the classroom – estimated at 80 to 90% – depends upon textbooks (Kilpatrick, 2006; Wright, 1996).

Ultimately, what is included and excluded in curricula and in textbooks is a political decision. Around 150 years ago, in 1854, Herbert Spencer argued that the 'question of questions' for all educational endeavours was 'what knowledge is of most worth?' and noted that before there can be a rational curriculum, we must settle which things it most concerns us to know. This is a sound suggestion, but raises the question of how these matters are settled. Addressing this issue, Michael Apple (1991) formulated a slightly different question: 'Whose knowledge is of most worth?' The very title of Apple's paper (*The politics of curriculum and teaching*) suggests that politics play a key role in deciding whose knowledge is of most worth and which knowledge is marginalized. We submit that these two questions, the first posed 150 years ago and the second 15 years ago, are still relevant today when we look at the portrayal of the social economy in our textbooks. As Myers and Stocks (2008) points out, in omitting or minimizing the social and non-competitive forms of the economy, textbooks and textbook companies are in effect 'selling' to students the free market values of competition and profit rather than representing the economy as a complex system with multiple forms and purposes.

Recommendations

We will conclude with four recommendations. First, we suggest complementing the findings of the studies discussed in this chapter with more research across different subject areas, historical periods, and educational levels. Indeed, it would be insightful to further explore the representation of the social economy in subject areas other than business and economics (e.g., social studies, civic studies, career planning). It would also be useful to generate a better understanding of the representation of the social economy in textbooks over time through qualitative and quantitative studies that examine changes in coverage and treatment. In this regard, it would be particularly interesting to conduct studies in different countries to confirm or disconfirm the hypothesis arising from Kalmi's study that a key social economy actor (co-operatives) had a larger presence in economics textbooks in the past. Also, as we develop a stronger knowledge base on high school and undergraduate courses in economics and business, it would be pertinent to expand that base by exploring curricular content and textbooks in graduate courses.

Our second recommendation is to complement our knowledge of the portrayal of the social economy in textbooks and curricula by engaging in research about the particularities of the teaching-learning process in business and economics courses in high schools and universities. This is important because we know that although textbooks and curricula are the main drivers of the classroom experience, instructors have relative autonomy to incorporate additional content or propose extracurricular activities (e.g., visits to social economy organizations, guest speakers).

Our third recommendation is to do more research on what youth actually know and think about the social economy. This is relevant because students acquire knowledge and attitudes from a variety of sources that certainly include textbooks, but they also learn from teachers, classmates, family, friends, mass media, alternative media, online groups, social economy organizations, social movements, political parties, and the like. A potential study on this could be undertaken with incoming university students.

Our fourth recommendation deals with policy and practice. One of the main purposes of education is to open possibilities and alternatives. The marginalization of the social economy in textbooks narrows learning opportunities instead of expanding them. Hence, it is reasonable to request that future revisions of curricula and textbooks consider the inclusion of more explicit references to this important sector. As it becomes clearer that the current coverage of the social economy in textbooks is incommensurate with its presence in society, it is timely to build a network of textbook writers, educators, publishers, students, key social economy actors, and the public at large interested in broadening and deepening content on the social economy in high school and university textbooks.

NOTES

1 Human Rights Watch (2007) argues that Wal-Mart uses a wide range of anti-union tactics to violate its workers' legal right to freedom of association, including using illegal techniques to gather information about union activity while pressuring workers to stop organizing, refusing to allow workers to bargain collectively, and coercively interrogating workers about their and their co-workers' union sympathies. It also complains about wage and hour violations, sex discrimination of workers in promotions, pay, job assignments, and training, disability discrimination, and the firing of long-term workers.

REFERENCES

Adams, Roy J. (2005). Organizing Wal-Mart: The Canadian campaign. *Just Labour 6&7*, 1–11.

Antonelli, Fabrizio. (2003). *Manufacturing the responsible citizen: A textual analysis of the civics and career studies texts in Ontario's secondary schools.* Unpublished Master's thesis, Ontario Institute for Studies in Education, University of Toronto.

Apple, Michael. (1991). *The politics of curriculum and teaching.* NASSP Bulletin, Vol. 532, 39–50.

Austen, Ian. (2007). Canada: Court rejects Wal-Mart. *The New York Times*, World Business Section, May 4.

Babin, P., & Knoop, R. (1975). *Bias in textbooks regarding the aged, labour unions, and political minorities.* Retrieved December 8, 2009, from ERIC database http://www.eric.ed.gov/ERICDocs/data/ericdocs2sql/content_storage_01/0000019b/80/39/c6/3f.pdf

Balderson, W. (1998). *Canadian entrepreneurship and small business management.* (3rd ed.). Toronto: McGraw-Hill Ryerson.

Barnes, J.G. (Ed.). (2001). *Fundamentals of marketing.* (9th Canadian ed.). Toronto: McGraw-Hill Ryerson.

Bekken, J. (1994, August). *The portrayal of labor in reporting textbooks: Critical absences, hostile voices.* Paper presented at the Annual Meeting of the Association for Education in Journalism and Mass Communication. Atlanta, GA

Brooks, L.M., & Lynch, R.G. (1944). Consumer problems and the co-operative movement in the curricula of Southern Negro colleges. *Social Forces, 22*(4), 429–36.

CBC News. (2005). *Wal-Mart ordered to stop harassing workers in Quebec.* Retrieved November 15, 2009, from http://www.cbc.ca/money/story/2005/02/25/walmart-050225.html

Chamard, John (2004). Co-operatives and credit unions in economics and business texts: Changing the paradigm. *The International Journal of Co-operative Management 1*(2), 34–40.

Co-operatives Secretariat. (2006). *Top 50 non-financial co-operatives in Canada 2006 (revised).* Retrieved October 28, 2009 from http://www.coop.gc.ca/COOP/display-afficher.do?id=1233159280930&lang=eng

Co-operatives Secretariat. (2007). *Co-ops in Canada (Situation – 2004).* Retrieved October 28, 2009, from http://www.coop.gc.ca/COOP/display-afficher.do?id=1232741407551&lang=eng

Cormode, S., McKitrick, A., & Smith, J. (2008). *Assessment of social economy content in prescribed learning outcomes of British Columbia curriculum.* The Social Economy Hub, University of Victoria (unpublished manuscript).

Davidson, A., Quarter, J., & Richmond, B.J. (1996). Business textbooks: Telling half the story. *Education Forum 22*(2), 28–31.

Desjardins (2009). *Desjardins figures.* Retrieved November 3, 2009, from http://www.desjardins.com/en/a_propos/qui-nous-sommes/chiffres.jsp

Friedman, M. (1970). The social responsibility of business is to increase its profits. *New York Times Magazine*, 32–3.

Gunn, C. (2004). *Third sector development: Making up for the market.* Ithaca, NY: Cornell University Press.

Hall, M., de Wit, M.L., Lasby, D., McIver, D., Evers, T., Johnson, C., et al. (2004). *Cornerstones of community: Highlights of the national survey of nonprofit and voluntary organizations* (Statistics Canada Publication No. 61–533-XIE).

Hamdad, M., & Joyal, S. (2005). *Satellite account of nonprofit institutions and volunteering* (Statistics Canada Publication No. 13–015-XIE).

Hill, Roderick. (2000). The case of the missing organizations: Cooperatives and the textbooks. *Journal of Economic Education 31*(3), 281–95

Human Resources and Social Development Canada (2005). *Social Economy: Questions and answers.* Retrieved November 15, 2009, from http://www.hrsdc.gc.ca/en/cs/comm/sd/social_economy.shtml

Human Rights Watch. (2007). Discounting rights: Wal-Mart's violation of US workers' right to freedom of association. *Human Rights Watch* HRW Index No.: G1902.

International Cooperative Alliance. (2006). *The world's major co-operatives and mutual business*. International Cooperative Alliance, Geneva, Switzerland.

International Cooperative Alliance. (2009). *Statistical information on the cooperative movement*. Retrieved November 15, 2009, from http://www.ica.coop/coop/statistics.html

Independent Sector. (2004). *Employment in the nonprofit sector*. Washington, DC: Independent Sector.

International Labour Organization. (2008). *ILO says global financial crisis to increase unemployment by 20 million*. Retrieved October 24, 2009, from http://www.ilo.org/global/About_the_ILO/Media_and_public_information/Press_releases/lang--en/WCMS_099529/index.htm

Kalmi, Panu. (2006). *The disappearance of co-operatives from economics textbooks*. Helsinki School of Economics Working Papers, W-398 (February).

Kilpatrick, Jimmy. (2006). An interview with Frank Wang: About the beauty of mathematics. *Education News*, September 17. Retrieved November 15, 2008, from http://www.ednews.org/articles/1233/1/An-Interview-with-Frank-Wang-About-The-Beauty-of-Mathematics/Page1.html

Lynch, L., Urban, M., & Somner, R. (1989). De-emphasis on cooperatives in introductory economics textbooks. *Journal of Agricultural Cooperation 4*, 89–92

Mook, L., Quarter, J., & Richmond, B.J. (2007). *What counts: Social accounting for nonprofits and cooperatives*. (2nd ed.). London: Sigel Press.

Murphy, T., Kelley, R., McMillan, R., Williams, B., & Wilson, J. (1987). *The world of business*. (2nd ed.). Toronto: John Wiley and Sons.

Murphy, T., Kelly, R., McMillan, B., & Wilson, J. (1994). *The world of business*. (3rd ed.). Toronto: Nelson Canada.

Murphy, T., Wilson, J., & Notman, D. (2001). *The world of business: A Canadian profile*. (4th ed.). Scarborough, ON: Nelson Thomson Learning.

Myers, J.P., & Stocks, J.L. (2010). Fostering the common good: The portrayal of the social economy in secondary business and economic textbooks. *The Journal of Social Studies Research 34*(2).

Nembhard, J.G. (2008). Alternative economics: A missing component in the African American studies curriculum. *Journal of Black Studies 38*(5), 758–82.

Nickles, W.G., McHugh, J.M., McHugh, S., Berman, P., & Cosa, R. (2003). *Understanding Canadian business*. (4th ed). Toronto: McGraw-Hill Ryerson.

Ontario Co-operative Association. (2008). Summary of report by the Ministry of Economic Development, Innovation and Export in Québec: Survival rate of co-operatives in Québec, 2008 edition. Retrieved December 8, 2009, from http://www.ontario.coop/upload/Summary%20of%202008%20Quebec%20Survival%20Report%20.pdf

Panel on the Nonprofit Sector. (2005). Report to Congress and the nonprofit sector on governance, transparency, and accountability. Retrieved December 8, 2009, from http://www.nonprofitpanel.org/Report/final/Panel_Final_Report.pdf

Parnell, Edgar. (1995). *Reinventing the co-operative: Enterprises for the 21st century*. Oxford: Plunkett Foundation for Cooperative Studies.

Ross, S.W. (2001). *Portrayal of organized charitable activity in high school American history textbooks*. Dissertation Abstracts International, vol. 62–11A.

Seley, J.E., & Wolpert, J. (2002). *New York City's nonprofit sector*. Toronto: University of Toronto Press.

Shaffer, R. (2002). Where are the organized public employees? The absence of public employee unionism from U.S. history textbooks, and why it matters. *Labor History*, 43(3), 315–34.

Spencer, Herbert. (1854). What knowledge is of most worth? *West-minster Review*.

Statistics Canada. (2006). Satellite account of non-profit institutions and volunteering. Retrieved December 8, 2009, from http://www.statcan.ca/Daily/English/061208/d061208a.htm

Thompson, David. (1997). Cooperative America (1997) from International Cooperative Information Centre. Retrieved October 23, 2002, from www.wisc.edu/uwcc/icic/def-hist/country/us/Cooperative-America – 1997–1.html

Van Til, J. (2000). *Growing civil society: From nonprofit sector to third space*. Bloomington: Indiana University Press.

Wright, Ian (1996, July). Critically thinking about the textbook. Paper presented at the International Conference on Critical Thinking, Sonoma, CA.

8 Mandatory High School Community Service in Ontario: Assessing and Improving Its Impact

PAULETTE PADANYI, MARK BAETZ, STEVEN D. BROWN, AND AILSA HENDERSON

The growing recognition that there is a social economy highlights the increasing role of the voluntary and not-for-profit sector in what was once largely the domain of the public and private spheres. As governments have come to appreciate the contribution of this sector to the health of the community, they have also been made aware of the importance of civic engagement among young people – the very people who in coming decades will be responsible for sustaining the social economy.

One approach seized upon by many jurisdictions in North America to encourage youth volunteerism has been to introduce mandatory high school community service programs. Viewed from the perspective of chapter 1 (Mook, Quarter, and Ryan), mandatory community service is an attempt by a public service organization to introduce students to participation in the social economy, primarily through civil society organizations.

As noted in chapter 6 (Brock), Ontario introduced such a program into its high school curriculum in 1999, and all graduates since 2003 have completed 40 hours of required public service. Unfortunately, this program is not well structured compared to others operating in Canada or abroad (Meinhard, Brown, Ellis-Hale, Foster, & Henderson, 2007). Details such as the types of community service eligible for credit, the extent of assistance to be provided by school personnel, and the relationship of the program to school curricula are left up to local school boards. This, in combination with the fact that many of these school boards have difficulty funding their core programs because of changes made in the 1990s to Ontario's funding formulae for education, has resulted in many high schools providing only minimal support. For example, a school's involvement often consists simply of collecting the sheets required to confirm each student's individual community activity and recording basic data for transcript purposes (Brown, Meinhard, Ellis-Hale, Henderson, & Foster, 2007).

Despite this lack of structure, the Ontario Ministry of Education's stated purpose for making participation in 40 hours of community service a requirement for high school graduation is ambitious: it is to 'encourage students to develop awareness and understanding of civic responsibility and of the role they can play in supporting and strengthening their communities' (Ontario Ministry of Education, 2009).

This chapter focuses on Ontario's mandatory community service program and its effectiveness to date. A multi-university team of researchers led by Steven Brown of Wilfrid Laurier University conducted three studies over 2007 and 2008 which collectively address two key areas of concern:

1. Basic program impact – specifically,

A Does the program result in exposure to community service for high school students who would not otherwise become involved?
B Does exposure to community service through Ontario's mandatory high school program affect subsequent civic engagement?

2. Student response – specifically,

A Do students consider the service they undertook to fulfil their high school requirement to be significant and positive?
B Do students vary in their response to community service and, if so, why?

Although all three research studies contribute to findings and conclusions related to more than one of the above questions, each study was distinct and conducted by different team members. This chapter therefore begins with an overview of each study's focus, research methodology, and theoretical framework. Findings and conclusions are subsequently discussed by research question rather than by study. The chapter concludes with a discussion of the policy implications of these findings concerning how the program is structured and how it is positioned to all stakeholders.

It is important to note that the data for all three studies were collected from university students rather than from high school students. This was done to ensure that all respondents were reflecting upon complete, rather than partial, experiences with the mandatory community service program. However, because it is likely that the experiences of these university participants are not representative of all high school graduates, the conclusions from these studies should be limited to the population of university-bound high school graduates.

Study Overviews

Study 1

FOCUS

This study focused on one basic program impact question and one student response question, specifically: 'Does the program result in exposure to community service for high school students who would not otherwise become involved?' and 'Do students consider the service they undertook to fulfil their high school requirement to be significant and positive?'

RESEARCH METHODOLOGY

An in-class survey was conducted in Fall 2007 among recent high school graduates. Specifically, this survey was completed by 198 undergraduate business students enrolled in a core second-year course on Organizational Behaviour at Wilfrid Laurier University in Waterloo, Ontario. The survey asked students to indicate the extent to which they were involved in volunteering/community service during various educational periods in their life and to comment on how any of the experiences affected them personally, either negatively or positively.

THEORETICAL FRAMEWORK

This study was designed around the assumption that Dewey's principle of continuity has relevance to student volunteering. This principle states that 'all experience occurs along a continuum ... (and) experiences build on previous ones' (Dewey, 1938). Given that students may have long volunteering/community service pathways that involve elementary school, high school, and university, there is the potential for students to build on these various experiences for personal growth and development.

Three aspects of the concept of community service learning were used to provide a basis for organizing and understanding student responses regarding the personal impact of their volunteering/community service experiences. These three aspects are:

1 the principle of reciprocity - both the server and served must profit from the experience (Kendall, 1990). Importantly, in its rationale for instituting mandatory community service in high schools, the Ontario Ministry of Education recognized a possible reciprocal outcome whereby the server can develop personal 'awareness, understanding (and) responsibility' and the served can be strengthened. A similar point about the dual benefits of volunteering is made in chapter 11 (Meinhard, Handy, and Greenspan), which notes that employer-supported volunteering can be both self-beneficial and socially beneficial.
2 reflection - a pedagogical mechanism to help students integrate their experiences and their learning (Ash, Clayton, and Moses, 2007). There are three categories of learning goals identified with service learning reflection: (a) personal growth, (b) civic engagement, and (c) academic enhancement. The Ontario Ministry of Education's objective for its high school community service requirement relates to two of these three goals - personal growth (awareness of and understanding of civic responsibility) and civic engagement (the role and the contributions they can make in strengthening communities).
3 development of the five skills of responsible citizenship (Godfrey, 1999). These skills are: (a) awareness of the scope and magnitude of societal problems, (b) humanization of the problem to dismantle preconceived notions and stereotypes, (c) grappling with issues of social justice and personal compassion as requisite elements of a good and moral life, (d) moral skills of compassion, patience, and true concern for others, and (e) intention to continue to serve their communities (Godfrey, 1999). The Ontario Ministry of Education's objectives for the community service requirement relate to all five of these responsible citizenship skills because each skill is associated with civic responsibility.

Study 2

FOCUS
This study sought to address the two basic program impact questions cited above. Specifically: 'Does the program introduce high school stu-

dents to the voluntary sector who would not otherwise have had that exposure?' and 'Does exposure to community service through Ontario's mandatory high school program affect subsequent civic engagement?'

RESEARCH METHODOLOGY

In Winter 2007, all fourth-year students at Wilfrid Laurier University in Waterloo and the University of Guelph were invited to complete an online survey dealing with student experiences and perspectives in both university and high school. The questionnaire also elicited information about the breadth and duration of their high school volunteering experiences, the enjoyment associated with service placements, and the apparent motivation for undertaking community service. The final sample for this study was 820 students.

Importantly, this composite sample was drawn from two high school cohorts: students from the first Ontario high school cohort that was required to complete community service in order to graduate, and students from the last high school cohort in Ontario that had no such graduation requirement. However, both entered university in the same year – 2003 – because the high school curriculum had been shortened from five to four years at the same time that the mandatory service requirement was introduced. As a consequence, surveying this Ontario double cohort as the students finished their fourth year of university studies approximates a quasi-experimental design, allowing the researchers to examine the effects of mandating high school community service on civic engagement by comparing the attitudes and behaviour of these two groups regarding volunteering four years after their high school graduation.

THEORETICAL FRAMEWORK

The introduction of mandatory community service into high school curricula essentially exploits the school system as an agent of socialization (Schachter, 1998). Evidence is now accumulating about the effectiveness of these programs, and a modest consensus is emerging on several issues. However, there are still a number of open questions.

One issue central to this study is the impact of *mandating* service in high school rather than simply encouraging or facilitating it. Indeed, chapter 6 (Brock) cites mandatory programs as examples of the government acting as an enforcer. Proponents of mandated programs argue that the positive effects of service accrue regardless of why it was undertaken in the first place. They argue that the net effect of a mandated program can only be positive because of the impact it has on those students who would not enter the voluntary sector of their own accord (Avrahami & Dar, 1993; Giles & Eyler, 1994; Sobus, 1995). On the other hand, critics question the premise that one's motivation to get involved is not a relevant factor, and worry that compelling service may even have negative effects on subsequent volunteering (for example, Batson, Jasnoski, & Hanson, 1978; Kunda & Schwartz, 1983; Chapman, 2002; Stukas, Snyder, & Clary, 1999).

A second issue is the longevity of the effects of high school community service. While there is enormous empirical support for the general thesis that activism in adolescence predicts adult civic involvement (e.g., Fendrich, 1993; Hanks & Eckland, 1978; Jennings, 2002), support for the longevity of effects associated with *mandated community service* is less well established. Some researchers (Brown, Pancer, Henderson & Ellis-Hale, 2007; Henderson, Brown, Pancer, & Ellis-Hale, 2007) have reported that mandated students were as likely to volunteer again about a year after graduation as students who volunteered in high school without such a requirement. However, other researchers (Hart et al., 2007) found that those who did no more than their required high school service were no more likely to volunteer with civic or youth organizations eight years later than those who did no high school service at all.

Study 3

FOCUS
This study was based on the premise that understanding the differences among high school students can provide a basis for improving the program to enhance its likelihood of achieving its goals. Therefore, its primary purpose was to address one of the student response questions, specifically 'Do students vary in their response to community service in high school and, if so, why?'

RESEARCH METHODOLOGY
An online survey was conducted in Winter 2007 among all first-year university students at four post-secondary institutions in Southwestern Ontario (University of Guelph, University of Waterloo, Wilfrid Laurier University, and Conestoga College). The final sample of 1,299 respondents answered questions dealing with their attitudes towards society, helping others, and volunteering. In Winter 2008, in-depth interviews

were then conducted with 20 first-year University of Guelph students to probe their specific high school volunteering experiences and their attitudes towards helping others.

THEORETICAL FRAMEWORK
The effectiveness of mandatory high school community service has been the subject of much debate. Some scholars believe that forced civic engagement does not help student development. They feel that, rather than strengthening community ties and deepening civic commitment, it can create resentment, thereby decreasing civic and moral engagement (Stukas, Snyder, and Clary, 1999). Others take the opposite view, that mandatory community service can have a positive effect because it provides youth with 'outlets to ... instill a sense of civic responsibility, reduce apathy and cynicism, and promote a lifelong commitment to service' (Planty, Bozick, and Regnier, 2006).

Both positions may be correct, since high school populations are quite heterogeneous. High school students differ substantially in terms of basic demographics (e.g., household income, social class), family background (e.g., ethnicity, religious affiliation, and orientation), their attitudes towards others, and their inherent sense of altruism. They also vary widely in terms of their going-in experience with, and commitment to, volunteerism. Therefore, it may be possible to segment high school students into groups that have a greater or lesser likelihood of being affected positively by mandatory community service in high school.

Grouping high school students for this purpose is supported by helping behaviour theory (Schwartz, 1977, as cited in McCarthy and Tucker, 1999, and McCarthy and Tucker, 2002). This theory proposes that both cognitive and affective influences motivate people to assist others. These two influences work through a multi-step process involving three phases: activation, obligation, and defence. Activation involves becoming aware of others' needs. Feelings of moral obligation are the result of an individual's norms and values as they relate to taking action to helping others. Defence involves assessing potential helping responses based on costs and benefits to one's self. It can negate an individual's sense of moral obligation to help if the cost of responding is felt to be high.

For some Ontario high school students, helping behaviour is activated by role models such as parents, while, for others, it is solely activated by the requirement to undertake mandatory community service.

The fact that there are different catalysts for community service in high school suggests that students fall into groups which may respond quite differently to the requirement for mandatory community service.

Findings and Data Analysis

1. *Basic Program Impact*

A Does the Ontario program result in exposure to community service for high school students who would not otherwise become involved?

According to the 1997 National Survey of Giving, Volunteering and Participation (NSGVP), over 35% of Ontario youth reported volunteering in the previous twelve months. The percentage with university degrees doing so was much higher at 62% (Febbraro, 2001). Since the 1997 NSGVP was conducted just prior to Ontario's introduction of the mandatory high school program in 1999, its findings suggest that a mandated program might have the potential to introduce a solid majority of the high school student population -- including a substantial minority of those who were university-bound -- to the voluntary sector.

As noted, the three studies reported here deal only with university-bound students. Their collective results suggest that the mandatory program played a very modest role in the community service experience of these students:

- Of the 198 second-year university students surveyed in study 1, 91% participated in the province's mandatory high school program; however, almost all of them – 88% – had also been involved in other volunteering experiences.
- Of the first-year university students who completed study 3's online survey, virtually all had completed service as part of Ontario's mandatory program, and 85% had also been involved in other volunteering experiences.
- Study 2, which surveyed Ontario's double cohort in their fourth year of university, did find that more mandated than non-mandated students completed some service in high school – 94% vs. 77% – but the high levels of participation for both cohorts suggest that most university-bound students tend to enter the voluntary sector without being forced to by the province.

Additional findings from both study 1 and study 2 reinforce the conclusion that the mandatory program serves as an entrée to the voluntary sector for only a few university-bound students. There were 163 respondents involved in study 1 who provided information on their entire volunteering/community service pathway (35 other respondents were not able to or did not provide the requested information). Of these 163 respondents, 88% did community service during at least two levels of school, and 55% were involved at all three educational levels of elementary school, high school, and university. In other words, most students had a volunteering/community service pathway which involved at least two different educational periods in their lives. The alternative pathways undertaken by the student respondents in study 1 are illustrated in figure 8.1.

If, as this exhibit indicates, 77% of students who enter high school gain volunteering experience in elementary school and only 23% of students enter high school without prior volunteering experience, the mandatory high school program provides, at most, initial exposure to community service for only a minority of students and supplementary or reinforcing exposure for the majority of these university-bound high school students. Study 2 tells a similar story. Among the mandated students in the study, about 75% indicated that the mandated service they completed was not their introduction to the community service field.

Both sources of data clearly indicate that the mandated program exposes more students to the voluntary sector. However, they also suggest that, for most students, it may play only a secondary or reinforcing role in achieving the Ontario Ministry of Education's stated goal of encouraging students to 'develop awareness and understanding of civic responsibility and of the role they can play in supporting and strengthening their communities.' We will return to this issue again when we address Student Response questions.

B Does exposure to community service through Ontario's mandatory high school program affect subsequent civic engagement?

To examine the unique effects on subsequent attitudes and behaviour that might be attributed to Ontario's program, study 2 put study participants into four groups. The purpose was to isolate the key target population for the program – those students who would not have otherwise done volunteer work in high school. The four groups were

Figure 8.1. Alternative volunteering/community service pathways

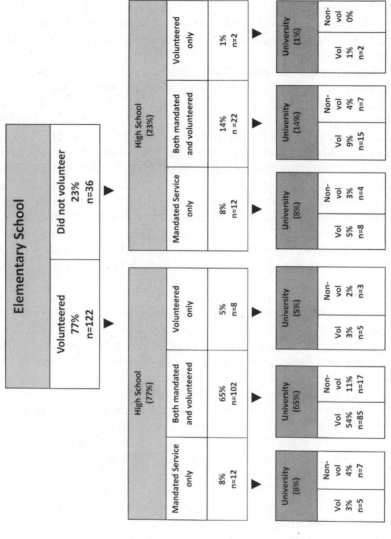

Note: (1) 158 students included in this analysis (remaining students surveyed had neither high school mandatory community service nor high school volunteering, or the responses were unusable for this analysis because of incomplete information); (2) some percentages may not add up due to rounding.

- *no service* – students who did no community service in high school (n = 123; 15% of respondents);
- *mandated only* – students who were apparently mobilized to volunteer in high school only by the graduation requirement (n = 104; 13% of respondents);
- *mandated and volunteered* – students who completed mandated service but had volunteered in high school beforehand (n = 280; 34% of respondents); and
- *volunteered* – students who volunteered freely during high school and had no community service requirement to graduate (n = 312; 38% of respondents).

A comparison of mean current community service activity levels across these four groups (i.e., activity four years after graduation from high school) was conducted using four measures of civic engagement:

- Community service activity undertaken in the last 12 months;
- Level of community service external to the university in the last 12 months;
- Level of university-based charitable activity in the last 12 months;
- Current attitude towards volunteering (3 item-scale).

Results (see figure 8.2) reveal that the mandated only and no service groups do much less volunteering four years after high school than the mandated and voluntary and non-mandated groups. Only with regard to attitude towards volunteering is the mandated only group similar to the latter two groups. Thus, there is little support here for the thesis that forcing high school students to volunteer pays off in subsequent community service down the road.

If the Ontario program had few positive effects on subsequent attitudes and behaviour, did it have any negative effects? Specifically, did it poison the well to future volunteering as some have worried it might? Study 2 addressed this question using OLS regression to estimate the independent effect of the mandated/non-mandated distinction on current community service activity. To isolate the independent effect of the program, the analysis also included controls for other high school service characteristics (duration of volunteer experiences and level of enjoyment of volunteering experiences) and potential confounding social background variables (sex, religious attendance, high school activity

Figure 8.2. Current volunteering: Comparing student groups based on their high school volunteering experience

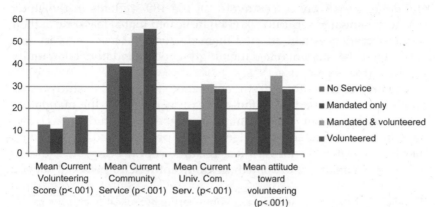

level, urban-rural residence, and parents' community service activity level).[1]

The analysis revealed that some aspects of a student's high school community service experience are significant predictors of current service activity. Specifically, duration of service (greater than a year) and the level of enjoyment that they associate with their service experiences – both of which talk to the quality of high school placements - are positively associated with civic engagement after high school. On the other hand, the analysis indicated that whether the service is mandated or freely chosen is not related to current activity levels. Therefore, study 2 suggests that the Ontario program may not have a negative effect on subsequent volunteering as posited by previous researchers (for example, Batson, Jasnoski, & Hanson, 1978; Kunda & Schwartz, 1983; Chapman, 2002; Stukas, Snyder, & Clary, 1999).

2. *Student Response*

A Do students consider the service they undertook to fulfil their high school requirement to be significant and positive?

Information gathered through both study 1 and study 3 indicates that the mandatory service experience that students undertook to graduate was *not* felt to be significant, in a positive sense, by most students.

Participants in study 1 were asked if at least one of their various volunteering/community service experiences had affected them personally either negatively or positively. Of the 180 students in the study who did mandated service, 83% (149) indicated that at least one of their service experiences had affected them personally. However, very few (22) of these 149 students cited their high school mandatory community service as that experience.

Similarly, several of the 20 students who participated in study 3's indepth interviews made spontaneous comments about the mandatory high school program. These comments suggest that students may not be willing or able to acknowledge that the program had an impact on them because they do not view it as genuine volunteering, but rather as either a forced activity or something done entirely for personal benefit:

Respondent 2: The 40 hours was not volunteering because students are receiving something in return and they were told they had to.

Respondent 5: (I) definitely (went) beyond the 40. I knew it looked better … If an employer knew you only needed 40, and saw that you only did the minimal, it looks very bare minimal and getting 40 looked very entry [sic] and doesn't look like you're doing it for the right causes.

Respondent 11: In high school, it just meant graduating. I guess I got something out of it but the majority of time we were forced into it … For high school, I don't know how voluntary it actually is … I think the majority of people just volunteered because they needed to graduate. Maybe one or two volunteered out of the goodness of their heart. But for most people I think they felt like they were forced. They felt it was just another class or credit that they needed to graduate.

Respondent 12: 40 hours forces students to give back to the community and it can help people start doing that. Some people don't put in the effort because they have to do it.

Respondent 15: (Volunteering is) something you do on your own time and that you do for someone else … so you are not forced like the hours you do in high school.

Respondent 20: What you find yourself doing for 40 hours is not really volunteering. I think there are two different types (of volunteering) – something that gets you 40 hours versus what you want to do. The 40 hours you do in high school gets you going and leads you into more volunteering.

The above comments were made by students whose high school community service experience ranged from doing only what was required to graduate to doing extensive volunteering above the required level. Therefore, attitude towards the existing program may be broadly negative and not a strong differentiating factor among students.

B Do students vary in their response to community service and, if so, why?

Based on a question asked in the study 3 online questionnaire about the number of hours of volunteering done in high school, this study's 1,299 survey respondents were segmented into three groups:

- Segment 1 - those who did the required 40 hours only
- Segment 2 - those who did the required 40 hours plus an additional amount less than 40 hours, and
- Segment 3 - those who did the required 40 hours plus an additional 40 hours or more.

Demographics confirm that these are distinct groups because they differ substantially in terms of variables known to be key characteristics of volunteers, i.e., gender, parents' volunteering practices, and the extent that religion is stressed in their home. See table 8.1.

Comparing the segments based on their top two box (agree and strongly agree) responses to questions about personal community service plans reveals that these groups also differ substantially in that they represent low (segment 1), medium (segment 2), and high (segment 3) levels of intention to undertake community service. See table 8.2.

Table 8.1
Segment demographics

	Segment 1 – High school requirement only	Segment 2 – Both required and on own - some	Segment 3 – Both required and on own – a lot
Total	195 (15%)	470 (36%)	634 (49%)
Male	40%	30%	27%
Parents volunteer	25%	44%	53%
Religion stressed at home	44%	50%	54%
Attend church > once a month	11%	15%	32%

Table 8.2
Segment volunteer plans

	Segment 1 – High school requirement only	Segment 2 – Both required and on own - some	Segment 3 – Both required and on own – a lot
Total	195 (15%)	470 (36%)	634 (49%)
Plan to do some volunteer work	39%	64%	87%
Plan to become involved with community	36%	61%	81%
Plan to participate in community service org	30%	51%	71%

Having established that the segments were different in ways relevant to possible attitudes towards community service, comparisons were made based on their top two box (agree and strongly agree) responses to specific attitudinal questions related to: (a) civic responsibility, (b) personal responsibility for one's own circumstances and welfare, (c) how people treat others, and (d) their tolerance of immigrants and cultural groups. The respondents who only did 40 hours of service (segment 1) were less inclined to believe that people have a civic responsibility to volunteer or otherwise help others, more inclined to feel that people are responsible for their own circumstances and welfare, more inclined to be less trusting of other people, and had a lower tolerance for people who are different. The respondents who did a lot of volunteering in addition to the 40-hour requirement (segment 3) held the polar opposite views, while the respondents who did some volunteering in addition to their 40 hours (segment 2) were in-between on all counts. See table 8.3.

Twenty in-depth interviews were conducted in Winter 2008 to supplement the above findings and better understand the roots of student helping behaviour (activation, obligation, and defence). The respondents included eight students from segment 1, six from segment 2, and six from segment 3.

In terms of activation, segment 1 students became involved with volunteering only through the mandatory high school program. In terms of obligation, they planned to volunteer in the future but only 'if there is time' or if it involves 'something of personal interest' to them. In terms of defence, the segment 1 respondents did not currently volunteer and all cited multiple reasons for not doing so, such as not having enough

Table 8.3
Segment attitudes toward others

	High school requirement only	Both required and on own – some	Both required and on own – a lot
Total	195 (15%)	470 (36%)	634 (49%)
Everybody should volunteer some time for the good of the community	65%	83%	89%
People have a responsibility to help those who are less fortunate	52%	62%	73%
People who don't get ahead should blame themselves, not the system	40%	32%	33%
In our society, you should be responsible for your own welfare and others for theirs	36%	30%	24%
Most people can be trusted	24%	36%	38%
Most of the time, people try to be helpful	27%	39%	39%
Recent immigrants should have as much to say about our country's future as people born and raised here	36%	49%	53%
A society with a variety of ethic and cultural groups is more able to tackle new problems as they occur	49%	61%	64%

time, not having connections, preferring to use their time earning money, and not being aware of the volunteer opportunities available.

Segment 2 students typically started volunteering when they were 11–13 years old because they were asked to by someone they knew. They want to volunteer in the future primarily to help others. While most do not volunteer at the present time, their excuses for not doing so are primarily due to being too busy or not being aware of the volunteer opportunities available.

Segment 3 students also started volunteering when they were 11–13. They thought it was a fun way to keep busy. Because of their love of volunteering, these respondents not only put in many hours of service, but they did so with a larger number of organizations and by undertaking a much wider variety of activities than the other segments' respondents did. Segment 3 students definitely plan to volunteer because it's natural, and part of their personality or lifestyle. As a result, they currently volunteer and they made no 'defensive' comments that suggested that they felt there were costs associated with volunteering.

Combining all of the above quantitative and qualitative information leads to the following student profiles:

- Segment 1 (high school students who do only enough community service to graduate) come from families that do not emphasize the importance of volunteering or religion. These students are not very interested in volunteering or working with a community service organization. They do not feel that people have a strong sense of civic responsibility towards others and, in fact, tend to feel that people are responsible for themselves. From a helping behaviour perspective, they have been activated by outside forces, have a low sense of obligation, and are highly defensive, associating many costs with volunteering.
- Segment 2 (high school students who do a little more community service than is required to graduate) have parents who do some volunteering and, although these students don't attend church services regularly, religion was stressed at home when they were growing up. They have a moderate sense of civic responsibility and are somewhat trusting of people and tolerant of those from different backgrounds. From a helping behaviour perspective, they were activated prior to high school, they have a moderate sense of obligation, and cite fairly pragmatic costs (too busy, don't know of opportunities) as their defence for not volunteering at the present time.
- Segment 3 (high school students who do a lot more community service than is required) have parents who volunteer and/or they come from homes where religion was stressed to a great extent when they were growing up. They believe that people should help others, and tend to be very trusting of others and open-minded about people who come from different backgrounds. From a helping behaviour perspective, they were activated prior to high school; they have a high sense of obligation, and are not defensive about volunteering. Indeed, they love volunteering and fully endorse it as a way for their peers to contribute to society.

Clearly, these findings suggest that high school students cannot be treated as a homogeneous group. There are relevant group differences that contribute to differences in student willingness to fully participate in the program and therefore influence its subsequent personal impact on them.

Policy Implications – Proposed Changes to the Program

Program Structure

All three of the studies discussed in this chapter confirmed that the mandatory high school community service program in Ontario is somewhat successful in that it exposes more students to the voluntary sector. Among university-bound graduates, the proportion may be small, given that 88% of the second-year student participants in study 1 and 85% of the first-year student participants in study 3 who had undertaken mandatory high school service had also been involved in other community service (as noted previously in the Findings section).

However, study 2 also found that the students who probably would not have volunteered while they were in high school if they were not required to – i.e., the students for whom the high school program was most intended – were no more likely to volunteer post-high school than students who did no volunteering whatsoever in high school. Thus, the current Ontario program may not be effective at all with its key target population. Study 2's additional finding that qualitative aspects of the service placement – especially the enjoyment factor – are important predictors of future volunteering points to a likely reason for this ineffectiveness: the Ontario program is very weakly structured and does little to facilitate student placements that are suitable and satisfying. This supports earlier research on the subject (Padanyi, Meinhard, & Foster 2003).

Suggestions for specific types of structural improvements arise from all three studies. The pathways uncovered in study 1 suggest that the program should exploit Dewey's principle of continuity, encouraging students to build on their variety of volunteering/community service experiences. That this is not occurring with the existing program is suggested by the fact that only 13 of the 175 students who had volunteering experiences beyond mandatory service felt that personal impacts occurred at more than one educational level. The Ontario program needs to acknowledge that many students enter high school with prior community service experience. For these students, a high school community service program could help them better grasp: (a) the importance of what they have done to date and (b) how they can build on their previous experiences both to do more good for the community and to enhance their own personal growth and development. This would require integrating the program more formally into the curriculum, perhaps through required courses and/or by encouraging publishers to correct the current under-representation of the social economy in business and economics textbooks (as found in chapter 7, Schugurensky and McCollum). Students cannot be expected to figure this out for themselves as the current program expects them to do.

Study 2 revealed that volunteering, by itself, is not an effective means of mobilizing young people to become more active and engaged citizens. In the medium term at least, the high school community service experience will have an impact only if it is a satisfying and enjoyable experience for the student and/or it involves a relatively broad exposure to the voluntary sector. Since only 22 of study 1's 180 student respondents claimed that their mandated service had affected them personally either negatively or positively, it is apparent that high schools and their boards *must* become involved with helping students find suitable and satisfying placements.

However, study 3 reminds us that all students cannot be treated the same. In re-structuring the program, program designers must also recognize that there are key differences within the student population that must be taken into consideration in setting up both prior instruction and means to find and match students with appropriate placements.

The students who will benefit most from integrating the program more formally into the curriculum will likely be the 49% who do many more hours of volunteering beyond the 40-hour requirement (segment 3). They have such a strong pre-existing sense of civic responsibility and willingness to volunteer that lectures and discussion on the importance and value of community service will likely reinforce and strengthen their going-in attitudes towards community service. The same characteristics will help any placement assistance find good matches for them.

The students who may have the greatest potential to be changed by integrating the program more formally into the curriculum are the 36% who do a little more community service than the required 40 hours (segment 2). Although the current program appears to have little impact on them, i.e., they enter and exit the current high school program with a modest sense of civic responsibility, instruction may help build upon the sense of moral obligation towards others that they gained prior to high school. As well, since this group is not as proactive about find-ing service placements as the above group, they will also likely benefit from placement assistance, such as volunteer fairs and counselling ar-ranged and/or provided by high school administration.

The students who are least positively impacted by the current pro-gram and may not be very receptive to either instruction on community service or placement assistance at the high school level are the 15% of high school students who do only the required 40 hours (segment 1). The current mandatory program serves primarily to make them feel guilty and defensive about volunteering. Improving their sense of civic responsibility and willingness to participate in community serv-ice may require not only making the current program more structured and supportive, but also changing some aspect of their lives prior to high school. This may be accomplished, for example, by instituting an introduction to community service course in grade school rather than waiting until high school. Governments could also encourage more employers to require their employees to participate in volunteer activi-ties, possibly with their families.

These recommended changes in program structure should result in the mandatory program having far greater short- and long-term im-pacts on Ontario's student population. However, the impact of these changes may be further enhanced by better explaining and position-ing the program to students, their parents, high school administrations, and all of the others directly involved in its implementation.

Program Positioning

All three of the studies discussed in this chapter also point to the need to better educate students and other stakeholders about the goals and objectives of mandatory community service in high school. This might be best achieved by positioning the program as a form of community service-learning (CSL).Of the 22 students indicating a personal impact from their mandated community service, 20 described that impact in terms that can be readily associated with CSL. Examples of their com-ments are as follows:

REFLECTION EXAMPLE 1: (It is) hard to explain but it made me feel good inside that I was helping people. Like I was a part of a cause ... for something good.

This illustrates a recognition of the potential for reciprocity in a service experience, i.e., that there is a benefit both to the student ('made me feel good inside') and others ('helping others').

REFLECTION EXAMPLE 2: For community service, I helped in a soup kitchen and I was surprised how many people showed up. I didn't realize that ... that many people needed that service in my community. This had encouraged me to help out more now that I knew how much they needed it.

This illustrates the development of three responsible citizenship skills: (1) gaining awareness of the scope and magnitude of societal problems (' I didn't realize that ... that many people needed that service in my community') , (2) developing critical moral skills of compassion, patience, and true concern for others ('now that I knew how much they needed help') and (3) creating behavioural intention to continue to serve their communities ('This had encouraged me to help out more').

REFLECTION EXAMPLE 3: Volunteering has really helped me grow as a person. I developed a lot of skills and became more confident in myself through these experiences. I would never have seen myself doing some of the things I am had it not been for volunteering. Even how I volunteer has changed. I went from helping out to taking on leadership roles and running events.

This illustrates how much personal growth, such as skill development and increased self-esteem and self-efficacy, can occur from volunteering/community service.

REFLECTION EXAMPLE 4: (Volunteering/community service) taught me more than I learn in the classroom. Met amazing people and lifelong friends.

This speaks to the issue of academic enhancement through volunteering/community service.

Positioning the high school requirement as community service learning (CSL) will elevate the exercise in the minds of all stakeholders. CSL is a well-recognized pedagogical approach that allows students to work directly with community-based social purpose organizations such as nonprofits, service clubs, co-operatives, and government offices on projects or activities that these organizations need help with. It helps students better understand academic theories and how they are applied in the real world while increasing their personal sense of social responsibility and their civic-mindedness. CSL is an approach to education that has more obvious outcomes and more direct benefits for both students and the community organizations they work with than the current unstructured, mandated program in Ontario. Restructuring and repositioning this program based on the CSL model should result in increasing the program's impact well above its current level.

NOTES

1 Table 8.4 is the summary table for the regression of students' current volunteer activity level on aspects of their high school service experience with controls for other social background variables. Cell entries are unstandardized b coefficients with associated standard errors. Asterisks indicate the level of statistical significance associated with each coefficient.

REFERENCES

Ash, S., Clayton, P., & Moses, M. (2007, October). *Teaching and learning through critical reflection*. The Seventh International Research Conference on Service-Learning and Community Engagement, Tampa, Florida.

Avrahami, A., & Dar, Y. (1993). Collectivistic and individualistic motives among kibbutz youth volunteering for community service. *Journal of Youth and Adolescence, 22*(6), 697–714.

Barber, B.R. (1992). *An aristocracy of everyone*. New York: Ballantine.

Batson, C.D., Jasnoski, M.L., & Hanson, M. (1978). Buying kindness: Effect of an extrinsic incentive for helping on perceived altruism. *Personality and Social Psychology Bulletin, 4*(1), 86–91.

Brown, S.D., Meinhard, A., Ellis-Hale, K., Henderson, A., & Foster, M. (2007). *Community service and service learning in Canada: A profile of programming across the country*. Report prepared for the Knowledge Development Centre, Imagine Canada.

Brown, S.D., Pancer, S.M., Henderson, A., & Ellis-Hale, K. (2007). *The impact of high school mandatory community service programs on subsequent volunteering*

Table 8.4
Regression of current volunteer activity on high school community service variables, and socio-demographic background variables.

Independent Variables	Index of Current Volunteer Activity (range 0–21)	
	b coefficient	Std Error of b
(Constant)	.347	.493
Female (0 – 1, 1=female)	.158	.239
Attend Religious Services (0 – 1, 1 = once a week)	1.938***	.357
Active in High School (0 – 1, 1 = heavily)	1.075***	.278
Family Income (0 – 1, 1 = $150,000+)	–.715*	.335
Mother's Community Involvement (0 – 1, 1 = high)	1.94**	.622
Father's Community Involvement (0 – 1, 1 = high)	1.678**	.626
Any HS Service (0 – 1, 0 = no,1 = yes)	–.121	.330
HS Service Quality Index (0, 1, 1 = most positive)	2.022***	.567
Sustained Service (0 – 1, 0 = no, 1 = at least a year)	–.003	.245
Non-Mandated-Mandated Cohort (0–1, 1 = mandated)	.005	.205
Adjusted R^2 for Regression Equation	.220***	

*p < .05   **p < .01   ***p < .001

and civic engagement. Laurier Institute for the Study of Public Opinion and Policy (LISPOP) Working Paper Series.

Chapman, B. (2002). A bad idea whose time is past: The cases against universal service. Brookings Review, 20, 10–13.

Dewey, J. (1938). Experience and education. The Kappa Delta Pi Lecture Series. New York: Macmillan Publishing Company.

Febbraro, A. (2001). Encouraging volunteering among Ontario youth. Toronto: Canadian Centre for Philanthropy.

Fendrich, J.M. (1993). Ideal citizens: The legacy of the civil rights movement. Albany: State University of New York Press.

Giles, D.E., Jr., & Eyler, J. (1994). The impact of a college community service laboratory on students' personal, social and cognitive outcomes. Journal of Adolescence, 17(4), 327–39

Godfrey, P. (1999). Service-learning and management education: A call to action. Journal of Management Inquiry, 8(4), 363–78.

Hanks, M., & Eckland, K.B. (1978). Adult voluntary associations and adolescent socialization. Sociological Quarterly, 19(3), 481–90.

Hart, D., Donnelly, T.M., Youniss, J., & Atkins, R. (2007). High school community service as a predictor of adult voting and volunteering. *American Educational Research Journal, 44* (1), 197–219.

Henderson, A., Brown, S.D., Pancer, S.M., & Ellis-Hale, K. (2007). Mandated community service in high school and subsequent civic engagement: The case of the 'Double Cohort' in Ontario, Canada. *Journal of Youth and Adolescence, 36*(7), 849–60.

Jennings, M.K. (2002). Generational units and student protest movements in the United States: An intra- and inter-generational analysis. *Political Psychology, 23*(2), 303–24.

Kendall, J.C. (Ed.). (1990). *Combining service and learning: A resource book for community and public service (Vol.1).* Raleigh, NC: National Society for Internships and Experiential Education.

Kunda, Z., & Schwartz, S. (1983). Undermining intrinsic moral motivation: External reward and self-presentation. *Journal of Personality and Social Psychology, 45*(4), 763–71.

McCarthy, A.M., & Tucker, M.L. (1999). Student attitudes toward service learning: Implications for implementation. *Journal of Management Education, 23*(5), 554–73.

McCarthy, A.M., & Tucker, M.L. (2002). Encouraging community service through service learning. *Journal of Management Education, 26*(6), 629–47.

Meinhard, A., Brown, S.D., Ellis-Hale, K., Foster, M., & Henderson, A. (2007). Best practices in school community service programs: Evidence from Canada and abroad. Knowledge Development Centre, Imagine Canada.

Ontario Ministry of Education. (2009) *Ontario secondary school diploma requirement: Community involvement activities in English-language schools.* Policy/ Program Memorandum No. 124a. Ontario Ministry of Education. Retrieved December 8, 2009, from http://www.edu.gov.on.ca/extra/eng/ppm/124a .html

Padanyi, P., Meinhard, A., & Foster, M. (2003, November). *A study of a required youth service program that lacks structure: Do students really benefit?* 32nd Annual ARNOVA (Association of Research on Nonprofit Organizations and Voluntary Action) Conference, Denver, Colorado.

Planty, M., Bozick, R., & Regnier, M. (2006). Helping because you have to or helping because you want to: Sustaining participation in service work from adolescence through young adulthood. *Youth and Society, 38*(2), 177–202.

Schachter, H.L. (1998). Civic education: Three early political science association committees and their relevance for our times. *PS-Political Science and Politics, 31*(3), 631–5.

Sobus, M.S. (1995). Mandating community service: Psychological implications of requiring pro-social behaviour. *Law and Psychology Review, 19*, 153–82.

Stukas, A., Snyder, M., and Clary, G. (1999). The effects of mandatory volunteerism on intentions to volunteer. *Psychological Science, 10* (1), 59–64.

9 Strategic Partnerships: Community Climate Change Partners and Resilience to Funding Cuts

TRAVIS GLIEDT, PAUL PARKER, AND JENNIFER LYNES

Nonprofit environmental service organizations create and deliver services designed to improve environmental performance and to mitigate climate change through increased water efficiency, better waste management, and reduced greenhouse gas emissions. These green community organizations embody the four criteria that capture the 'social' dimension of the social economy identified in chapter 1: they are motivated by the social and environmental objectives in their mission statements (Green Community Canada, 2008); they utilize volunteer labour; they initiate and facilitate civic engagement; and their structure represents a form of social ownership (e.g., nonprofit). Like many social economy organizations, environmental service organizations face unstable funding environments, making their capacity to adapt to sudden changes in funding a critical challenge. Some organizations are vulnerable and their continued operation is put in doubt when a major funding source is lost. Others adapt and diversify. What accounts for these differences in the capacity to change?

In 2006, dozens of environmental service organizations faced a crisis when the Canadian federal government suddenly cancelled their major funding source, the EnerGuide for Houses program (Gliedt & Parker, 2007; Parker & Rowlands, 2007). In response, environmental service organizations diversified services and funding sources, and relied on partnerships with municipal governments and for-profit utility companies to survive. Using the framework presented by Mook, Quarter, and Ryan in chapter 1, these organizations shifted from being public sector nonprofits that entered into a partnership with government to deliver a service and became a form of community economic development with more diversified forms of funding. Employing a case study approach, this chapter examines the strategic partnerships of one successful southern Ontario organization (ESO) to understand how they facilitate the creativity and flexibility necessary to drive innovation and enhance organizational resilience.

This study follows the conception and definition of the social economy described in chapter 1 of this book; namely, that the social economy contains organizations driven by social (and environmental) objectives that can 'produce and market services' and 'generate market value' (p. 3). As social economy organizations often rely upon partners for funding and other resource exchanges, organizational stability is dependent on the priorities and continued operation of external public, private, and social economy partnership organizations. Therefore, it is important to examine whether resilience is affected by changes in the mix of primary funding partners used by the ESO.

This chapter concludes that the ESO used *crisis partnerships* to overcome immediate shocks, *stability partnerships* to facilitate long-term operations, and *green community entrepreneurship* to innovate in order to diversify funding sources. The combination of the two forms of partnership, the entrepreneurship process, and the timing of their use enhanced organizational resilience in the face of funding uncertainty.

The following sections examine climate change mitigation partnerships, define the forms of partnership found in the social economy and in the case study, describe the features of partnerships that enable change, and review the concept of organizational resilience. A brief description of the methodology and results will be followed by a concluding section that summarizes the case study and its implications for the social economy.

Local Climate Change Partnerships

According to Backstrand (2006), 'partnerships are innovative forms of governance that can pool together diverse expertise and resources from civil society, government and business sectors' (p. 303). Many local partnerships are characterized by 'a high level of commitment, mutual trust, equal ownership, and the achievement of a common goal' (Stern & Green, 2005, p. 270). Local climate change partnerships help integrate mitigation objectives into sustainable development planning in order to enhance local capacity for action (Bizikova, Robinson, & Cohen, 2007). Partnerships also play an important role in local climate change and energy policy-making and implementation (Bulkeley & Betsill, 2005;

Bulkeley & Moser, 2007; Environmental Protection Agency, 2008; Fleming & Webber, 2004; International Council for Local Environmental Initiatives, 2007, 2008; Karlsson, 2007; Kellett, 2007; Lindseth, 2004; Moss, 2008; Natural Resources Canada, 2007a, 2007b; Robinson et al., 2006).

Climate change mitigation partnerships involve relationships between different stakeholders across multiple scales. This includes public-public partnerships between different levels of government (Mason, 2007; Orans, Price, Williams, Woo, & Moore, 2007), and public-private partnerships between governments and corporations. For example, the Federation of Canadian Municipalities, which provides grants through the Green Municipal Fund for sustainable community planning, brownfield redevelopment, energy services, renewable energy development, and sustainable transportation (Federation of Canadian Municipalities, 2008a, 2008b), favours cities that create partnerships with the private sector because such partnerships can 'leverage greater sources of capital for joint projects' (Hilton, 2007, p. 107). While public-public and public-private partnerships are important to local climate change mitigation, the current case study focuses on partnerships between a social economy organization and partners in the public and private sectors. Therefore, private–social economy, public–social economy, and partnerships connecting all three sectors are now reviewed.

Private–social economy partnerships designed to meet environmental objectives are viewed favourably by for-profit organizations that recognize the benefits of building resource exchange relationships with environmental service organizations (Cook & Barclay, 2002; Hartman & Stafford, 1997; Kumar & Malegeant, 2006; Rondinelli & Berry, 2000; Rondinelli & London, 2003). Glasbergen and Groenenberg (2001) describe two case studies of private–social economy partnerships designed to reduce greenhouse gas emissions. The first involves a partnership for the development and diffusion of solar collectors in the Netherlands between a nonprofit (Greenpeace), a for-profit installer of the technology (Stork Infra Techniek), a for-profit financial institution to provide 'green' financing (Rabobank), and a for-profit energy consulting firm (Ecofys). This partnership led to the sale and delivery of 3,000 systems, far less than the target of 20,000. Glasbergen and Groenenberg argue that the decision by Greenpeace to lend its logo and support to other solar collector firms in direct competition with Stork Infra Techniek, despite signing a partnership agreement, reduced the likelihood for success of this partnership. This case highlights the potential conflict between a nonprofit organization's desire to achieve an environmental objective and its responsibilities to partners that operate in the competitive economy.

The second case involves the World Wildlife Fund partnering with private sector builders. The goal was to develop energy efficient building projects to demonstrate their construction with minimal additional cost. This partnership was successful, leading to the development of five subdivisions of energy efficient houses as per the original agreement. World Wildlife Fund carried out its part of the agreement by lending its name and logo, and handling public relations for the five projects.

In both cases, the contribution of the nonprofit environmental organization to the partnership was mostly symbolic, lending names and logos, and providing public relations services (Glasbergen & Groenenberg, 2001). This is in contrast to the ESO under examination here, which partnered with external organizations initially to increase participation rates in its core program, a residential energy rating service, and then to facilitate entrepreneurship and innovation. This ESO used resources mobilized through partnerships to create new services and programs that they then delivered for a fee.

Public–social economy partnerships are commonly used to tackle climate change at the local level. Walker, Hunter, Devine-Wright, Evans, and Fay (2007) and Mander (2007) discovered that federal funding policy objectives for renewable energy development were linked to community partnerships in order to create joint ownership of green energy in the UK. A community-based approach was used to overcome local opposition to wind farms while incorporating citizens into the decision-making process. Conversely, this approach was viewed by the community as a way to achieve social and economic benefits while contributing to sustainable energy development (Mander, 2007).

Multi-sector, multi-scale partnerships are used by local governments to develop community energy plans to reduce emissions (Environmental Protection Agency, 2008; Fleming & Webber, 2004; Natural Resources Canada, 2007a, 2007b). Many Cities for Climate Protection participants, including climate change mitigation leaders like Portland, Oregon (International council for Local Environmental Initiatives, 2006), credited successful climate change action to 'partnerships with state, provincial, and national governments, as well as with private financial institutions' that enabled the mobilization of key financial resources (Lindseth, 2004, p. 330). Holgate (2007) found that multi-sector partnerships including environmental nonprofit organizations, coupled with an energy supply crisis, helped Cape Town, South Africa successfully implement climate change mitigation policies. In contrast, Johannesburg lacked strong partnerships and did not experience an energy crisis, and has been unsuccessful at achieving climate change objectives.

Environmental service organizations are also using multi-sector, multi-scale partnerships to create solutions to climate change (Gliedt & Parker, 2007). The Community Environmental Council, a nonprofit environmental organization in California, used formal relationships with for-profit and public partners to create a plan to eliminate Santa Barbara County's use of fossil fuels. The plan involves conservation, efficiency, and renewable energy development and deployment, and is designed to help mitigate climate change while reducing dependence on oil. Community Environmental Council also uses partnerships to create and deliver services including a green business program, and to influence changes in local government policies to improve the efficiency of new and existing homes (Community Environmental Council, 2007; Hunt, 2008).

This section has highlighted an international pattern of local partnerships for climate change programs. These studies provide insight into the motivations for creating partnerships (e.g., mobilize and exchange resources, engage citizens, achieve social, economic, and environmental benefits), as well as their outputs (e.g., policies, plans, services, programs) and outcomes (e.g., greenhouse gas emissions reduced, jobs created). The next section will construct a definition of partnerships based on a set of criteria established from the literature.

Partnerships in the Social Economy

Partnerships can be categorized as strategic, operational, or collaborative. Based on Lasker and Weiss (2003), Boydell and Rugkasa (2007) define strategic partnerships as broad 'multi-issue' relationships with 'agenda-setting capacity.' Boydell and Rugkasa contrast strategic partnerships with operational partnerships, the latter representing 'a more focused and local remit to deliver projects to address specific problems' (p. 219). Collaborative partnerships are 'those in which each partner exercises power in the decision-making process' (Mason, 2007, p. 2366). Therefore, a broad multi-issue partnership where each partner has decision-making authority represents a *collaborative-strategic partnership*, while a narrow single-issue partnership with shared decision-making authority is a *collaborative-operational partnership*. If the ESO does not possess significant decision-making authority, the partnership is termed *weak-strategic* or *weak-operational*.

Partnerships can also be classified based on partnership relations and forms of control. Polson (2008, p. 52) categorizes relationships based on the degree of independence maintained by each organization, the extent that organizational boundaries remain distinct, the level of interaction between the organizations, and which organization initiated the relationship. Gazley (2008) subdivides partnerships involving nonprofit organizations based on the form of control in the relationship: (1) presence of a formal (signed) agreement, (2) funding dependence, and (3) the source of decision-making authority (nonprofit, government, private, or shared). If partnerships have formal agreements, success may depend on whether the nonprofit partner upholds the conditions of the agreement (Glasbergen & Groenenberg, 2001). In partnerships without formal agreements, Gazley (2008) found that the government partner can maintain control through funding arrangements, cultural conventions, the desire to achieve a common objective, and trust factors.

To this point we have identified the motivations, outputs, outcomes, relations, and forms of control within partnerships. While these factors are important to classifying partnerships, Boydell and Rugkasa (2007) recommend investigating 'the ways in which partnerships create the conditions that make change possible' (p. 225). The following section will examine the components of successful partnerships that encourage change.

Partnerships and the Conditions for Change

A number of attributes of successful partnerships have been identified. They include the ability to generate connections with other partners, leverage access to information and expertise, and build relationships that accelerate the implementation of new programs and services (Boydell & Rugkasa, 2007). Open and active communication among all partners, support and participation from government, effective framing and selling of the benefits of participating in the partnership, and the length of partnership existence also increase the chances that partnerships will successfully facilitate change (Schweitzer & Ogle-Graham, 2005). Successful partnerships between churches and other social economy organizations demonstrate strong social bonds, 'frequent interaction and communication,' and 'shared responsibility' for the success of services (Polson, 2008).

In addition to the aforementioned commonly cited characteristics, successful partnerships are founded on the basis of 'complementary resources' that each partner organization needs to achieve a strategic objective (Rondinelli & London, 2003). Gazley and Brudney (2007) conclude that 'governments principally appear to offer their non-profit partner financial resources, whereas non-profit organizations offer specialized expertise beyond the scope of government' (p. 399). This is supported by Keiner and Kim's (2008) finding that partnerships 'are structured to take advantage of the fact that each participating entity brings different aspects to the fore' (p. 195).

Partnership development and success may depend on the ability of individual champions to overcome institutional barriers (Cheadle et al., 2008; Schweitzer & Ogle-Graham, 2005). Additionally, individuals called 'boundary people' (Stern & Green, 2005) may help prevent a reduction in nonprofit organizational independence, a weakening of its ability to advocate on behalf of citizens, and a compromising of its social objectives; limitations of public-social economy partnerships identified by Salamon (1995). Boundary people work at the margins of the partnership to achieve a common goal while maintaining allegiance to the values and objectives of their parent organization (Stern & Green, 2005).

This section has identified a number of factors which help partnerships facilitate change: complementary resources, open communication, access to information and expertise, length of partnership, shared decision-making power, shared responsibility for the success of services, and individual champions and boundary people. The partnerships in this case study are analysed to determine if they contain the necessary ingredients to facilitate and drive change. Equally important is the role partnerships play in allowing the ESO to adapt to change in order to survive. Therefore, the following section examines whether partnerships can enhance organizational resilience to future shocks.

Organizational Resilience through Partnerships

Based on an extensive literature review of physical, ecological, social, community, and individual resilience studies, Norris, Stevens, Phefferbaum, Wyche, and Phefferbaum (2008) conclude that resilience generally refers to 'an ability or process' rather than 'an outcome,' and should be viewed as 'adaptability' rather than 'stability.' They define community resilience as 'a process linking a set of networked adaptive capacities to a positive trajectory of functioning and adaptation in constituent populations after a disturbance' (p. 131). Therefore, resilience in our study is measured by the ability of the ESO to adapt to, rather than resist, change. Resilience would be demonstrated by a recovery to a state of operations which can be considered 'healthy' based on a given set of criteria, rather than a return to the pre-shock state (Norris et al., 2008).

Relationships, partnerships, and social capital can increase organizational resilience to shocks. Gittell (2008) found that relationship networks helped a collection of healthcare organizations in the U.S. enhance organizational resilience to an external threat. Organizational resilience is therefore fostered by 'institutionalized memory,' the stocks and flows of human and social capital (Andersen, 2008) that exist in and between environmental service organizations. King (2008) broadens this conception to the community scale by suggesting that agricultural-ecological systems enhance local resilience through the use of relationships, participation, mobilization of resources, and knowledge dissemination.

Homer-Dixon (2007) and Norris et al. (2008) argue that the most effective means of enhancing resilience may be partnerships that are 'loosely coupled' (rather than 'tightly coupled') in order to 'respond to local needs' and 'facilitate access to resources' (Norris et al., 2008). This is similar to Granovetter's (1983) 'weak ties' argument, and Hauser, Tappeiner, and Walde's (2007) finding that loosely coupled relationships can positively influence innovation. Relationships which are too tightly coupled, however, 'can lead to premature convergence on solutions' (Norris et al., 2008, p. 138) and unnecessary complexity that could make the community more vulnerable to systemic collapse (Homer-Dixon, 2007).

Norris et al. (2008) define four 'resilience resources' as social capital, information and communication, community competence, and economic development. Based on Bruneau et al.'s (2003) properties of resilient systems, Norris et al. argue that these resources must be 'robust' (strong and unlikely to disappear), 'rapidly deployable/accessible,' and 'redundant' (having a degree of 'substitutability') in order to promote resilience. Therefore, the partnerships in our case study will be examined to determine if they meet the criteria for resilience resources. The following methodology was employed to test the hypothesis that partnerships contribute to the resilience of the ESO.

Methodology

Semi-structured interviews with the executive directors of 12 Canadian environmental service organizations connected by a national network were used to identify responses to the EnerGuide for Houses cancellation. Environmental service organizations responded by creating new services and programs through green community entrepreneurship, and strategic partnerships were identified as a key facilitating factor in this process (Gliedt & Parker, 2007). An intensive case study was then used in this chapter to examine whether partnerships contribute to organizational resilience. Zahran, Grover, Brody, and Vedlitz's (2008) suggestion for the use of intensive case study tools when examining local organizations developing climate change programs was applied to one successful environmental service organization (ESO) in Southern Ontario. A three-hour in-person interview with the executive director of the ESO was combined with a detailed analysis of internal budgets and strategic plans from 2004–8, as well as external documents published by the ESO.

Results

The ESO drew upon established partnerships with local electric and natural gas utility companies by reaching out for funding and resource support to replace the federal funding that had been cancelled with one day's notice (Parker & Rowlands, 2007). In return, the ESO provided its credibility as an established environmental leadership organization to the for-profit utilities for use in their demand management programs. The ESO also supplied a marketing service by mentioning the 'partner support' to citizens during residential energy efficiency evaluations. This exchange of complementary resources strengthened the relationships between the ESO and the local partners. The scale of the local partnerships increased rapidly as the utility companies provided a large amount of funding, demonstrating their support for the continued operation of the ESO. This local funding allowed the organization to retain staff, and supported the development of many new services that they continue to offer two years after the funding shock (e.g., solar energy evaluations, Greening Sacred Spaces, Well Aware).

The local utility companies played a critical role after the federal government's cancellation of the ESO's primary funding program. The utilities had partnered with the ESO as secondary funders over the previous seven years. They stepped in and replaced the federal funding to help keep the cost of the residential energy efficiency evaluations low enough to maintain community demand for the service. These partnerships represented 'longstanding relationships' because the utilities

consistently funded the ESO for seven years, while managers from the
utilities acted as 'boundary people' by sitting on the advisory board of
the organization. The municipal council also played an important role
in supporting the ESO by passing resolutions and pressuring the federal government to reinstate the EnerGuide for Houses Program (Parker
& Rowlands, 2007).

These established local partnerships acted as social, knowledge, and
financial capital exchange channels to quickly funnel resources between
organizations. This discovery is supported by Rottman's (2008) conclusion that the network of relationships between an organization and
its partners represents a 'social capital resource' which has 'an exploit-
able value' in addition to financial and knowledge resources which are
exchanged. Mu, Peng, and Love's (2008) finding that 'reciprocal trust
enables knowledge to flow efficiently from one partner to another,
(while) greater trust significantly increases the flow of knowledge'
(p. 95) supports our argument that established relationships built on
mutual trust can be drawn upon quickly to transfer the three forms of
capital resources. Polson (2008) agrees, arguing that partnerships 'create institutionalized avenues that allow congregations to more easily
invest the human, social, and financial capital that they have into local
social service efforts' (p. 59). Local 'crisis' partnerships were adaptive
and quick to react to help overcome an unforeseen shock.

While local partners kept the ESO operating until the federal government brought back a modified version of EnerGuide for Houses called
the ecoENERGY program (ecoENERGY, 2008), an additional partnership was required as demand for the ecoENERGY service was below
EnerGuide for Houses levels. As the executive director explains, the 'initial response to the federal grants for ecoENERGY was lukewarm, with
some customers saying that the amount of the grant was not worth the
cost of the evaluation' (personal communication, June 17, 2008). Under
the previous program, the federal government had reduced the cost of
the evaluations by purchasing the residential data files for $120-$150.
This purchase agreement made evaluations more affordable to citizens
($100-$200). The ecoENERGY program did not include the payment for
files, but still required their delivery to the federal government. The
result was a higher cost to clients, typically $250-$350 per evaluation.
However, a new partnership between the ESO, its parent organization
Green Communities Canada, and the province of Ontario provided the
missing incentive to drive demand for the residential energy efficiency
service. According to the executive director, 'when the province an-

Table 9.1
Total number of initial and follow-up evaluations conducted by the ESO annually

Year	Pre-EGH[a] Cut 2004	EGH Cut 2005	ecoENERGY 2006	ecoENERGY+ 2007	Province 2008
Initial	1,162	1,025	636	901	1,724
Follow-up	431	402	658	334	677
Total	1,593	1,427	1,294	1,235	2,401

[a]EGH: EnerGuide for Houses

nounced it would match the grants and cover half the cost of the initial evaluation to a max of $150, demand shot through the roof and is still going strong' (personal communication, June 17, 2008). Therefore, the new provincial partnership helped scale up the residential energy efficiency service to a level which exceeded the previous peak EnerGuide for Houses demand. Table 9.1 displays the total number of evaluations conducted by the ESO annually for the years prior to the EnerGuide for Houses cancellation (2004, 2005); the year the program was cut (2006); the year the new federal government introduced the ecoENERGY program as a modified version of EnerGuide for Houses (2007); and the following year in which the provincial government began matching and thus doubling the size of grants to homeowners (2008). This table highlights the rapid increase in demand for initial evaluations in 2008 compared to previous years.

Table 9.2 highlights the drastic change in funding partners and amounts between 2004 and 2008. Several factors caused the changes. In 2004, the federal government's purchase of EnerGuide for Houses files accounted for nearly half of the organization's revenue. Much of the rest of the revenue (client fees and some local partner contributions) was dependent upon delivery of the same service. In 2005, local utilities partnered with the ESO to deliver some demand side management programs as part of province-wide initiatives to conserve electricity. In 2006, the federal government cut core program funding partway through the year and local partners stepped in to enable local residents to still receive the service. The overall result was a 10% decline in total revenue for the year instead of the potential loss of most revenue. The year 2008 saw the provincial government become a direct funder of residential energy evaluations and well inspections. Federal funds were

Table 9.2
Revenue by source (percent)

	2004	2005	2006	2007	2008
Client fees	30	21	14	35	70
Federal	47	34	18	5	1
Provincial	–	–	5	24	5
Local	23	45	63	36	24
Total (%)	100	100	100	100	100
Total ($000)	449	628	564	613	904

still received from Human Resources and Skill Development Canada, but at a dramatically reduced level from 2004. The relative funding contributions from the provincial and federal governments were reversed from 2006 to 2007. In 2007, the ESO had a balanced mix of funding with approximately one-third of funding coming from client fees, upper-level government, and local partners, respectively. This diversity of funding partnerships has enabled the organization to successfully respond to changes in core funding and to add new services. Total revenue in 2007 returned to 2005 levels, while further growth in 2008 led to total revenues exceeding the previous high-water mark of 2005 by nearly a third.

Finally, the percentage of revenue from client fees rendered for services delivered by the ESO more than tripled from 2005 to 2008, reflecting the loss of federal funding and a shift towards a more entrepreneurial approach. This 'green community entrepreneurship' was facilitated by partnerships as discussed by Gliedt and Parker (2007). Green community entrepreneurship is the 'collective ability to mobilize resources, including social capital, to provide products or services that achieve environmental rather than profit maximizing goals' (Gliedt & Parker, 2007, p. 543). This process allowed the case study organization to survive a major funding shock by creating new energy services to meet immediate citizen needs for affordable energy and climate change mitigation. As the executive director explains, local partners delivered timely financial capital resources which provided the organizational stability necessary for creative thinking. The stability created by the partnership resources allowed the ESO to free-up and draw upon its existing human capital resources to develop new services. In addition to partnerships and human capital, social capital networks connecting this ESO to other environmental service organizations across Canada

Figure 9.1. Green community entrepreneurship

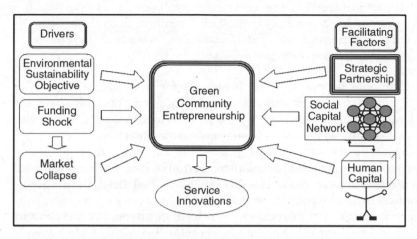

Source: Based on Gliedt and Parker, 2007

helped facilitate green community entrepreneurship through the sharing of knowledge and expertise (figure 9.1).

Local crisis partnerships helped facilitate green community entrepreneurship. The executive director accentuates this point by describing
one new service created by the ESO as a House for Sustainable Living.
The objective is to promote deeper energy retrofits. The standard measures taken by customers after an energy evaluation achieve a 25–30%
reduction in energy use; however, much greater savings are possible.
The ESO approached the regional government to enter a new partnership. The region agreed and provided two small side-by-side 1,200
square foot century old houses in the downtown core.

The first house will demonstrate a set of retrofits that reduce energy
consumption and costs by 50% with a budget of $30,000. This '30/50
House' highlights what can be achieved with targeted retrofits on
a budget that many century home owners invest in their property. In
this case, the house will be returned for use as regional housing and
its energy performance monitored. The second house will be retro-
fitted with insulation, weather stripping, solar photovoltaic panels,
solar water heating, an air-to-air heat pump, an urban wind turbine, environmentally friendly products and materials, and energy and water
saving landscaping techniques. As the executive director explains:

the House for Sustainable Living will be open to the public for tours and workshops, and will be a net-zero energy house, and Leadership in Energy and Environmental Design (LEED) certified. So one is the 'accessible to most people house', and the other is the 'house of the near future.' (personal communication, June 17, 2008)

Additional proposals were developed for new partnerships with local groups to design and deliver education programs. In 2009, the federal government decided to become a partner in the House for Sustainable Living as part of its Community Adjustment Fund.

To classify the partnerships in this study, findings from the literature were combined with an adapted version of Polson's typology. Each partnership was analysed based on the identified criteria and categorized as *crisis* or *stability* (table 9.3).

The ESO initiated discussions with local partners after the funding shock in an attempt to expand existing relationships. The ESO quickly became dependent on these partners, and communications increased in frequency after the EnerGuide for Houses cancellation. *Crisis partnerships* with utilities and local governments are characterized by shared decision-making and a broad focus on many objectives (e.g., reduce greenhouse gas emissions, energy demand, and cost of energy, install compact fluorescent light bulbs, sit on board of directors, exchange research data) and services (e.g., energy efficiency, renewable energy, conservation, education, and demonstration house). Crisis partners were concerned with the day-to-day operations of the ESO in addition to the delivery of specific services. Therefore, local governments and for-profit utilities formed collaborative-strategic partnerships with the ESO. In contrast, nonprofit organizations formed collaborative-operational partnerships with the ESO because of a shared decision-making authority but a narrow focus on the delivery of individual services (e.g., energy efficiency evaluations of churches).

Stability partnerships displayed a lower level of interaction, which occurred indirectly via Green Communities Canada. The government initiated stability partnerships and was the dominant decision-making authority in the relationship. Prior to the EnerGuide for Houses cancellation, the ESO was highly dependent on the federal government. However, a new partnership with the province reduced the level of ESO dependence on individual stability partners. Federal stability partnerships are focused on single programs (e.g., ecoENERGY) rather than broadly supporting the ESO's daily operations. Because of the federal

Table 9.3
Categorization of partnerships in case study

	Vertical Stability Partnerships			Horizontal Local Crisis Partnerships		
Criteria	Fed. Govt. EnerGuide	Fed. Govt. ecoENERGY	Prov. Govt. ecoENERGY	Nonprofit	Local Govt.	For-Profit Utility Companies
Partnership Relations						
Distinct boundaries?	Yes	Yes	Yes	Yes	Yes	Yes
Level of interaction between organizations	Medium indirect interaction via GCC	Medium indirect interaction via GCC	Medium indirect interaction via GCC	Medium	High after EGH[a] cut; medium currently	High after EGH cut; medium currently
Which partner initiated relationship?	Gov.	Gov.	Gov.	ESO	ESO	ESO
Forms of Control						
Formal (signed) agreement	Yes	Yes	Yes	Yes	Yes	Yes
How dependent is the ESO on the partner?	High	Medium	Medium	Low	High after EGH cut; low currently	High after EGH cut; low currently
Partnership Category	weak-operational	weak-operational	weak-strategic	collaborative-operational	collaborative-strategic	collaborative-strategic

[a]EGH: EnerGuide for Houses

partner's dominant decision-making authority and the narrow focus on one program, federal stability partnerships are weak-operational. While the provincial stability partner also has control of decision-making, the province supports more than one program delivered by the ESO (e.g., ecoENERGY, Well Aware, Energy Efficiency Assistance for Houses). Therefore, the provincial partnership is termed weak-strategic.

Partnerships, Entrepreneurship, and Organizational Resilience

Two processes of change occurring in the ESO are similar to Jones's (2006) theory of evolutionary entrepreneurship. The first is analogous to 'strategic determination' as discussed by Andersen (2008), where partnerships mobilize human and social capital (institutionalized memory) to 'release creativity' necessary to generate 'incremental and inconspicuous' innovations. This is a continuous process that fluctuates in intensity depending on the resource support from *stability partnerships*. The second takes the form of emergency entrepreneurship (Johannisson & Olaison, 2007), where new services and programs emerge in response to a sudden external shock through the timely support of *crisis partnerships*. The combination of stability and crisis partnerships is comparable to Capello and Faggian's (2005) 'relational space,' a landscape which leads to innovation and the collective achievement of social and environmental objectives in the local community.

The ESO used partnerships and entrepreneurship to overcome the traditional market dilemmas that limit many communities to taking only climate change actions that are economic in the short-term. Diversification through partnership and entrepreneurship improves organizational resilience to ensure continued delivery of climate change and energy management services to the community. Collaboration between sectors may lead to multi-sector governance structures that increase the collective capacity to survive and adapt to fiscal and climate changes, while providing the resilience necessary for the development of sustainable energy systems. This conclusion is supported by three emerging trends in local climate change policy identified by Bulkeley and Moser (2007):

- A shift in the roles of government and non-state actors where 'state actors take on roles of promotion, facilitation, encouragement and advocacy long associated with civil society actors, while actors from outside the state are becoming responsible for the development of policy goals and their regulation' (p. 2),

- A shift towards multi-scale, multi-sector climate change policy-making that uses 'different forms of influence, regulation, and sanction' (p. 5), and
- A shift in how climate change is framed and debated in the policy process, as 'the mobilization of different actors requires finding common languages, and common visions of what is to be achieved ... for example, linking climate to sustainability, or climate and social justice' (p. 9).

These trends suggest a growing integration between the social economy, for-profit business, and local government sectors in creating and implementing climate change programs. They also imply a more prominent role for social economy organizations in defining problems and influencing policies.

Conclusion

This chapter discussed three forms of partnership: private–social economy, public–social economy, and social economy–social economy. The case study revealed a general shift in the strength of partnerships, as measured by amount of funding dollars, over a five-year period which encompasses pre–funding shock, funding shock, and post–funding shock/adapted periods. The shift in dominant partners from public in the first period to private in the second, and then to a combination of public and private partners in the third, supports our hypothesis that some partnerships are critical during times of crisis (crisis partnerships) while others provide long-term stability but fluctuate in their degree of support due to political changes (stability partnerships).

Crisis partnerships are important to green community entrepreneurship, the process of creating new environmentally beneficial programs and services in the social economy, while stability partnerships are important for scaling-up new and existing services to reach an expanded market. We conclude that crisis partnerships can be characterized as 'resilience resources' because they were stable and enduring, quickly mobilized, and substituted for the federal funding withdrawal. Redundancy was enhanced by diversifying partnerships and funding sources, as well as the scope of services and programs offered by the

ESO. Diversification increases the resilience of the ESO to future shocks, as 'resilience depends not only on the volume of economic resources but also on their diversity' (Norris et al., 2008, p. 137). The coupling of crisis and stability partnerships with the process of entrepreneurship has enhanced organizational resilience to sudden changes in the funding environment.

REFERENCES

Andersen, O.J. (2008). A bottom-up perspective on innovations. Mobilizing knowledge and social capital through innovative processes of bricolage. *Administration & Society, 40*(1), 54–78.

Backstrand, K. (2006). Multi-stakeholder partnerships for sustainable development: Rethinking legitimacy, accountability and effectiveness. *European Environment, 16*(5), 290–306.

Bizikova, L., Robinson, J., & Cohen, S. (2007). Linking climate change and sustainable development at the local level. *Climate Policy, 7*(4), 271–7.

Boydell, L.R., & Rugkasa, J. (2007). Benefits of working in partnership: A model. *Critical Public Health, 17*(3), 217–28.

Bruneau, M., Chang, S., Eguchi, R., Lee, G., O'Rourke, T., Reinhorn, A., et al. (2003). A framework to quantitatively assess and enhance the seismic resilience of communities. *Earthquake Spectra, 19*(4), 733–52.

Bulkeley, H., & Betsill, M.M. (2005). Rethinking sustainable cities: Multilevel governance and the 'urban' politics of climate change. *Environmental Politics, 14*(1), 42–63.

Bulkeley, H., & Moser, S.C. (2007). Responding to climate change: Governance and social action beyond Kyoto. *Global Environmental Politics, 7*(2), 1–10.

Capello, R., & Faggian, A. (2005). Collective learning and relational capital in local innovation processes. *Regional Studies, 39*(1), 75–87.

Cheadle, A., Hsu, C., Schwartz, P.M., Pearson, D., Greenwald, H.P., Beery, W.L., et al. (2008). Improving local health departments in community health partnerships: Evaluation results from the Partnership for the Public's Health Initiative. *Journal of Urban Health: Bulletin of the New York Academy of Medicine, 85*(2), 162–77.

Community Environmental Council (2007). A new energy direction. A blueprint for Santa Barbara County. Bold local solutions to a global problem. Retrieved October 15, 2009, from http://www.cecsb.org/storage/communityenvironmentalcouncil/documents/completeblueprint.pdf

Cook, E., & Barclay, E. (2002). Sound climate, sound business. *Corporate Environmental Strategy, 9*(4), 338–44.

ecoENERGY. (2008). ecoENERGY Retrofit for Homes. ecoACTION Program. Government of Canada. Retrieved October 16, 2009, from http://www .ecoaction.gc.ca/ecoenergy-ecoenergie/retrofithomes-renovationmaisons-eng.cfm?ecoenergy_main

Environmental Protection Agency. (2008). Green Communities Program. Five step planning process. Retrieved October 16, 2009, from http://www.epa .gov/greenkit/index.htm

Federation of Canadian Municipalities. (2008a). Partners for Climate Protection. Retrieved October 16, 2009, from http://www.sustainablecommunities. fcm.ca/Partners-for-Climate-Protection/

Federation of Canadian Municipalities. (2008b). The Green Municipal Fund. Investing in Leadership, Inspiring Change. Federation of Canadian Municipalities. Retrieved October 16, 2009, from http://gmf.fcm.ca/_ pvw7ce56679/gmf/default.asp

Fleming, P.D., & Webber, P.H. (2004). Local and regional greenhouse gas management. *Energy Policy 32*(6), 761–71.

Gazley, B. (2008). Beyond the contract: The scope and nature of informal government-nonprofit partnerships. *Public Administration Review, 68*(1), 141–54.

Gazley, B., & Brudney, J.L. (2007). The purpose (and perils) of government-nonprofit partnership. *Nonprofit and Voluntary Sector Quarterly, 36*(3), 389–415.

Gittell, J.H. (2008). Relationships and resilience: Care provider responses to pressures from managed care. *The Journal of Applied Behavioural Science, 44*(1), 25–47.

Glasbergen, P., & Groenenberg, R. (2001). Environmental partnerships in sustainable energy. *European Environment 11*(1), 1–13.

Gliedt, T., & Parker, P. (2007). Green community entrepreneurship: Creative destruction in the social economy. *International Journal of Social Economics, 34*(8), 538–53.

Granovetter, M. (1983). The strength of weak ties: A network theory revisited. *Sociological Theory, 1*, 201–23.

Green Communities Canada. (2008). Mission and Values. Retrieved October 16, 2009, from http://www.gca.ca/indexcms/index.php?mission

Hartman, C., & Stafford, E. (1997). Green alliances: Building new business with environmental groups. *Long Range Planning, 30*(2), 184–96.

Hauser, C., Tappeiner, G., & Walde, J. (2007). The learning region: The impact of social capital and weak ties on innovation. *Regional Studies, 41*(1), 75–88.

Hilton, R. (2007). The path to local sustainable development: Two approaches. In G.B. Doern (Ed.), *Innovation, science, environment: Canadian policies and performance* (pp. 98–117). Montreal and Kingston: McGill-Queen's University Press.

Holgate, C. (2007). Factors and actors in climate change mitigation: A tale of two South African cities. *Local Environment, 12*(5), 471–84.

Homer-Dixon, T. (2007). *The upside of down: Catastrophe, creativity, and the renewal of civilization.* Toronto: Vintage Canada.

Hunt, T. (2008). Freedom from fossil fuel and nuclear power: The scope for local solutions in the United States. In P. Droege (Ed.), *Urban energy transition: From fossil fuels to renewable power* (pp. 619–30). New York: Elsevier.

International Council for Local Environmental Initiatives. (2006). Combating climate change: A comprehensive look at local climate protection programs. *International Council for Local Environmental Initiatives* (pp 1–32).

International Council for Local Environmental Initiatives. (2007). Progress Report. International Council for Local Environmental Initiatives. Cities for Climate Protection. Retrieved October 16, 2009, from http://www.iclei.org/documents/USA/documents/CCP/ICLEI-CCP_International_Report-2006.pdf

International Council for Local Environmental Initiatives. (2008). International Council for Local Environmental Initiatives. Cities for Climate Protection Campaign. Retrieved October 16, 2009, from http://www.iclei.org/index.php?id=800

Johannisson, B., & Olaison, L. (2007). The moment of truth – reconstructing entrepreneurship and social capital in the eye of the storm. *Review of Social Economy, 65*(1), 55–78.

Jones, C. (2006). Contemplating an evolutionary approach to entrepreneurship. *World Futures, 62*(8), 576–94.

Karlsson, S.I. (2007). Allocating responsibilities in multi-level governance for sustainable development. *International Journal of Social Economics, 34*(1, 2), 103–26.

Keiner, M., & Kim, A. (2008). City energy networking in Europe. In P. Droege (Ed.), *Urban energy transition: From fossil fuels to renewable power* (pp. 193–210). New York: Elsevier.

Kellett, J. (2007). Community-based energy policy: A practical approach to carbon reduction. *Journal of Environmental Planning and Management, 50*(3), 381–96.

King, C.A. (2008). Community resilience and contemporary agri-ecological systems: Reconnecting people with food, and people with people. *Systems Research and Behavioral Science, 25*(1), 111–24.

Kumar, S., & Malegeant, P. (2006). Strategic alliance in a closed-loop supply chain, a case of manufacturer and eco-non-profit organization. *Technovation*, 26(10), 1127–35.

Lasker, R.D., & Weiss, E.S. (2003). Broadening participation in community problem solving: A multidisciplinary model to support collaborative practice and research. *Journal of Urban Health, 80*(1), 14–47.

Lindseth, G. (2004). The Cities for Climate Protection Campaign (CCPC) and the framing of local climate policy. *Local Environment, 9*(4), 325–36.

Mander, S.L. (2007). Regional renewable energy policy: A process of coalition building. *Global Environmental Politics, 7*(2), 45–63.

Mason, M. (2007). Collaborative partnerships for urban development: A study of the Vancouver Agreement. *Environment and Planning A, 39*(10), 2366–82.

Moss, L.R. (2008). Local governments reduce costs through pollution prevention. *Journal of Cleaner Production, 16*(6), 704–8.

Mu, J., Peng, G., & Love, E. (2008). Interfirm networks, social capital, and knowledge flow. *Journal of Knowledge Management, 12*(4), 86–100.

Natural Resources Canada. (2007a). Community energy planning. A guide for communities. Volume 1 – Introduction. CANMET Energy Technology Centre, Ottawa.

Natural Resources Canada. (2007b). Factor-2 Communities: Planning your community with energy in mind. Community Energy Planning Guide. CANMET Energy Technology Centre, Ottawa.

Norris, F.H., Stevens, S.P., Phefferbaum, B., Wyche, K.F., & Phefferbaum, R.L. (2008). Community resilience as a metaphor, theory, set of capacities, and strategy for disaster readiness. *American Journal of Community Psychology, 41*(1–2), 127–50.

Orans, R., Price, S., Williams, J., Woo, C.K., & Moore, J. (2007). A Northern California–British Columbia partnership for renewable energy. *Energy Policy, 35*(8), 3979–83.

Parker, P., and Rowlands, I.H. (2007). City partners maintain climate change action despite national cuts: Residential Energy Efficiency Program valued at local level. *Local Environment, 12*(5), 505–17.

Polson, E.C. (2008). The inter-organizational ties that bind: Exploring the contribution of agency-congregation relationships. *Sociology of Religion, 69*(1), 45–65.

Robinson, J., Bradley, M., Busby, P., Connor, D., Murray, A., Sampson, B., et al. (2006). Climate change and sustainable development: Realizing the opportunity. *A Journal of the Human Environment, 35*(1), 1–8.

Rondinelli, D.A., & Berry, M.A. (2000). Environmental citizenship in multinational corporations: Social responsibility and sustainable development. *European Management Journal, 18*(1), 70–84.

Rondinelli, D.A., & London, T. (2003). How corporations and environmental groups cooperate: Assessing cross-sector alliances and collaborations. *Academy of Management Executive, 17*(1), 61–75.

Rottman, J.W. (2008). Successful knowledge transfer within offshore supplier networks: A case study exploring social capital in strategic alliances. *Journal of Information Technology, 23*(1), 31–43.

Salamon, L.M. (1995). *Partners in public service. Government-nonprofit relations in the modern welfare state.* Baltimore: Johns Hopkins University Press.

Schweitzer, M., & Ogle-Graham, L. (2005). A search for factors related to successful performance by Rebuild America partnerships. *Energy Policy, 33*(15), 1957–68.

Stern, R., & Green, J. (2005). Boundary workers and the management of frustration: A case study of two Healthy City partnerships. *Health Promotion International, 20*(3), 269–76.

Walker, G., Hunter, S., Devine-Wright, P., Evans, B., & Fay, H. (2007). Explaining and evaluating community-based localism in renewable energy policy in the UK. *Global Environmental Politics, 7*(2), 64–82.

Zahran, S., Grover, H., Brody, S.D., & Vedlitz, A. (2008). Risk, stress, and capacity: Explaining metropolitan commitment to climate protection. *Urban Affairs Review, 43*(4), 447–74.

10 The Online Social Economy: Canadian Nonprofits and the Internet

SHERIDA RYAN

This chapter describes a study undertaken to identify Canadian non-profit organizations that meet a broad definition of the social economy, as outlined in the first chapter of this book, and that rely on the Internet to meet their primary organizational objectives. Although face-to-face nonprofit enterprises are beginning to turn to the Internet to enhance their outreach and public profile, organizations that rely on information technology for their work are rarely included in any mapping of the social economy sector. The purpose of this exploratory research was to find and shed light on these online organizations in order to begin to explore their human, social, economic, and political contributions to the social economy.

Background

The Internet is the fastest growing medium of social and economic activity. It has changed the way Canadians work, bank, shop, and entertain themselves. Canadian surveys show that 80% of the population have Internet access (Statistics Canada, 2010), with 64% of households having at least one person who regularly uses the Internet at home (Ipsos Canada, 2005). Internet usage by Canadians between the ages of 16 and 24 has reached 98% (Statistics Canada, 2010), with computer-mediated social interaction being the most popular online activity (Media Awareness Network, 2005). In terms of economic activity, a recent American survey reported that 66% of Internet users engage in online commerce, which is roughly double the number reported in a similar survey in 2000 (Horrigan, 2008).

The rapid growth of the Internet has attracted the attention of social scientists and prompted considerable debate about its impact on society (Castells, 1996; Wellman et al., 1996). Critics of this trend argue that people's absorption in individualized technical environments increases the fragmentation and alienation that is prevalent in today's society and contributes to the decline of face-to-face associational activity (Kraut et al., 1998; Putnam, 2000). Utopian views of this technology claim that it can facilitate new forms of association that transcend the limitations of space and time (Baym, 1997; Rheingold, 1993). Some Internet scholars have suggested that the Internet is a democratizing medium that increases egalitarian interaction and social change (Deibert, 2000). They argue that online associations are characterized by voluntary, public, interaction, which encourages democratic participation and civic engagement (Barraket, 2005; Jensen, Danziger, & Venkatesh, 2007). These characteristics suggest that social economy organizations that share these attributes would feel at home in online environments.

Online groups and organizations have attracted research interest in a number of academic disciplines; for example, sociology (Wellman & Haythornthwaite, 2002), psychology (McKenna & Seidman, 2005), political science (Deibert, 2000), business, and management (Jarvenpaa, Tractinsky, & Vitale, 2000; McLure Wasko & Faraj, 2000). In comparison, these types of enterprises have received little attention from nonprofit researchers (Brainard & Brinkerhoff, 2004), perhaps because nonprofit organizations, with exception of public sector nonprofits and large organizations, have been slow to adopt information technology (Spencer, 2002). The reasons for this lag are rooted in the everyday reality of these types of organizations.

The majority of nonprofit associations have limited resources, both human and financial. They rely with varying degree on volunteers, who may have an uneasy relationship with technology, especially if they have had limited experience with information and communication technology (Corder, 2001). This lack of familiarity with information and communication media has also been a characteristic of many nonprofit managers and decision-makers in funding agencies. Organizations that do not have technology champions in positions of leadership tend to be wary of emerging technology (Corder, 2001). Added to this, nonprofit organizations have traditionally engaged in hands-on activity, often with the disadvantaged, who have limited, if any, access to the Internet. All of these factors can make it difficult for nonprofits to justify investment in technology as a priority.

This situation, however, is changing. Spurred by the increasing prevalence of Internet-based technology in everyday life and the mainstream success of online advocacy organizations such as MoveOn.org and the World Wildlife Fund, many nonprofits are beginning to build a web presence. These organizations are using the Internet to promote their mission, to enhance their fundraising, and to communicate efficiently with their constituencies (Brainard & Siplon, 2004). Many nonprofits maintain websites that resemble glossy brochures or magazines, and a few innovative associations participate actively with their members in online discussions, polls, and campaigns (Kenix, 2007). Some of these organizations have begun to experiment with the next generation of participatory platforms, such as social networking sites (e.g., Facebook) and Internet based 3D virtual worlds (e.g., Second Life).

Groups that have an established offline presence and that use the Internet to enhance their outreach potential are becoming more commonplace in nonprofit circles. However, enterprises that rely on the Internet to support their mission and objectives and that maintain little face-to-face presence run the risk of becoming, to borrow a term from Smith (2000), dark matter associations (Brainard & Brinkerhoff, 2004). They tend to attract little research attention because they do not obviously fit the prevailing paradigm applied to mainstream nonprofits (Brainard & Brinkerhoff, 2004; Smith, 2000). Online nonprofits, characterized by fluid boundaries, widely fluctuating and partially committed membership, and informal organizational structures (Wellman, 2001), challenge traditional views of nonprofit enterprises. These online associations are rarely included in any mapping of the nonprofit sector, which in turn, renders them nearly invisible to social economy research.

Challenges

There are a number of challenges to including online nonprofit enterprises within the study of the social economy. The first challenge is that there are no universally accepted definitions of the social economy and its constituent organizations, which complicates the identification of online social economy enterprises. Some researchers apply a narrow definition of the concept and do not include, for example, civil society or self-help groups (Bouchard, Ferraton, & Michaud, 2006). Others favour a broad inclusive perspective (Quarter, Mook, & Armstrong, 2009) that incorporates a wide variety of organizations such as co-operatives, social enterprises, community development initiatives, public sector nonprofits, nonprofit member associations, and civil society organizations. Since this research was exploratory, a broad, inclusive, definition, based on the work of Quarter, Mook, and Armstrong (2009), was employed to identify potential online social economy enterprises, specifically nonprofits engaged in community development, public or member service, and civil society organizations.

To add to the definitional challenge, the concept of the social economy has not been popularized outside of select academic and practitioner circles. Few online nonprofits have sufficient familiarity with the concept to self-identify as social economy organizations. For example, Wikipedia is an online nonprofit enterprise with a social mission, 'a multilingual, Web-based, free content encyclopedia project [which] attempts to collect and summarize all human knowledge in every major language' (Wikipedia, 2009). It provides a service to the public through content developed online by volunteers who are engaged in active community consensus building in order to fulfil the organization's goals. Although Wikipedia contributors have developed content pages about the social economy, there remains insufficient familiarity with the concept for them to propose that Wikipedia itself is a social economy project.

The study has also had to grapple with the offline versus online dichotomy that is frequently applied to organizations and communities in discussions about the Internet and its impact on society. This is a false dichotomy because the Internet does not have a separate existence outside of what we define as the 'real world' (Wellman, 2002) and it has become part of everyday activity. It is increasingly difficult and, perhaps, counterproductive to separate organizations into face-to-face and online enterprises.

For example, some organizations are reliant on the Internet to support extensive place-based projects. GiveMeaning.com is a Canadian online donation and fundraising enterprise that supports, among other things, community development projects in Africa (GiveMeaning, 2009). Other organizations make limited use of a physical place to support their largely online enterprise. For instance, TakingITGlobal has an office in Toronto; however, its mission is to inform, inspire, and connect youth around the world (TakingITGlobal, 2009). Still others blend environments and platforms. The International Freedom of Expression eXchange, IFEX, based in Toronto, is an email hub that monitors and collects evidence of freedom of expression abuses around the world, alerts a long list of place-based advocacy associations, and advises them about what actions could be taken to address freedom of speech issues locally and globally (International Freedom of Expression eXchange, 2009) . The challenge for this research has been to identify the degree of online presence that would qualify a nonprofit as being an online social economy organization.

Selection of online social enterprises for this study was based on characteristics suggested by Quarter, Mook, and Armstrong (2009), which include a strong social mission; social ownership; and dependence in varying degrees on volunteer/social participation and member civic engagement. For the purpose of this study, civic engagement was defined as member interaction and connection to each other through content creation and through online democratic decision-making processes. In order to identify these enterprises, an additional characteristic, a reliance on Internet technology to achieve primary organizational objectives, was added. Since this research was exploratory, the study was inclusive of organizations with varying levels of face-to-face and online presence.

To manage the scope of this initial exploration of online social economy organizations, the study limited its search to organizations that originated in Ontario or that have distinct Ontario sub-units or chapters. A few potential online social economy enterprises outside of Ontario, recommended by participants in the study, were also included.

Methods

Search engines, key informants, and snowball sampling were employed to find potential online nonprofit organizations. Snowball sampling was employed in this study because it is often useful in identifying populations that are difficult to find (Atkinson & Flint, 2001). Search engines were used to identify a variety of online organizations that broadly matched the study criteria. Key experts in the field of social and community informatics, as well as social activists involved in the nonprofit sector, were asked about the enterprises found through the search engines and were canvassed for their suggestions of other online associations that might fit the study's criteria. The organizations identified in this manner were then contacted and asked for their recommendations of other potential online social economy type groups. Several organizations posted a description of the study in their online newsletters and forums, and word of the research began to circulate through a variety of networks.

Organizations identified by this method were grouped according to

Table 10.1
Categories of website stages

Stage	Characteristics
Brochure	Basic information: organizational mission, names of staff/board directors and contact information
Magazine	More content: monthly/quarterly newsletters or magazines, list of events, articles of special interest to organization's mission, links to other organizations, donation or membership option online
Direct Appeal	Organizational mission and membership aggressively promoted Depth of content: searchable and downloadable articles, including research articles, content changed or updated frequently, relevant news, polls, surveys, offers RSS link Limited member content creation, may have online forum
Community	Members develop content for the website, forums, chat, blogs, social networks, platforms for collaborative work (wikis) Potential for online volunteering Incorporation of multiple types of media and applications: webcasting, podcasting, webinars, YouTube, Facebook, SlideShare, etc. Facilitates members' use of the Internet in support of organization's mission and/or social change

Note: Based on categories developed by Christ (2003); Cravens (2009)

the International Classification of Nonprofit Organizations, a classification system developed by the Johns Hopkins Comparative Nonprofit Sector Project and modified to better represent the context of the Canadian nonprofit sector (Hall, Barr, Easwaramoorthy, Sokolowski, & Salamon, 2005). After classification, the websites of the online enterprises were analysed to assess the degree to which they met the proposed criteria of the study. Member civic engagement and participation were also evaluated by employing a categorization framework (see table 10.1) based on models of website stages or levels of maturity (Christ, 2003; Cravens, 2009). Four categories, brochure, magazine, direct appeal, and community, were used to assess organizational online presence and the degree of member participation. Brochure and magazine type websites have little capacity for member active participation, with the exception of online donations and membership subscription. Direct appeal type websites offer more participation options, for example surveys and simple online forums. Community type websites support member content creation and frequently have the capacity for multi-media content. Civic engagement was assessed by evaluating a website's capacity and support for member interaction and content creation.

In order to develop a more in-depth understanding of the online social economy, leaders from five identified enterprises were interviewed to explore their organizations' similarity to traditional social economy enterprises, their use of information technology, and their perceptions of online social economy enterprises. Three of the interviews were carried out by email and two by telephone. Five short case studies based on the website analysis and the interviews are presented in the next section of the chapter.

Findings

Snowball sampling, search engines, and key informants identified 75 nonprofit organizations as potential online social economy enterprises. The organizations were grouped as follows: Culture and recreation (11), Education and research (4), Health (3), Social services (9), Environment (5), Development and housing (17), Law, advocacy, and politics (17), Philanthropic intermediaries and voluntarism promotion (4), International (2), Religion (1), Business and professional associations and unions (1), and Not elsewhere classified (1). Analyses of the organizations' websites revealed many similarities to traditional social economy enterprises. The organizations had social missions, were either public or member oriented, and had varying degrees of volunteer participation. The online enterprises, however, differed in the degree of member civic engagement, online participation, and content creation (see table 10.2).

Organizations with limited brochure type websites accounted for 16% of the online enterprises identified. Magazine and direct appeal organizations accounted for 23% and 28% of the sample. A number of the direct appeal enterprises exhibited rich, specialized content and were encouraging online member engagement. These organizations appeared to be moving towards the next stage of website maturity, where members have more presence and voice. Online community type nonprofits with member content creation and multiple means of online communication represented 31% of the groups examined. Although community type online enterprises remained in the minority, member online participation appeared to be growing.

Five leaders from the identified organizations volunteered to be interviewed. The study findings continue with short case studies of the

Table 10.2
Classification and member engagement/interactivity

Classification	Organizations	Brochure	Magazine	Appeal	Community	Closed
Culture & Recreation	11	1	4		5	1
Education and Research	4		2	1		1
Health	3		1	2		
Social services	9		1	2	6	
Environment	5			2	3	
Development & Housing	17	7	2	5	3	
Law, Advocacy, & Politics	17	3	5	6	3	
Philanthropy, Volunteers	4			2	2	
International	2		2			
Religion	1			1		
Business & Professional	1				1	
Other	1	1				
Total	75	12	17	21	23	2

Note: The term 'closed' refers to groups where member engagement could not be assessed because the group was closed to non-members.

Toronto Social Purchasing Portal, the Ontario Women's Health Network, Torontothebetter, the DisAbled Women's Network Ontario, and the Kuhkenah Network. In reference to the Venn diagram presented in chapter 1, the Toronto Social Purchasing Portal and the Kuhkenah Network could be viewed as community economic development; Torontothebetter is a social economy business; and the Ontario Women's Health Network and the DisAbled Women's Network Ontario are civil society organizations. These enterprises represented a continuum in member active engagement.

Toronto Social Purchasing Portal

A Social Purchasing Portal (SPP) is an Internet-accessed business-to-business database that connects socially responsible companies with local businesses that have agreed to employ people who need support to enter or to succeed in the workforce. It is based on a model that incorporates a blended financial and social bottom line in an attempt to facilitate economic development in a targeted community (Social Purchasing Portal Canada, 2009). Purchasers can search the database by keyword, by type of goods or services, and by location. The search produces a list of vendors that match the purchaser's criteria and includes more in-depth information about these businesses. In addition, the SPP system supports advertisements and job postings.

The first SPP, the Vancouver SPP, was developed in 2003, has generated over $1 million of new commercial activity in the downtown east side, and has facilitated the employment of 75 individuals (LePage, 2006). The success of Vancouver's SPP has been a catalyst for the creation of other SSPs across Canada.

Toronto Social Purchasing Portal was created in 2004 to assist the city's long-term unemployed, immigrants, and urban Aboriginal people. It was developed through a partnership between three nonprofit organizations, the Learning Enrichment Foundation, an established community organization that provides programs and services for the disadvantaged, Miziwe Biik, an organization that provides Aboriginal employment and training programs, and the Information Technology Association of Canada for Ontario (Toronto Social Purchasing Portal, 2008a). This partnership is described as a true collaboration as each of the participating nonprofits contributes its specific strengths, expertise, and networks to the enterprise and is actively engaged in overall decision-making for the venture. The long-term goal of this enterprise is to become self-sustaining and to make social purchasing an accepted form of economic transaction for Toronto's corporate community.

To join, companies fill out a purchasing partnership form that asks them to make a commitment to support job creation by privileging suppliers who are members of the portal. Suppliers must also submit a form and commit to hiring the hard to employ. Representatives from the Social Purchasing Portal follow up on these applications offline to make sure that the applicants understand their commitment and the premise behind the SPP program (Toronto Social Purchasing Portal, 2008b). At this point, the Toronto SPP requires substantial face-to-face relationship building by portal representatives in order to develop a base of purchasers and suppliers.

Although the Toronto SPP requires face-to-face activity, it is dependent on Internet-based technology to fulfil its objectives. The interviewee felt that the initiative was a useful example of a developing online social economy project. He also cautioned that the phrase 'online social economy' was confusing and that many community economic development groups may not consider themselves online or social, even if they fit the criteria for the study.

Ontario Women's Health Network

The Ontario Women's Health Network (OWHN), incorporated in 1997, is a provincial nonprofit that advocates for women's equitable access to health services (Ontario Women's Health Network, 2009a). The organization's mission is to

- Give voices to women's health issues;
- Link women to resources and tools;
- Build and strengthen the ability of individual women and communities to act on their health issues;
- Conduct research on women's health issues;
- Advocate on behalf of women's health concerns.

OWHN believes that information about women's health and the resources that support wellness must be shared publicly. With the help of volunteers, it has developed a website that provides up-to-date information and resources that can assist women in making informed health decisions. OWHN has created a regularly updated Internet directory of Ontario women's services and programs so that women can find health resources close to home (Ontario Women's Health Network, 2009b). The website also provides general information about common female health concerns and links to more in-depth articles and publications (Ontario Women's Health Network, 2009a).

In addition to sharing information through its website, the OWHN publishes a weekly E-Digest and a quarterly E-Bulletin. The E-Digest features health-related news, announcements, and events. It is an open, unmoderated list and all OWHN members may post to it. The E-Bulletin provides more in-depth coverage of particular health-related topics such as poverty and women's health, violence against women, and HIV/AIDS information. The website also has an extensive alphabetical list of links to other Ontario women's organizations.

OWHN does not have any core funding. It relies on money from contracted, often research type, projects to cover the salaries of its 1.5 FTE (4 part-time employees), to maintain its office, and to operate its website and email outreach. This work involves considerable face-to-face activity; for example, conducting focus groups for organizations such as the Hospital Report Research Collaborative, Women's College Hospital, Women's Health Matters, and York University. Even though OWHN relies on this type of work for financial survival, it employs Internet technology to fulfil much of its organizational mission.

The OWHN interviewee could appreciate her organization as a type of online social economy project. She reported, however, that the organization engaged in little future planning about the employment information technology. The organization was surviving from project to project and did not have the resources to investigate how emerging technology could further benefit the organization or the women that it serves.

Torontothebetter.net

In early 2004, Torontothebetter.net became the city's first online progressive business directory (Torontothebetter, 2009b). Torontothebetter is an initiative of Libra Knowledge and Information Services Co-op Inc., a unionized worker's co-op. The goal of this enterprise is to facilitate informed shopping based on an individual's principles. Torontothebetter helps people put their money where their values are (Torontothebetter, 2005b). Torontothebetter is supported primarily by the profits earned by the Libra Co-op. Fees for business listings and a shoppers' card program account for only a third of Torontothebetter's funds. Libra Co-op has made the decision to develop Torontothebetter slowly, as a unique, debt-free, value-driven project.

Purveyors of goods and services can be nominated by customers or they can get a listing directly if they meet certain criteria. Aside from regional rules (no U.S. head offices), the businesses are assessed by the degree to which they exhibit the following principles:

- Involve excluded or inadequately served sections of the community (community category);
- Educate consumers and offer them economic participation in business benefits (consumer category);
- Actively support environmental improvement (environment category);
- Provide workers with the right to participate in business management and economic benefits (worker category);
- Specialize in services to the types of business identified above (services category). (Torontothebetter, 2005a, ¶ 2)

The interviewees reported that they make use of the Internet to research a new enterprise's credibility and fit. They begin by reviewing the potential participant's website and then they search for any news, blogs, reviews, etc. that have information about the business. If there are doubts, Libra workers are canvassed for their opinions. Libra workers come from activist backgrounds and are connected to other progressive organizations, including the Social Investment Organization. The information embedded in these networks provides third-party assurance of a potential vendor's bona fides. As of January 2008, Torontothebetter had 248 participating businesses in its directory.

Potential customers can search the site by product, service, category, or name. Once they have located a business they can find out more about the enterprise, such as its mission, services, special offers, location, and contact information (Torontothebetter, 2009a). The website supports a blog for news, events, and comments about social shopping and businesses. Shoppers and businesses make some use of the blog as an interactive communication environment.

Libra has been a worker co-operative since 1989 and has supported this mission- and values-driven online project since 2004. The interviewees were familiar with social enterprises and with information technology and perceived Torontothebetter as a good example of online social economy enterprise.

DisAbled Women's Network Ontario

Formed in 1992, the DisAbled Women's Network Ontario (DAWN) is a volunteer, feminist organization that advocates inclusion and equality for women and girls with disabilities (DAWN Ontario, 2009a). Its mission is to empower its members to advocate for their unmet needs, to engage in coalition building with other sympathetic organizations, and to bridge the digital divide. DAWN has attempted to achieve its mission through education, research, resource development, capacity building, and knowledge sharing (DAWN Ontario, 2009d). DAWN has 426 registered members and women with disabilities make up 100% of the board.

DAWN launched its website in 1998. In 2000, it began to develop online discussion forums so that members could share information and support, and build their individual and group capacity for self-advocacy (DAWN Ontario, 2009b). In addition to the above online activities, the website also includes an updated news and campaigns section and access to a variety of resources such as a Media Kit, an Advocacy Tool Kit, a Disability Access Checklist, a Virtual Activist Training Reader, and a Violence Against Women section that focuses on women with disabilities (DAWN Ontario, 2009a). The organization also hosts and maintains websites for organizations with less technical expertise.

One of DAWN's major strengths is its ability to form cross-sectoral networks with organizations that share their concern for social justice. The organization has developed links with 185 like-minded Canadian groups (DAWN Ontario, 2009c). An abbreviated list of organizations with whom it has worked closely includes Ontario Social Safety Network, National Association of Women and the Law, Cross Sectoral Violence against Women Strategy Group, Lesbian and Breast Cancer Project, and the Canadian Research Institute for the Advancement of Women. DAWN uses these collaborative opportunities to raise awareness of accessibility issues and to promote the full and equal participation of women with disabilities. Much of this activity occurs online, and DAWN Ontario has developed a positive reputation for its effectiveness in mobilizing its members and allies through its website and forums.

DAWN Ontario has been operating without funding or paid staff since January 1999 (DAWN Ontario, 2009a). This lack of funding has severely limited the organization's face-to-face activity, its ability to provide copies of print or video material, and, recently, its telephone access. In 2007, DAWN received a donation from the Elementary Teachers' Foundation of Ontario to offset some of the website's hosting fees.

DAWN Ontario is a good example of an online social economy enterprise in that it has a social mission; it is a public social property that is governed by volunteers who are actively engaged in civic participation. A quote from the interviewee poignantly illustrates the experience of DAWN members.

> I think for many of our members and even for our board, it was the first time any of us had engaged in such meaningful work (outside our families) ... the bulk of us are ordinary women, many without formal education, many socially isolated and many too accustomed to living in our own little worlds. The new world that had opened for us via online activism was incredibly empowering and for the first time, many of us felt like we were contributing to a great cause ... helping in some small way to work to positively affect social change.

Kuhkenah Network

Kuhkenah Network (K-Net) is an information and communication initiative of Keewaytinook Okimakanak (KO), a nonprofit, non-political, tribal Chiefs council that represents the First Nations in the Sioux Lookout region of northwestern Ontario (K-Net, 2009a; Keewaytinook Okimakanak, 2009). K-Net provides telecommunication infrastructure, services, training, and support to remote communities, some of which can only be reached by small aircraft. In doing so, it enhances local health, education, social, and economic initiatives. K-Net is governed by the KO council that sets the long-term goals for the enterprise, ensuring that the service supports local cultural self-determination (Ramirez, Aitkin, Jamieson, & Richardson, 2003). K-Net projects are funded through a combination of provincial and federal programs and, like other nonprofit organizations, are susceptible to yearly pressure for ongoing funding for their various initiatives.

K-Net was established in 1994 and immediately began work to provide communication resources to the KO communities. Starting with a Bulletin Board System, the organization has evolved to a point where it now offers a range of digital communication services, including sophisticated multi-media applications (Fiser, Clement, & Walmark, 2006). From the beginning, KO and K-Net understood that community development meant more than economic development. K-Net supports a variety of projects that enhance the quality of life in these remote communities.

To address the healthcare needs of KO communities, K-Net developed the capacity to support a set of telemedicine services and health education resources (K-Net, 2009c). Rather than travelling hundreds of miles to get service, people can now stay in their community, in their homes, and receive quality healthcare. Educational support was also seen as a priority for the people in these remote communities, especially since 50% of the region's population is less than 20 years of age. K-Net's educational initiatives include the operation of a SchoolNet helpdesk that provides technical assistance for First Nation K-12 schools that have Internet connectivity, the development of Keewaytinook Internet High School for grades 9 and 10 as well as access to other distance education opportunities (K-Net, 2009b). These programs strengthen the community by enabling young people to engage in learning activities with their peers in a familiar environment and to share their knowledge with the rest of the community.

In addition to the above, K-Net's portal supports a variety of online services from chat rooms and individual websites to band office programs and promotion of Aboriginal arts, crafts, and culture (K-Net, 2009a). The organization is recognized as an international leader in the provision of information and communication technology in support of First Nation community self-determination. KO and K-Net have recently created a research institute (KORI) to study the uses of information and communication technology for the advancement of Aboriginal issues (Okimakanak, 2009).

K-Net is a social economy enterprise that uses a wide range of emerging Internet technology to achieve the health, education, social, and economic objectives of the KO First Nations communities. When asked how he would describe an online social economy enterprise, the interviewee responded:

> I would use words like engaging, transformative, innovative, empowering, etc. I use these descriptive words to highlight how these communication tools provide a means for the remote and rural communities to now have a voice that can be heard anywhere in the world. They are now able to share and market their knowledge, experience, and products as they see fit instead of depending on others to be taking care of them. They are now able to create new opportunities, services, and products for themselves, their community and for others in far away places. They now have choices of how, where, and when they can receive support services including education, justice, health, counselling, and other applications that most urban dwellers take for granted.

Discussion

The purpose of this study was to identify online enterprises that fit the broad definition and characteristics of social economy organizations and that fulfilled their primary organizational objectives using Internet technology. Seventy-five organizations were found by employing Internet search engines, key informants, and a snowball sampling technique. This preliminary search suggested that advocacy and civil society organizations (Law, advocacy, and politics) and community development projects (Development and housing) appeared to be the most prevalent types of online social economy organizations identified in this study. This finding supports previous research, which reported that advocacy groups had been successful in harnessing Internet-based technology to the benefit of their respective constituencies (Child & Grønbjerg, 2007). The social service category had the largest number of participatory, community type, organizational websites. This finding reflects the number of online youth and social support groups identified in this study and is in line with research about online self-help groups (Eysenbach, Powell, Englesakis, Rizo, & Stern, 2004).

A secondary purpose of this study was to examine potential online social economy enterprises, their use of information technology, and their understanding of the concept of an online social economy enterprise and to explore their 'fit' with the characteristics employed to describe traditional social economy organizations. Although the identified organizations fitted most of the study criteria, 29 of these nonprofits were categorized as having brochure or magazine type websites. These types of websites do not normally support active online member participation, and an argument can be made that these organizations do not fulfil the study criteria. However, including these nonprofits in preliminary research may be worthwhile in developing a more nuanced perspective of the online social economy

The five case studies were illustrative of the range of online presence found in the nonprofits identified in the study. Each employed Internet-based technology to achieve its organizational objectives; however, the nonprofits' use of this technology lay on a continuum in terms of the amount of face-to-face activity in which they engaged and the type and degree of active online participation that they supported. At one end of the continuum, Toronto SPP interacted with their purchasers and suppliers mostly through face-to-face contact, using online forms to initiate the SPP process and to provide a database of services. OWHN reached out to its members through an email list that disseminated e-digests and e-bulletins. Members could respond to the circulated information; however, this rarely occurred. In the middle, Torontothebetter used a blog to communicate news and events and to highlight certain progressive businesses and their practices. Members were encouraged to comment and contribute their own content, and this occurred several times a month. At the other end of the continuum, DAWN Ontario and K-Net made extensive use of their Internet-based communication platforms to interact with their members and the public. Both organizations employed technology not only to achieve their missions but also to accomplish day-to-day activity. DAWN Ontario accomplished its work primarily by email, while K-Net, because of its funding, was able to incorporate many emerging technology platforms.

The enterprises analysed in this study appear to be representative of the general state of online nonprofit development; that is, only a minority of innovative associations actively participate online with their members and with like-minded organizations (Kenix, 2007). Active member participation is a key characteristic of social economy type enterprises and a key descriptor of the degree of organizational online presence. An important question to be considered in future research is whether the criteria applied to online social economy organizations in this study should be made more stringent and limited to groups that support a certain level of Internet-mediated interaction. Unfortunately, this would effectively exclude many online associations that contribute to the social economy and that may not yet have the resources to sustain a more interactive online environment. This study represents a snapshot of the identified nonprofits, and a recent review of the 29 organizations that had brochure and magazine type websites revealed that three of them now have the capacity for member online interaction.

Given that research about online nonprofit organizations is still relatively novel, the framework presented above may be useful in the development of a classification system for other studies. As noted, online organizations operate face to face as well, but for some the Internet is the primary mechanism for serving their clientele and for others this medium is used as an entrée for a service that is primarily face-to-face. This classification system could be viewed in categorical terms or as a continuum, the latter requiring more precise distinctions.

One issue that arises with respect to this classification system is that there appeared to be a difference between organizations that serve the public and those that serve a membership in where they fall in the classification system. Our sample for this study was too small to make a determination, but it is interesting that the organizations serving a membership were able to undertake their services online whereas the organizations serving the public required face-to-face transactions. It would be interesting to determine whether this is a generalizable finding and, if so, what the explanation is.

The interview participants exhibited a mixed understanding of the concept of online social economy organizations. With the exception of Torontothebetter and K-Net, the other organizations found the terms 'online social economy' confusing. Sometimes it was a matter of the word 'social,' other times the word 'economy' was difficult for participants to apply to their organization, and one person questioned their organization's online presence. Future studies will need to clarify these terms when recruiting participants.

Although these findings are interesting, it should be noted that the study represents baseline research and is only an initial step in identifying online social economy enterprises. One of the limitations of snowball sampling is its inherent bias towards over-representing certain findings due to similar social identities or homophily within accessed social networks (Atkinson & Flint, 2001). In addition, this type of sampling does not allow for any generalization. The study did not have sufficient time to replicate the procedures and continue the search to find, for example, peer-to-peer online professional groups, social purpose organizations, micro-finance projects, and avocational interest groups that may fit the criteria for online social economy enterprises.

This study is an initial step in understanding online social economy enterprises and opens the door for more research into this neglected corner of the sector. More potential social economy enterprises that incorporate emerging Internet technology need to be identified, and more in-depth case studies are required to develop a better picture of these types of organizations. Future online social economy research can then begin to explore the contributions of these enterprises to an evolving Internet-mediated society.

REFERENCES

Atkinson, R., & Flint, J. (2001). Accessing hidden and hard-to-reach populations: Snowball research strategies [Electronic Version]. *Social Research Update*, 33. Retrieved October 2, 2009, from http://sru.soc.surrey.ac.uk/SRU33.html

Barraket, J. (2005). Online opportunities for civic engagement? An examination of Australian third sector organisations on the Internet. *Australian Journal of Emerging Technologies and Society*, 3(1), 17–30.

Baym, N.K. (1997). Interpreting soap operas and creating community: Inside an electronic fan culture. In S. Kiesler (Ed.), *Culture of the Internet* (pp. 407–30). Mahweh, NJ: Lawrence Erlbaum.

Bouchard, M.J., Ferraton, C., & Michaud, V. (2006). Database on social economy organizations: The qualification criteria. *Working Papers of the Canada Research Chair on the Social Economy* Retrieved October 22, 2009, from http://www.chaire.ecosoc.uqam.ca/Portals/ChaireEcoSoc/docs/pdf/cahiers/R-2006–03.pdf

Brainard, L.A., & Brinkerhoff, J.A. (2004). Lost in cyberspace: Shedding light on the dark matter of grassroots organizations. *Nonprofit and Voluntary Sector Quarterly, Supplement to vol. 33* (3), 32S-53S.

Brainard, L.A., & Siplon, P.D. (2004). Toward nonprofit organization reform in the voluntary spirit: Lessons from the Internet. *Nonprofit and Voluntary Sector Quarterly*, 33(3), 435–57.

Castells, M. (1996). *The rise of the network society* (Vol. 1). Cambridge, MA: Blackwell Publishers.

Child, C.D., & Grønbjerg, K.A. (2007). Nonprofit advocacy organizations: Their characteristics and activities. *Social Science Quarterly, 88*(1), 259–81.

Christ, R. (2003). *The stages of site development: The evolution of nonprofit web sites.* Retrieved October 20, 2009, from TechSoup http://www.techsoup.org/learningcenter/webbuilding/page5443.cfm

Corder, K. (2001). Acquiring new technology: Comparing nonprofit and public sector agencies. *Administration & Society, 33*(2), 194–219.

Cravens, J. (2009, July). *Stages of maturity in nonprofit organizations' use of online technologies.* Retrieved October, 2009, from http://www.coyotecommunications.com/outreach/online3.html

DAWN Ontario. (2009a). DAWN Ontario: *DisAbled Women' Network Ontario.* Retrieved October 31, 2009, from http://dawn.thot.net/

DAWN Ontario. (2009b). *Herstory.* Retrieved November 3, 2009, from http://dawn.thot.net/herstory.html

DAWN Ontario. (2009c). *Organizations we work with.* Retrieved November 2, 2009, from http://dawn.thot.net/what.html#whom

DAWN Ontario. (2009d). *What we do.* Retrieved November 2, 2009, from http://dawn.thot.net/what.html

Deibert, R. (2000). International plug'n play? Citizen activism, the Internet, and global public policy. *International Studies Perspectives, 1*(3), 255–72.

Eysenbach, G., Powell, J., Englesakis, M., Rizo, C., & Stern, A. (2004). Health related virtual communities and electronic support group: Systematic review of the effects of online peer to peer interactions. *British Medical Journal, 328*(7449), 1166–71.

Fiser, A., Clement, A., & Walmark, B. (February 2006). The K-Net development process: A model for first nations broadband community networks. *CRACIN Working Paper No 12* Retrieved October 19, 2009, from http://www3.fis.utoronto.ca/research/iprp/cracin/publications/workingpapersseries.htm

GiveMeaning. (2009). *Home.* Retrieved November 29, 2009, from http://www.givemeaning.com/

Hall, M.H., Barr, C., Easwaramoorthy, M., Sokolowski, S.W., & Salamon, L.M. (2005). *The Canadian nonprofit and voluntary sector in comparative perspective.* Toronto: Imagine Canada.

Horrigan, J.B. (2008). *Online Shopping.* Retrieved October 22, 2009, from Pew Internet and American life Project http://www.pewinternet.org/Reports/2008/Online-Shopping.aspx

International Freedom of Expression eXchange. (2009). *IFEX Home.* Retrieved October 29, 2009, from http://www.ifex.org/

Ipsos Canada. (2005). *Canadian Inter@ctive Reid Report: Internet access and profiles*. Retrieved October 13, 2009, from http://www.ipsos.ca/reid/interactive/intAccessProfiles.cfm

Jarvenpaa, S.L., Tractinsky, N., & Vitale, M. (2000). Consumer trust in an Internet store. *Journal of Information Technology and Management, 1*(1–2), 45–71.

Jensen, M.J., Danziger, J.N., & Venkatesh, A. (2007). Civil society and Cyber society: The role of the Internet in community associations and democratic politics. *The Information Society, 23*(1), 39–50.

K-Net. (2009a). *Home*. Retrieved October 26, 2009, from http://knet.ca/

K-Net. (2009b). *Keewaytinook Internet High School*. Retrieved October 21, 2009, from http://kihs.knet.ca/drupal/

K-Net. (2009c). *KO Telemedicine*. Retrieved October 21, 2009, from http://telemedicine.knet.ca/

Keewaytinook Okimakanak. (2009). *Keewaytinook Okimakanak*. Retrieved November 8, 2009, from http://knet.ca/info/

Kenix, L.J. (2007). In search of utopia: An analysis of non-profit web pages. *Information, Communication & Society, 10*(1), 69–94.

Kraut, R., Patterson, M., Lundmark, V., Kiesler, S., Mukophadhyay, T., & Scherlis, W. (1998). Internet paradox: A social technology that reduces social involvement and psychological well-being? *American Psychologist, 53*(9), 1017–31.

LePage, D. (2006). The Social Purchasing Portal: A tool to blend values [electronic version]. *Horizons, 8*(2). Retrieved November 3, 2009, from Policy Research Initiative, Government of Canada http://www.policyresearch.gc.ca/doclib/HOR_v8n2_200602_e.pdf

McKenna, K.Y.A., & Seidman, G. (2005). You, me, and we: Interpersonal processes in electronic groups. In Y. Amichai-Hamburger (Ed.), *The social net: Understanding human behavior in cyberspace* (pp. 280). Oxford: Oxford University Press.

McLure Wasko, M., & Faraj, S. (2000). 'It is what one does': Why people participate and help others in electronic communities of practice. *The Journal of Strategic Information Systems, 9*(2–3), 155–73.

Media Awareness Network. (2005). *Young Canadians in a wired world: Phase II*. Retrieved October 21, 2009, from http://www.media-awareness.ca/english/research/YCWW/

Okimakanak, K. (2009). Keewaytinook Okimakanak Research Institute. Retrieved November 4, 2009, from http://www.research.knet.ca/

Ontario Women's Health Network. (2009a). *About us*. Retrieved October 19, 2009, from http://www.owhn.on.ca/who.htm

Ontario Women's Health Network. (2009b). *OWHN resource database*. Retrieved October 21, 2009, from http://www.owhn.on.ca/directory.htm

Putnam, R.D. (2000). Bowling alone: The collapse and revival of American community. New York: Simon & Schuster.

Quarter, J., Mook, L., & Armstrong, A. (2009). *Understanding Canada's Social Economy*. Toronto: University of Toronto Press.

Ramirez, R., Aitkin, H., Jamieson, R., & Richardson, D. (2003). *Harnessing ICTs: A Canadian First Nations experience*. Retrieved October 15, 2009, from http://www.crdi.ca/uploads/user-S/11660372751KNET-Final_light_ENG.pdf

Rheingold, H. (1993). *The virtual community: Homesteading on the electronic frontier*. Reading, MA: Addison-Wesley Pub. Co.

Smith, D.H. (2000). *Grassroots organizations*. Thousand Oaks, CA: Sage.

Social Purchasing Portal Canada. (2009). *About*. Retrieved November 3, 2009, from http://www.sppcanada.org/elgg/

Spencer, T. (2002). The potential of the Internet for non-profit organizations [electronic version]. *First Monday*, 7(8). Retrieved October 20, 2009, from http://firstmonday.org/htbin/cgiwrap/bin/ojs/index.php/fm/article/view/976/897

Statistics Canada. (2010). Canadian Internet use survey. The Daily. Retrieved from http://www.statcan.gc.ca/daily-quotidien/100510/dq100510-eng.htm

TakingITGlobal. (2009). *Home*. Retrieved October 29, 2009, from http://www.tigweb.org/index.html

Toronto Social Purchasing Portal. (2008a). *About SPP Toronto*. Retrieved June 1, 2008, from http://www.spptoronto.org/aboutus.cfm

Toronto Social Purchasing Portal. (2008b). *How you can partner with us*. Retrieved June 1, 2008, from http://www.spptoronto.org/placeAnAd.cfm#1

Torontothebetter. (2005a). *Inclusion Criteria*. Retrieved November 5, 2009, from http://www.torontothebetter.net/criter1.html

Torontothebetter. (2005b). *Why TorontotheBetter.net*. Retrieved October 30, 2009, from http://www.torontothebetter.net/2whyttbetter.htm

Torontothebetter. (2009a). *Directory*. Retrieved October 30, 2009, from http://www.torontothebetter.net/2tgbd-sh.html

Torontothebetter. (2009b). *Home*. Retrieved October 30, 2009, from http://www.torontothebetter.net/home.html

Wellman, B. (2001). *The persistence and transformation of community: From neighbourhood groups to social networks*. Retrieved October 18, 2009, from http://www.chass.utoronto.ca/~wellman/publications/index.html

Wellman, B. (2002). Little boxes, glocalization, and networked individualism. In M. Tanabe, P. Van Den Besselaar, & T. Ishida (Eds.), *Digital cities II: Computational and sociological approaches* (pp. 10–25). Berlin: Springer.

Wellman, B., & Haythornthwaite, C. (2002). *The Internet in everyday life.* Oxford: Blackwell.

Wellman, B., Salaff, J., Dimitrova, D., Garton, L., Gulia, M., & Haythornthwaite, C. (1996). Computer networks as social networks: Collaborative work, telework, and virtual community. *Annual Review of Sociology, 22,* 213–38.

Wikipedia. (2009). *Wikipedia: About.* Retrieved October 25, 2009, from http://en.wikipedia.org/wiki/Wikipedia:About

11 Corporate Participation in the Social Economy: Employer-Supported Volunteering Programs in Canada's Financial Institutions

AGNES MEINHARD, FEMIDA HANDY,
AND ITAY GREENSPAN

The term 'social economy' has been used for years to describe a segment of the economy that is neither driven by the profit motives of private interests nor owned by the state to serve public interests. However, definitions of the term defy clear boundaries, at times excluding certain types of organizations and at others including them (Moulaert & Ailenei, 2005). In Quebec, for example, as described in chapter 3 (p. 00), social economy goes beyond a mere description of organizations and refers to 'an alternative model of economic development' governed by democratic processes and contributing to the democratization of society in partnership with the state; however, it excludes most nonprofit organizations. In Ontario and the rest of Canada, reference to social economy includes co-operatives, nonprofit organizations, and social enterprises with an emphasis on the market economy (Mook, Quarter, & Richmond, 2007; Quarter, 1992; Quarter, Mook, & Armstrong, 2009). Irrespective of these variations, there is general agreement that the social economy is made up of organizations whose abiding purpose is social in nature even though they may make economic contributions.

Increasingly, as indicated in the Venn Diagram in chapter 1, social economy organizations straddle all three sectors of society. There is a blurring of boundaries between nonprofit, for-profit, and public organizations; nonprofits adopting business models and engaging in profit-making activities (Dart, 2004; Meinhard, Foster, Moher, & Fitzrandolph, 2006) and for-profits engaging in the production of social goods as part of their corporate social responsibility (Foster, Meinhard, Berger, & Krpan, 2009). Bi-sector and tri-sector collaborative partnerships, in which nonprofits and for-profits, or nonprofits, for-profits, and government, bring their strengths to the collaborations, are also on the rise.

These collaborations enhance efficiencies and are becoming more prevalent with the growing recognition that resolving entrenched social problems requires a concerted effort by all sectors (Rocha, 2009).

Given these developments, we propose to adopt a broader perspective in this chapter; we view the social economy in terms of *activities* (rather than organizations) aimed at enhancing 'the social good.' For example, volunteering for and donating to organizations that engage in enhancing the social good would be indicative of participation in the social economy. This approach implies that corporations can participate in the social economy by engaging in community-enhancing activities through donations, joint ventures, partnerships, and *employer-supported volunteering* (ESV) initiatives wherein corporations encourage and support community volunteering among their employees. This chapter examines the concept of ESV and presents findings from our research to illustrate this aspect of corporate participation in the social economy.

Employer-Supported Volunteering

Employer-supported volunteering (ESV) – variously called *corporate volunteering* or *employee volunteering* – refers to a range of initiatives provided by for-profit employers to encourage and support community volunteering among their employees. According to Graff (2004, p. 6), 'ESV can range from simple acknowledgement that employees perform volunteer work in the community, through to ongoing staff time-off and in-kind support of community efforts and charitable causes.' Some ESV initiatives mentioned in the Canadian literature include *sponsoring events* such as fundraising runs/walks, where employee participation is encouraged thorough organized teams (Hall, Easwaramoorthy, & Sandler, 2007; Rog, Pancer, & Baetz, 2004); *liaising with local volunteer centres* (Easwaramoorthy, Barr, Runte, & Basil, 2006); *forming long-term partnerships* with community agencies to share expertise through the volunteering of their employees (Rog et al., 2004); *providing resources and allowing volunteers to use company equipment or facilities* for their programs (NSGVP, 2004); *modifying work hours or giving time off* for employee volunteers (Easwaramoorthy et al., 2006);[1] and *honouring volunteers* for exemplary community work and *rewarding them* by donating to their organization of choice (Graff, 2004).

With the exception of a few studies that examine ESV within a theoretical or analytical framework (e.g., de Gilder, Schuyt, & Breedijk, 2005; Peloza, Hudson, & Hassay, 2009; Safrit & Merrill, 1998), most of the ESV literature, both in Canada and elsewhere, is either descriptive or prescriptive, with the general aim of making a business case for corporate volunteering programs. These studies either intuit or rely on interviews with corporate officials to identify the benefits that accrue to corporations from ESV programs. They point, first and foremost, to the competitive advantages ESV affords companies in terms of external stakeholders – customers, clients, investors – and internal stakeholders – employees, managers, and board members.

Because the volunteers are out in the community performing 'organizational citizenship behavior' (Peloza et al., 2009) and representing their companies, they serve as organizational ambassadors. The personal contacts of employee volunteers and their exposure to non-profits and the community at large help to increase brand recognition, improve client relations, enhance the corporation's reputation among potential investors, and build customer loyalty (Graff, 2004; Hall et al., 2007; Points of Light Foundation, 2005; Rog et al., 2004). Furthermore, volunteers can provide feedback to their organizations about community needs for new product development (Graff, 2004; Points of Light Foundation, 2005). In the long run, such involvement helps to create stronger communities, providing a more stable base for businesses (Hall et al., 2007).

In making the business case for ESV, most of the literature focuses on the recruitment, retention, productivity, and skill improvement of employees. The contention is that companies with good community involvement records are able to attract and recruit the most talented people (Hall et al., 2007; Rochlin & Christoffer, 2000). Once hired, employees develop increased goodwill towards employers who provide opportunities for community involvement (Points of Light Foundation, 2005). ESV also improves employee satisfaction, loyalty, team spirit, and morale, and provides opportunities for enhancing existing skills and/or acquiring new ones (Easwaramoorthy et al., 2006; Graff, 2004; Hall et al., 2007; Peloza & Hassay, 2006; Points of Light Foundation, 2005; Rog et al., 2004). As a result, employee productivity is increased and turnover rates are decreased (Easwaramoorthy et al., 2006; Graff, 2004; Peloza & Hassay, 2006; Rog et al., 2004). Benefits to the employee volunteer include possibilities for career advancement, workplace recognition, meeting other employees, increasing work variety, and acquiring new knowledge and skills that are transferable to the workplace, especially 'people skills' (Graff, 2004; Peloza & Hassay, 2006).

Corporations have been shown to benefit financially from good corporate citizenship. Employee satisfaction has been positively linked with increased earnings and shareholder returns (Edmans, 2009). A meta-analysis of corporate social responsibility and financial perform-ance clearly indicates that investment into social responsibility yields financial benefits in the long run (Orlitzky, Schmidt, & Rynes, 2003).

However, these benefits are not universally achieved in all ESV pro-grams. Peloza and colleagues (2006, 2009) demonstrate that volunteer credit programs like 'Dollars for Doers' (i.e., programs that give a mon-etary reward to the organization in which the employee volunteers) do not afford the individual or the company as many benefits as volun-teering done in company teams for a specific cause or for a charitable organization adopted by the company.

Lest we think that corporations engage in philanthropic activities only for their own benefit, Hall and his colleagues (2007) found that several of their corporate respondents reported that their activities in the social economy were motivated 'primarily because of their phil-anthropic commitment to communities' (ibid., p. 9). However, this is self-reporting, and hence subject to overestimation of altruistic motives. Regardless of motives, in a time of decreasing intensity of volunteer participation (NSGVP, 2004), the benefits of ESV to the social economy are significant. ESV programs provide nonprofit organizations with ac-cess to reliable and motivated volunteers often with skills that match their needs (Graff, 2004; Peloza et al., 2009; Rog et al., 2004).

ESV programs also pose some challenges for companies, testing their commitment to support the volunteering activities of their em-ployees. For example, covering absentee workers who leave work to volunteer was the most commonly mentioned challenge among 990 businesses surveyed; almost one-quarter of them saw this as a problem (Easwaramoorthy et al., 2006). There are also challenges in program administration. For example, the costs of the program, time and staff-ing constraints, selling the program to employees, lack of good models, and adjusting to the expectations of community agencies were some of the key challenges mentioned by a sample of 34 ESV program directors interviewed by Rog and her colleagues (2004). Another study reported complaints by volunteer co-ordinators about insufficient resources for dealing with multiple stakeholder expectations (Hall et al., 2007).

Prevalence of ESV in Canada

ESV is not a new phenomenon in the Canadian corporate world. Surveys indicate that 14%-25% of Canadian companies have some kind of formal volunteering policy (Rostami & Hall, 1996; Easwaramoorthy et al., 2006), but more than 70% of them support their employees' volunteering efforts in an informal manner (Easwaramoorthy et al., 2006). In all, 27% of Canadian volunteers reported receiving some type of support for volunteering from their employer (Hall, McKeown, & Roberts, 2000). On average, volunteers whose employers support them volunteer more hours to more organizations (151 hours for 1.8 organizations) than volunteers who do not receive such support (131 hours for 1.5 organizations) (Hall et al., 2000). This suggests that receiving support from one's employer may intensify volunteering rates; however, given the cross-sectional nature of the data, this is a tentative conclusion.

Canada's financial institutions are at the vanguard of employer-supported volunteer programs. In 2001, in response to concerns over mergers in the Canadian financial sector, amendments to the Bank Act, the Insurance Companies Act, and the Trust and Loans Companies Act were passed requiring all financial institutions with over $1 billion in equity to 'annually publish a statement [Public Accountability Statements, or PAS] describing the[ir] contribution ... to the Canadian economy and society' (Bank Act 459.3[1]).[2] This legislation requires corporations to report their economic and social contributions to the community. Writing a cheque to the CEO's favourite charity no longer suffices; financial institutions are expected to ensure that, whatever philanthropy they practise, it must accrue to the community in which they do business. These amendments seem to have an impact on company efforts to meet their community responsibilities, one of which is the creation or expansion of ESV programs.

This research examines ESV programs undertaken by large financial institutions that are required to publish Public Accountability Statements. We examine the structure of these programs, how they fit into the overall corporate philanthropic strategy, and how these activities can be perceived as contributing to the social economy as defined above.

Methodology

We used two main methods to achieve these goals: first, we conducted in-depth key informant interviews with eight ESV program directors in the major financial institutions, and second, we surveyed the employee volunteers in one financial institution to better understand their motivations and involvement in the social economy.

In-Depth Key Informant Interviews

We contacted eleven financial institutions whose Public Accountability Statements (PAS) indicated that they have ESV programs. Of these, eight agreed to have related staff interviewed: five of Canada's major banks and three of the large insurance companies. Interviews were arranged at a time and place of convenience with senior staff – volunteer program directors and/or corporate philanthropy managers – at each of the eight responding corporations. With the exception of one interview conducted over the telephone, the interviews took place in corporate offices and lasted from an hour to an hour and a half. The interviews were semi-structured to cover the research questions listed below. In some cases, more than one representative of the company was present.

In order to understand how ESV programs fit into the philanthropic strategy of the corporation and how these activities are perceived as contributions to the social economy, our semi-structured interviews were guided by the following research questions:

- What types of ESV programs are offered and how are they run?
- What is the reason for encouraging employee volunteering?
- What are the benefits to the employer and employee?
- Have ESV programs generated an increase in volunteering?
- How do employees perceive their contribution?
- What are the opportunities and challenges faced by employer and employees?
- What are the successful and not successful experiences of ESV programs?

Employee Survey Questionnaire

As part of an in-depth analysis of a single institution, we conducted a survey of employee volunteers. The questionnaire was custom designed in collaboration with the officer in charge of ESV. It examines the demographic profile of the employee volunteers, describes their volunteering activities both outside of and through their company's ESV program, and probes their motivations for volunteering. The survey questions were mainly forced-choice, closed-ended; however, opportunities for elaboration and comments were made available throughout. The survey was administered on an online independent platform (SurveyMonkey) accessed through the company's internal email system between May and August 2007. It was sent to all employees at the corporation's headquarters who volunteered in that year. The response rate was close to 60% as almost 300 employees completed the online survey. The median age of survey respondents was 35, two-thirds of whom were females and two-thirds of whom were married. An overwhelming majority (93%) had at least some post-secondary education, while two-thirds of the respondents were university graduates. Almost half of the respondents were earning in excess of $100,000.

Data Analysis

All the interviews were transcribed, coded to maintain confidentiality, and analysed to identify common themes and to better understand the essence of the ESV programs. Quantitative results of the survey questionnaire were analysed, and open-ended, qualitative questions were content coded.

Methodological Limitations

Since we were only able to survey employee volunteers, we are unable to compare their attributes to non-volunteering employees; nevertheless, the data from the surveys does give us valuable insight into the attitudes and motivations of ESV participants. This study would have been more complete had we investigated the perspective of organizations benefiting from the employee volunteers. This is a subject for future research.

Findings

Overall, the impression we gained from the interviews was how remarkably similar the ESV programs are across the entire sample. Differences were noted mostly in the details of program administration and variety of program options. With the exception of two institutions, ESV is not pivotal in a company's corporate philanthropy strategy. The low priority of ESV is reflected both organizationally and fiscally. Organizationally, ESV is peripheral in many institutions to the main focus of the department that houses it, be it Human Resources, Corporate Social Responsibility, Public Relations, or Community Relations. Budgetary allotments for ESV programs are minuscule relative to the companies' total philanthropic contributions. In two institutions, however, ESV is part of a long-term strategic vision for partnering with social economy organizations in order to improve society.

> Maybe what I should say at the outset is that it [ESV] is hugely important for us … not only to acknowledge the wonderful work that our employees are doing but to encourage that in our corporate culture. And it speaks to the values of the organization. [3]

> It [ESV] is about doing good for the sake of doing good. I don't discount companies who profile themselves or who do press releases or put their logos on things. They have reasons. Some of them are business reasons and some of them make a lot of sense, but for us, for our business, we don't need to do it. [7]

This notwithstanding, the relative success of ESV programs seems to stem more from the energetic efforts of their managers and employee commitment than from corporate strategic commitment to the programs.

Types of Employer-Supported Volunteering Programs

Similar to the typology offered by Peloza and Hassay (2006), the programs described in our interviews can be broadly categorized as (a) *credit-for-volunteering programs*, also referred to as inter-organizational volunteering, and (b) *institutional* (in-house) *projects*, also referred to as intra-organizational volunteering.

CREDIT FOR VOLUNTEERING

These programs are designed to recognize and encourage employee volunteering by making a monetary donation to a nonprofit organization at which the employee volunteered at his or her own discretion. The program is based on the American equivalent 'Dollars for Doers,' although only one of our respondents named it as such. The importance of this type of program is indicated by the fact that it was usually the first one mentioned when interviewees were asked to describe their ESV programs. In this form of ESV, the employer recognizes the volunteering efforts of employees by rewarding the nonprofit organization at which they volunteered with a donation in the range of $250 to $1,500, depending on the policy of corporation. Credit-for-volunteering programs are normally run on a basis of trust (i.e., with no required proof of volunteering). On average, about 500 to 600 employees in each company take advantage of this program yearly.

Although most institutions have some guidelines with respect to the kinds of social economy organizations they are ready to support, the range is very broad and diverse, encompassing community sports teams and public school projects on the one hand, and large formally registered charitable organizations on the other hand. In general, there is no monetary cap on the total amount donated to organizations and initiatives through ESV programs. Our respondents indicated that they would readily distribute more awards than they presently do, if only more employees would take advantage of the program.

> I'm not even sure what a reasonable goal is ... To me, 4% [of employees participating at the credit-for-volunteering program] seems low, and I'm sure if our employees started using it [applying for credit], we'd move up to 10% or whatever. The company would continue to pay that amount, well I would hope. [6]

It is clear in the interviews that, from the administrators' perspective (shared by all the respondents), the credit-for-volunteering programs are under-utilized.

Our interviewees do not think that this program actually encourages employees to volunteer more; rather, they see it as a way to reward employees for activities they are already doing on their own time, in their own communities.

> I think it's a bit more of an after-the-fact recognition ... especially with this program, where they're doing it on their own time ... We are giving them some money in recognition, but they're the ones putting in the time and the sweat work, right? [3]

Nevertheless, the survey results presented below suggest differently. At the same time, the institution garners visibility in the community, as the cheque presentation ceremony is accompanied by some form of internal and external publicity. So the benefits of the program to the company, the employees, and the community are greater than our interviewees suggest.

INSTITUTIONAL PROJECTS
This refers to volunteering efforts initiated in the workplace, either by the employees, or as part of the overall philanthropic strategy of the

corporation. They are characterized by the establishment of volunteer teams working for a specific cause, such as raising funds for a hospital or volunteering at a food bank. These team projects are more likely than individual volunteering to be accompanied by some time off during working hours for planning or even implementation.

Employee-generated programs most often occur at the branch level, and do not require approval or oversight from ESV administrators at corporate headquarters. Approvals of projects are left to the discretion of the branch managers, as long as the institution's general guidelines are followed.

> Our belief has been that we need to let our staff in local communities get behind whatever is passionate to them. So for me to sit here in Toronto and say, 'thou will volunteer for [such and such] ... Why should they not be able to fundraise for [what is] important in their local community? So, we purposefully have left it quite decentralized ... There is the distinct feeling that we should not be driving the agenda, they need to get behind what they want to get behind.[2]

The companies often contribute towards the fundraising efforts of their employees by promising to match each dollar raised with a contribution of their own.

> Our executives are very strongly supportive of the localized community and grassroots reach that it gets us. That 'grassroots' word, it becomes a buzzword. The team puts on some sort of fundraising initiative ... If they do those things [as a team], the monies that they raise are matched by [the company]. [2]

These team-building efforts are strongly supported by the corporations because they see them directly benefiting employee morale. Thus, corporations are more ready to be flexible in giving employees time off for team volunteering than for volunteering on an individual basis. Three of the institutions have formal time-off policies for individual volunteering; however, all of them claim time off is available on an *ad hoc* basis, negotiated between the individual and his or her manager.

> I don't think that there's a specific policy saying if you're volunteering for a charity, you can take time off. But I know [our company] is really good on flex hours, and you come in a little early and leave a little early

as long as you're getting your work done and it's basically up to you or your manager. [6]

Although most employee-initiated volunteering is focused on fundraising, there are definitely other types of volunteer activities. For example in one institution, employees took

> a day of their time to build homes ... so they go out for the day and build for a day ... again, subject to their managers' approval. [7]

This kind of direct volunteering, as opposed to fundraising, is more likely to be initiated by the employers than by the employees, often in response to requests from nonprofit agencies. These institution-wide initiatives are part of strategic partnerships established with other for-profit and nonprofit organizations. Examples of this are mentoring programs or providing expertise to nonprofit organizations in specific areas such as human resources management or financial management, or tutoring/mentoring youth at local schools. These 'expertise partnerships' may be expressed in the form of lectures or workshops, or one-on-one counselling delivered at regular intervals or on an 'as needed' basis. Some of these partnerships involve secondments, where an employee actually joins the staff of the nonprofit organization for a specified time. For example, one institution paid an employee to work at a nonprofit organization for a year to help establish a long-term joint venture for the benefit of society.

Costs and Challenges of Running ESV Programs

During our conversations with corporate key informants, it was clear that ESV programs entail both explicit and implicit costs. For example, direct costs include monetary awards given in recognition of employee volunteering (credit-for-volunteering programs) and matching donations in their employees' fundraising drives. Implicit costs include employee time involved in organizing and volunteering in institutional projects and staff time for disseminating, promoting, and managing ESV programs. At the time of the interviews, respondents were unable to share the actual costs of these programs, although they admitted that such costs are real but difficult to estimate as they are embedded among other programs related to corporate philanthropy or public relations.

Without question the biggest challenge mentioned by most of the ESV administrators is reaching out to employees and informing them of the many opportunities that are available to serve their communities. Compounding this challenge is the fact that volunteering is not systematically tracked, either locally at the branch level or nationally at the corporate headquarters; nor are employees regularly surveyed about their volunteering experiences through the ESV program. Thus although our interviewees know how many volunteer credit cheques are issued each year (i.e., the annual financial cost to the company), they are unable to determine the overall rate of volunteering in their institutions. Their estimates range from 10% of the workforce to 'pretty much reflecting the national average,' with most estimating on the lower end of the range.

Several of our key informants speculated that volunteering rates could be improved with better internal communications. This is true of both the credit programs and the institutional programs. Although information about programs is thought to be readily available through the internal company website, brochures, and other communication means, judging from the participation rates, the messages aren't reaching enough employees. As two of the interviewees explained:

Right, so that's [communication] one of the battles, especially in a big company like this, there are so many communications on the intranet, and so many emails … It fills up people's inboxes, and you know it's hard. [2]

I actually think that there would be a greater uptake if we more broadly communicated it. People are busy. I think that they, for whatever reason, may not know that this program is available … We know that more employees work in the community and they have not yet applied for funding. [4]

The programs run at the branches, or initiated in departments, seem to be more successfully communicated as they rely on word-of-mouth dissemination among much fewer employees with a strong emphasis on team building motivating the programs.

We're not dealing with great numbers of individuals, so there's a different dynamic that occurs in the field offices; it depends on the size, the nature of the office, whether or not they hold monthly meetings; it can be as simple as that. [8]

Working for the Social Good

In this section we examine the motivations of both the institutions and their employees for engaging in community projects that involve volunteer activities on the part of their employees.

INSTITUTIONAL PERSPECTIVE

Despite the costs associated with ESV programs, as outlined in the section above, the corporations in our sample are willing to support employee-related volunteer activities because they recognize the real, even if un-measurable, benefits accruing to the organization from these activities relating to (a) employee recruitment, satisfaction, and retention, (b) competitive business advantages, and (c) healthy communities.

ESV is generally seen as more important for employee morale than for its contribution to the social good: 'What has been most important to me is the surge in employee pride in the organization' [1]. ESV administrators also speculated that their programs would make their company more competitive in recruiting good candidates as well as helping to retain them.

> I think we can safely say that it has been a point of attraction for potential employees. Just the general data available to us completely supports that. [1]

> I can't say whether or not we've recruited more employees because of this ... [but] I think with respect to volunteerism, it does help in recruiting ... also retention. I think people want to work for an organization that has certain social responsibilities and corporate citizenship. [4]

ESV programs are credited with putting their companies on the local map. As one interviewee said, 'We get ... high profile in lots of small communities and [it is] very important' [5]. Another one added:

> I think the corporation also benefits when community organizations benefit. When you talk about the corporation, it's in everyone's interest, [to] have a strong healthy community.' [4]

Thus ESV programs are seen as enhancing the corporation's image as a good corporate citizen, especially at a time when the public is increasingly demanding some social accountability from them. But, some respondents pointed out that recognition was not the most important gain.

> This is certainly a very important part of what we do, but I don't necessarily think there's been an enormous surge in recognition in the community. [1]

Interestingly, none of the respondents saw the new legal requirement to publish a Public Accountability Statement as a driving force in these programs, 'I don't think the PAS is driving it. I think word-of-mouth of our staff is driving it'[2].

Be this as it may, our key informants recognized the need for corporate social responsibility and saw it as their mission to help their institutions contribute to the social economy. ESV is one way of achieving this through direct engagement in the social economy of their communities. As one respondent said, 'Philanthropy is really about building communities' [4].

INDIVIDUAL PERSPECTIVE

From the institutional perspective, employees participating in ESV programs are seen as 'ambassadors to the community' not only bringing intangible benefits to their institutions but also engaging in the production of social goods. In order to ascertain some of the benefits and motivations of employees engaged in volunteering programs, we conducted a survey of employee volunteers in one of the financial institutions in our sample. The survey probed the volunteering practices of employees, the extent of their participation, their motivations for and satisfaction with the volunteering experience, and their perceived benefits.

In general, volunteering has an element of personal choice and an element of individual cost. The element of choice is at the heart of the notion of volunteering (Handy, Cnaan, Brudney, Meijs, Ascoli, & Ranade, 2000), even for employee volunteers who might experience pressure from their employer or peers to participate. For volunteers there is always a cost of supplying labour without receiving monetary remuneration. Despite the many intangible benefits that accrue to the volunteer, the costs exceed the benefits, which is the defining aspect of volunteering (Handy et al., 2000). Thus, if volunteering that takes place at the employee's own discretion and time is compared with a similar activity done in the framework of a company ESV program, the latter might yield greater benefits to the individual in terms of career enhancement, or positive recognition by the employer. This is especially true if the company seeks to promote such activity among its employees and uses it to showcase its performances in social responsibility publications. Examining why employees choose to get involved in such activities might shed light on whether this method of promoting the social good is indeed an important way to rethink corporate/nonprofit partnership in the social economy.

The surveyed company engages their employees in volunteering through both types of ESV programs identified above: credit-for-volunteering and institutional projects. As mentioned earlier, institutional programs are usually team-based and run on a regular and recurring basis, although there are some *ad hoc* projects initiated by employees often at the local level. In addition to the typical ESV programs, outstanding community contributions by employees are recognized in the company each year in a special awards ceremony.

Of those who are involved in ESV programs, a vast majority of respondents (92.0%) participate only in company-initiated projects, while 1.3% participate in the matching program only, and nearly 7% participate in both programs (6.7%). The rate of participation varies, with most employees (74.0%) volunteering only occasionally and the remaining volunteering on a regular basis – weekly (16%), or monthly (7%). Seventy percent of respondents volunteer for less than 10 hours a month. Reasons given for volunteering through the ESV programs are, in order of frequency: 'it provides an opportunity to help others' (98%), 'it is part of the company's culture' (61%), 'because my co-workers volunteer' (29%), 'because senior management encourages it' (26%), and 'because of the matching grants' (25%).

Our survey demonstrates that employer-supported volunteering programs do have an impact on volunteering rates of employees, thus indirectly contributing to the social economy. Close to half of the respondents (42%) report that ESV was their first volunteering experience; almost one-third (32%) claim that their ESV experience motivates them to volunteer outside the workplace; and one in five volunteers (20%) report that the ESV matching grant program (credit for volunteering) encourages them to increase their hours of volunteering in order to receive the grant. Nonetheless, nearly half (45%) state that the ESV initiatives make no difference in the intensity of their volunteering.[3] This latter finding corresponds to the fact that not all volunteering reported by our respondents is supported by the company. Although over half (57%) of the volunteers receive full company support, the other half receive only partial support or no support at all (34% and 9%, respectively). This suggests that participation in the ESV programs does not preclude employees from additional volunteering on an individual basis outside their workplace, or in other words contributing to the overall social economy irrespective of their employer contribution.

Company officers do not doubt the impact of ESV in creating a culture of volunteering and encouraging employees to participate. Open-ended comments by respondents indicate this to be so.

> In making volunteering arrangements, the company helped me to identify a 'legitimate, deserving charity.'

> [As] most of the arrangements are made by the company this is easy and available to fit in my schedule.

> [The company's] strong support for variety of volunteer works makes it easy for us to be involved.

In terms of benefits that accrue from their volunteering, respondents focus on the community rather than themselves. Their activities, according to their self-reported beliefs, 'increase a sense of community' and 'build trust' in society. Career enhancement and professional networking are both ranked low in importance. The lowest-ranked benefit is 'getting recognition from co-workers,' despite the fact that 85% of respondents say they volunteer alongside their co-workers and colleagues and 29% see this as an important reason for volunteering. Our findings indicate that respondents' satisfaction with their workplace improved significantly following their participation in ESV initiatives. Employees not only see the company as contributing to the social good and caring for their community, but also take pride in this image of their company. However, not many respondents agree that ESV programs are likely to contribute to company loyalty or employee retention.

In some of the open-ended questions, respondents give further details on how they perceive the ESV programs. Although they were not asked directly whether such activities contribute to the social economy, the sentiment is captured in the following quotes.

> To me it is the XX Public School because it is in our community. I live in the area so it is especially important to me.

Giving back to the kids through ... The results are seen almost immediately and they directly impact the lives of those around us.

Community activities are the most meaningful initiatives by [the company].

I am proud of what my company does to give back to the community.

They always have something we can volunteer in and they are very community-oriented.

[The company] takes an active part in community relations and activities.

Discussion and Conclusions

Our point of departure in this chapter was to view the social economy not only in terms of participating organizations but also as *activities* aimed at enhancing the 'the social good' in communities and society. This view broadens our perspective of what constitutes social economy to include social and/or economic activities beyond those conducted, promoted, or championed by nonprofit organizations, co-operatives, and social enterprises. Our overarching argument is that certain activities within the public and corporate spheres should also be considered as part of the social economy. In fact, part of every government's mandate is to provide for the good and welfare of its citizens and it may do so in a variety of ways. Thus when government partners with nonprofits to provide social services and achieve social goals, it is indirectly contributing to the social economy.

More recently, the corporate sector, too, has been taking an interest in promoting 'social good,' perhaps in response to external forces. In the past couple of decades there has been an increasing demand by the public to see for-profit corporations 'giving back' to their communities (Berger, Cunningham, & Drumwright, 2006). Then, in 2001 government enacted legislation requiring high-earning financial institutions to prepare an annual Public Accountability Statement (PAS), reinforcing the growing consensus that corporations have a social obligation to the communities in which they operate and cannot disassociate themselves from the social challenges facing our country. And finally, changes to the tax law regarding charitable donations have furnished a more favourable climate for charitable giving. When a corporation makes donations, or encourages employees to volunteer, or collaborates with nonprofit organizations in other ways, it is promoting, and in a sense participating in, the social economy.

We focus on a relatively new, and certainly growing, form of corporate participation in the social economy – employer-supported volunteering. Using the three motivational categories identified by Foster and her colleagues (2009) – reactive, creating goodwill for the company, and improving society – we found that the practice of ESV in our sample is motivated by the latter two. None of the corporations in our sample is motivated only by a reaction to expectations. Most organizations are concerned with creating goodwill for their company. Their ESV programs are informed by some planning and have clear goals; their primary motive is to present their organization in a favourable light for the benefit of both their internal and external stakeholders. Only two organizations are truly motivated by a desire to improve society. These organizations are involved in company-initiated, long-term partnerships with nonprofit organizations where their employees proffer assistance over a longer period of time. They are genuinely motivated by 'doing good.' Clearly, the lines between the categories are not absolute. Whether they admit it or not, all organizations gain self-benefit from participating in the social economy.

Some may argue, as Milton Friedman did, that philanthropic activities have no place in the corporate sector. And indeed, only 30% of commercial organizations in the United States contribute to social, cultural, educational, and other causes (KPMG & Peat Marwick, 1997). Others may claim that corporate participation in the social economy is simply a guise to 'buy' satisfied employees and gain consumer goodwill (Reich, 2007). But this is to miss the point. Social economy activities occur in all sectors, and if such activity promotes the social good, then it should not matter whence the spring of goodwill arises.

Given this, we can point to some policy implications that may further integrate for-profit organizations into the social economy through activities that promote the social good alongside the company's own agenda. First, improved in-house communication would engage more employees in the community through volunteering. The current low participation rates suggest that the ESV programs are either not 'heard' by many of the employees, or are of little interest to them. Better communications strategies need to be devised to engage employees; the use of the intranet may be counterproductive when most employees already receive far too many emails on busy working days. Furthermore, combing two trends in volunteering research – greater evidence for the rise of episodic volunteering and the importance of volunteering done in teams (especially those initiated by the employer) – suggests opportunities for nonprofits to partner with for-profits. Nonprofits that require volunteer labour to handle specific tasks can turn to for-profits with opportunities of utilizing skilled volunteers for a specific time and not expect them to return over a long period. This requires nonprofits to find innovative ways to satisfy their needs using teams of volunteers in a one-off situation such as fundraising, preparation of holiday meals, or seashore clean-ups. There is a role for a co-ordinating umbrella organization that encourages nonprofit and for-profit partnerships in such manners. It would list the various types of events requiring teams of volunteers and market these opportunities among for-profits, playing the role of a broker. Volunteer Canada, for example, has started an initiative in this direction by establishing the Corporate Council on Volunteering (Mitchell, personal communication, 2006)

In conclusion, the premise of this chapter is that corporate support of employee volunteering constitutes an important and significant contribution to the social economy. ESV programs have the potential to raise awareness and generate conversations between the various stakeholders in the different sectors that give rise to opportunities for sustained cross-sectoral partnerships. In a period where multinational financial institutions are suspected of creating the largest of financial crises, ESV provides a useful mechanism and a ready channel of communication and engagement with local communities. Employee-supported volunteers give a human face to the for-profit institution and lend authenticity, credibility, and legitimacy to these institutions while contributing in meaningful ways to the social economy – areas that were not traditionally within the realm of the for-profit world.

Directions for future research would involve integrating the perspectives of leaders of social economy organizations in an evaluation of the contribution of ESV programs towards the public good. At present, corporate ESV programs are limited to a very small number of social economy organizations, mostly supporting larger, more well-known organizations. Smaller organizations serving needier populations and more controversial causes are seldom chosen for support by corporations; yet it is these very organizations that may benefit most from this kind of volunteer support. Future research may help point the way to integrating more of the social economy into the volunteer efforts of corporate volunteers.

NOTES

1 The authors note that 'the most common forms of [volunteer] support are adjusting work schedules (78%), providing time-off without pay (71%), and allowing access to company facilities and equipment (70%)' (p. iii).
2 Subsection 459.3(1) of the Bank Act; Public Accountability Statements (Banks, Insurance Companies, Trust and Loan Companies) Regulations P.C. 2002–402 March 21, 2002. http://laws.justice.gc.ca/en/ShowDoc/cr/SOR-2002–133/bo-ga:s_1::bo-ga:s_2//en?page=1&isprinting=true
3 These figures are not mutually exclusive, as respondents could reply positively to more than one option.

REFERENCES

Berger, I., Cunningham, P., & Drumwright, M. (2006). Identity, identification, and relationship through social alliances. *Journal of the Academy of Marketing Science, 34*(2), 128–37.

Dart, R. (2004). Being 'business-like' in a nonprofit organization: A grounded and inductive typology. *Nonprofit and Voluntary Sector Quarterly, 33*(2), 290–310.

de Gilder, D.D., Schuyt, T.N.M., & Breedijk, M. (2005). Effects of an employee volunteering program on the work force. *Journal of Business Ethics, 61*(2), 143–52.

Easwaramoorthy, M., Barr, C., Runte, M., & Basil, D. (2006). *Business support for employee volunteers in Canada: Results of a national survey.* Retrieved from Imagine Canada http://library.imaginecanada.ca/files/kdc-cdc/imagine_business_support_report.pdf

Edmans, A. (2009). Does the stock market fully value intangibles? Employee satisfaction and equity prices. Retrieved December 9, 2009, from the Social Science Research Network http://ssrn.com/abstract=985735

Foster, M., Meinhard, A., Berger, I., & Krpan, P. (2009). Corporate philanthropy in the Canadian context: From damage control to improving society. *Nonprofit and Voluntary Sector Quarterly, 38*(3), 441–66. DOI: 10.1177/0899764008316249.

Friedman, M. (1970, September 13). The social responsibility of business is to increase profits. *The New York Times Magazine.*

Graff, L. (2004). *Making a business case for employer-supported volunteerism.* Retrieved from Volunteer Canada http://www.volunteer.ca/files/ESVThinkPiece.pdf

Hall, M., Easwaramoorthy, M., & Sandler, W. (2007). *Business contributions to Canadian communities: Findings from a qualitative study of current practices.* Retrieved November 13, 2009, from Imagine Canada http://nonprofitscan.imaginecanada.ca/files/en/misc/business_contributions_en.pdf

Hall, M., McKeown, L., & Roberts, K. (2000). *Caring Canadians, involved Canadians: Highlights from the 2000 National Survey of Giving, Volunteering and Participating.* Catalogue no 71-542-XIE. Retrieved from http://www.givingandvolunteering.ca/pdf/n-2000-hr-ca.pdf

Handy, F., Cnaan, R.A., Brudney, J., Meijs, L., Ascoli, U., & Ranade, S. (2000). Public perception of 'who is a volunteer': An examination of the net-cost approach – a cross-cultural perspective. *Voluntas, 11*(1), 45–65.

KPMG & Peat Marwick. (1997). *Organizations serving the public: Transformation to the 21st century.* New York: KPMG & Peat Marwick.

Meinhard, A., Foster, M., Moher, L., & Fitzrandolph, S. (2006). Commercial ventures in nonprofit organizations: Strategic change or natural evolution? *The Hungarian Journal of Marketing & Management, 40*(6), 147–54.

Mitchell, W. (2006, June 26). Personal communication.

Mook, L., Quarter, J., & Richmond, B.J. (2007). *What counts: Social accounting for nonprofits and cooperatives.* London: Sigel Press.

Moulaert, F., & Ailenei, O. (2005). Social economy, third sector and solidarity relations: A conceptual synthesis from history to present. *Urban Studies, 42*(11), 2037–54.

NSGVP. (2004). *Employer-supported volunteering.* Fact sheet from the 2000 National Survey of Giving, Volunteering and Participating. Retrieved from http://www.givingandvolunteering.ca/files/giving/en/factsheets/employer_support_volunteering.pdf

Orlitzky, M., Schmidt, F., & Rynes, S. (2003). Corporate social and financial performance: A meta-analysis. *Organization Studies, 24*(3), 403–41.

Peloza, J., & Hassay, D.N. (2006). Intra-organizational volunteerism: Good soldiers, good deeds and good politics. *Journal of Business Ethics, 64*(4), 357–79.

Peloza, J., Hudson, S., & Hassay, D. (2009). The marketing of employee volunteerism. *Journal of Business Ethics, 85*(2), 371–86. DOI 10.1007/s10551-008-9734-z

Points of Light Foundation. (2005). *Measuring employee volunteering programs:*

The human resources model. Points of Light Foundation & The Centre for Corporate Citizenship at Boston College.

Quarter, J. (1992). *Canada's social economy: Co-operatives, non-profits, and other community enterprises.* Toronto: James Lorimer.

Quarter, J., Mook, L., & Armstrong, A. (2009). *Understanding Canada's social economy.* Toronto: University of Toronto Press.

Reich, R. (2007). *Supercapitalism: The transformation of business, democracy and everyday life.* Toronto: Random House of Canada.

Rocha, C. (2009). Developments in national policies for food and nutrition security in Brazil. *Development Policy Review, 27*(1), 51–66.

Rochlin, S., & Christoffer, B. (2000). *Making the business case: Determining the value of corporate community involvement.* The Center for Corporate Citizenship.

Rog, E., Pancer, S.M., & Baetz, M.C. (2004). *Community and corporate perspectives on corporate volunteer programs: A win-win approach to community betterment.* Toronto: Canadian Centre for Philanthropy.

Rostami, J., & Hall, M. (1996). *Employee volunteers: Business support in the community.* Toronto and Ottawa: Canadian Centre for Philanthropy and Conference Board of Canada.

Safrit, D., & Merrill, M. (1998, November). *An exploratory study of corporate volunteer motivations for baby boomers and Generation X: Critical issues in nonprofit management and leadership.* Paper Presented at the 27th Annual Conference of the Association for Research on Nonprofit Organizations and Voluntary Action (ARNOVA), Seattle, WA.

12 Work Stoppages in Canadian Social Economy Organizations

KUNLE AKINGBOLA

This study examines the causes, impacts, and dimensions of work stoppages resulting from strikes and lockouts in social economy organizations (SEOs) in Ontario between 1994 and 2005. It provides insight into the state of labour relations and, to some extent, human resource management in the sector. I suggest that due to the underlying social values of these organizations (Quarter, 1992; Quarter, Mook, & Richmond, 2003) and the type of workers they tend to attract (Brown & Yoshioka, 2003; McMullen & Schellenberg, 2003), these stoppages may be consistent with the collective voice explanation of strikes and explain strike proneness in subsectors of the social economy (Godard, 1992; Hyman, 1989).

Although the literature on labour relations in Canada has largely omitted the social economy, the associated organizations offer a unique context for the study of industrial relations. With a vibrant civil society, the second largest nonprofit and voluntary sector in the world (Hall, Barr, Easwaramoorthy, Sokolowski, & Salamon 2005), and a co-operative sector that includes some of the top employers in the country (Quarter et al., 2003), Canada provides an excellent context for the study of labour relations in social economy organizations. The conception of the social economy used in this chapter is similar to that presented in chapter 1 by Mook et al. and in chapter 2 on Ontario's social economy by Lasby et al.

Work Stoppages

An underlying characteristic of employment relationship from a pluralist perspective is that conflict is inevitable (Edwards, 2003). Work stoppages are manifestations of this unavoidable conflict, which occurs when there is a temporary breakdown in the relationship between employers and employees. Employees therefore embark on a strike to compel the employer to address a grievance, demand, or position (Hyman, 1989). Similarly, employers use lockouts in an attempt to induce or compel employees to accept their terms of employment (Hyman, 1989).

Three theoretical approaches are relevant to explain work stoppages in social economy organizations. The neoclassical economic literature examines the effect of strikes in terms of productivity, profitability, capital investment, and employment growth (Budd, 1994; Hanrahan, Kushner, Martinello, & Masse, 1997; Hirsch, 1997). The primary conclusion of this perspective is that strikes reduce profitability and capital investment (Hirsch, 1997). Institutional and organizational explanations of why strikes occur highlight social and behavioural dimensions of labour disputes (Darlington, 2004; Hyman, 1989; Kerr & Siegel, 1954). This perspective posits that some industries and occupations are more prone to strike because of the inherent social characteristics of the work that enables collective consciousness and community integration (Kerr & Siegel, 1954).

Social movement unionism aligns workplace goals and social change through partnership with social groups. However, until recently, industrial relations literature has characterized social movement unionism mainly as another means to enhancing trade unionism, which has achieved limited social objectives (Bellemare, Gravel, Briand, & Vallée, 2006). The new form of social movement unionism extends the objectives to include coalitions with civil society to achieve broader objectives in social change, public policy, and working conditions (Bellemare et al., 2006; Mathers, Taylor, & Upchurch, 2004; Turner, 2004). The proponents of the new social movement unionism see opportunities for better and long-term integration of strategy between unions and civil society. This has been interpreted as the effect of a neo-liberal agenda in North America (Mathers et al., 2004; Robinson, 2000).

Human Resource Management and Labour Relations Context of Social Economy Organizations

For many social economy organizations, their human resources, consisting of employees and volunteers, are truly their most important asset. Studies in Canada and the U.S. have substantiated the critical importance of human resources to the effectiveness of these organizations (Barbeito & Bowman, 1998; Hall, Andrukow, & Associates, 2003; Light, 2002). While there is limited research on human resources management in co-operatives in Canada, available literature points to the critical importance of human resources to the performance and growth of the organizations (Arcand, Bayad, & Fabi, 2002).

Moreover, there are other factors that contribute to the added importance of human resources to social economy organizations and nonprofits in particular. First, the personal services provided by many social economy organizations mean that they cannot replace employees with investment in physical capital. In most cases, employees are the services.

Second, more than in other organizations, employees of nonprofits (and by extension social economy organizations) are attracted and are motivated by intrinsic factors such as a belief in the organization's mission and opportunity to actualize individual values (Brandel, 2001; Brown & Yoshioka, 2003; McMullen & Schellenberg, 2003). Chaves and Moreno (2004) suggest that as a result of the consistency between managers' beliefs, value systems, and management style, behaviour patterns that are detrimental to business organizations are less likely in social economy organizations. Nonprofit employees are deeply committed; they are known to informally volunteer their time as part of their job and to participate in other activities of the organizations. In addition to their employment role, employees are also an invaluable component of the volunteer productive capacity of many social economy organizations.

Third, employees of social economy organizations are likely to participate in the decision-making process because many of these organizations embrace democratic culture (Arcand et al., 2002; Brandel, 2001). Consistent with the value orientation of social economy organizations, employees are more likely to be encouraged to generate or contribute ideas for service delivery and work in project teams and committees, and they have more varied tasks in their work. This intrinsic benefit gives employees a sense of purpose (Brandel, 2001). The opportunity for participation could also be explained in terms of size and the close-knit environment of many social economy organizations. Since many nonprofits are small (McMullen & Schellenberg, 2002), there seem to be more opportunities for employees to participate in decision-making. Co-operatives embrace participation and communication as key components of their human resources management practices (Arcand et al., 2002).

Beyond the social objectives and values of social economy organizations, the economic reality of increased dependence on government funding, the related political reality of increased accountability, and demands for efficiency (Akingbola, 2006) have added weight to the importance of human resources. The need for the professional delivery of services and the accountability requirements of the new funding environment suggest that employees are critical stakeholders in the strategy of social economy organizations.

Together, the social objectives and values of nonprofits and co-operatives and the operating realities of funding for nonprofits in particular have made human resource management of utmost importance. But there is more: new findings are emerging that point to increasing challenges for human resource management in the sector. Although research is scarce on labour relations in social economy organizations, where employees are unionized or covered by a collective agreement, labour relations is an integral part of human resource management. Thus, the human resource management challenges are very likely to shape labour relations, and furthermore, some authors have predicted that these challenges will increase the rate of unionization in the sector (Peters & Masaoka, 2000; Pynes, 1997). I briefly review the challenges below.

An interesting observation about the challenges of human resource management and labour relations in social economy organizations is that they are related to the same factors that make their context unique – social objectives, values, funding, and civil society. It has been suggested that nonprofit employees are more likely to experience job dissatisfaction if (a) they perceive that their organization is not achieving the public good that attracted them; (b) the mission is de-emphasized or derailed by other exigencies; (c) the espoused values are inconsistent with those in use in the organization (Akingbola, 2006; Kim, 2005). The increased accountability requirement has been identified as a source of stress and job dissatisfaction among child welfare employees (Howe & McDonald, 2001). Similarly, Peters and Masaoka (2000) found that disgruntlement among employees, particularly relating to lack of participation in the decision-making process, contributed to increased unionization in nonprofits.

Bearing in mind that nonprofits tend to be value driven and attract employees who have identified with their values (Brown & Yoshioka, 2003: Handy & Katz, 1998), there are questions about what unionization will mean to their values and mission. However, Akingbola (2005) found that union status was not associated with the importance of mission in the decision to develop new services. But more importantly, the study found that unionized nonprofits were more likely to depend on government funding than non-unionized nonprofits, thus highlighting that unionized nonprofits are more likely to be in services that were previously provided directly by the government. Unions could assist nonprofits in their advocacy activities to government and in enhancing the egalitarian values of the organization.

Regardless of the attraction of employees to the values and social objectives of social economy organizations, compensation is an important human resources management factor. There are two views on compensation in social economy organizations. While many studies have reported that compensation is generally low in nonprofit organizations in particular (Barbeito & Bowman, 1998; Brandel, 2001; Handy & Katz, 1998; McMullen & Schellenberg, 2003), other studies found that there is no wage differential (Handy, Mook, Ginieniewicz, & Quarter, 2007). McMullen and Schellenberg reported that the average earnings of managerial, professional, and technical/trades categories of nonprofit employees are lower than those of their comparative categories in the other sectors. The comparatively low pay in nonprofit organizations is a major human resource management and labour relations concern.

Together these factors highlight the need to examine the causes, impacts, and dimensions of work stoppages. The implications of strikes for employees, management, and customers/clients as well as the impact on the community are important if we are to understand the dynamic interplay of forces in the sector. The study aims to explore whether the underlying social values of these organizations are consistent with the neoclassical economic, structural, and institutional theoretical explanations of strikes, and whether there is an indication of social movement unionism.

Based on these factors, the paper examines the following research questions:

1 Are wages and conditions of service the major causes of work stoppages in social economy organizations?
2 Are service quality and advocacy issues a rationale for work stoppages in social economy organizations?
3 What are the impacts of work stoppages in social economy organizations on clients and the community?

Data and Method

The study is based on two sets of data, one quantitative and the other qualitative. The quantitative data are the official record of work stoppages of the Ontario Ministry of Labour between 1994 and 2005. There were 196 work stoppages resulting from labour disputes involving social economy organizations. The quantitative data provides the context for the research questions. For the qualitative data, two case studies were conducted to examine the questions above. These cases offer in-depth insight into the frontline and backroom drivers of labour disputes in nonprofits. One of the case studies was a 34-day strike action while the second was a labour dispute that resulted in a 93% vote in favour of strike action. The case studies were part of a larger study that examined unionization in nonprofit organizations. Since the two case studies involved union locals of the Canadian Union of Public Employees (CUPE), interviews were conducted with CUPE local executives of four organizations and three executive directors of organizations with CUPE locals. The case studies provided details and perspectives that could not be obtained in a survey. The qualitative data were analysed using open coding (Strauss & Corbin, 1998), and the text was combed for descriptive categories based on themes relevant to the research.

Measures and Analysis

The Ministry of Labour data include three main dimensions of work stoppages: incidence, duration, and size. Measures relevant to this study include type of work stoppages, days out, industry, names of unions, and location. As explained below, additional variables were created from the dataset to examine work stoppages in the sector.

The dependent variables are (1) incidents of work stoppage and (2) days out. *Work stoppage* includes strike, illegal strike, or lockout. The average number of work stoppages for the study was 1.12 (SD = .39). *Days out* is the duration or number of days that the work stoppage lasted. The average number of days was 45.76 (SD = 60.44).

There were five independent variables. (1) Type of organization was measured based on three categorizations relevant to the social economy sector:

i *Social Economy Organizations*: social economy organizations are classified into their two main types: nonprofits and co-operatives.

One hundred and seventy-six (89.9%) of the social economy organizations were nonprofits while 20 (10.2%) were co-operatives;
ii *Industrial sector code*: the Ontario Ministry of Labour classified
organizations into four main groups – private (33.7%), municipal
(5.6%), provincial (60.7), federal and various;
iii *Association Canada categories*: these define organizations based on
their type of service: transportation (3.1%), religion (2%), recreation
(9.2%), public service (17.3%), law and justice (1%), labour (9.2%),
industry (1.4%), health (44.4%), education (2%), Canadians and
society (1.5%), business and finance (6.6%), arts and culture
(2%).

Other independent variables are (2) *Size*: number of employees involved in the work stoppage. The average number of employees was
159 (*SD* = 727.61); (3) *Economic region*: classification of the province
into economic regions using government data; (4) *Union classification*:
whether the union represents bargaining units primarily in the public, private, nonprofit, or various sectors; (5) *Year*: the calendar year in
which the work stoppage occurred.

Simple descriptive statistics were completed to examine the relevant
scale, frequency, and dimension of work stoppages in social economy
organizations between 1994 and 2005.

The case studies data were examined to answer research questions
1, 2, and 3. The data were analysed extensively to elicit themes that
were specific to the research. The interviews and data were coded into
descriptive categories. First the entire interview text was combed for
descriptive categories, which were then reviewed to highlight themes
relevant to the research questions. A brief description of the two organizations in case studies is provided below.

Case 1 was established in 1911. The organization provides services
for youth, new Canadians, low-income families, women, and seniors.
Involvement and engagement of neighbours across class, culture, and
generations are the central operating philosophy of the organization.
As a multi-service organization, the organization also provides workshops for stroke survivors and operates a daycare that accommodates
children with special needs and autism. About 150 employees were
members of the CUPE local at the time of the strike in 2003.

Case 2 is a multi-service downtown Toronto nonprofit organization
with a core operational mandate to assist disadvantaged individuals,
families, and groups in the community to have greater control of their

lives by promoting personal and social change. The services of the organization include settlement, adult literacy programs, a high school diploma equivalency program for mature students, a drop in, employment skills development programs, supportive housing, and support programs for families, children, the elderly, and abused women. The organization was founded in 1912.

Results

The findings suggest that between 1994 and 2005, social economy organizations in Ontario lost 490,190 person days to 196 work stoppages. The number of employees involved in the work stoppages ranged from 2 to 10,000, highlighting the significant variation in organizational size and work stoppage duration.

There was significant variability in work stoppages by year. As shown in figure 12.1, the most extensive work stoppages, as measured by person-days lost, occurred in 1996, 1998, and 2000. The person-days lost in each of these three years varied from the Cerminara Boys' Residence strike involving nine employees with 830 person-days lost to the industrial action of 575 nursing staff of Victoria Order of Nurses (VON) across the province involving 5,240 person-days lost.

Another important observation relevant to the discussion of the person-days lost in 1996, 1998, and 2000 is that these strikes occurred at a tumultuous time, for nonprofit organizations in particular, because of the implementation of neo-liberal policies by the government in Ontario. The Victorian Order of Nurses was particularly affected by the opening of competition for home healthcare to for-profit companies.

As expected, the most common form of work stoppage was strike. Within the period, 180 strikes (including four that were illegal) constituted 91.8% of work stoppages. Most of the work stoppages (155 occurrences, 79%) lasted between one and 60 days. Between 1994 and 2005, there were 16 lockouts representing 8.2% of work stoppages. More than in any other year, 2004 seems to have been a year of lockouts, with seven (43.8%) of the 16 lockouts recorded. Although small compared to strikes, the lockouts by management were as diverse as the Kennedy House Youth Services and the Ontario Jockey Club.

Sub-Sector

Nonprofits account for 176 (89.9%) work stoppages recorded between

Figure 12.1. Person-days lost

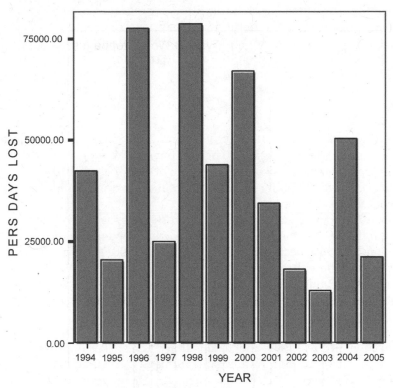

1994 and 2005; co-operatives experienced 20 (10.2%) work stoppages. Using the 12 classifications of organizations by Association Canada, the data indicate that 87 (44.4%) of the work stoppages occurred in health organizations, followed by public service organizations with 34 (17.3%) work stoppages (see figure 12.2). It is unclear whether this finding is due to greater strike proneness among health organizations or their larger representation in the sample. However, it is important to note that healthcare and social services have the largest number of employees among nonprofit subsectors.

Another interesting and perhaps paradoxical finding is that labour unions as employers experienced the third largest number of work stoppages among social economy organizations. Between 1994 and 2005, labour unions experienced 18 (9.2%) work stoppages – the Sheet Metal Workers, Canadian Auto Workers' Union, and Service Employees'

Figure 12.2. Work stoppages by organization type (Association Canada Categories)

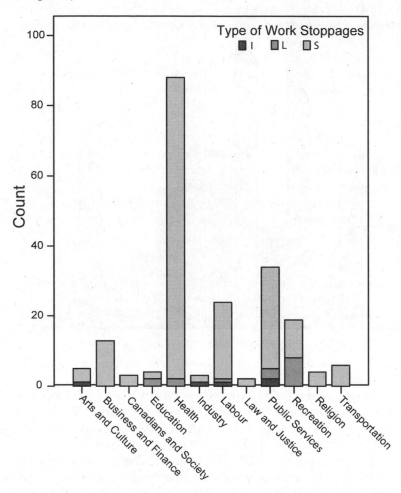

International Union each experiencing more than one strike within the period and the Service Employees' International Union local 204 locking out 25 employees for 36 days in 1997.

Other sub-sectors that experienced a relatively large number of work stoppages were recreation and gaming organizations, and business and finance associations. By comparison, law and justice organizations had only two work stoppages, the lowest rate over the period.

While the Ministry of Labour data may not provide sufficient information to draw conclusions, the test of association between variables below provides a good insight on work stoppages and enhances our understanding of the research questions (Tashakkori & Teddlie, 1998).

WORK STOPPAGES

A linear regression analysis was conducted to explore the relationship between work stoppage and each of the independent variables. The results indicate that the Ministry of Labour industrial sector classification modestly predicts work stoppage, $R^2 = .03$. adjusted $R^2 = .02$. $p < .05$, but the relationship is weak. Organizations classified as provincial by the Ministry of Labour were more likely to experience work stoppages than those classified as private or municipal. The federal and various categories were not present in the sample.

None of the other predictors (the two other measures of organizational type, economic region, union classification, and year) was related to work stoppages.

DAYS OUT

Consistent with the findings on incidents of work stoppages, the results on days out – the duration of the work stoppage – indicate that the Ministry of Labour industrial sector classification does predict how long a work stoppage will last $R^2 = .05$. adjusted $R^2 = .04$. $p < .01$. Another variable that predicted days out is union classification $R^2 = .02$. adjusted $R^2 = .02$. $p < .05$. Year also modestly predicted days out $R^2 = .02$. adjusted $R^2 = .01$. $p < .10$, thus indicating that the number of days work stoppages lasted was significantly higher in some years. Days out was unrelated to any of the other variables including size.

Qualitative Results from Case Studies

As indicated above, the case studies were analysed to examine research questions: (1)Are wages and conditions of service the major causes of work stoppages in social economy organizations? (2) Are service quality and advocacy issues rationale for work stoppages in social economy organizations? (3) What are the impacts of work stoppages in social economy organizations on clients and the community?

Cases 1 and 2 are both multi-service organizations that have been in operation for close to 100 years. As a result, it is evident that they have experienced the transformation of the nonprofit sector in Canada.

Unionization appears to be part of the new experience for the organizations. Case 1 became unionized in 1999 while case 2 was unionized in the late 1980s. According to case 2 union local executive, there was no document of the actual date because the structure was informal and mostly led by individuals.

CAUSES OF LABOUR DISPUTES

The union executives explained that wage rate was a central issue in the labour disputes. Case 1 union executive explained that

> We have also managed to make increases in wages and benefits for our workers. So that has been an important success with where the union is at. We had gone close to ten years without a wage increase at the agency and we got a wage increase and as well the majority of our workers didn't receive any benefits at all and we were actually on strike last summer and those were the two key issues--monetary issues and we were able to get a better wage benefit package for workers.

Although case 2 union executive attributed part of the challenge to the inactivity of the union in the organization for many years, he noted that employees did not receive any increase for many years.

> when I came to the agency about six years ago they had a collective agreement for seven years. Even the union was certified. There was nobody that was doing the union work, so that means there hadn't been any increase in salaries, there hadn't been any kind of changes to salary structure for staff, no negotiations about that. What we are trying to achieve now is a little bit of harmony in terms of salaries they get paid, benefits for part-time and full-time.

Union local executives and executive directors who have not been involved in work stoppages appear to corroborate the findings from the case studies. They explained that although wage rate was the top item in their collective bargaining, both the management and union parties were aware that funding may not support an increase in wages. As one of the management executives noted, 'the fact that we have a union does not mean that funders will give us more.'

SERVICE QUALITY AND ADVOCACY ISSUES AS RATIONALE
FOR WORK STOPPAGES

On the one hand, the case studies provided evidence that wage rate was the primary driver of work stoppages in nonprofit organizations. On the other hand, there was also evidence that wage rate was coupled with issues such as condition of service, quality of care or client issues, and funding. In other words, it was not all about wages. The following responses from two union local executives involved in the work stoppages reiterate this point.

> So, there have been monetary gains and I know as well from my past I find that the union is at the place where I could engage in work that I want to do and on issues that impact on the community and also the people that I work with like on issues of homelessness, issues of immigration, issues of poverty, issues of racism. The union I find is a very -- a concept I guess what they call it is social unionism, and that is something that many of us who are active in our local have been activists, or community activists already and we now use our union locals as a tool for that purpose as well.

> We are always talking about issues and the community right, we are talking about the social values, and we are always concerned about serving communities, help[ing] communities rather than kind of like, you know, giving our service ... based on how much money you have to pay. The more money you have the better service you can get, you know, trying to equalize the service delivery. So what happens is that when a sector is under-funded and we struggle with management about, you know, how best to manage that under-funding and where do you compromise? Do you compromise on program delivery, you compromise on organization or the structure, you compromise on salaries for staff?

One of the executive directors noted that, ultimately, union and work stoppages may work for the advantage of the organization and clients. The executive director noted that

> a major advantage of being unionized is that the union could (pressure) the Ontario government. They pressure government to fund subsidies for the agency's pay equity program. They have the ability to do that because they are powerful, they can get together and work together collaboratively to address the systems' issues.

IMPACT OF WORK STOPPAGES

Since the Ministry of Labour database does not include the cause and impact of the labour disputes, the research relied on the case studies, particularly information on whether and how the services were provided during the labour disputes. While case 2 did not include this information because a strike was avoided, case 1 and interviews of executive directors provided sufficient examples of how labour disputes affected clients, the organization, and mitigating strategies of the social economy organizations during work stoppages.

In case 1, the organization was faced with complete closure of all its services including homecare support, shelter and youth services, and childcare because of the strike. To avert and mitigate the impact of the strike on the homeless, the organization paid the homeless clients to perform some of the duties of employees who were on strike. The union executive who was involved in the work stoppage offered this insight:

> Yes, I guess what we say, you know, as workers, the things that we talk about like when we are having our drop-in exposure we took on the organization to keep it open and we made it clear that yes it was about saving jobs, jobs that have a decent pay, they have benefits, unionized jobs, but it is also about the service, right? If we have a job of serving 200 people a day what happens when the service is stopped, you know, that means people are going to be out on the street; where are they going to get meals, where are they going to get care access? We talk about yes we have a right to a job, but we are also providing a service out of necessity, and we talk about what happens when you try to take away those kinds of services, right?

From the interviews, it appears that labour disputes affected clients either directly or indirectly. While management was able to mitigate the impact of the dispute in case 1, the organization did not have any alternative way of delivering services. The employer either used replacement workers or introduced other contingency plans to mitigate the impact of the work stoppage. This may explain why case 2 initially resisted the inclusion of part-time and casual employees in the union.

However, considering the finding above that work stoppages and unionization may help to highlight issues such as condition of service, quality of care, and funding, one may posit that the outcomes appeared to benefit not only the employees but also the clients. Issues that affect clients such as quality of care, advocacy, and funding are blended into labour relations. As one union executive noted,

> Social advocacy work? Some of us as well within the union local find that the union then has become a place for that work to be done since it is not the culture of the agency anymore particularly.

Discussion

This study sets out to explore work stoppages in social economy organizations with the aim of providing insight on the state of labour relations and human resource management; explaining the impact on clients, employees, and the community; and examining whether the work stoppages are consistent with major theoretical explanations of strike and lockout (Bellemare et al., 2006; Darlington, 2004; Godard, 1992; Kerr & Siegel, 1954; Mathers et al., 2004; Shorter & Tilly, 1974; Turner, 2004).

The findings on the dimensions of work stoppages in Ontario indicate that social economy organizations lost 490,190 person-days to 196 work stoppages that occurred mainly in smaller organizations with up to 50 employees. In the sample, healthcare and public service organizations experienced significantly more work stoppages. Healthcare organizations account for almost half of the recorded labour disputes. Public service organizations also experience a significant number of work stoppages, but less than half of the number reported for healthcare organization.

The possible linkage between healthcare organizations and work stoppages requires additional explanation. While hospitals operate under extensive regulatory legislation including labour relations – the Hospital Labour Disputes Arbitration Act – which replace the right to strike with binding arbitration, it is possible that community healthcare organizations, which are funded differently and have the right to strike, may resort more to work stoppages. Because of the similarities with the quasi–public-sector hospitals, community healthcare organizations are good examples of an area where Pynes (1997) predicted that unionization would increase. The higher incidence of work stoppages resulting from labour disputes could be an indication of the public nature of their services, professionalization, and more opportunity for collective voice (Freeman & Medoff, 1984).

Since most healthcare and social services are within the jurisdiction of the provincial government, our finding on healthcare organizations and the relationship between work stoppages and Ministry of Labour industrial sector classification could suggest that social economy organizations that are dependent on government, i.e., those that provide public services, *may* be more prone to work stoppages than others. As with the healthcare organizations, additional research would be required to validate the relationship. However, nonprofit research has emphasized the blurring of the boundaries between nonprofits and the public sector and the change the sector has been experiencing over the past two decades (Akingbola, 2005; Hall et al., 2003; Peters & Masaoka, 2000; Pynes, 1997). These factors have contributed to the increased rate of unionization among social economy organizations (McMullen & Brisbois, 2003) and could explain the work stoppages in those classified as provincial. Employees appear not only to be using the collective voice they have acquired through unionization (Freeman & Medoff, 1984) to press for increased wages and conditions of service, but also to be using it for advocacy to the government (Akingbola, 2005).

The analysis of the case studies suggests that while wages and conditions of service appear to be the primary causes of the labour disputes, the stoppages were tied to issues that reflect the values and operational challenges of nonprofits in particular. In fact, the root causes of the work stoppages were related to funding and cutbacks. This result corroborates the previous quantitative findings on the connection between social economy organizations' work stoppages and public services and further highlights the underlying role of public policy (Clark, 2007; Reed & Howe, 1999; Salamon, 1995).

The related causes of work stoppages such as quality of care, advocacy, and safety for clients reflect the values of social economy organizations and are important to our understanding of labour relations in the sector. Employees appear to be using their collective voice through the collective bargaining process to advocate for quality care, raise safety concerns, and advocate on behalf of the organization to government. The importance employees are attaching to these issues by raising them at the collective bargaining table highlights two emerging elements of the nature of labour relations in the sector.

First, it provides evidence of the increasingly lopsided nature of employment relations and the resulting adoption of a collective voice (Godard, 1992; Hyman, 1989). With managers forced to act more as agent of funders, there is increased mission drift, and organizations are not achieving the public good that attracted employees (Akingbola, 2006; Kim, 2005). As a result, employees appear to be embracing the collective voice option offered by work stoppages to show discontent with the encroachment on mission and values. The adoption of the collective voice approach is further supported by the labour dispute at Yellow Brick House, Aurora, Ontario, which one of the union executives highlighted in the interviews. The dispute, which was underway during the study, involved the lockout of employees by management over a restructuring plan the union claimed would affect nine employees who are union activists.

Second, the findings on the causes of work stoppages resulting from labour disputes show a potential opportunity for social movement unionism in Canada (Bellemare et al., 2006; Mathers et al., 2004; Turner, 2004). While proponents of social movement unionism see an opportunity for moving unions away from business unionism and towards reconnecting unions to civil society, I see increased unionization in social economy organizations as an opportunity to spread the values of social movement unionism from within the civil society. As unionization in the sector increases and unions continue to advocate for issues other than wages and conditions, this may create increased consciousness about civil society issues and set the stage for partnership between the sector and unions (Mathers et al., 2004).

The results suggest that the work stoppages affected clients either directly or indirectly because, as expected, the organizations were not able to provide substitute services, and clients were left with reduced or no services. Owing to either the small size and limited resources capacity of many organizations, or to the specialized nature of the services, social economy organizations could not feasibly mitigate the impact of the labour disputes. Thus in the short term, the work stoppages affect the primary stakeholders – the organization, clients, employees, and the community.

From the perspective of a neoclassical explanation of strike, social economy organizations affected by the work stoppages experienced reduced productivity and were not able to contribute to the economy (Budd, 1994; Hirsch, 1997) or to the social well-being of clients during the strike period. However, the impact will vary from organization to organization. In the two case studies examined in this research, since the organizations provide services in conjunction with or on behalf of government agencies, the impact of the work stoppages threatened the survival of the organizations.

If one considers the causes of the labour disputes, the work stoppage and strike vote deadline could be seen as 'short-term pain for long-term gain.' A win for the employees in collective bargaining on issues such as quality of care, workload, and safety could be beneficial not only to clients but also to employees, the organization, and the community. From the qualitative review, there are multidimensional benefits of collective bargaining in social economy organizations. For example, a security concern raised as a major issue during a labour dispute will not only affect clients but also compromise the safety of employees and the bottom line of the organization. This view of work stoppages in social economy organizations could be explained using the counter-vailing collaboration model of labour relations in which unions and management recognize and work together to develop a complimentary relationship that benefits employees, the organization, and the union, while acknowledging their different roles, values, and goals (Blackard, 2000). In effect, when unions raise issues relating to safety and quality of care in collective bargaining in social economy organizations, man-agement could leverage it as an opportunity to address an issue that is in their mutual interest.

Conclusion

To conclude, this study explored the dimension of work stoppages resulting from labour disputes in social economy organizations. The findings show that some organizations, particularly in healthcare and public services, may experience more work stoppages than their coun-terparts. As noted, more research on this point is needed. This would extend the literature on the degree of closeness of nonprofits with the public sector. Similarly, the causes and impact of work stoppages high-light important factors that could define labour relations in the sector, especially the use of collective voice and opportunity for social move-ment unionism that connects unions to civil society. These two theoreti-cal orientations appear to be relevant frameworks for explaining work stoppages in social economy organizations.

REFERENCES

Akingbola, K. (2004). Staffing, retention and government funding: The Cana-dian Red Cross, Toronto Region. *Nonprofit Management and Leadership, 14*(4), 453–67.
Akingbola, K. (2005). Unionization and non-profit organizations. In K.S. De-vine & J. Grenier (Eds)., *Reformulating industrial relations in liberal market economies.* Selected Papers from the XLI Annual CIRA Conference. Captus University Publications.
Akingbola, K. (2006). Strategy and human resource management in nonprofit

organizations: Evidence from Canada. *International Journal of Human Resource Management, 17*(10), 1707.

Alvi, S. (2001). The impact of strikes on Canadian trade balance. *Applied Economics Letters, 8*(6), 389–96.

Arcand, M., Bayad, M., & Fabi, B. (2002). The effects of human resources management practices on the organizational performances of Canadian financial co-operatives. *Annals of Public and Cooperative Economics, 73*(2), 215–40.

Barbeito, C.L., & Bowman, J.P. (1998). *Nonprofit compensation and benefits practices.* New York: John Wiley.

Belcourt, M., & McBey, K.J. (2000). *Strategic human resources planning.* Toronto: Nelson.

Bellemare, G., Gravel, A.R., Briand, L., & Vallee, L. (2006). Le syndicalisme de transformation sociale (social movement unionism). Voie de renouvellement des théories du syndicalisme? Le cas des services de garde. *Économie et solidarités, 36*(2), 192–218.

Blackard, K. (2000). Countervailing collaboration, change model. In *Managing change in a unionized workplace: Countervailing collaboration* (pp. 59–89). Westport: Quorum Books.

Brandel, G.A. (2001). The truth about working in not-for-profit. *CPA Journal, 71*(10), 13.

Brown, A.W., & Yoshioka, C. (2003). Mission attachment and satisfaction as factors in employee retention. *Nonprofit Management & Leadership, 14* (1), 5–18.

Budd, J. (1994). The effects of multinational institutions on strike activity in Canada. *Industrial and Labor Relations Review, 47*(3), 401–16.

Chaves, R., & Moreno, A. (2004). Social economy managers: Between values and entrenchment. *Annals of Public & Cooperative Economics, 75* (1), 139–61.

Clark, J. (2007). *The UK voluntary sector almanac.* London: NCVO Cooperative secretariat. Retrieved December 6, 2009, from http://www.ncvo-vol.org.uk/products-services/publications/uk-voluntary-sector-workforce-almanac-2007

Darlington, R. (2004). *Wildcats and agitators: The relationship between spontaneity and leadership within workplace strike activity.* Paper presented at Canadian Industrial Relations Association Conference. University of Manitoba, Winnipeg.

Edwards, P. (2003). *Industrial relations: Theory and practice.* Oxford: Blackwell Publishing.

Eldridge, J.E.T. (1968). *Industrial disputes: Essays in the sociology of Industrial relations.* London: Routledge.

Franzosi, R. (1989). One hundred years of strike statistics: Methodological and theoretical issues. *Industrial and Labor Relations Review, 42* (3), 348–62.

Freeman, R.B., & Medoff, J.L. (1984). *What do unions do?* New York: Basic Books.

Gittell, J.F., von Nordenflycht, A., & Kochan, T.A. (2004). Mutual gains or zero sum? Labour relations and firm performance in the airline industry. *Industrial and Labour Relations Review, 57*(2), 163–80.

Godard, J. (1992). Strikes as collective voice: A behavioural analysis of strike activity. *Industrial and Labor Relations Review, 46* (1), 161–75.

Hall, M., Barr, C., Easwaramoorthy, M., Sokolowski, S., & Salamon, L.M. (2005). *The Canadian nonprofit and voluntary sector in comparative perspective,* Toronto: Imagine Canada.

Hall, M.H., Andrukow, A., & Associates. (2003). *The capacity to serve: A qualitative study of the challenges facing Canada's nonprofit and voluntary organizations.* Toronto: Canadian Centre for Philanthropy.

Hameed, S.M.A., & Lomas, T. (1975). Measurement of production losses due to strikes in Canada: An input-output analysis. *British Journal of Industrial Relations 13*(1), 86–93.

Handy, C. (1988). *Understanding voluntary organizations.* Harmondsworth, UK: Penguin.

Handy, F., & Katz, E. (1998). The wage differential between nonprofit institutions and corporations: Getting more by paying less. *Journal of Comparative Economics, 26*(2), 246–61.

Handy, F., Mook, L., Ginieniewicz, J., & Quarter, J. (2007). The moral high ground: Perceptions of wage differentials among executive directors of Canadian nonprofits. *Philanthropist 21*(2), 109–27.

Hanrahan, R., Kushner, J., Martinello, F., & Masse, I. (1997). The effects of work stoppages on the values of firms in Canada. *Review of Financial Economics, 6*(2), 151–66.

Hirsch, B.T. (Ed.). (1997). *Unionization and economic performance: Evidence on productivity, profits, investment, and growth.* Vancouver: The Fraser Institute.

Howe, P., & McDonald, C. (2001). Traumatic stress, turnover and peer support in child welfare. Washington, D.C. Child Welfare League of America. Retrieved November 17, 2009, from http://www.cwla.org/programs/trieschman/2001fbwPhilHowe.htm

Hyman, R. (1989). *Strikes.* London: Macmillan.

Jalette, P. (1997). *The impact of human resource management and industrial relations practices on the organizational performance of credit unions in Quebec.* (No. Working Paper W-97–6E). Ottawa: HRDC Applied Research Branch.

Kaufman, B. (1982). The determinants of strikes in the United States, 1900–1977. *Industrial and Labor Relations Review, 35*(4), 473–90.

Kehoe, F., & Archer, M. (2002). *Canadian industrial relations* (10th ed.). Oakville, ON: Century Labour Publications.

Kerr, C., & Siegel, A. (1954). The inter-industry propensity to strike: An international comparison. In A. Kornhauser, R. Dubin, & A.M. Ross (Eds.), *Industrial conflict*. New York: McGraw Hill.

Kim, S. (2005). The big management challenges in nonprofit human services agencies. *International Review of Public Administration, 10*(1), 85–93.

Light, P. (2002). The content of their character: The state of the nonprofit workforce. *The Nonprofit Quarterly, 9*(30), 6–16.

Mathers, A., Taylor, G., & Upchurch, M. (2004, June). *Opening up civil society: Prospect for social movement unionism in the UK*. Paper presented at the Canadian Industrial Relations Association Conference, Winnipeg, Manitoba.

McMullen, K., & Brisbois, R. (2003). *Coping with change: Human resource management in Canada's nonprofit sector* (No. 4). Ottawa: Canadian Policy Research Network.

McMullen, K., & Schellenberg, G. (2002). *Mapping the nonprofit sector* (No. 1). Ottawa: Canadian Policy Research Network.

McMullen, K., & Schellenberg, G. (2003). *Job quality in nonprofit organizations* (No. 2). Ottawa: Canadian Policy Research Network.

McHugh, R. (1991). Productivity effects of strikes in struck and nonstruck industries. *Industrial & Labor Relations Review, 44*(4), 722–32.

Nolan, P., & O'Donnell, K. (Eds.). (2003). *Industrial relations, HRM and performance*. (2nd ed.). Malden, MA: Blackwell Publishing.

Odgers, C.W., & Betts, J.R. (1997). Do unions reduce investment? Evidence from Canada. *Industrial & Labor Relations Review, 51*(1), 18–36.

Peters, J.B., & Masaoka, J. (2000). A house divided: How nonprofits experience union drives. *Nonprofit Management & Leadership, 10*(3), 305–17.

Pynes, J.E. (1997). The anticipated growth of nonprofit unionism. *Nonprofit Management & Leadership, 7*(4), 355–71.

Quarter, J. (1992). *Canada's social economy: Co-operatives, nonprofits and other community enterprises*. Toronto: James Lorimer.

Quarter, J., Mook, L., & Richmond, B.J. (2003). *What counts: Social accounting for nonprofits and cooperatives*. Upper Saddle River, NJ: Prentice Hall.

Reed, P. B., & Howe, V. J. (1999). *Voluntary Organizations in Ontario in 1990s*. Ottawa: Statistics Canada.

Robinson, I. (2000) Neo-liberal restructuring and U.S. unions: Towards social movement unions. *Critical Sociology, 26* (½), 109–38.

Rose, J.B. (2004). Public sector bargaining: From retrenchment to consolidation. *Relations Industrielles, 59*(2) 271–95.

Salamon, L. (1995). *Partners in Public Service: Government-Nonprofit Relations in the Modern Welfare State*. Baltimore, MD: The Johns Hopkins University Press.

Scott, K. (2003). *Funding matters: The impact of Canada's funding regime on nonprofit and voluntary organizations*. Ottawa: Canadian Council on Social Development.

Shorter, E., & Tilly, C. (1974). *Strikes in France, 1830–1968*. London: Cambridge University Press.

Strauss, A., & Corbin, J. (1998). *Basics of qualitative research: Grounded theory procedures and techniques*. Thousand Oaks, CA: Sage.

Tashakkori, A., & Teddlie, C. (1998). *Mixed methodology: Combining qualitative and quantitative approaches* (Vol. 46). Thousand Oaks, CA: Sage.

Tucker, D.J., & Sommerfeld, D.H. (2006). The larger they get: The changing size distributions of private human service organizations. *Nonprofit and Voluntary Sector Quarterly, 35*(2) 183–203.

Turner, L. (2004). Labor and global justice: Emerging reform coalitions in the world's only superpower. *German Journal of Industrial Relations, 11*(1–2), 92–111.

13 Organic Farmers and the Social Economy: Positive Synergies for Community Development

JENNIFER SUMNER AND SOPHIE LLEWELYN

Since its inception, organic agriculture has always been part of the social economy. Its reasons for emergence, philosophical basis, and expressions in practice have easily aligned with the vision of transformation associated with the social economy. Like other forms of the social economy, its social values stand alongside and indeed precede its economic import (Quarter, 1992). But, unlike many other forms of the social economy, its environmental values mesh with both its social and economic commitments.

When conceptualizing the social economy, Lévesque and Mendell (2004) divide it into four quadrants: response to urgent social needs, response to new opportunities, social development, and economic development. At the intersection of economic development and responses to new opportunities, they have placed organic farming, along with social enterprises, worker co-operatives, natural food co-operatives, and recycling. In this way, organic agriculture is clearly recognized as a vibrant part of the social economy, particularly as a new form of social-economic development. In chapter 1 of this book, Mook, Quarter, and Ryan refer to these forms of social-economic development primarily as social economy businesses, a label that could be applied to the co-operative that is central to this study.

This chapter looks at organic farmers' participation in social economy organizations in southern Ontario. After outlining a brief history of organic agriculture, the chapter will discuss the changes in organics and the challenges faced by organic farmers. It will then explain how organic farmers address these challenges through the social economy and conclude with some positive synergies for community development. In this way, we hope to add both breadth and depth to the concept of the social economy, and familiarize readers with two mutually reinforcing phenomena: organic agriculture and the social economy.

Organic Agriculture

Organic agriculture began as a social movement in Britain in 1926 (Conford, 2001). Like many other movements of protection (Polanyi, 2001), it arose as a reaction to the negative consequences of industrialization – in this case, the industrialization of agriculture. These consequences included deteriorating public health, soil infertility problems, pest and disease outbreaks, and rural community breakdown. The organic pioneers shared an ethic in which soil, crop, livestock, human, and community health were all interconnected (Howard, 1943). In this way, organic agriculture was not originally designed as a market niche or a business opportunity, but as a defence against increasing industrialization and as a vision of a more sustainable way of life.

The organic pioneers espoused a set of values that promoted the health and welfare of people, animals, communities, and the environment (Howard, 1943). These values correspond to the alternative paradigm posited by Beus and Dunlap (1990), who put forward an argument for two socio-cultural paradigms influencing agriculture. They proposed, on the one hand, a conventional paradigm of large-scale, highly industrialized agriculture and, on the other hand, an increasingly vocal alternative agriculture movement, which advocates major shifts towards a more ecologically sustainable agriculture. The authors sought to clarify and synthesize the core beliefs and values underlying these two approaches to agriculture and outlined six major dimensions: (1) centralization vs. decentralization, (2) dependence vs. independence, (3) competition vs. community, (4) domination of nature vs. harmony with nature, (5) specialization vs. diversity, and (6) exploitation vs. restraint. To this list, Chiappe and Flora (1998) added two more dimensions to the alternative agriculture approach – quality family life and spirituality – while Sumner (2003) added a third – conscious resistance to corporatization. Although there is undoubtedly a range of approaches to agriculture, these two paradigms not only illustrate the tensions within agriculture today, but also help us to understand the vital role that organic farmers play in the alternative paradigm.

Unlike the conventional paradigm, characterized by a growing industrialization that concentrates power and wealth, commodifies the environment, exploits labour, and undermines food security (DeLind, 2000), the alternative paradigm exemplified by the organic pioneers disperses power and wealth, works with the environment, treats labour fairly, and supports food security (IFOAM, 2008). As Fromartz (2006) noted, the attraction of organics was not nostalgia for a simpler time, but rather, a refusal to sacrifice all other values to the singular push for yield and profit. In this way, the social economy credentials of organic agriculture were established early.

Challenges to Organic Farmers

Over time, however, the exponential growth in market share of organic products caught the attention of the same powerful interests that had industrialized agriculture in the first place, prompting Blobaum (in Rigby & Bown, 2007, p. 81) to comment that 'the organic sector is becoming what we hoped it would be an alternative to.' Under the formidable pressures of industrialization, organic farmers face a series of challenges that are moving organics towards the conventional paradigm and placing the entire movement in jeopardy. A study of organic farmers in southern Ontario reveals the extent of these challenges. Chosen by systematic selection from lists provided by the community partners in this project – Organic Meadow Co-operative and FoodShare Toronto – 49 farmers participated in qualitative, open-ended interviews, each of which lasted between one and three hours. Analysis of the data shows a series of five interconnected challenges in the areas of production, processing/storage, marketing, regulations, and community.

Production Challenges

Like other forms of the social economy, organic agriculture, by definition, questions the status quo. Its philosophy is based on the alternative paradigm's ethic of co-operation and working with nature, not the conventional paradigm's ethic of competition and dominating nature. Its farming methods prohibit inputs like synthetic pesticides and fertilizers, the mainstays of industrial agriculture. The low-input, high-management orientation of organic agriculture contravenes the high-input, low-management requirements that produce the endless profits that the industrialization of agriculture brings to agribusiness and the institutions it supports. For this reason, organics has been ignored, vilified, and marginalized by corporate, government, and academic interests (Sumner, 2008). Unable to receive support on any level, organic farmers face a number of access problems that affect the production of food.

First, organic farmers lack access to knowledge about organic production methods. With the rise of neo-liberal policies within universities, most public monies for agricultural research have become unavailable unless first matched by private monies (Clark, 2000). However, no corporate-sponsored research will support organic farmers because they do not create demand for corporate products. The majority of funds that do become available are linked to value-chain research, which supports the agri-food industry, not to production research, which would investigate actual organic farming methods (Smith, 1993). As a result, the bulk of agricultural research is no longer carried out for the public good, but for corporate enrichment, through the generation of private goods and/or private knowledge. In this way, organic farmers have been unable to benefit from the traditional knowledge-generating sources such as universities, which have ended up supporting the conventional paradigm through the promotion of industrial agriculture.

Second, organic farmers lack access to production inputs, including organic grain, hay, and manure. Based on intensive management rather than corporate products, these inputs offer no incentives to agribusiness. Lack of such inputs can seriously restrict the holistic management practices required by organic agriculture.

Third, organic farmers lack access to labour. Within agriculture in general, it has become increasingly difficult to attract seasonal labour because of falling commodity prices, diminished returns for farmers, the widespread exit from agriculture, and the transformation of rural communities into satellite communities for urban centres, which reduces the number of people familiar with agricultural production. In addition, organic agriculture in particular requires a holistic approach and most seasonal labourers are not trained in this type of farming.

Storage and Processing Challenges

Organic farmers looking for storage and processing facilities are often out of luck because there is, generally speaking, a lack of certified organic processors. This is partly due to regulations that favour the conventional paradigm, which have had the effect of driving small and medium-sized operations out of business, leaving the field to large-scale operators who only handle large batches. For example, in the Niagara region, the last canning factory recently closed in a province that used to boast many such businesses. A similar situation exists with respect to slaughterhouses: regulations have driven all but the biggest players out of business, and these large operations will not process smaller batches of product.

Marketing Challenges

During the 1980s, organic farmers faced a number of marketing challenges. First, they had difficulty capturing the value of 'ecological products' and distinguishing them from conventional products. Second, they faced the challenge of selling to a market unfamiliar with the benefits of organic production. And third, the farmers had limited access to wholesale organic marketing and distribution channels for grain crops and milk.

While they have been largely successful in meeting these challenges over the last 20 years, a new set of marketing challenges is emerging. One challenge involves lack of access to markets for higher-priced organic meat and produce. Although such markets now exist in urban areas, shipping costs can be prohibitive. In addition, the growing acceptance of organic products means increased competition within the organic sector, especially in the grain market. Such competition contributes to the erosion of the co-operative values inherent in the alternative paradigm.

Regulatory Challenges

Regulation involves the creation of rules to govern the whole, or a sector, of society. Agricultural regulations focus on the details or procedures required in the production of food and fibre. Like all forms of governance, regulations benefit some while handicapping others. In the case of agricultural regulations, they often reinforce the conventional paradigm by benefiting large players at the expense of small and medium-sized operations. For example, the quota system is designed with industrial agricultural practices in mind. In effect, it protects industrial practices at the expense of small-scale, ecologically sustainable production systems and direct-marketing approaches. In a similar vein, health and safety standards are prohibitively expensive for smaller-scale operations. Within the organic movement itself, the organic certification process can be an intimidating and confusing regulatory system for many organic farmers.

Community Challenges

Organic farmers face a number of situations that challenge the social side of their existence. First, in their relations with neighbours, they face conflicts over issues such as chemical drift and contamination from genetically modified organisms. And, with the majority of farmers in Canada still farming conventionally, organic farmers experience social ostracism, exclusion, loneliness, and isolation. Second, access to neighbourly support is limited for organic farmers. Because organic agriculture is fundamentally different from conventional agriculture, those organic farmers who do have friendly neighbours can't always count on the kinds of support – advice, help with labour-intensive activities like haying, help in times of emergency, and equipment sharing – that neighbours once provided to each other.

How Organic Farmers Use the Social Economy to Address Their Challenges

Overall, organic farmers face a series of challenges that threaten to undermine the whole organic movement and push it towards the conventional paradigm. Resourceful as they are, they cannot overcome these problems as individuals. To meet these challenges, they have returned to their roots in the social economy and come together to create, join, and spread a range of social economy organizations, such as co-operatives, public sector nonprofits, and nonprofit mutual associations. This solidarity gives them a form of collective power that they would not have individually, allowing them to act in ways that not only protect the organic farming movement, but also advance the alternative paradigm. While all farmers create, join, and spread a wide variety of social economy organizations, this section focuses on the specific ways that organic farmers use the social economy to address their particular challenges.

Organic farmers formed their first social economy organizations (SEOs) in the late 1970s and early 1980s. In many cases, they were producers with non-traditional backgrounds who were motivated by a desire to meet like-minded farmers and to learn more about organic

production. A significant number of Ontario's earliest organic farmers migrated to rural Ontario in the 1970s, either from urban centres
or from farming communities in Northern Europe (the latter bringing
with them Rudolph Steiner's biodynamic farming approach). As newcomers with unconventional values and different production ideals,
their start-up years were marked to some degree by a sense of isolation
from their conventional farmer neighbours. Recalling their first few
seasons, farmers with urban backgrounds highlighted the stress associated with learning to farm from scratch, their desire for a more cohesive
organic community, and their need for advice at a time when information on organic production was very difficult to find.

In the following pages, we draw from our interviews with organic
farmers to explore their engagement with social economy organizations in southern Ontario and to situate this activity as a response to
the challenges that organic farmers face. The study's 49 respondents
reported activities with over 100 different SEOs, including 19 producers' co-operatives, three consumers' co-operatives, 13 credit unions, 54
nonprofit mutual associations (including 13 economic associations and
41 social organizations), 13 public sector nonprofits, and 25 mutual insurers. While some of these organizations serve organic farmers exclusively, and could thus be termed 'organic SEOs,' many more contribute
to the livelihoods of farmers of all stripes and to rural communities
in general. A summary of each of these organizations' activities is neither feasible nor useful here; instead, we provide a brief account of the
five SEOs that were most significant to the study's respondents. Their
contributions to organic producers' lives and livelihoods are discussed
with reference to the challenges identified in the preceding section.

Nonprofit Mutual Associations

Nonprofit mutual associations are civil society organizations that are
oriented towards a membership who finance their services through
their fees and may also choose to take part in decision-making through
voting at meetings and, perhaps, even serving in the governance (Quarter, Mook, & Richmond, 2003). These social economy organizations can
be divided into two main categories: economic associations, such as
unions, professional associations, and producers' associations, and social associations, such as ethno-cultural groups, churches, social clubs,
neighbourhood groups, and mutual socio-political organizations, such
as political parties or environmental groups. Although organic farmers

in the study are active in both categories of nonprofit mutual associations, the economic associations have been most significant to them.

ORGANIC NONPROFIT MUTUAL ASSOCIATIONS

Two of the social economy organizations that we encountered in our research emerged from organic farmers' needs for access to knowledge, production inputs, marketing information, and social support: the Ecological Farmers Association of Ontario and Canadian Organic Growers.

The Ecological Farmers Association of Ontario's roots are in rural southwestern Ontario, where it was founded in 1979 as a vehicle for farmer-to-farmer knowledge sharing and social support. Since its inception, the Ecological Farmers Association of Ontario's membership has significantly expanded, and its activities have broadened to include a wide range of social economy initiatives such as training programs and knowledge-sharing opportunities. While the organization's Introduction to Organic Agriculture workshop has become a rite of passage for new and transitioning organic farmers, the learning needs of its members continue to drive the development of more advanced technical workshops. Active members have developed considerable expertise during the last 30 years, and the Ecological Farmers Association of Ontario has provided a forum for them to build and share this knowledge through farmer-facilitated workshops, one-on-one mentorship opportunities, monthly email bulletins, quarterly newsletters, and regular kitchen table meetings. Information about organic production methods is now available from a variety of commercial and (more recently) government sources, but Ecological Farmers Association of Ontario members value the organization's grassroots integrity and its unique contribution to Ontario's organic farming community.

While the Ecological Farmers Association of Ontario is a farmer-founded organization, and its membership remains primarily rural and farmer-based, the Canadian Organic Growers began as an urban organization with a mandate to support networking and education among organic gardeners, consumers, farmers, and supporters. Early Canadian Organic Growers initiatives included the Heritage Seed Program (now a separate organization, Seeds of Diversity), founded in 1984 as an effort to support organic agriculture by preserving the genetic capital essential to viable organic production. One early member of Canadian Organic Growers described the program as an attempt to promote intergenerational exchange between older farmers – 'hold outs' who had never adopted chemical agricultural methods – and what was then a new generation of organic farmers, including members of the 'back to the land' movement. For this member, Seeds of Diversity was an explicitly grassroots, social economy response to market pressures to reduce agricultural biodiversity.

The vision of organics as a social movement whose long-term viability is grounded in its independence was echoed in interviews with several other respondents who were involved in Ontario's early organic movement. However, the culture of organics has shifted over the past 20 years, largely in response to dramatic growth in market demand for organic products, and Canadian Organic Growers has changed with it. The organization has grown since the 1980s to become a national networking, education, and advocacy organization whose members include some of Canada's largest certified organic commercial producers. The organization has built a significant catalogue of publications on organic production techniques. It also publishes a quarterly glossy magazine, organizes and sponsors regular industry events, and has recently overseen the revision of the federal government's National Organic Production Standards, thus having a voice in the regulations that govern organic production. They also have published a guide to transitioning through the organic certification process.

But if its contemporary funding structure, commercial activities, and organizational culture suggest a departure from some of the principles that informed its earliest programs, Canadian Organic Growers nonetheless remains a social economy organization whose work is grounded in a strong volunteer base. Canadian Organic Growers' 15 regional chapters act as hubs where market gardeners, livestock farmers, and small-scale urban growers meet regularly to exchange knowledge, develop new skills, and promote organic agriculture through grassroots, chapter-based initiatives. Most of the Canadian Organic Growers members who participated in this study emphasized the value they draw from attending Canadian Organic Growers chapter meetings, connecting with fellow organic farmers and home gardeners, and sharing growing tips and marketing opportunities. Perhaps of greatest significance to these farmers was the sense of belonging and affirmation that they feel as a member of a nationwide network of organic farmers. Despite organics' new status as a multi-billion dollar industry, many of our respondents expressed feelings of isolation as organic growers, and many admitted to occasional bouts of self-doubt. Participating in an organization like Canadian Organic Growers can buoy organic farmers' confidence in their production choices and reaffirm the environmental, social, and economic values that guide their efforts.

OTHER NONPROFIT MUTUAL ASSOCIATIONS

Organic farmers in this study were also deeply involved with other social economy groups that qualify as nonprofit mutual associations. They include Ontario's three general farm organizations – the National Farmers Union, the Ontario Federation of Agriculture, and the Christian Farmers Federation of Ontario – which are provincially accredited agricultural advocacy groups whose funding is drawn primarily from yearly membership fees. All farmers in the province are required to register their farms annually under the Farm Registration and Farm Organizations Funding Act, 1993, and their mandatory registration fees ($157.50 in 2008) are channelled to the farm organization of their choice. Although the Ontario Federation of Agriculture is by far the largest of these organizations, most of the farmers who participated in this study belong to the National Farmers Union or Christian Farmers Federation of Ontario, smaller organizations that are explicit in their support for family farming and sustainable agricultural practices. These groups offer a forum for farmers to participate in political advocacy work and thereby respond to the structural forces that threaten rural communities and constrain organic farmers' ability to pursue sustainable rural livelihoods. Respondents who are involved in these farm organizations described this activity in terms of negotiating political representation at the provincial and national level, and/or building political capacity at the community level. The farmers belonging to the National Farmers Union were the most focused on community-level advocacy work, which helped them to meet their challenges with respect to community. As an organization with a social and environmental justice orientation, the National Farmers Union presents itself as a means for farmers 'to work collectively to assert their interests in an agricultural industry increasingly dominated by multi-billion-dollar corporations' (National Farmers Union, 2008).

The National Farmers Union is active in research and policy development at the national level, and engages in international advocacy work through its activities with La Via Campesina, a worldwide peasant movement. Although they expressed support for these activities and pride in the organization's national leadership, the farmers who participated in this study are more directly involved in community-level activities, under the auspices of National Farmers Union locals. For example, one respondent sees her work with the National Farmers Union as a means of fostering a sustainable local food system and contributing to a viable future for the family farm. She pursues these goals by engaging in activities that build community among farmers and consumers, and educate people about the challenges faced by family farms and the benefits of 'eating local.' She describes her activities with the National Farmers Union as a natural extension of her work as an organic farmer, a means of practising her values beyond the farm gate.

Many of the organic farmers who participated in this study shared their fears about the effects of economic globalization and corporate consolidation on the social, economic, and environmental health of Ontario's rural communities. Respondents worried most about corporate control over the seed supply, the increasing prevalence of genetically modified crops, competition from cheap agricultural imports, and the long-term security of Canada's supply management systems – 'big picture' issues in the face of which individual farmers can feel powerless. Organic farmers' activity with these social economy organizations can be understood as a proactive response both to these pressing policy issues themselves and to the psychological toll that living with these worries can take on farming families. Involvement with a nonprofit mutual association like the National Farmers Union is an assertion of personal agency, a means of building community capacity, and a way to support and inform a collective movement for change.

Public Sector Nonprofits

Public sector nonprofits serve a constituency external to the organization rather than a membership (Quarter et al., 2003). Social economy organizations such as the United Way, the YM/YWCA, 4-H Clubs, soup kitchens, and homeless shelters provide a suite of services to a wide range of people in Canada.

Organic farmers who participated in this study were active with a variety of public sector nonprofits, including 4-H, the Children's Aid Society, and local food banks. But, FoodShare Toronto provides the most interesting case study. A social economy organization that works with communities to ensure access to healthy food, FoodShare Toronto has over ten years' experience collaborating with organic farmers in the city's foodshed. Some of the farmers we interviewed sell their produce to FoodShare Toronto for use in the organization's organic food box program. However, their dealings with FoodShare Toronto are not bounded by the typical conventions of a grower-wholesaler relationship. Instead, respondents described the organization as a vehicle for learning and a catalyst for urban-rural exchange.

A pioneer in the movement for sustainable food systems, FoodShare Toronto has paved the way for a number of other social economy organizations – Local Food Plus, AfriCan Food Basket, the Stop, and Evergreen in Toronto; Eat Local organizations in Hamilton, Sudbury, and elsewhere; Just Food in Ottawa; and food box schemes across Ontario, among others – all of which promote healthy food 'from field to table' as a means of supporting rural and urban community development. Not all of our respondents' reflections on FoodShare Toronto were positive: some expressed frustration at changes in staff, and complained about the organization's fluctuating capacity to serve local organic suppliers. These comments tended to be qualified by recognition of the funding constraints which impede nonprofits' ability to consistently fulfil their objectives.

Co-operatives

A co-operative is an autonomous association of persons united voluntarily to meet their common economic, social, and cultural needs and aspirations through a jointly owned and democratically controlled enterprise (International Co-operative Association, 2008). There are three main types of co-operatives: producer co-ops, worker co-ops, and consumer co-ops. Among other benefits, co-operatives offer people a united voice in an economic climate where individuals are easily dominated by powerful corporate players.

Most of the farmers who participated in this study are members of Organic Meadow – a producers' co-operative that markets eggs, grain, and dairy, and a community partner in the research project. The co-op was formed in Grey County in 1989 by a small group of organic grain producers who were brought together by their grain broker's unexpected exit from the business. After a decade of educational activity through organizations like the Ecological Farmers Association of Ontario and Canadian Organic Growers, Ontario's organic farming community had significantly increased its production capacity by the late 1980s; however, the marketing infrastructure for organic products remained severely underdeveloped. With the closure of the region's only organic grain mill imminent, the Grey County group assessed their marketing options and decided that their interests – and those of the organic movement more generally – would best be served if they marketed the grain themselves. They elected to join together, lease the grain mill from their former broker's creditors, and establish a co-operative to handle their marketing collaboratively. In his history of the co-op, Organic Meadow president Ted Zettel describes the farmers' frustration with conventional marketing models, and articulates their desire to create a new food system, rooted in social economy activity.

> Organic Meadow was born out of urgent need, powerful vision and persistent determination. The urgent need was to have a means of getting our crops to the market. The entire organic food business was only in its infancy at the time, with no reliable infrastructure. While regular farmers had many marketing options, the pioneers of organics were very much on their own, unnoticed by the business world and shunned by the powerful academia-government alliance that was insistent on moving agriculture toward industrialization. The radical vision of the founders was of a separate model, a totally new food system that would deliver highest quality, certified organic, local food to a willing, well informed citizenry, who were more than happy to support the stewards of the land. We were a unique mixture of new converts from chemical farming and 'dyed in the wool' environmentalists with one belief in common; the thing was not working and we would rebuild it, from the ground up. (Zettel, 2008)

Today, the co-op is best known for its organic dairy line, a venture launched in 1995. Prior to 1995, organic dairy farmers in Ontario had no means of differentiating their milk from the conventional dairy pool: organic milk was mixed with conventional milk, organic farmers received no price premium, and consumers were essentially unable to access organic dairy products. Remembering those days, the long-time organic farmers we interviewed told us how frustrating it was to produce organic milk but to receive no recognition for their hard work, good stewardship practices, and the high quality of their product. Organic dairy farmers found themselves working harder than their conventional neighbours to produce lower milk yields[1] for less remuneration. In launching their dairy line, Organic Meadow members responded to this situation by building a new marketing infrastructure for organic milk. Since that time, the co-op has directed much of its energy both to developing new products and to increasing production volume by actively recruiting new members, coaching them through their transition to organic production, and providing numerous forms of support. Although the focus on dairy has contributed over time to some volatility in the co-op's grain pool, Organic Meadow has nonetheless remained a dynamic co-operative enterprise and a force for innovation, change, and growth in Ontario's organic sector.

MEMBER SUPPORT THROUGH TRANSITION AND BEYOND

Although Organic Meadow's dairy pool initially grew by incorporating farmers who were already producing organically, it was not long before the co-op began recruiting conventional dairy farmers to organic production. Transitioning to organic dairy production is a complex, protracted process that requires farmers to spend three to four years transforming their production systems before they can earn the price premiums associated with a certified organic label. Respondents who had transitioned from conventional production described the process as risky and stressful: while the steep learning curve can make for a stimulating challenge, the production risks incurred by abandoning conventional weed and pest management techniques are typically harrowing. The success of the co-op's recruitment efforts has therefore hinged on the group's ability to provide support through the transition to organic production.

Much of this support is informal, offered by fellow Organic Meadow members. The co-op invests significant resources in building a cohesive, knowledgeable member base. It holds social events, sponsors farm tours, hosts speakers, runs a mentorship program, organizes bus trips to dairy operations in the US, publishes a newsletter, provides production information through its website, and consciously employs an 'Organic Meadow family' rhetoric to build social capital among farmer-members. The co-op also employs a team of field staff who counsel new members through the transition process, assist with the paperwork associated with organic certification, and provide ongoing support in the form of production advice and referrals. Organic Meadow members were overwhelmingly appreciative of not only the practical help, but also the moral support and camaraderie provided by co-op field staff and fellow co-op members.

MANAGING GROWTH AND CHANGE

The co-op's investment in recruitment and member support has enabled its dairy pool to grow from six farms in 1995 to 42 farms in

2007, when this research was conducted. Growth in membership, production, and distribution has had benefits for both the farming families involved in Organic Meadow and organic consumers across Canada. The co-op's success has also helped support the independently owned, rural processing plants to which Organic Meadow contracts its processing of milk, cheese, and other products; it has also benefited the organic events, research institutes, and rural charities to which the co-op provides financial support.

However, expansion has entailed significant changes and challenges for Organic Meadow. Although most of the Organic Meadow farmers interviewed were enthusiastic about the co-op's growth, some members were critical of a process that they feel has led to a departure from the group's founding principles. Other members welcomed the growth in membership, but expressed dismay over the compromises that the co-op has made in order to market its products on a large scale. Several farmers identified the co-op's use of packaging as a source of particular concern. Organic Meadow's new mini-yogurts are packaged in little plastic containers; its chocolate milk drinking boxes are sold as 250ml tetra packs with plastic straws attached. Respondents who objected to the environmental impacts of such packaging often raised the possibility of adopting refillable glass bottles for their fluid milk. However, glass bottles cannot offer the extended shelf-life required for dairy products with national distribution.

Organic Meadow members generally felt that if their goods are to appeal to mainstream consumers, the co-op needs to offer products and packaging that meet conventional expectations. But, some worried about the extent of these concessions to mainstream retail practice. While Organic Meadow has become a major force in facilitating the conversion of conventional acreage to organic production in Ontario, its members wondered how to reconcile the co-op's increasing ecological footprint with the environmental values so central to organic agriculture. The co-op's leadership is receptive to these concerns, and is actively seeking to reduce the distance that Organic Meadow ships its products (and thereby shrink its carbon footprint), by supporting the formation of organic dairy co-operatives in western Canada and the Maritimes. But, it is unlikely to make the dramatic changes to its product packaging that some members would like to see. This debate raises the larger issue of the problems that social economy organizations face as they grow and thrive within the context of corporate capitalism.

DEMUTUALIZATION THREATS

One of the greatest problems co-operatives face in the current global market is demutualization, the process by which members of a mutual company, such as a co-operative, accept an external takeover. At the end of this process, the owners are no longer the members of the organization, but the people who buy stocks in it. Demutualization is associated with raising capital or participating in mergers, and can endanger the co-operative movement. Organic Meadow helps to illustrate the pressures that co-operatives face with respect to demutualization.

As a producer co-operative, Organic Meadow has grown and thrived since its founding. The co-op has invested an enormous amount of energy and capital into increasing organic production, processing, marketing, and distribution capacity in Ontario, and this investment continues to pay off as demand for organic product rises. However, with success has come competition from corporate actors looking to enter and profit from the market for organic dairy. Co-op leaders cited corporate interest in the co-op as a critical threat to its integrity. According to one respondent:

> We get almost every week a call from a big organization that says, 'We want organic milk, and we understand you guys have the supply.' And we say, 'Well, we're short; we don't have enough supply.' 'Well, then we're buying you out.' 'Well, we're a co-op, you cannot buy us.' 'Why not?' 'Because we're owned by the farmers.' 'Well, then we buy the farmers, too.' Well, farmers don't want to farm for somebody else. [These companies] don't have any understanding. They think money buys everything. And so there is a big threat - an underlying threat that I don't really want to talk that much about. But our co-op becomes worth a lot now, because we have a big market share. And so the big boys could even start offering our members to buy out, right? To sell out their shares. And that could become a danger. Now, they're not doing that yet. So for us, it's even more reason to become more a family. You don't wanna sell your family, right?

The co-op's strategy for responding to the threat of demutualization includes educating its members about corporate designs on the co-op, and reminding farmers of the long-term benefits of participating in an organization whose objectives include ensuring fair, consistent financial returns to farmers. The term 'family' recurred again and again in interviews, particularly with co-op leaders, who use the word both to articulate the strong social ties that bind co-op members together, and to reinforce those ties.

In the age of globalization, the importance of social economy organizations such as co-operatives in the farming sector is crucial, given the impacts of the conventional paradigm's industrial agriculture on small and medium-sized farms, as well as rural communities. According to agricultural economist John Ikerd (2003, p. 1), 'agriculture as we have known it, with family farms and viable rural communities, is being rapidly transformed into an industrial agriculture, with factory farms and dying rural communities.' While it is evident that organic farmers use social economy organizations to address the challenges they face, can these organizations also support rural communities deeply affected by the detrimental impacts of industrial agriculture?

The Social Economy and Community Development

A community is most frequently understood as 'a social network of interacting people, usually concentrated into a defined territory' (Johnston, 2000, p. 101). These groups of people are also referred to as communities of place, or geographical communities. But there can also be communities of practice, in which people with similar work or interests come together to form a community that is not based on a defined territory, such as an academic community or an online community. Organic farmers belong to both sorts of communities: they live near rural communities and they belong to the organic community – a community of practice formed around the shared interest of organic farming. Their allegiance to community not only reinforces the alternative paradigm, but can also contribute to its growth through community development.

Community development is the process of creating or increasing shared identity and agency (Bhattacharyya, 1995) among community members. As an approach to social, environmental, and economic change, community development aims to build capacity within communities to realize or expand their potential. The social economy has long been connected to community development in Canada. Indeed, 'an important aspect of activities within the social economy has been to strengthen geographic communities, particularly in the underdeveloped regions of the country' (Quarter, 1992, p. 89). While rural communities have always suffered from underdevelopment, over the last 30 years they have been seriously affected by the impacts of corporate globalization (Sumner, 2005b). Agricultural communities have been particularly hard hit by the ongoing industrialization of agriculture, backed by government policy to move small and medium-sized farmers off the land – both characteristics of the conventional paradigm. As farms fail and farm families move away, rural communities face a vicious downward spiral of decreased tax revenues, lack of attendance at local schools, churches, and clubs, loss of customers for local businesses, and diminishing social capital, which reduces the possibilities of building capacity for the shared identity and agency so necessary to community development.

In contrast to the ongoing crisis in agriculture and agricultural communities, organic farmers have not only been succeeding, but also making vital contributions to rural community development, thus reinforcing the alternative paradigm. Several studies have already shown the benefits organic farmers bring to rural communities. In Europe, Pugliese (2001) found a multifaceted and promising convergence between organic farming and sustainable rural development. Using four basic aspects of sustainable rural development – innovation, conservation, participation, and integration – the author concluded that 'organic farming systems can effectively contribute to all these aspects, thanks to their dynamism, multivalence, and networking activities' (p. 125).

In Canada, a study of organic farmers and rural development found that organic farmers made significant economic, social, and environmental contributions to rural communities (Sumner, 2005a). Economically, they contribute both on the supply side, through direct sales, and on the demand side, through local purchasing. Socially, they make social, cultural, political, and human-development contributions. And environmentally, they contribute to rural development by such activities as lowering the chemical burden on the land, selling their produce locally (thereby reducing food miles), and speaking publicly about environmental issues.

Another Canadian study of farm-community linkages found both economic and social contributions by organic farmers (MacKinnon, 2006). Economically, organic farmers contributed to rural development through local purchasing, job creation, and viable farms. Socially, organic farmers showed a strong involvement in education, networking, and leadership. The study also found strong indicators of social capital, which is the invisible social infrastructure thought to underlie a community's capacity for development. Overall, the research findings suggest that support for the organic sector – at the local and policy level – can offer substantial benefits for the future of rural communities.

While it is clear that organic farmers contribute to community development, does their involvement in the social economy enhance this development? Our study of organic farmers and the social economy provides some answers to this question. We use Pugliese's (2001) four aspects of sustainable rural development – innovation, conservation, participation, and integration – to investigate the links between organic farmers, the social economy, and rural community development.

First, *innovation* is 'a mental attitude, capable of combining creativity with the spirit of initiative and taste for risk' (Pugliese, 2001, p. 119). Innovative solutions include 'new methods of organizing and managing processes and information within and between sectors' (p. 118). By creating social economy organizations that encourage education and knowledge sharing, such as the Ecological Farmers Association of Ontario and Canadian Organic Growers, organic farmers have enhanced their communities of practice by building a creative and dynamic learning environment that moves their practice forward. In addition, by joining existing social economy organizations, such as the National Farmers Union, they make valuable contributions to their communities of place.

Second, *conservation* balances innovation in sustainable rural development, helping to 'avoid the erosion of the rural comparative advantage and limit unwanted transformations' (Pugliese, 2001, p. 120). Guided by a principle regarding environmental conservation carried out through use, conservation has the intention of producing natural and human landscapes that live and work. By joining social economy organizations such as Organic Meadow, which promote sustainable production practices, organic farmers contribute to these living, working landscapes through their organic farming methods. By learning to farm in nature's image, they combine natural and human landscapes into a holistic, dynamic system, which benefits their communities of place, while reinforcing their communities of practice.

Third, *participation* is part of a people-centred development model, in which local people are 'helped to identify their needs and viable solutions,' as well as 'encouraged and enabled to contribute to the planning and implementation of the development process' (Pugliese, 2001, p. 121). In addition to networking, she argues, rural development needs animators, leading actors, and catalysing figures. Organic farmers within this study actively engaged with a wide range of social economy organizations, as well as other community organizations, all of which emphasize member participation. In this way, they help to weave the fabric of community development, creating and/or increasing agency and identity in communities of both place and practice.

And fourth, Pugliese (2001) argues that *integration* highlights the idea that many factors make up the kind of community development that contributes to the growth of the local system as a whole. In particular, the creation of synergies with other sectors contributes to an integrated rural development. Synergies have been defined as 'linkages between two or more entities, whose joint effort produce[s] effects that are quantitatively and qualitatively more far reaching than the effects of similar entities when they operate alone' (Brunori & Rossi, 2000, p. 410). Organic farmers promote synergies by meeting their challenges through the social economy. They create or join social economy organizations that help them address their production, storage, processing, marketing, regulatory, and community problems. In doing so, they forge linkages among themselves, between organic and nonorganic farmers, and within their rural communities.

According to Latour (in Brunori & Rossi, 2000, p. 416), synergy is power 'in potentia,' which has to be mobilized by action – it has to be transformed into power 'in actu' in order to produce effects. By their participation in the social economy, organic farmers mobilize potential power into actual power to not only meet their challenges, but also contribute to community development, in both communities of place and communities of practice. In all these ways, the participation of organic farmers in the social economy results in long-term, sustainable community development, which also helps to reinforce the alternative paradigm.

Conclusion

From this study, it is clear that organic farmers are active participants in the social economy. They create, join, and spread social economy organizations such as co-operatives, public sector nonprofits, and nonprofit mutual associations. However, as organic agriculture becomes more industrialized and begins to operate out of the conventional paradigm, with fewer and larger farms, these contributions will disappear. Industrial agriculture, whether organic or not, often bypasses rural communities altogether by looking to urban centres and the global market.

In addition, it is driven by private monetary interests, not the health and well-being of farmers, animals, rural communities, or the environment. As organics begins to reflect the demands of the global market and become more conventionalized, the benefits organic farmers offer to rural community development risk being diminished. For example, MacKinnon (2006) found that while both local and export-oriented organic farms played a strong economic role in rural communities, only locally oriented organic farms played a strong social role. Without the capacity to build social capital, a community's ability to develop and prosper is seriously compromised.

This overall challenge can be found in one way or another in all social economy organizations. The pressures to think and act within the bounds of the conventional paradigm erode the breadth and depth of alternatives to it. And yet, the social economy exists because of the massive shortcomings of the very paradigm that can end up undermining it. In spite of these tensions, the social economy continues to survive and thrive. This highlights its capacity to address basic social, economic, and environmental needs. In this way, the social economy is not merely a complement to the current neo-liberal economy, but the portal to another way of life – 'a vision of social transformation' (Quarter, 1992, p. x) that we can work together to collectively create.

NOTES

1 Organic dairy herds generally yield slightly less milk than conventional herds, which are pushed to the limits of their production capacity.

REFERENCES

Beus, C.E., & Dunlap, R.E. (1990). Conventional versus alternative agriculture: The paradigmatic roots of the debate. *Rural Sociology, 55*(4), 590–616.

Bhattacharyya, J. (1995). Solidarity and agency: Rethinking community development. *Human Organization, 54*(1), 60–8.

Brunori, G., & Rossi, A. (2000). Synergy and coherence through collective action: Some insights from wine routes in Tuscany. *Sociologia Ruralis, 40*(4), 409–23.

Chiappe, M.B., & Flora, C.B. (1998). Gendered elements of the alternative agriculture paradigm. *Rural Sociology, 63*(3), 372–94.

Clark, E.A. (2000). Academia in the service of industry: The ag biotech model. In J.L. Turk (Ed.), *The corporate campus: Commercialization and the dangers to Canada's colleges and universities* (pp. 69–86). Toronto: James Lorimer.

Conford, P. (2001). *The origins of the organic movement*. Edinburgh: Floris Books.

DeLind, L.B. (2000). Transforming organic agriculture into industrial organic products: Reconsidering national organic standards. *Human Organization, 59*(2), 198–208.

Fromartz, S. (2006). *Organic, INC.: Natural foods and how they grew*. Orlando, FL: Harcourt.

Harvey, D. (1990). Between space and time: Reflections on the geographical imagination. *Annals of the Association of American Geographers, 80*(3), 418–34.

Howard, Sir A. (1943). *An agricultural testament*. New York: Oxford University Press.

IFOAM. (2008). *The principles of organic agriculture*. Retrieved November 11, 2009, from http://www.ifoam.org/about_ifoam/principles/index.html

International Co-operative Association. (2008). *What is a co-operative?* Retrieved November 11, 2009, from www.ica.coop/coop/index.htmlIkerd, J. (2003). Destructive factory farms rapidly displacing family farmers. *CCPA Monitor, 10*(6), 1–8.

Johnston, R. (2000). Community. In R.J. Johnston, D. Gregory, G. Pratt, & M. Watts (Eds.), *The Dictionary of Human Geography* (4th ed.) (pp. 101–2). Malden, MA: Blackwell Publishers.

Lévesque, B., & Mendell, M. (2004). *The social economy: Diverse approaches and practices*. Working document for SSHRC President. Montreal, July 2.

MacKinnon, S. (2006). *Identifying and differentiating farm-community linkages in organic farming in Ontario*. Unpublished Master's thesis, Department of Geography, University of Guelph, Ontario, Canada.

National Farmers Union. (2008). *About us*. Retrieved November 11, 2009, from http://www.nfu.ca/about.html

Polanyi, K. (2001). *The great transformation: The political and economic origins of our time*. Boston: Beacon Press.

Pugliese, P. (2001). Organic farming and sustainable rural development: A multifaceted and promising convergence. *Sociologia Ruralis, 4*(1), 112–30. Quarter, J., Mook L., & Richmond, B.J. (2003). What counts: Social accounting for nonprofits and cooperatives. Upper Saddle River, NJ: Prentice Hall.

Quarter, J. (1992). *Canada's social economy*. Toronto: James Lorimer & Company.

Rigby, D., & Bown, S. (2007). Whatever happened to organic?: Food, nature and the market for 'sustainable' food. *Capitalism, Nature, Socialism, 18*(3), 81–102.

Smith, S. (1993). Sustainable agriculture and public policy. *Maine Policy Review,* 2(1), 68–78.

Sumner, J. (2005a). *Organic farmers and rural development: A research report on the links between organic farmers and community sustainability in Southwestern Ontario.* Retrieved from http://oacc.info/DOCs/org_farmers_rural_dev.pdf

Sumner, J. (2005b). *Sustainability and the civil commons: Rural communities in the age of globalization.* Toronto: University of Toronto Press.

Sumner, J. (2008). Protecting and promoting indigenous knowledge: Environmental adult education and organic agriculture. *Studies in the Education of Adults, 40*(2), 207–23.

Zettel, T. (2008). *Our history.* Retrieved November 11, 2009, from Organic Meadow, Inc. http://www.organicmeadow.com/auh.sz

14 On the Challenges of Inclusion and the Co-operative Movement for Francophone Immigrants in Ontario

GINETTE LAFRENIÈRE, MAIKE ZINABOU,
MATT RIEHL, AND SANDY HOY

Francophones in Ontario have a strong interest in maintaining their socio-political and economic status as a means to preserve their cultural identity and their hard-won French-language services that are guaranteed federally and provincially. The successful inclusion of visible minority francophone immigrants within francophone minority communities in Ontario not only helps to sustain the size of the communities but also provides a diverse base to support francophone identity and ongoing advocacy for language rights. Within the context of an increasingly diversified francophone community, the Franco-Ontarian co-operative movement presents one promising model moving towards building a more inclusive community through the elaboration of common social values and economic goals. Understanding the ways in which Franco-Ontarian co-operatives can foster the integration of visible minorities within francophone communities contributes to a greater understanding of how the social economy might be adapted and utilized to address the pressures and changing nature of an increasingly multicultural society. (Throughout this chapter, we will refer to visible minority Francophones as 'francophone immigrants,' 'Francophones from racial minority backgrounds,' or 'francophone newcomers.' The 'Franco-Ontariens de souche' or 'Franco-Ontarians' are those Francophones who are characterized as belonging to the dominant white francophone community. 'Minority Francophones' or 'Francophones' refer to both the white and the visible minority Francophones who together constitute a linguistic minority within various anglophone-dominated communities outside Quebec.)

Data from the 2001 Census (OFA, 2005a) indicate that a small increase within the Franco-Ontarian population occurred between 1996 and

2001 because of the settlement of francophone immigrants and refugees. Recent demographic trends point to increasing numbers of francophone immigrants arriving yearly in Ontario either from their countries of origin or from the province of Quebec. Francophone immigrants settling in francophone minority communities in Ontario strive for a successful settlement in Canada, anticipating that their knowledge of one of Canada's official languages will benefit them. However, current census data illustrate that francophone immigrants to Ontario, despite above average educational credentials and official language skills, are most often unemployed or underemployed and have a higher likelihood of living in poverty (OFA, 2005b). Quell (2002) argues that the challenges of inclusion are compounded in the case of francophone immigrants in Ontario, for whom not only 'moving to Canada is a complex venture' but 'moving into a minority community adds another complexity' (p. 25).

The process of francophone immigrants attempting to integrate within traditionally insular Franco-Ontarian communities is challenging. While great strides have been made to integrate these 'new Franco-Ontarians' into various Ontario communities, the process has been politically and socially difficult. The 'Franco-Ontariens de souche' have been slow to share their socio-political space, but have gradually formed alliances with newcomers. A changing social reality produced by increased rates of immigration has required Franco-Ontarians to re-define themselves as a transforming heterogeneous francophone community living outside Quebec. This melding of different francophone actors within a larger dominant anglophone social context has been and continues to be both a challenging and textured social experience.

As researchers, we set out to learn whether the co-operative model of economic development – a model that promotes the values of equity and civic engagement in meeting the economic, social, and cultural needs of the actors involved in the joint ownership and democratic control of the co-operative – was one that could enhance social and economic inclusion for visible minority francophone immigrants in Ontario. To date, very little has been written on the subject of co-operatives, inclusion, and immigrants, particularly within a minority francophone context. This chapter focuses on some of the issues specific to francophone immigrants settling in Ontario and is based on the findings of our research conducted during the past two years. Our findings confirm our prediction that the co-operative model could potentially offer much to support inclusion for francophone immigrants in Ontario, but there are a number of challenges that must be faced if we are to realize the full potential presented by this opportunity. To that end, our investigation produced a number of recommendations that could facilitate greater uptake of the co-operative model by francophone immigrants. The recommendations are a call to action to both francophone and anglophone co-operative communities in Ontario to support the inclusion of immigrants and newcomers.

The Francophone Community in Ontario

Of all the provinces and territories in Canada, Ontario has the largest number of Francophones in a minority situation. Ontario is home to 548,940 Franco-Ontarians, comprising 4.8% of the province's population, with the percentage of Francophones varying significantly across the different regions of the province (OFA, 2005a). In 2001, 58,520 Francophones from racial minority backgrounds lived in Ontario. Of the newcomers born outside of Canada, 31.5% were born in Africa, 30.5% in Asia, 18% in the Middle East, 8.5% in the Caribbean, and 7.8% in Central and South America (OFA, 2005b). The biggest proportion of francophone immigrants and refugees coming to Ontario settle in Central (55%) or Eastern Ontario (36%), with most of them in Ontario's major cities: Toronto (31.3%) and Ottawa (40.2%) (OFA, 2005b).

Francophones from racial minority backgrounds have generally attained high levels of education – 'higher than for Francophones in general, all racial minorities combined and for the province's population as a whole' (OFA, 2005b, p. 10). Francophone newcomers are often educated in fields where francophone Canadians are underrepresented (OFA, 2005a; OFA, 2005b), a fact which should theoretically increase their chances of becoming employed. When it comes to employment, however, newcomers face many significant barriers in Canada. Although language fluency is 'considered to be the predominant variable that determines a successful outcome in the integration process' (Madibbo, 2005, p. 16), a study of Black francophone Ontarians found that race was also a crucial factor (Madibbo, 2005). As part of a racial *and* linguistic minority, Francophones from racial minority backgrounds face particularly problematic and oppressive settlement conditions (Madibbo, 2005; Quell, 2002). While francophone newcomers enter the country highly educated and trained (OFA, 2005b) – in some instances having mastered French despite emigrating from 'countries where French is not even an official language' (Chevalier, 2000, n.p.) – the benefit of having advanced linguistic skills appears to be countered by the prevalence of racial discrimination that generates severe socio-economic disadvantages for Francophones from racial minority backgrounds. For example, the unemployment rate for Francophones from racial minority backgrounds is almost double that of Francophones in general (11.2% compared to 6.1%) and their employment income is lower (OFA, 2005a). In addition, an intolerable portion of Francophones from racial minority backgrounds live below the low-income cutoff (33.7%) compared to that of Francophones in general (14.1%) and all racial minorities combined (25.9%) (OFA, 2005a).

The Challenges of Inclusion within Francophone Communities in Ontario

There are various dynamics that impede the process of inclusion for francophone immigrants. First, discrimination against newcomers from racial minority backgrounds appears to be intensified in minority francophone communities. This could be explained in several ways. For example, Quell (2002) cautiously articulates that francophone communities lack experience with the integration of immigrants from non-European countries and are reserved about the integration of francophone immigrants and refugees from racialized communities, because 'for minority francophone communities, diversity is a new phenomenon' (p. 6). Diallo and Lafrenière (1998) describe how francophone communities are threatened by the addition of new francophone actors within the francophone fabric of Ontario, and Quell (2002) suggests that 'there is a natural tendency to try and maintain the community from within' (p. 36). Quell (2002) further adds that fear is likely informing the community's response to 'the prospect of [its] identity being redefined through the integration of newcomers who share the same language but come from very different cultural backgrounds' (p. 36).

A second factor that impacts the inclusion of minority Franco-Ontarians is the pressure to learn English in order to succeed within a dominant anglophone culture. Quell (2002) describes the extent to which bilingualism facilitates social life and economic activities for Francophones in anglophone society. Francophone newcomers with limited or no English proficiency soon become aware that their access to education and employment opportunities is restricted. The knowledge of French as an official language is not sufficient when settling in a francophone minority community surrounded by an anglophone majority; indeed, additional English skills are essential (Madibbo, 2005; Quell, 2002). This reality comes as an unwelcome surprise to many newcomers (who had assumed they would face few barriers speaking French within an officially bilingual nation) and leads to about half of the French-speaking immigrants who settle outside Quebec adopting English as their primary language (Quell, 2002).

Third, there is an overall inadequacy of settlement services available in French, which 'may be the most critical impediment to the smooth settlement' of those francophone immigrants from racial minority backgrounds who rely heavily on these services, particularly during the first years of settlement (Madibbo, 2005, p. 36). The inadequacy of these services and other barriers to inclusion are unlikely to be addressed if visible minority Francophones continue to be excluded from government decision-making around funding for minority language communities within Ontario and marginalized within Franco-Ontarian social and economic organizations themselves.

It is evident that the francophone community in Ontario needs to increase its numbers in order to sustain the community and its institutions in Ontario. Visible minority Francophones have an important role to play in the survival of the community. As Madibbo (2005) argues, francophone racial minorities 'can be counted upon to support claims for more francophone institutions and services' (p. 17). Despite the willingness of francophone racial minorities to 'participate in the francophone struggle,' a common perception among them is that 'when it comes to sharing the fruits there is no room for us' (francophone immigrant, cited in Quell, 2002, p. 7). However, recent political shifts have occurred provincially for Francophones – most notably the reconfiguration towards greater inclusivity of the provincial francophone association, l'Assemblée de la francophonie de l'Ontario – indicating an acknowledgment that the political space within the larger Franco-Ontarian community is increasingly being shaped and informed by Francophones who are members of visible minority communities and who are from diverse cultural backgrounds. This is significant because Franco-Ontarians and racial minority francophone newcomers to Ontario share the experience of attempting to defy assimilation and strive towards successful political and economic integration within the majority anglophone culture.

Co-operatives, Social Entrepreneurship, and Newcomer Inclusion

Co-operatives are 'autonomous associations of persons united voluntarily to meet their common economic, social, and cultural needs and aspirations through a jointly-owned and democratically-controlled enterprise' (International Co-operative Alliance, 2009). Most of the early co-operatives originated in farming communities and informal saving institutions. Co-operatives today may be involved in the provision of financial services in credit unions or caisses populaires, housing services, employment services, childcare services, and settlement opportunities (Ontario Co-operative Association, 2006). Important reasons for developing and maintaining co-operatives include both keeping a community or business alive and empowering individuals and the community by keeping profits and control of a business within the community. Consumer co-ops, worker co-ops, and producer or marketing co-ops are examples of co-operatives that can help sustain the community in these significant ways (Ontario Co-operative Association, 2006).

Co-operative entrepreneurship has been and remains an important part of the social economy for Francophones, both within and outside of Quebec. For Francophones in Ontario, co-operatives are a vehicle with which francophone communities can ensure linguistic, economic, and political survival (Lafrenière, 1987). As Breton (1984) argues, patterns of inequality within a society are largely based on inequitable distribution and access to material resources. Given the comparatively higher rates of unemployment among Franco-Ontarians, co-operative involvement can be seen as benefiting the larger francophone community by providing jobs and resources that individuals may not be able to secure on their own (OFA, 2005a).

The most compelling evidence that co-operatives can and do have an impact on Francophones' lives is the emergence of the Mouvement Desjardins in Quebec and francophone communities in Ontario. In 1900 in Lévis, Québec, Alphonse Desjardins conceptualized a credit union model aimed at combating the exploitive money-lending practices that were crushing French Canadian farmers at that time. In about 100 years, the Desjardins Group evolved into the largest integrated co-operative financial institution in Canada with assets of $152 billion (Desjardins, 2009). Interestingly, the social economy in Quebec is not without its legitimate critiques and challenges, particularly those related to issues of citizenship engagement, democracy, and state intervention in community development initiatives (Boivin & Fortier, 1998). Francophones both inside and outside the province of Quebec have been for the past century the recipients of both the challenges and benefits of the co-operative model of social and economic development. In what follows, we outline some of the challenges inherent within the social economy, and by extension the co-operative movement, while also exploring the benefits as they pertain to vulnerable francophone immigrants in Ontario.

Contrary to popular belief, the francophone co-operative movement in Ontario is strong and vibrant. (It is also notable that English-speaking caisses populaires have recently emerged in various communities across Ontario, most notably in southern Ontario.) At a recent conference in Ontario attended by the authors, it was evident that anglophone practitioners in the Ontario social economy were largely unaware of the francophone co-operative movement in the province. Unfortunately, there truly are two solitudes in Ontario when it comes to co-operative development, but this reality is gradually changing because of the leadership of provincial co-operative organizations.

Table 14.1, prepared by the national francophone co-operative organization the Conseil canadien de la coopération et de la mutualité (2008), demonstrates the vibrancy of francophone co-operatives in Ontario and the rest of Canada. There are 66 co-operatives in francophone milieus in Ontario with over 264,000 members and assets over $2 billion. These co-operatives include caisses populaires, a funeral co-op, and agricultural and housing co-operatives, most clustered in northeastern and eastern Ontario. While New Brunswick has more francophone co-operatives than any other province outside Quebec, there are more francophone co-op members in Ontario, doing substantially more business than in any other area outside of Quebec.

Methods

As mentioned above, the current study was designed to explore whether the co-operative model of economic development serves as a tool for social and economic inclusion for francophone immigrants living in Ontario. There were three main objectives in this study: first, to increase understanding of the complexities that francophone immigrants experience in Canada and how the reality of intersecting language and race issues can present challenges to social and economic inclusion within minority francophone spaces; second, to examine the co-operative model in order to understand the possibilities of this model in enhancing francophone immigrants' economic sustainability and creating nurturing support networks; and, third, to understand the experiences of visible minority francophones living in Ontario in relation to the co-operative movement.

Table 14.1
Francophone co-operative membership

Province	Number of Co-operatives	Number of Members	Number of Employees	Number of Directors	Sales $	Assets $
Prince Edward Island	12	7,335	63	95	7,925,879	55,620,637
Nova Scotia	18	17,300	217	164	97,200,000	133,000,000
New Brunswick	117	230,000	2,500	550	2,250,000,000	2,300,000,000
Québec	3,196	7,795,665	81,189	28,000	20,497,000,000	128,748,000,000
Ontario	66	26,645	1,263	399	5,038,317,696	2,75,492,411
Manitoba	26	38,700	385	120	67,861,200	661,675,289
Saskatchewan	6	2,000	50	56	4,243,000	19,693,000
Alberta	8	8 250	130	61	13,202,000	205,602,000
British Columbia	2	8,500	35	15	s/o	43,705,000
Total	3,484	8,372,407	86,227	29,446	28,123,349,775	135,458,588,337

Adapted from Conseil canadien de la cooperation et de la mutualité, 2008

The study employed a range of qualitative research methods: (a) literature reviews; (b) semi-structured interviews with key informants; and (c) focus groups.

Literature Reviews

Extensive literature reviews were conducted on immigration in Canada, issues related to minority francophones in Canada, and the history and evolution of the co-operative movement in Canada and Quebec.

Individual Semi-Structured Interviews

There were 43 individual interviews conducted with key informants. A few informants were involved with co-ops in their countries of origin as well as here in Canada. Each interview took between 45 to 120 minutes, depending on the individual being interviewed.

Focus Groups

Two focus groups were conducted as part of the research study, with a total of 16 participants. Six of the participants were in some way involved in the co-operative movement either here in Canada or in their country of origin.

Participants

The study participants were selected through purposeful sampling as well as the snowball method, which involves the identification of new potential key informants by those already participating in the study. Sixteen participants were key informants from the francophone community who had worked either within the francophone co-operative movement in Ontario or with francophone immigrants in some capacity in the past 10 years. Those key informants who had worked within the co-operative movement in Ontario had done so between 10 and 30 years. Six key informants were visible minority Francophones who were working in some capacity within the social economy either as practitioners or as individuals working with newcomers in southern Ontario. Finally, 21 research participants were newcomers who were attempting to integrate within francophone milieus in Ontario and were in the process of looking for employment or attending some type of

training program. Research participants who were newcomers came
to Canada from countries such as Rwanda, Congo, Burundi, Guinée,
and other North African and French-speaking countries. Five of the
research participants who were newcomers were also on their second
migration from Quebec to Ontario. Most research participants lived in
the southern Ontario cities of Kitchener-Waterloo, Toronto, Hamilton,
and Welland. Four study participants lived in Sudbury, Ottawa, and
Montreal – two of whom had worked in some capacity with francophone community groups in southern Ontario.

Further specifics regarding the key informants are deliberately ob-
scured to protect their anonymity (this is particularly important given
the small numbers of participants drawn from the leadership base within francophone and co-operative communities in Ontario).

Emerging Themes

The data collected within the context of this study were very rich, in-
formative, and, at times, provocative. Employing a diversity lens and
critical theory, we found that four overarching themes emerged, all of
which were consistent with the information collected by our literature
review. The themes that emerged repeatedly within the context of our
research and that served to highlight the legitimacy of our interest in
co-operatives and inclusion were (a) the co-operative model as a tool
for social and economic inclusion; (b) challenges of integration with
minority francophone communities; (c) challenges related to co-operatives and newcomers; and (d) issues related to education and leadership within the Franco-Ontarian community. In the discussion that follows, the themes are succinctly described and accompanied by recommendations from the research participants.

*Legitimacy of the Co-operative Model as a Tool for Social and
Economic Inclusion*

Participants were generally positive about the possibilities presented
by the co-operative model as a potential tool for social and economic
inclusion. Many noted that the principles of the co-operative model
harmonized well with newcomers' values of family and solidarity that
had informed their experiences in their countries of origin. Several informants had some experience with co-operatives in their country of
origin. Some had been connected to agricultural co-ops and others were

part of women's lending circles. A few were critical of co-operatives because in their countries of origin co-operatives were often controlled by the state and had exploited farmers. Overall, however, most of the research participants understood the nature of a co-operative and welcomed the idea of working within a framework that prioritized the collective over the individual. Many believed in social justice values, which they understood to be inherent within the co-operative model. One participant explained:

> Co-op activity is a locus of people who otherwise may not have collided socially in other milieus. Co-ops provide a crossroads for all kinds of people who come together; language is the common denominator, the need is the service.

Despite the recognition by participants that co-operatives may offer opportunities for francophone immigrants and refugees, the overwhelming messages we heard were that many challenges are faced by francophone newcomers to Ontario and that systems, including co-operatives, pose a significant challenge to integration. As one participant stated, supports are crucial if francophone immigrants are to develop any type of co-operative initiative:

> Without money, guidance, and someone who can speak French and listen to our needs and hopes, it will be very difficult to encourage someone in my milieu to develop a co-operative or any other type of self-employment initiative.

In discussing this theme, the following comment illustrates one woman's conclusion after attempting to initiate a co-operative:

> The women in our group had tried to initiate a consumer co-operative in our city. We had decided to do so because we felt and still feel that there is no place for us within the larger Franco-Ontarian society. Many of us are educated and have degrees but no one will hire us even though we speak French very well. At first there was a lot of enthusiasm, but it took no time at all to realize that what the project expected of us and what we were prepared to give was totally different. We had underestimated how difficult and long it would take to actually set up our project. People lost interest and after a while people withdrew. It doesn't mean that our

idea wasn't a good one; it just was a question I guess of supports and timing.

Challenges of Integration with Minority Francophone Communities

It came as no surprise that issues relative to racism and discrimination were realities that shaped the lived experience of francophone immigrants in Ontario. Our research participants shared stories of marginalization, but they also spoke of the hope that one day they would take their rightful place within the context of the larger francophone community. Additionally, participants working with vulnerable immigrants or refugees who came from war-torn countries shared their concern that issues involving physical and mental health were factors impeding the newcomers' capacity to embrace self-employment initiatives through the co-operative model.

A recommendation emerging from discussion around the challenges of integration was to educate Franco-Ontarians about the needs, aspirations, and contributions that francophone immigrants could bring to francophone communities, while informing francophone newcomers about the battle for French language rights in Ontario. What became clear was that there needs to be a mechanism in place whereby visible minority Francophones and Franco-Ontarians can dialogue on a regular basis, not only enabling a demystification of one another but also encouraging a process whereby both francophone groups come to a space of mutual recognition and respect.

Challenges Related to Co-operatives and Newcomers

Some participants had little background knowledge of co-operatives and how such models of social and economic development might speak to the needs of newcomers. For those participants with co-operative experience, there were a number of factors that repeatedly emerged as having compromised visible minority Francophones' capacity to engage fully in co-operative development projects. First, a common factor was the inability to access credit or venture capital loans from a financial institution; several participants stated that they simply didn't feel that the banks perceived them as 'credible' entrepreneurs. Second, participants reported experiencing a lack of support from francophone consultants in settlement services who did not have either the time or

the expertise to assist emerging groups that expressed a wish to initiate a co-operative venture. Third, there were challenges involved in recruiting business-minded members who also had social goals. Fourth,
conflicts (historical and current) in people's countries of origin sometimes spilled over into Canadian contexts and issues of trust therefore
impeded a group's ability to develop co-operative ventures. Other participants lacked the tolerance for risk needed to initiate a co-operative
venture and expressed reluctance to assume yet another challenge in
addition to their ongoing struggle for integration. Two participants
spoke to this issue:

> The consequence of failure is significant to newcomers who often sup-
> port family members in the country of origin, and as such taking a risk in
> starting a co-operative venture may be too risky and therefore some im-
> migrants prefer traditional forms of employment even if they are poorly
> paid.

> During this time of integration, they cannot dream, they are simply in
> survival mode.

Another research participant shared her cumulative negative experience from involvement with a co-operative in her community:

> There was a lot of paperwork and we had to put in a lot of volunteer hours
> on top of our paid work. It was very stressful and as immigrants we are
> already dealing with so much stress. Having the added stress of starting
> our co-op was just too much.

According to most of the research participants, the following five recommendations were considered important for greater inclusion of francophone immigrants within co-operatives: (a) community consultations
with visible minority francophones regarding their needs as potential
co-operative developers would provide a good starting point for engaging these communities; (b) work with immigrants within the context of
co-op development must be part of a larger co-op development strategy
among all of the co-op actors in the province of Ontario; (c) financial
supports and mentoring programs (in French) regarding how to operate
a co-operative venture should be developed; (d) education on the co-op
model should be provided to newcomers who do not know the model
or who have had a negative experience with it in their countries of ori-

gin; and (e) case studies of other successful cultural groups who have thrived with the co-op model should be made available.

Issues Related to Education and Leadership within Franco-Ontarian Communities

According to several research participants, there should be more dialogue between the leadership of the francophone co-operative movement in Ontario and prominent members of francophone immigrant communities. Several research participants shared their frustration with the current leadership of the francophone co-operative movement.

> There is a lack of education about co-ops; the main problem with the caisses populaires is that they've gotten big; their human resources are coming out of business schools where they do not study anything about co-operatives. Their reference point is the capitalist system and how it operates.

Some participants also felt that a few leaders in Desjardins appeared to be out of touch with the needs of Francophones in Ontario and were not aware of any particular needs of francophone immigrants. Participants experienced a lack of commitment to education and support for both francophone organizations and individuals wishing to develop co-operative projects. Some participants also suggested that a reconnection with the fundamental values of the co-operative movement was essential in order to continue thriving as a community. The data collected from participants revealed a number of issues pertaining to education and leadership in Ontario and led to the development of the following recommendations to address these issues: (a) educational support for the co-operative model in French; (b) more contributions from caisses populaires towards co-operative development within francophone communities in Ontario; and (c) a renewal in leadership within francophone milieus in Ontario so that the diverse composition of the francophone community will be better reflected in the leadership. This would mean more effective outreach strategies, particularly towards women, immigrants, and youth.

Many research participants, when questioned about the legitimacy of having bilingual services made available to francophone newcomers, described having negative experiences with bilingual services (or the lack thereof) in the past and voiced a preference for having French-only education and supports around co-operative development. As one research participant stated, 'Bilingual co-ops are perfect tools of assimilation.' This sentiment is important to understand as it illustrates a desire to maintain linguistic homogeneity for the education surrounding the purposes and development of co-operatives.

There are a number of recommendations for the francophone co-operative movement that flow from our findings: (a) the co-op movement itself must return to its foundational values of education, solidarity, and co-operation; (b) there is a need to engage the leadership within the co-op movement in order to create spaces for women, young people, and immigrants, as they will be the future champions of the co-operative movement within francophone spaces in Ontario; (c) a conference or series of discussions should be organized whereby Francophones can debate fundamental questions relative to co-op development in Ontario; and (d) research is needed to provoke and stimulate debate within and across francophone communities in Ontario.

Discussion of the Findings

Despite enormous challenges relative to co-operatives and francophone immigrants, the idea that co-operatives could be viewed as a tool to stimulate social and economic inclusion as well as the development of social networks was very appealing to many of the research participants. According to the participants, if provided with enough education, supports, and venture capital, francophone newcomers would welcome the co-operative model as a healthy alternative to individualized work. Those seeking to work in a collective fashion seemed to think that co-operatives could provide a supportive space for newcomers to work within the context of a group with similar goals. Additionally, the co-operative was seen as a means for cross-cultural interaction.

This study produced a complex portrait of the multiple layers of inclusion and exclusion and challenges facing minority Francophones within various contexts. The research outcomes taught us that there is more to the co-op model than we had initially understood or anticipated going into this project. While the co-operative model is attractive to the francophone diaspora, supports must be in place in order for development and expansion to occur. Co-operatives themselves must be situated within a larger community economic development context in order to deal effectively and efficiently with the numerous needs that francophone newcomers have shared with us around economic sustainability and social inclusion. It is simply not enough to believe that francophone co-operatives as they are currently envisioned offer a panacea of social and economic inclusion for francophone immigrants in Ontario. Not surprisingly, Francophones in Ontario neither wish for nor seek out bilingual services, and this too must be considered by the larger co-operative movement in Ontario.

What we have learned through this study is that thoughtful and purposeful attention must be given to the needs of all immigrants wishing to settle successfully within Canadian society. This takes time, energy, and co-ordinated efforts between all social service and governmental bodies committed to the integration of new Canadians in Ontario. The data collected in this study were consistent with the literature on the challenges and goals relative to integration, particularly with respect to employability issues and the values of social justice and solidarity inherent within co-operatives and the social economy. Where we feel this research is most helpful is in generating healthy and authentic dialogue among Francophones (francophone immigrants and Franco-Ontarians) in Ontario. There is a need to address various tensions among Francophones, but there is also a need to address the perceived lack of leadership within some co-operative circles in Ontario. Future discussions should address the roles that the francophone leadership must play in creating welcoming spaces for francophone immigrants who have much to share and contribute to the larger francophone community. A renewal of the leadership within the co-op movement, particularly as it pertains to youth, women, and immigrants, is an important first step in this process.

Additionally, we would submit the following recommendations, some of which go beyond the needs of immigrants in Ontario and speak to the entire collective of Ontarians searching for ways to address social and economic exclusion. There needs to be a co-ordinated education model at all educational levels in Ontario that promotes an understanding of alternative economic models in order that transformative change may occur. It simply is not enough to hope that somehow people in Ontario will share our enthusiasm for the social economy if these same individuals are not exposed to its benefits from an early age. For us, education imbued with the values of the social economy is the most significant determining factor that could effect social change. Finally, the formalized creation of a Social Economy Secretariat is an idea whose time has come. For francophone immigrants and racial minority communities in Ontario, the path to inclusion may arise via the emergence of more co-operatives and within the context of a better supported social economy.

Conclusion

Traditionally, Francophones in Quebec and minority francophone communities across Canada have benefited from various co-operative initiatives that have ensured their economic and cultural survival. It is incumbent upon the francophone co-operative leadership in Ontario to extend this opportunity and experience to francophone allies from immigrant communities. Current relations between francophone immigrants and the larger francophone community indicate a significant need to form partnerships, address tensions, and work collaboratively. Our study suggests that productive collaborations can be nurtured through the social economy within francophone communities. Based on this preliminary research, we believe that further in-depth investigation regarding the legitimacy of the co-operative model as a tool for inclusion for francophone immigrants in Ontario will confirm that co-operatives' inherent values relative to social inclusion, collective solidarity, respect for the individual, and viewing capital as a tool (not as an end) are conducive to the inclusion of francophone immigrants who seek to integrate within francophone milieus in Ontario.

REFERENCES

Boivin, L., & Fortier, M. (1998). *L'économie sociale – L'avenir d'une illusion.* Québec : FIDES.

Breton, R. (1984). The production and allocation of symbolic resources: An analysis of the linguistic ethnocultural fields in Canada. *Canadian Review of Sociology and Anthropology, 21*(2), 123–44.

Chevalier, A.C. (2000, winter). *Rapport statistique d'Educacentre.* Vancouver: Educacentre.

Conseil canadien de la coopération et de la mutualité. (2008). Les effectifs cooperatives francophones. Retrieved November 14, 2009, from http://www.cccm.coop/site.asp?page=element&nIDElement=2641

Desjardins. (2009). About Desjardins. Retrieved November 14, 2009, from http://www.desjardins.com/en/a_propos/qui-nous-sommes/chiffres.jsp

Diallo, L., & Lafrenière, G. (1998). Les minorités et l'espace francophone à

Sudbury, Ontario – Perspectives. *Reflets: Revue ontaroise d'intervention sociale et communautaire*, 4(1).

International Co-operative Alliance. (2009). What is a co-operative? Retrieved December 9, 2009, from http://www.ica.coop/coop/index.html

Lafrenière, G. (1987). La coopération et les Franco-Ontariens. Unpublished Master's thesis, IRECUS, Université de Sherbrooke.

Madibbo, A. (2005). *Immigration, race, and language: Black Francophones of Ontario and the challenges of integration, racism, and language discrimination.* CERIS Working Paper Series. Toronto: Ryerson University.

OFA (Office of Francophone Affairs). (2005a). *Francophones in Ontario: Statistical profile.* Retrieved November 14, 2009, from http://www.ofa.gov.on.ca/en/franco-stats-1999general.html

OFA (Office of Francophone Affairs). (2005b). *Francophone racial minorities in Ontario: Statistical profile.* Retrieved November 14, 2008, from http://www.ofa.gov.on.ca/en/franco-stats-2005minorities-h.html

Ontario Co-operative Association (ON Co-op). (2006). *Co-op history.* Retrieved December 9, 2009, from http://ontario.coop/pages/index.php?main_id=311

Quell, C. (2002). Official languages and immigration: Obstacles and opportunities for immigrants and communities. Office of the Commissioner of Official Languages. Retrieved August 1, 2008, from http://www.ocol-clo.gc.ca

15 Conclusion

LAURIE MOOK, JACK QUARTER, AND SHERIDA RYAN

As indicated in the first four chapters of this book, there are differing perspectives on the social economy. The perspective articulated in the introductory chapter and utilized in chapter 2 by David M. Lasby, Michael Hall, R. Mark Ventry, and Denyse Guy on Ontario's social economy takes a broad perspective and includes all organizations with a social mission that generate some economic value. In contrast, chapter 3 about Quebec by Marguerite Mendell and Nancy Neamtan articulates the view that the social economy is a movement with a transformative vision. As such, the criteria that are utilized in Quebec by the apex organization, le Chantier de l'économie sociale, are more restrictive and are limited to organizations that fit the movement criteria. Chapter 4 by Roger Spear on the social economy in Europe indicates that this same difference of opinion exists in Europe with CIRIEC articulating the movement perspective and the European Commission embracing a broader perspective, as suggested in the chapters by Mook, Quarter, and Ryan and Lasby et al.

The design of this research collection follows the broader perspective of the social economy. However, as indicated in the introductory chapter, the debate about what organizations fit the criteria of the social economy misses an important issue: how the organizations in the social economy interact with the public and private sectors and what functions social economy organizations utilize in this context. As stated in chapter 1, the organizations in the social economy are an infrastructure for society as a whole. Their members may work in the private and public sectors, and their financing may come in part from government and in part from private sector donors. In other words, even though organizations in the social economy have some distinct characteristics,

Figure 15.1. Venn diagram of social economy

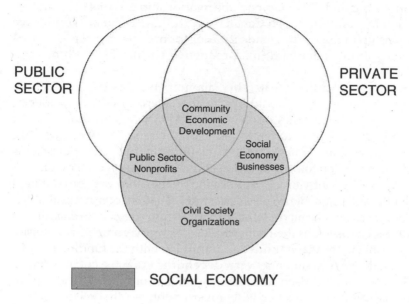

they are not a world unto themselves but one part of a society that in-cludes government and the private sector. To highlight this point, we illustrate the relationship between the social economy and the other sectors using a Venn diagram (see figure 15.1).

One of the important contributions of this book is to highlight the many ways that the organizations in the social economy interact with the other sectors. In this brief concluding chapter, we illustrate this point and also suggest ways that this line of inquiry could be devel-oped further.

Two of the chapters – 'A Comparative Analysis of Voluntary Sector/ Government: Relations in Canada and England' by Peter Elson and 'Capturing Complexity: The Ontario Government Relationship with the Social Economy Sector' by Kathy Brock – discuss specifically the interactions between social economy organizations and government. The focus in both papers is on what are referred to as public sector non-profits in figure 1, that is, nonprofits that rely upon government for funding and that also are guided to some degree by government policies. Such organizations are not an insignificant part of the social economy.

The Elson chapter highlights the importance of government for such organizations and illustrates how the relationship to social economy organizations differs between Canada and the UK. The more supportive relationship in the UK has made it easier for organizations in the social economy to move forward in a productive partnership with government.

As discussed in the research by Salamon (1987, 1995), the relationship with government should not be characterized as a dependency, as government also relies upon social economy organizations for the delivery of services. Quarter, Mook, & Armstrong (2009) characterize nonprofits as intermediaries in this relationship, but whatever label is used there is an ongoing interaction and reliance upon each other.

Chapter 6 by Kathy Brock explores the relationship with government in depth, utilizing Ontario as a case study. That chapter notes that the relationship can take many different forms from coercion to encouragement. Brock discusses the challenge faced by government in ensuring that organizations that it funds are complying with the funding criteria, and that the relationship may vary, depending upon the circumstances.

The chapters by Elson and Brock were the only ones that specifically discussed relationships with government, but that relationship is implied in other chapters. Chapter 7, 'Notes in the Margins: The Social Economy in Economics and Business Textbooks' by Daniel Schugurensky and Erica McCollum, discusses the systematic bias against social economy organizations in business and economics high school textbooks. The reasons for this are not completely clear, but this bias also appeared in a study by Davidson, Quarter, and Richmond (1996). It is not evident that education policies have influenced this direction in textbooks, and it may be that textbook authors are simply articulating norms, as they understand them. Nevertheless, textbooks and the curriculum more generally are an important influence on how people view the social economy, particularly organizations that operate in the market. This chapter underlines the importance of the interaction with the public sector on the development of social economy organizations.

Chapter 8,'Mandatory High School Community Service in Ontario: Assessing and Improving Its Impact' by Paulette Padanyi, Mark Baetz, Steven D. Brown, and Ailsa Henderson, also discusses the interaction between public education institutions and the community – in this case through an analysis of a mandatory community service program for secondary school students. Volunteers are a major human resource for nonprofit organizations, and public education programs that seek to encourage volunteering are of great importance to social economy organizations. However, as this carefully researched project suggests, mandatory community service does not appear to enhance the likelihood of volunteering.

Chapter 9, 'Strategic Partnerships: Community Climate Change Partners and Resilience to Funding Cuts' by Travis Gliedt, Paul Parker, and Jennifer Lynes, discusses some of the challenges in interactions between government and community organizations, in this case a nonprofit assisting with the dissemination of information about climate change. As a result of the change in government priorities, the program upon which this nonprofit relied was cut, but the chapter discusses how the nonprofit reoriented itself and started covering the cost for its service from the marketplace; in other words, a different form of interaction.

Chapter 10, 'The Online Social Economy: Canadian Nonprofits and the Internet' by Sherida Ryan, analyses social economy organizations in an entirely different context; that is, as organizations that function online primarily. The paper analyses one organization that functions in the market, another that serves a co-ordinating function between conventional businesses and social economy organizations, and three others that are civil society organizations. In two cases they assist groups with health challenges and in another they provide a vital communications link for relatively isolated Aboriginal communities. Again, the chapter provides a wide range of illustrations between the social economy and other parts of society.

Chapter 11, 'Corporate Participation in the Social Economy: Employer-Supported Volunteering Programs in Canada's Financial Institutions' by Agnes Meinhard, Femida Handy, and Itay Greenspan, illustrates the importance of interaction with the private sector, in this case large financial institutions and their support for volunteering in the social economy. Without this important form of support, social economy organizations could face labour shortages. Yet, a question that arises is whether this form of support causes social economy organizations to vary their priorities or whether the support is conditional on particular priorities.

Chapter 12, 'Work Stoppages in Canadian Social Economy Organizations' by Kunle Akingbola, is a unique piece of research. There is much research on the work stoppages in the private and public sectors, but very little on the social economy. Yet social economy organizations are guided by the same labour laws as businesses and public sector organizations and like organizations in the other sectors have employees and management. Therefore, work stoppages should be expected, and as with organizations in the other sectors, these stoppages affect the broader society, particularly if the organization is large.

Chapter 13, 'Organic Farmers and the Social Economy: Positive Synergies for Community Development' by Jennifer Sumner and Sophie Llewelyn, discusses a form of social economy organization that functions in the marketplace and the challenges it faces from the dynamics of the market in maintaining its distinctive features – a challenge faced by social economy organizations in general that function in the market. Such organizations are different, but they are governed by the same norms as conventional businesses, and they must struggle to maintain their distinctiveness.

Chapter 14, 'On the Challenges of Inclusion and the Co-operative Movement for Francophone Immigrants in Ontario' by Ginette Lafrenière, Maike Zinabou, Matt Riehl, and Sandy Hoy, discusses specifically the role of co-operatives in integrating immigrants whose first language is French into Ontario's economy. This chapter suggests that co-operatives should serve a bridging function in integrating French-speaking immigrants into the economy.

These chapters all differ, but their commonality is the differing functions served by social economy organizations relative to the broader society. The range of possibilities is vast, and these chapters are simply scratching the surface. However, they point to a different approach to understanding the social economy – one that departs from the emphasis on the distinctiveness of social economy organizations and instead focuses upon how they interact with other parts of society. Doing this implies that the social economy is part of a broader society. Part of the function that it serves is to challenge norms and to articulate a vision for social change, as the chapter by Mendell and Neamtan suggests and as is also articulated to a degree in other chapters. However, some organizations in the social economy are conservative, rather than challenging social norms and articulating a vision for social change. Business associations such as chambers of commerce, for example, are simply the voice of private sector interests. Religious congregations are usually a conventional force in society, but they do serve the important function of bringing people with a common bond together for a shared need.

Mapping these varied interactions is essential to a better understanding of the social economy and its many functions in society. These interactions affect social economy organizations and they also affect organizations in the private and public sectors to which they relate.

REFERENCES

Davidson, A., Quarter, J., & Richmond, B.J. (1996). Business textbooks: Telling half the story. *Education Forum* 22(2), 28–31.

Quarter, J., Mook, L., & Armstrong, A. (2009). *Understanding Canada's social economy: A Canadian perspective*. Toronto: University of Toronto Press.

Salamon, L.M. (1987). Partners in public service: The scope and theory of government-nonprofit relations. In W.W. Powell (Ed.), *The independent sector: A research handbook* (pp. 99–117). New Haven: Yale University Press.

Salamon, L.M. (1995). Partners in public service: Government-nonprofit relations in the modern welfare state. Baltimore: Johns Hopkins University Press.